CAPITAL PUNISHMENT

Recent Titles in
Documentary and Reference Guides

Substance Abuse in America: A Documentary and Reference Guide
James A. Swartz

The Iraq War: A Documentary and Reference Guide
Thomas R. Mockaitis

Animal Rights and Welfare: A Documentary and Reference Guide
Lawrence W. Baker

Water Rights and the Environment in the United States: A Documentary and Reference Guide
John R. Burch Jr.

Endangered Species: A Documentary and Reference Guide
Edward P. Weber

9/11 and the War on Terror: A Documentary and Reference Guide
Paul J. Springer

Vaccination and Its Critics: A Documentary and Reference Guide
Lisa Rosner

Arab-Israeli Conflict: A Documentary and Reference Guide
Priscilla Roberts

Modern Slavery: A Documentary and Reference Guide
Laura J. Lederer

Poverty in the United States: A Documentary and Reference Guide
John R. Burch Jr.

Afghanistan War: A Documentary and Reference Guide
Ryan Wadle

Modern Genocide: A Documentary and Reference Guide
Paul R. Bartrop

Cyber Warfare: A Documentary and Reference Guide
Paul J. Springer

Attacks on the American Press: A Documentary and Reference Guide
Jessica Roberts and Adam Maksl

Free Speech and Censorship: A Documentary and Reference Guide
Cari Lee Skogberg Eastman

CAPITAL PUNISHMENT

A Documentary and Reference Guide

David L. Hudson Jr.

Documentary and Reference Guides

BLOOMSBURY ACADEMIC
NEW YORK • LONDON • OXFORD • NEW DELHI • SYDNEY

BLOOMSBURY ACADEMIC
Bloomsbury Publishing Inc
1385 Broadway, New York, NY 10018, USA
50 Bedford Square, London, WC1B 3DP, UK
29 Earlsfort Terrace, Dublin 2, Ireland

BLOOMSBURY, BLOOMSBURY ACADEMIC and the Diana logo are trademarks of Bloomsbury Publishing Plc

First published in the United States of America 2023

Library of Congress Cataloging-in-Publication Data
Names: Hudson, David L., 1969– author.
Title: Capital punishment : a documentary and reference guide / David L. Hudson Jr.
Description: New York : Bloomsbury Academic, an imprint of Bloomsbury Publishing Inc., [2023] | Includes bibliographical references and index.
Identifiers: LCCN 2022048273 (print) | LCCN 2022048274 (ebook) | ISBN 9781440875779 (hardback) | ISBN 9781440875786 (ePDF) | 9788216170921 (eBook)
Subjects: LCSH: Capital punishment—United States | BISAC: LAW / Criminal Law / Sentencing | SOCIAL SCIENCE / Violence in Society
Classification: LCC KF9227.C2 H83 2023 (print) | LCC KF9227.C2 (ebook) | DDC 345.73/0773—dc23/eng/20230403
LC record available at https://lccn.loc.gov/2022048273
LC ebook record available at https://lccn.loc.gov/2022048274

ISBN: HB: 978-1-4408-7577-9
ePDF: 978-1-4408-7578-6
eBook: 979-8-2161-7092-1

Series: Documentary and Reference Guides

Typeset by Apex CoVantage, LLC

To find out more about our authors and books visit www.bloomsbury.com and sign up for our newsletters.

CONTENTS

READERS' GUIDE TO RELATED DOCUMENTS AND SIDEBARS

U.S. Supreme Court Decisions

Wilkerson v. Utah 1879
In Re Kemmler 1890
Williams v. Mississippi 1898
Davis v. Burke 1900
Franklin v. South Carolina 1910
Powell v. Alabama 1932
Watts v. Indiana 1949
Alcorta v. Texas 1957
Rudolph v. Alabama 1963
Boykin v. Alabama 1969
Furman v. Georgia 1972
Gregg v. Georgia 1976
Gilmore v. Utah 1976
Coker v. Georgia 1977
Lockett v. Ohio 1978
Eddings v. Oklahoma 1982
Strickland v. Washington 1984
Darden v. Wainwright 1986
Ford v. Wainwright 1986
McCleskey v. Kemp 1987
Whitmore v. Arkansas 1990
Payne v. Tennessee 1991
Callins v. Collins 1994
Atkins v. Virginia 2002
Miller-El v. Dretke 2005
Roper v. Simmons 2005
Kennedy v. Louisiana 2008
Thompson v. McNeil 2009
Hinton v. Alabama 2014
Hall v. Florida 2014
Glossip v. Gross 2015
Jordan v. Mississippi 2018
Bucklew v. Precythe 2019

Statements from Lawmakers

President Nixon State of the Union 1973
President Clinton's Stay of Execution 2000
Illinois Governor George Ryan's Commutation 2003
Washington Governor Issues Moratorium 2014
California Governor's Executive Order 2019

Statements from Advocates of Capital Punishment

John Stuart Mill in Favor of the Death Penalty 1868
Paul Cassell's Pro-Death Penalty Testimony 1993
John McAdams' Pro-Death Testimony 2006
Testimony of Heritage Foundation Analyst (pro) 2007

Statements from Opponents of Capital Punishment

Dr. Pat Robertson's Death Penalty Speech 2000
Professor David Baldus' Testimony 2001

Statements from Exonerated Death Row Inmates

This reference guide also includes nine sidebars. These sidebars add additional information to certain entries. For example, the sidebar on Clarence Norris provides more information about one of the Scottsboro Boys, the defendants in the Supreme Court decision *Powell v. Alabama* (1932). The sidebars included in this text comprise:

Clarence Norris	Sidebar to *Powell v. Alabama* (Document 8)
William Brenan's Concurring Opinion	Sidebar to *Furman v. Georgia* (Document 13)
David Kendall	Sidebar to *Coker v. Georgia* (Document 17)
John Charles Boger	Sidebar to *McCleskey v. Kemp* (Document 23)
Hugo Bedau	Sidebar to Paul Cassell's Testimony (Document 26)
Clinton and Ricky Ray Rector	Sidebar to Clinton's Execution Stay (Document 31)
Scalia's Dissent	Sidebar to *Atkins v. Virginia* (Document 33)
Kirk Bloodsworth	Sidebar to Richard Dieter's Testimony (Document 38)
Seth P. Waxman	Sidebar to *Hall v. Florida* (Document 48)

PREFACE

Welcome to the Documentary and Reference Guide on Capital Punishment—one of the most enduringly controversial issues in American society.

The format of this reference guide is designed to provide readers with illuminating excerpts from a wide range of essential and representative primary sources on capital punishment. The types of documents featured within these pages include essays, testimonies, and speeches to Congress; landmark legislation; and pivotal U.S. Supreme Court decisions. The latter are particularly well represented because of the weight those opinions have had in shaping the trajectory of capital punishment in the United States. As French author Alexis De Tocqueville wrote in his classic work *Democracy in America* (1835) after traveling all around the country, "I am unaware that any nation of the globe has hitherto organized a judicial power in the same manner as the Americans," he wrote. "A more imposing judicial power was never constituted by any people."

There is another reason why the U.S. Supreme Court plays such a prominent role in capital punishment. The Supreme Court is truly the "Court of Last Resort" for a defendant who is appealing his or her death sentence. Most death penalty defendants start with a trial before a state judge. That decision then winds its way through the state and federal court systems as lawyers for the defendant file what is known as a "petition for writ of *habeas corpus*." This legalistic term means that the defendant contends that the state is illegally confining him. In plain terms, the defendant is arguing that his constitutional rights were violated at some point in his trial or appeal. In rare instances, these legal battles do not end until the case reaches the Supreme Court.

Many of the documentary entries in this book are not Supreme Court decisions, however. For example, the first entry in the book highlights the perspective of nineteenth-century English political theorist John Stuart Mill, a strong supporter of the idea that capital punishment was necessary in society. While this book examines the death penalty in the United States, our system of law largely arose from the English common law system. Mill remains an immensely important theorist in many areas of American law and political thought.

Other entries provide insights into the perspectives and arguments of death penalty opponents, death penalty proponents, former death penalty defendants, legislators, presidents, governors, and others. For example, one of the documents is former Illinois governor George Ryan's sensational 2003 announcement that he wants the death sentences of every death row inmate in Illinois to be changed to life in prison.

Each entry provides not only a prominent excerpt from the featured document but also an original contextual analysis. This analysis focuses on major messages and themes from the document, provides context for deeper understanding of the featured passages, and explains why the primary source is important. Each entry also concludes with a "Further Reading" section containing resources for further research and insights on a particular subject or topic.

Included in some of the entries are short "Sidebars" labeled "Did You Know," featuring interesting factoids or additional information about a key person or player in the case or controversy or examining legal concepts and precedents in additional detail.

This book examines the subject of capital punishment in the United States in six chronologically arranged chapters: (1) Early History of the Death Penalty; (2) Rising Usage of—and Opposition to—the Death Penalty; (3) The Supreme Court Abolishes—and Subsequently Reinstates—Capital Punishment; (4) Victims' Rights, Moratoriums, and Other Issues; (5) The Capital Punishment Debate Intensifies as Courts Narrow Its Application; and (6) Contemporary Capital Punishment Issues.

Chapter 1 focuses largely on the latter half of the nineteenth century. A notable document is a contribution from the English theorist John Stuart Mill, who was strongly supportive of capital punishment. Also included in this chapter are five early U.S. Supreme Court decisions on the death penalty—*Wilkerson v. Utah* (1879), *In Re Kemmler* (1890), *Holden v. Minnesota* 1890, *Williams v. Mississippi* (1898), and *Davis v. Burke* (1900).

Chapter 2 predominately focuses on cases and developments in the early twentieth century. These include the interesting death penalty cases of *Franklin v. South Carolina* (1910)—cases with disturbing racial aspects. It also includes the case of *Powell v. Alabama* (1932) when the U.S. Supreme Court first reversed the death sentences of several young African American defendants known as the "Scottsboro Boys."

Chapter 3 examines a very tumultuous time in the history of the death penalty. The National Association for the Advancement of Colored People (NAACP) and other groups vigorously sought to challenge the death penalty as unconstitutional for a number of reasons, including racial bias and other glaring disparities in its application. These efforts culminated in the Supreme Court striking down the death penalty in 1972—only to revive it again in 1976.

Chapter 4 examines a period of time when there were competing movements in the death penalty arena, ranging from increased attention to victims' rights to efforts to end the death penalty through state-level moratoriums. Some believed that there was too much coddling of criminals and more respect needed to be paid to those directly harmed by crime. Others countered that the death penalty was still troubling and unconstitutional.

Chapter 5 examines a period in American history in which the U.S. Supreme Court eliminated the death penalty for particular defendants. For example, the

Court ruled that it was cruel and unusual punishment to execute inmates who are intellectually disabled or who committed murder as juveniles.

Chapter 6 examines recent trends and developments in death penalty law, including measures to abolish the death penalty in California and Virginia. The latter move is seen by many observers as particularly noteworthy because it marked the first time in U.S. history that a southern state had formally ended the practice.

A final word about this reference work. The book is designed to present the issues around capital punishment in a neutral, informative fashion. It is the author's hope that its contents will be illuminating for death penalty opponents and proponents alike.

INTRODUCTION

Capital punishment, often called the death penalty, has a long lineage, tracing back to the Hammurabi Code from ancient Babylon in eighteenth century B.C.E. That code provided for a variety of methods of execution for crimes ranging from adultery to stealing slaves. In 621 B.C.E., the Athenian lawmaker Draco passed a code of laws that was so harsh his name created an eponym—draconian—for extreme or radical measures or behavior. The Draconian Code punished nearly all legal offenses with death. The death penalty was commonly employed during the Roman Empire and into the Middle Ages as well. During the Middle Ages, in fact, executions were attended by large masses of people. They were akin to a modern-day rock concert or sports event. Today, of course, executions are carried out by representatives of the state behind closed doors with very few witnesses.

The death penalty continued in England from the Middle Ages up through the colonial period. It is considered harsh by today's standards. The methods of death were often burning or hanging—methods that are considered barbaric or "cruel and unusual punishment" under the Eighth Amendment of the U.S. Constitution.

The early American colonies followed the English common law tradition and executed people for a variety of crimes. As early as 1608, George Kendall was executed in Jamestown, a village in modern-day Virginia that was the first permanent English settlement in North America, for allegedly scheming to help the Spanish. Many colonies put people to death for relatively minor crimes. While today the only crime eligible for a death sentence is murder or treason, in colonial America, offenses like counterfeiting, adultery, and smuggling tobacco were all death-eligible crimes.

After the United States came into being, a stark racial aspect to death penalty emerged, particularly in the southern states. In Virginia, for example, white people could only be executed for the crime of murder, while Blacks could be put to death for more than 70 offenses, including administering medicine or teaching other slaves to read.

In other states outside of the South, the racial disparity was not as stark. Another feature was that capital punishment was—at least on the books—capable of being used for crimes other than first-degree murder. Similar to the Middle Ages, executions were huge events in society, as thousands of people would gather to watch hangings of condemned criminals. Often, a prominent preacher would preside over the event and deliver a religious harangue, warning the audience about the wages of sin.

The Founding Fathers appeared to assume the validity of capital punishment in the Constitution. The Fifth Amendment provides that "[n]o state shall be held to answer for a capital, or otherwise infamous crime, unless on a presentment or indictment of a Grand Jury." Thus, the Constitution in the Fifth Amendment assumes that a defendant can be sentenced to a capital crime. This shows that many of the early Founders approved of the death penalty, at least in limited circumstances—a point Justice Antonin Scalia of the U.S. Supreme Court frequently pointed out during his years on the bench (1986–2016).

EARLY OPPOSITION TO CAPITAL PUNISHMENT

Even in the eighteenth century, some philosophers and other citizens began to question the death penalty. The most well-known opponent of the death penalty was an Italian philosopher named Cesare Beccaria whose treatise *Essay on Crimes and Punishments* was widely circulated and read in the United States. Beccaria argued that "the punishment of death is pernicious to society from the example of barbarity it affords." He also argued that the death penalty did not deter crime. This was a significant argument, because deterrence remains a primary justification for the death penalty. Beccaria argued that imprisonment was the proper way to deal with criminals.

Thomas Jefferson and other leading Americans were persuaded by Beccaria's writings on the death penalty. Pennsylvania physician Benjamin Rush, who signed the Declaration of Independence, argued against the death penalty with particular passion in the late eighteenth century. A brief period followed in which it appeared this activism might reduce or even eliminate use of the death penalty in America. Beginning with Massachusetts, several states built their first prisons in the 1780s. Between 1794 and 1798, five states abolished the death penalty for all crimes other than murder.

In the middle of the nineteenth century, opposition to capital punishment became so strong that the practice was abolished in several states. In 1846, Michigan became the first state to abolish the death penalty. Rhode Island followed suit in 1852 and Wisconsin in 1853. Tennessee governor John Sevier unsuccessfully campaigned for the abolishment of the death penalty in Tennessee in 1807. A century later, though, nine states rode a cresting wave of abolitionist sentiment to abolish the death penalty between 1907 and 1917. Even those who supported the death penalty in theory began to worry about holding public executions, which were usually hangings, for the general public to witness. Many believed that it desensitized people to violence. Some states, such as Connecticut in 1830, began to move executions from the public square to the jail yard. The last public hanging in the United States occurred in Kentucky in 1936.

Another development—one that still resonates today—is that states looked for more humane ways to execute individuals. Hangings often resulted in long, prolonged death struggles for the prisoner. On more than one occasion, hangings resulted in the decapitation of the inmate's head from his body. American lawmakers and community leaders increasingly sought out what authors Robert Linton and Greg Mitchell called "the ultimate oxymoron—the humane killing."

In the 1880s, New York's efforts to find a less painful way of killing death row inmates settled on the use of electricity. A new term, "electrocution," was coined, combining the words "electricity" and "execution." In 1890, William Kemmler of New York became the first person to die in the electric chair. The U.S. Supreme Court had ruled in *In Re Kemmler* (a case examined later in this book) earlier that year that death by electrocution was not cruel and unusual punishment.

Electrocution was not the only new method of execution. In 1921, Nevada became the first state to adopt the gas chamber to carry out capital punishment. Later in the twentieth century, lethal injection became a common method of execution. Today, most states that have the death penalty use lethal injection. However, there remains continued controversy over whether the use of specific drugs in the lethal injection process causes unnecessary and wanton pain to inmates.

Prohibition, World War I, and the Great Depression all led to a resurgence in the death penalty in the 1920s and 1930s. It was an era when gangsters like John Dillinger, Pretty Boy Floyd, and others robbed banks and shot law enforcement officers with seeming impunity.

In the 1950s and 1960s, however, the pendulum swung the other way, as more people began to question the death penalty. Many believed that the execution of Julius and Ethel Rosenberg for being Soviet spies was unjust. The Rosenbergs were accused of providing top secret information to the Soviets. Historical evidence now appears to confirm the validity of those charges. Californian inmate Caryl Chessman, who was convicted of various crimes including robbery and kidnapping, became somewhat of a death-row celebrity by writing several books that criticized the death penalty prior to his execution in 1960.

Expressions of doubt about the death penalty were also heard from the Supreme Court. In the early 1960s, Justice Arthur Goldberg openly questioned the death penalty and its application to the crime of rape. Goldberg also questioned whether a death penalty that was applied in such a racially disproportionate way could possibly be constitutional.

As the Civil Rights Movement gained strength, the National Association for the Advancement of Colored People (NAACP) and its Legal Defense Fund mounted a campaign to end the death penalty by casting a harsh light on the racist dimensions of its application. The NAACP pointed out there were far more African Americans facing the death penalty than white men. Before long eliminating capital punishment was a major civil rights cause.

These tireless efforts paid off. In 1966, for the first and only time, a national poll showed that death penalty opponents outnumbered its supporters 47% to 42%. In 1965, even the U.S. Department of Justice called for the abolition of the death penalty.

The NAACP's efforts culminated in the landmark decision *Furman v. Georgia* (1972) when the U.S. Supreme Court ruled 5–4 that the death penalty was unconstitutional. A narrow majority of the Supreme Court ruled that several states' death penalty statutes violated the Constitution because they did not provide enough guidance to juries. Justice Potter Stewart wrote, "These death sentences are cruel and unusual in the same way that being struck by lighting is cruel and unusual."

The decision vacated the sentences of 600 inmates on death row. This meant that these death row inmates' sentences were changed to life sentences. The electric chair in Arkansas was unplugged and used to give inmates haircuts. The execution chamber in New Hampshire was used to store vegetables. Death penalty opponents briefly rejoiced.

But it turned out that their victory was short-lived. Widespread public opposition to the *Furman* decision emerged as violent crime rates rose in the 1970s.

After *Furman*, 35 states reworked their death penalty statutes to provide more guidance. Some adopted so-called aggravating and mitigating factors for jurors to consider in a death penalty case. In 1976, the U.S. Supreme Court ruled in *Gregg v. Georgia* that the revised death penalty laws that provided more guidance to juries were constitutional. These statutes provided juries with aggravating and mitigating circumstances that supposedly would make death sentences less arbitrary. Justice Stewart, who had voted against the death penalty in *Furman*, wrote an opinion in favor of the newly drafted laws. He wrote in his *Gregg v. Georgia* opinion that "the concerns expressed in Furman that the penalty of death not be imposed in an arbitrary or capricious manner can be met by a carefully drafted statute that ensures that the sentencing authority is given adequate information and guidance."

Since *Gregg*, the death penalty has remained a constant on the American scene, but death penalty opponents did not give up. They focused their efforts on reducing the death penalty for certain kinds of inmates. This led to a series of victories, as the Supreme Court outlawed the death penalty for the insane, for those who were intellectually disabled, and for those who committed their crimes as juveniles.

Meanwhile, other countries began abolishing the death penalty too, including Canada (1967) and Great Britain (1969). Other countries abolished the death penalty for those who were intellectually disabled and juveniles. These developments sparked a deep divide on the U.S. Supreme Court on whether international law was relevant in interpreting the U.S. Constitution.

Another development was the introduction of DNA evidence—a kind of truth serum to the criminal process, including death penalty cases. DNA evidence led to quite a few exonerations of inmates on death row. There were so many exonerations on death row in Illinois that outgoing governor George Ryan famously commuted all death sentences in the state in 1999.

"Revelations of innocent persons on death row have permanently altered the death penalty debate," writes law professor and criminal law expert Brandon Garrett. "Regardless of whether one believes that the death penalty is justified in some circumstances, the knowledge that innocent people have been sentenced to death can shake one's confidence that the death penalty can be soundly imposed."

In recent years, more and more states have abolished the death penalty—23 (and the District of Columbia) as of 2021, according to the Death Penalty Information

Center. The thinking behind this trend is that life sentences cost less, remove and keep dangerous offenders off the street, serve as deterrence, get the state out of the business of killing its own citizens, and eliminate the possibility of putting innocent people to death.

The death penalty debate rages on, as more than 2,500 inmates remain on death row, according to the Death Penalty Information Center. Concerns still arise on whether the death penalty is infected with racial bias. Study after study has shown that those who kill white victims are sentenced to death much more often than those who kill non-white victims. There are still an alarming percentage of racial minorities on death row.

However, the death penalty still retains some strong support. Supporters point to the language of the Fifth Amendment in arguing that capital punishment is constitutional, and they remain adamant that the death penalty deters at least some would-be murderers and is an appropriate, moral punishment for particularly heinous crimes.

FURTHER READING

Banner, Stuart. *The Death Penalty: An American History*. Cambridge, MA: Harvard University Press, 2002.

Chammah, Maurice. *Let the Lord Sort Them: The Rise and Fall of the Death Penalty*. New York: Crown, 2021.

Death Penalty Information Center. "Facts about the Death Penalty." Updated May 4, 2022. https://documents.deathpenaltyinfo.org/pdf/FactSheet.pdf.

Garland, David. *Peculiar Institution: America's Death Penalty in an Age of Abolition*. Cambridge, MA: Harvard University Press, 2012.

Garrett, Brandon L. *Convicting the Innocent: Where Criminal Prosecutions Go Wrong*. Cambridge, MA: Harvard University Press, 2011.

Mitchell, Greg, and Robert Jay Lifton. *Who Owns Death? Capital Punishment, the American Conscience and the End of the Death Penalty*. New York: William Morrow & Co, 2000.

Steiker, Carol S., and Jordan M. Steiker. *Courting Death: The Supreme Court and Capital Punishment*. Cambridge, MA: Harvard University Press, 2016.

1

EARLY HISTORY OF THE DEATH PENALTY

The death penalty has long historical roots, tracing back to at least the Hammurabi Code of ancient Babylon in the eighteenth century B.C.E. Centuries later, the death penalty was a salient feature in the cultures and societies of ancient Greece and Rome. A prominent individual in the spread of the practice was the Greek leader Draco, who in 621 B.C.E. promulgated the Draconian Code, which punished a wide variety of crimes with the punishment of death. This code later inspired the eponym "draconian"—meaning unusually harsh or severe.

The death penalty remained a hallmark of the Middle Ages, with executions a fairly common occurrence. Executions were mass public events attended by thousands of people. Some historians have considered these massive death penalty spectacles as akin to a modern-day combat sport event or rock concert, given their popularity.

English law featured the death penalty with eighteenth-century British justice being one of the harshest in Europe. Under English law, even certain property crimes were considered death-eligible crimes. This pattern continued in the American colonies, which generally followed the British common-law system. The colonies differed in their application of the death penalty, but generally speaking, they embraced it as an appropriate punishment for a wide variety of crimes besides murder. For example, counterfeiting and adultery were considered death penalty crimes in some of the colonies. As legal historian Stuart Banner writes in his book *The Death Penalty: An American History*, "The death penalty circa 1700 was the equivalent of prison today—the standard punishment for a wide range of serious crimes."

Executions in early American history shared some similarities to executions in the Middle Ages in that they were spectacles and featured officials formally responsibly for carrying out the execution. Legal historian Lawrence Friedman referred to these events as "box office hits." People would come far and wide to watch these executions, which commonly featured remarks from ministers warning about the evils and dangers of sin and the importance of following a virtuous life.

The Founding Fathers clearly believed that capital punishment was a necessary evil. Look no further than the text of the Fifth Amendment to the Constitution, which begins with the following words: "No person shall be held to answer for a capital, or otherwise infamous crime, unless on a presentment or indictment of a grand jury . . ."

Yet abolitionists viewed the death penalty as a morally indefensible sanctioning of violence by the state. The famed Italian philosopher Cesare Beccaria famously wrote in his 1764 treatise *Essay on Crimes and Punishment* that "the punishment of death is pernicious to society from the example of barbarity it affords."

Similarly, Dr. Benjamin Rush, a prominent medical doctor from Pennsylvania who was a signatory to the Declaration of Independence, objected to the death penalty. "The punishment of murder by death, is contrary to reason, and to the order and happiness of society," he wrote. "It lessens the horror of taking away human life, and thereby tends to multiply murders."

In the late nineteenth century, critics of capital punishment increasingly sought to introduce more humane ways to carry out those sentences,—what authors Robert Lifton and Greg Mitchell called "the ultimate oxymoron—the humane killing." Different states considered other ways to execute the condemned other than hanging. These methods included firing squad, the electrocution, the gas chamber, and then lethal injection—which remains the most common method of execution today.

FURTHER READING

Banner, Stuart. *The Death Penalty: An American History*. Cambridge, MA: Harvard University Press, 2002.

Bowers, William J. *Legal Homicide as Punishment in America, 1864–1982*. Boston: Northeastern University Press, 1984.

Friedman, Lawrence M. *Crime and Punishment in American History*. New York: Basic Books, 1993.

Hudson, David L., Jr. *Does Capital Punishment Have a Future? A Resource Guide for Teachers*. Chicago: American Bar Association, 2004.

Lifton, Robert Jay, and Greg Mitchell. *Who Owns Death? Capital Punishment, the American Conscience, and the End of Executions*. 2nd ed. New York: HarperCollins, 2002.

- ***Document 1:*** Text of Speech to Parliament
- ***Date:*** April 21, 1868
- ***Where:*** London, England
- ***Significance:*** John Stuart Mill was one of the leading thinkers and intellectuals of his time. His writings and speeches influenced American thought and attitudes on issues ranging from freedom of speech to capital punishment.

DOCUMENT

John Stuart Mill Defends Capital Punishment

1). . . It would be a great satisfaction to me if I were able to support this Motion. It is always a matter of regret to me to find myself, on a public question, opposed to those who are called—sometimes in the way of honour, and sometimes in what is intended for ridicule—the philanthropists. Of all persons who take part in public affairs, they are those for whom, on the whole, I feel the greatest amount of respect; for their characteristic is, that they devote their time, their labour, and much of their money to objects purely public, with a less admixture of either personal or class selfishness, than any other class of politicians whatever.

2) On almost all the great questions, scarcely any politicians are so steadily and almost uniformly to be found on the side of right; and they seldom err, but by an exaggerated application of some just and highly important principle. On the very subject that is now occupying us we all know what signal service they have rendered. It is through their efforts that our criminal laws—which within my memory hanged people for stealing in a dwelling house to the value of 40s.-laws by virtue of which rows of human beings might be seen suspended in front of Newgate by those who ascended or descended Ludgate Hill—have so greatly relaxed their most revolting and most impolitic ferocity, that aggravated murder is now practically the only crime which is punished with death by any of our lawful tribunals; and we are even now deliberating whether the extreme penalty should be retained in that solitary case.

3) This vast gain, not only to humanity, but to the ends of penal justice, we owe to the philanthropists; and if they are mistaken, as I cannot but think they are, in the present instance, it is only in not perceiving the right time and place for stopping in a career hitherto so eminently beneficial. Sir, there is a point at which, I conceive, that career ought to stop. When there has been brought home to any one, by conclusive evidence, the greatest crime known to the law; and when the attendant circumstances suggest no palliation of the guilt, no hope that the culprit may even yet not be unworthy to live among mankind, nothing to make it probable that the crime was

an exception to his general character rather than a consequence of it, then I confess it appears to me that to deprive the criminal of the life of which he has proved himself to be unworthy—solemnly to blot him out from the fellowship of mankind and from the catalogue of the living—is the most appropriate as it is certainly the most impressive, mode in which society can attach to so great a crime the penal consequences which for the security of life it is indispensable to annex to it. I defend this penalty, when confined to atrocious cases, on the very ground on which it is commonly attacked—on that of humanity to the criminal; as beyond comparison the least cruel mode in which it is possible adequately to deter from the crime.

4) If, in our horror of inflicting death, we endeavour to devise some punishment for the living criminal which shall act on the human mind with a deterrent force at all comparable to that of death, we are driven to inflictions less severe indeed in appearance, and therefore less efficacious, but far more cruel in reality. Few, I think, would venture to propose, as a punishment for aggravated murder, less than imprisonment with hard labor for life; that is the fate to which a murderer would be consigned by the mercy which shrinks from putting him to death. But has it been sufficiently considered what sort of a mercy this is, and what kind of life it leaves to him? If, indeed, the punishment is not really inflicted—if it becomes the sham which a few years ago such punishments were rapidly becoming—then, indeed, its adoption would be almost tantamount to giving up the attempt to repress murder altogether.

5) But if it really is what it professes to be, and if it is realized in all its rigour by the popular imagination, as it very probably would not be, but as it must be if it is to be efficacious, it will be so shocking that when the memory of the crime is no longer fresh, there will be almost insuperable difficulty in executing it. What comparison can there really be, in point of severity, between consigning a man to the short pang of a rapid death, and immuring him in a living tomb, there to linger out what may be a long life in the hardest and most monotonous toil, without any of its alleviations or rewards—debarred from all pleasant sights and sounds, and cut off from all earthly hope, except a slight mitigation of bodily restraint, or a small improvement of diet? Yet even such a lot as this, because there is no one moment at which the suffering is of terrifying intensity, and, above all, because it does not contain the element, so imposing to the imagination, of the unknown, is universally reputed a milder punishment than death—stands in all codes as a mitigation of the capital penalty, and is thankfully accepted as such. For it is characteristic of all punishments which depend on duration for their efficacy—all, therefore, which are not corporal or pecuniary—that they are more rigorous than they seem; while it is, on the contrary, one of the strongest recommendations a punishment can have, that it should seem more rigorous than it is; for its practical power depends far less on what it is than on what it seems.

6) There is not, I should think, any human infliction which makes an impression on the imagination so entirely out of proportion to its real severity as the punishment of death. The punishment must be mild indeed which does not add more to the sum of human misery than is necessarily or directly added by the execution of a criminal. As my Hon. Friend the Member for Northampton (Mr. Gilpin) has himself remarked, the most that human laws can do to anyone in the matter of death is to hasten it; the man would have died at any rate; not so very much later, and on

the average, I fear, with a considerably greater amount of bodily suffering. Society is asked, then, to denude itself of an instrument of punishment which, in the grave cases to which alone it is suitable, effects its purposes at a less cost of human suffering than any other; which, while it inspires more terror, is less cruel in actual fact than any punishment that we should think of substituting for it.

7) My Hon. Friend says that it does not inspire terror, and that experience proves it to be a failure.

But the influence of a punishment is not to be estimated by its effect on hardened criminals. Those whose habitual way of life keeps them, so to speak, at all times within sight of the gallows, do grow to care less about it; as, to compare good things with bad, an old soldier is not much affected by the chance of dying in battle. I can afford to admit all that is often said about the indifference of professional criminals to the gallows. Though of that indifference one-third is probably bravado and another third confidence that they shall have the luck to escape, it is quite probable that the remaining third is real. But the efficacy of a punishment which acts principally through the imagination, is chiefly to be measured by the impression it makes on those who are still innocent; by the horror with which it surrounds the first promptings of guilt; the restraining influence it exercises over the beginning of the thought which, if indulged, would become a temptation; the check which it exerts over the graded declension towards the state—never suddenly attained—in which crime no longer revolts, and punishment no longer terrifies.

8) As for what is called the failure of death punishment, who is able to judge of that? We partly know who those are whom it has not deterred; but who is there who knows whom it has deterred, or how many human beings it has saved who would have lived to be murderers if that awful association had not been thrown round the idea of murder from their earliest infancy? Let us not forget that the most imposing fact loses its power over the imagination if it is made too cheap. When a punishment fit only for the most atrocious crimes is lavished on small offences until human feeling recoils from it, then, indeed, it ceases to intimidate, because it ceases to be believed in.

9) The failure of capital punishment in cases of theft is easily accounted for; the thief did not believe that it would be inflicted. He had learnt by experience that jurors would perjure themselves rather than find him guilty; that Judges would seize any excuse for not sentencing him to death, or for recommending him to mercy; and that if neither jurors nor Judges were merciful, there were still hopes from an authority above both. When things had come to this pass it was high time to give up the vain attempt. When it is impossible to inflict a punishment, or when its infliction becomes a public scandal, the idle threat cannot too soon disappear from the statute book. And in the case of the host of offences which were formerly capital, I heartily rejoice that it did become impracticable to execute the law.

10) If the same state of public feeling comes to exist in the case of murder; if the time comes when jurors refuse to find a murderer guilty; when Judges will not sentence him to death, or will recommend him to mercy; or when, if juries and Judges do not flinch from their duty, Home Secretaries, under pressure of deputations and memorials, shrink from theirs, and the threat becomes, as it became in the other cases, a mere *brutum fulmen*; then, indeed, it may become necessary to do in this case

what has been done in those—to abrogate the penalty. That time may come—my Hon. Friend thinks that it has nearly come.

11) I hardly know whether he lamented it or boasted of it; but he and his Friends are entitled to the boast; for if it comes it will be their doing, and they will have gained what I cannot but call a fatal victory, for they will have achieved it by bringing about, if they will forgive me for saying so, an enervation, an effeminancy, in the general mind of the country. For what else than effeminancy is it to be so much more shocked by taking a man's life than by depriving him of all that makes life desirable or valuable?

12) Is death, then, the greatest of all earthly ills? *Usque adeone mori miserum est?* Is it, indeed, so dreadful a thing to die? Has it not been from of old one chief part of a manly education to make us despise death—teaching us to account it, if an evil at all, by no means high in the list of evils; at all events, as an inevitable one, and to hold, as it were, our lives in our hands, ready to be given or risked at any moment, for a sufficiently worthy object? I am sure that my Hon. Friends know all this as well, and have as much of all these feelings as any of the rest of us; possibly more. But I cannot think that this is likely to be the effect of their teaching on the general mind. I cannot think that the cultivating of a peculiar sensitiveness of conscience on this one point, over and above what results from the general cultivation of the moral sentiments, is permanently consistent with assigning in our own minds to the fact of death no more than the degree of relative importance which belongs to it among the other incidents of our humanity.

13) The men of old cared too little about death, and gave their own lives or took those of others with equal recklessness. Our danger is of the opposite kind, lest we should be so much shocked by death, in general and in the abstract, as to care too much about it in individual cases, both those of other people and our own, which call for its being risked. And I am not putting things at the worst, for it is proved by the experience of other countries that horror of the executioner by no means necessarily implies horror of the assassin. The stronghold, as we all know, of hired assassination in the 18th century was Italy; yet it is said that in some of the Italian populations the infliction of death by sentence of law was in the highest degree offensive and revolting to popular feeling.

14) Much has been said of the sanctity of human life, and the absurdity of supposing that we can teach respect for life by ourselves destroying it. But I am surprised at the employment of this argument, for it is one which might be brought against any punishment whatever. It is not human life only, not human life as such, that ought to be sacred to us, but human feelings. The human capacity of suffering is what we should cause to be respected, not the mere capacity of existing. And we may imagine somebody asking how we can teach people not to inflict suffering by ourselves inflicting it? But to this I should answer—all of us would answer—that to deter by suffering from inflicting suffering is not only possible, but the very purpose of penal justice. Does fining a criminal show want of respect for property, or imprisoning him, for personal freedom? Just as unreasonable is it to think that to take the life of a man who has taken that of another is to show want of regard for human life. We show, on the contrary, most emphatically our regard for it, by the adoption of a rule that he who violates that right in another forfeits it for himself, and that while no other crime that he can commit deprives him of his right to live, this shall.

15) There is one argument against capital punishment, even in extreme cases, which I cannot deny to have weight—on which my Hon. Friend justly laid great stress, and which never can be entirely got rid of. It is this—that if by an error of justice an innocent person is put to death, the mistake can never be corrected; all compensation, all reparation for the wrong is impossible. This would be indeed a serious objection if these miserable mistakes—among the most tragical occurrences in the whole round of human affairs—could not be made extremely rare.

16) The argument is invincible where the mode of criminal procedure is dangerous to the innocent, or where the Courts of Justice are not trusted. And this probably is the reason why the objection to an irreparable punishment began (as I believe it did) earlier, and is more intense and more widely diffused, in some parts of the Continent of Europe than it is here. There are on the Continent great and enlightened countries, in which the criminal procedure is not so favorable to innocence, does not afford the same security against erroneous conviction, as it does among us; countries where the Courts of Justice seem to think they fail in their duty unless they find somebody guilty; and in their really laudable desire to hunt guilt from its hiding places, expose themselves to a serious danger of condemning the innocent. If our own procedure and Courts of Justice afforded ground for similar apprehension, I should be the first to join in withdrawing the power of inflicting irreparable punishment from such tribunals.

17) But we all know that the defects of our procedure are the very opposite. Our rules of evidence are even too favorable to the prisoner; and juries and Judges carry out the maxim, "It is better that ten guilty should escape than that one innocent person should suffer," not only to the letter, but beyond the letter. Judges are most anxious to point out, and juries to allow for, the barest possibility of the prisoner's innocence. No human judgment is infallible; such sad cases as my Hon. Friend cited will sometimes occur; but in so grave a case as that of murder, the accused, in our system, has always the benefit of the merest shadow of a doubt.

18) And this suggests another consideration very germane to the question. The very fact that death punishment is more shocking than any other to the imagination, necessarily renders the Courts of Justice more scrupulous in requiring the fullest evidence of guilt. Even that which is the greatest objection to capital punishment, the impossibility of correcting an error once committed, must make, and does make, juries and Judges more careful in forming their opinion, and more jealous in their scrutiny of the evidence. If the substitution of penal servitude for death in cases of murder should cause any declaration in this conscientious scrupulosity, there would be a great evil to set against the real, but I hope rare, advantage of being able to make reparation to a condemned person who was afterwards discovered to be innocent. In order that the possibility of correction may be kept open wherever the chance of this sad contingency is more than infinitesimal, it is quite right that the Judge should recommend to the Crown a commutation of the sentence, not solely when the proof of guilt is open to the smallest suspicion, but whenever there remains anything unexplained and mysterious in the case, raising a desire for more light, or making it likely that further information may at some future time be obtained.

19) I would also suggest that whenever the sentence is commuted the grounds of the commutation should, in some authentic form, be made known to the public.

Thus much I willingly concede to my Hon. Friend; but on the question of total abolition I am inclined to hope that the feeling of the country is not with him, and that the limitation of death punishment to the cases referred to in the Bill of last year will be generally considered sufficient. The mania which existed a short time ago for paring down all our punishments seems to have reached its limits, and not before it was time. We were in danger of being left without any effectual punishment, except for small of offences. What was formerly our chief secondary punishment—transportation—before it was abolished, had become almost a reward. Penal servitude, the substitute for it, was becoming, to the classes who were principally subject to it, almost nominal, so comfortable did we make our prisons, and so easy had it become to get quickly out of them. Flogging—a most objectionable punishment in ordinary cases, but a particularly appropriate one for crimes of brutality, especially crimes against women—we would not hear of, except, to be sure, in the case of garotters, for whose peculiar benefit we reestablished it in a hurry, immediately after a Member of Parliament had been garrotted. With this exception, offences, even of an atrocious kind, against the person, as my Hon. and learned Friend the Member for Oxford (Mr. Neate) well remarked, not only were, but still are, visited with penalties so ludicrously inadequate, as to be almost an encouragement to the crime.

20) I think, Sir, that in the case of most offences, except those against property, there is more need of strengthening our punishments than of weakening them; and that severer sentences, with an apportionment of them to the different kinds of offences which shall approve itself better than at present to the moral sentiments of the community, are the kind of reform of which our penal system now stands in need. I shall therefore vote against the Amendment.

SOURCE: Speech In Favor of Capital Punishment (americanliterature.com).

ANALYSIS

John Stuart Mill (1806–1873) was one of the leading intellectuals in the nineteenth century. A philosopher, Mill is perhaps best known for two works: *On Liberty* (1859) and *The Subjection of Women* (1869). *On Liberty* was a powerful meditation on the relationship between liberty and authority, while *The Subjection of Women* was a heartfelt criticism of how women were treated in society.

Mill served for three years in the British Parliament, the British legislative body that rules the country. In 1868, the Parliament considered a bill to ban capital punishment. A proponent of utilitarianism, Mill spoke out against the bill, asserting capital punishment was appropriate in cases where the defendant is clearly guilty of aggravated murder.

Mill's argument for a limited application of capital punishment is multilayered. He argues that the possibility of capital punishment can serve as a key deterrent to criminals who might otherwise commit violent or even homicidal offenses.

Mill also argues that the death penalty is not even the cruelest form of punishment. He contends that life sentence—where the prisoner knows that he or she will never be released—is a slower and more punishing kind of death. Mill explains, "If, in our horror of inflicting death, we endeavour to devise some punishment for the living criminal which shall act on the human mind with a deterrent force at all comparable to that of death, we are driven to inflictions less severe indeed in appearance, and therefore less efficacious, but far more cruel in reality."

Mill not only contends that punishment should be increased for certain types of crime but also emphasizes that in capital cases, judges and jurors need to be "scrupulous" in determining whether a defendant actually committed the crime. Mill explains, "The very fact that death punishment is more shocking than any other to the imagination, necessarily renders the Courts of Justice more scrupulous in requiring the fullest evidence of guilt. Even that which is the greatest objection to capital punishment, the impossibility of correcting an error once committed, must make, and does make, juries and Judges more careful in forming their opinion, and more jealous in their scrutiny of the evidence."

Of course, history has not always borne this out, as there have been inmates released from death row after DNA evidence confirmed that they could not have committed the crime. But Mill was writing in the nineteenth century, well before DNA evidence became a usable tool for investigators.

FURTHER READING

Cockburn, David. "Capital Punishment and Realism." *Philosophy* (April 1991), pp. 177–190.
Thoma, George A. "A Note on John Stuart Mill's Views on Capital Punishment." *A Journal of the History of Economic Thought* (1981), pp. 49–50.

- ***Document 2:*** Supreme Court decision in *Wilkerson v. Utah*
- ***Date:*** March 17, 1879
- ***Where:*** Washington, D.C.
- ***Significance:*** The Court's decision shows that the courts often defer to legislatures as to the methods of execution. The decision also points out that state legislatures of that time were moving away from hanging as the primary method of execution.

DOCUMENT

Supreme Court Finds Death by Shooting Is Not Cruel and Unusual Punishment

Duly organized territories are invested with legislative power, which extends to all rightful subjects of legislation not inconsistent with the Constitution and laws of the United States.

Congress organized the Territory of Utah on the 9th of September, 1850, and provided that the legislative power and authority of the territory shall be vested in the governor and legislative assembly.

Sufficient appears to show that the prisoner named in the record was legally charged with the willful, malicious, and premeditated murder of William Baxter with malice aforethought by indictment of the grand jury in due form of law, as fully set forth in the transcript, and that he, upon his arraignment, pleaded that he was not guilty of the alleged offense. Pursuant to the order of the court, a jury for the trial of the prisoner was duly impaneled and sworn, and it appears that the jury, after a full and fair trial, found, by their verdict, that the prisoner was guilty of murder in the first degree.

Regular proceedings followed, and the record also shows that the presiding justice in open court sentenced the prisoner as follows: that

> "you be taken from hence to some place in this territory, where you shall be safely kept until Friday, the fourteenth day of December next; that between the hours of ten o'clock in the forenoon and three o'clock in the afternoon of the last-named day, you be taken from your place of confinement to some place within this district, and that you there be publicly shot until you are dead."

Proceedings in the court of original jurisdiction being ended, the prisoner sued out a writ of error and removed the cause into the supreme court of the territory, where the judgment of the subordinate court was affirmed. Final judgment having been rendered in the supreme court of the territory, the prisoner sued out the present writ of error, the act of Congress providing that such a writ from this court to the supreme court of the territory will lie in criminal cases where the accused is sentenced to capital punishment or is convicted of bigamy or polygamy.

Appended to the proceedings is the assignment of error imputed to the court below, which is repeated in the same words in the brief of his counsel filed since the case was removed into this court. No exception was taken to the proceedings in either court prior to the sentence, the assignment of error being that the court below erred in affirming the judgment of the court of original jurisdiction and in adjudging and sentencing the prisoner to be shot to death.

. . .

Criminal homicide, when perpetrated by a person lying in wait, or by any other kind of willful, deliberate, malicious, and premeditated killing, or which is committed in the perpetration or attempt to perpetrate any one of the offenses therein enumerated, and evidencing a depraved mind, regardless of human life, is murder in the first degree.

. . .

Duly convicted of murder in the first degree as the prisoner was by the verdict of the jury, it is conceded that the existing law of the territory provides that he "shall suffer death;" nor is it denied that the antecedent law of the territory which was in force from March 6, 1852, to March 4, 1876, provided that

> "when any person shall be convicted of any crime the punishment of which is death, . . . he shall suffer death by being shot, hung, or beheaded, as the court may direct," or as the convicted person may choose. . . .

Construed as that provision must be in connection with the enactment that every person guilty of murder in the first degree shall suffer death, and in view of the fact that the laws of the territory contain no other specific regulation as to the mode of executing such a sentence, the court here is of the opinion that the assignment of error shows no legal ground for reversing the judgment of the court below. Authority to pass such a sentence is certainly not possessed by the circuit courts of the United States, as the act of Congress provides that the manner of inflicting the punishment of death shall be by hanging.

Punishments of the kind are always directed by the circuit courts to be inflicted in that manner, but organized territories are invested with legislative power which extends to all rightful subjects of legislation not inconsistent with the Constitution and laws of the United States. By virtue of that power the legislative branch of the territory may define offenses and prescribe the punishment of the offenders, subject to the prohibition of the Constitution that cruel and unusual punishments shall not be inflicted.

Good reasons exist for supposing that Congress never intended that the provision referred to, that the punishment of death shall be by hanging, should supersede the power of the territories to legislate upon the subject, as the congressional provision is a part of the first crimes act ever passed by the national legislature. Different statutory regulations existed in the territory for nearly a quarter of a century, and the usages of the army to the present day are that sentences of the kind may in certain cases be executed by shooting, and in others by hanging.

. . .

Capital punishment, says the author first named, may be either by shooting or hanging. For mutiny, desertion, or other military crime, it is commonly by shooting; for murder not combined with mutiny, for treason, and piracy accompanied with wounding or attempt to murder, by hanging, as the sentence in England must accord with the law of the country in regard to the punishment of offenders. Exactly the same views are expressed by the other writer, which need not be reproduced.

Cruel and unusual punishments are forbidden by the Constitution, but the authorities referred to are quite sufficient to show that the punishment of shooting as a mode of executing the death penalty for the crime of murder in the first degree is not included in that category within the meaning of the Eighth Amendment. Soldiers convicted of desertion or other capital military offenses are in the great majority of cases sentenced to be shot, and the ceremony for such occasions is given in great fullness by the writers upon the subject of courts-martial.

. . .

Such is the general statement of that commentator, but he admits that in very atrocious crimes, other circumstances of terror, pain, or disgrace were sometimes superadded. Cases mentioned by the author are where the prisoner was drawn or dragged to the place of execution, in treason; or where he was emboweled alive, beheaded, and quartered, in high treason. Mention is also made of public dissection in murder, and burning alive in treason committed by a female. History confirms the truth of these atrocities, but the commentator states that the humanity of the nation by tacit consent allowed the mitigation of such parts of those judgments as savored of torture or cruelty, and he states that they were seldom strictly carried into effect.

. . .

the extent of the constitutional provision which provides that cruel and unusual punishments shall not be inflicted; but it is safe to affirm that punishments of torture, such as those mentioned by the commentator referred to, and all others in the same line of unnecessary cruelty, are forbidden by that amendment to the Constitution.

Concede all that, and still it by no means follows that the sentence of the court in this case falls within that category, or that the supreme court of the territory erred in affirming the judgment of the court of original jurisdiction. Antecedent to the enactment of the code which went into operation March 4, 1876, the statute of the territory passed March 6, 1852, provided that when any person was convicted of any capital offense he shall suffer death by being shot, hanged, or beheaded, as the court may direct, subject to the qualification therein expressed, to the effect that the person condemned might have his option as to the manner of his execution, the meaning of which qualification, as construed, was that the option was limited to the modes prescribed in the statute, and that if it was not exercised, the direction must be given by the court passing the sentence.

Nothing of the kind is contained in the existing code, and the legislature in dropping the provision as to the option failed to enact any specific regulation as to the mode of executing the death penalty. Instead of that, the explicit enactment is that every person guilty of murder in the first degree shall suffer death, or, upon the recommendation of the jury, may be imprisoned at hard labor in the penitentiary for life, at the discretion of the court.

Beyond all question, the first clause of the provision is applicable in this case, as the jury gave no such recommendation as that recited in the second clause, the record showing that their verdict was unconditional and absolute, from which it follows that the sentence that the prisoner shall suffer death is legally correct.

Had the statute prescribed the mode of executing the sentence, it would have been the duty of the court to follow it, unless the punishment to be inflicted was cruel and unusual, within the meaning of the Eighth Amendment to the Constitution, which is not pretended by the counsel of the prisoner. Statutory directions being given that the prisoner when duly convicted shall suffer death, without any statutory regulation specifically pointing out the mode of executing the command of the law, it must be that the duty is devolved upon the court authorized to pass the sentence to determine the mode of execution and to impose the sentence prescribed.

Persons guilty of murder in the first degree "shall suffer death," are the words of the territorial statute, and when that provision is construed in connection with sec. 10 of the code previously referred to, it is clear that it is made obligatory upon the court to prescribe the mode of executing the sentence of death which the code imposes where the conviction is for murder in the first degree, subject, of course, to the constitutional prohibition, that cruel and unusual punishment shall not be inflicted.

Other modes besides hanging were sometimes resorted to at common law, nor did the common law in terms require the court in passing the sentence either to prescribe the mode of execution or to fix the time or place for carrying it into effect, as is frequently if not always done in the federal circuit courts. At common law, neither the mode of executing the prisoner nor the time or place of execution was necessarily embodied in the sentence. Directions in regard to the former were usually given by the judge in the calendar of capital cases prepared by the clerk at the close of the term; as, for example, in the case of murder, the direction was "let him be hanged by the neck," which calendar was signed by the judge and clerk, and constituted in many cases the only authority of the officer as to the mode of execution.

Reference is made to the cases . . . as supporting the theory of the prisoner that the court possessed no authority to prescribe the mode of execution; but the court here is entirely of a different opinion, for the reasons already given.

Judgment affirmed.

SOURCE: *Wilkerson v. Utah*, 99 U.S. 130 (1879).

ANALYSIS

In the *nineteenth* century, the traditional method of execution was hanging, usually in the town square in front of a significant number of people. In the latter part of the *nineteenth* century, there was a movement to find different ways of executing persons. Many people began to see public hanging as too barbarous and cruel. One such method included death by firing squad.

In his book *The Death Penalty: An American Experiment* (2003), historian Stuart Banner explains that the movement to death by firing squad arose from the Mormon belief that one could not atone for one's crime without shedding blood. Hanging usually did not result in bloodshed. Therefore, the territory of Utah allowed death by firing squad. The state of Nevada later allowed shooting as well in 1912.

Utah's law initially provided that a condemned prisoner could choose his *or her* method of death among three choices: hanging, firing squad, or beheading. Beheading was later dropped, so the choice was between hanging or firing squad.

The U.S. Supreme Court reasoned that death by firing squad was not cruel and unusual punishment under the Eighth Amendment in a murder case in featuring a perpetrator named Wilkerson and a victim named William Baxter. The Court reasoned that it was not the job of the courts to second-guess a state legislature as to the preferred methods of execution.

The Court also reasoned that since firing squads were used by the military, their use could not be considered cruel and unusual under the Eighth Amendment. The Court did acknowledge that torture and other forms of grossly barbaric treatment could violate the Eighth Amendment but that death by firing squad did not fall into that category. In other words, death by firing squad was a constitutional form of punishment.

Between 1896 and 1972, *34* men were executed by firing squad in Utah. The most famous inmate executed by firing squad was Gary Gilmore, who was put to death in Utah in 1977 for the murder of two men. Gilmore's case became famous around the country when he demanded that he be put to death for his crimes. Utah later dropped death by firing squad in 2010 out of growing concern that *this* method of execution gave too much attention to death row inmates. The Utah governor, however, signed a bill in 2015 that provided that death by firing squad could be used in case the state could not procure the drugs necessary for lethal injection.

Currently, the only other states to allow for death by firing squad are Oklahoma and Mississippi. As in Utah, death by firing squad can only be used in those states if lethal injection, the gas chamber, or electrocution *is* not available or has been declared unconstitutional.

A law review article in 2019 advocated for the use of firing squads for the federal death penalty. The author, Stephanie Moran, wrote in "A Modest Proposal: The Federal Government Should Use Firing Squads to Execute Federal Death Row Inmates" (2019): "The use of firing squads is arguably the most humane and efficient method of execution. The firing squad results in a quicker, less painful death. Not only would the use of firing squads likely result in fewer botched executions, but it would also force society to accept what we are authorizing the state to do."

FURTHER READING

Banner, Stuart. *The Death Penalty: An American Experiment*. Cambridge, MA: Harvard University Press, 2002.

Moran, Stephanie. "A Modest Proposal: The Federal Government Should Use Firing Squads to Execute Federal Death Row Inmates." 74 *University of Miami Law Review* 276 (2019).

- ***Document* 3:** *In Re Kemmler*
- ***Date:*** May 19, 1890
- ***Where:*** Washington, D.C.
- ***Significance:*** The Court's ruling in this case that electrocution was a constitutional method of execution was momentous in terms of its impact on a number of states. Public hangings dropped and use of the electric chair increased in penitentiaries across the country.

DOCUMENT

Supreme Court Rules Electrocution Is Not Cruel and Unusual Punishment

This is an application for a writ of error to bring up for review a judgment of the supreme court of the state of New York, affirming an order of the county judge of Cayuga county, remanding the relator to the custody of the warden of the state-prison at Auburn, upon a hearing upon habeas corpus.

. . .

The petition was filed by one Hatch, and stated that William Kemmler, otherwise called John Hort, is imprisoned or restrained in his liberty at Auburn state-prison, in the city of Auburn, county of Cayuga, state of New York, by Charles F. Durston, agent and warden of Auburn state-prison, having charge thereof; that he has not been committed and is not detained by virtue of any judgment, decree, final order, or process issued by a court or judge of the United States, in a case where such courts or judges have exclusive jurisdiction under the laws of the United States, or have acquired exclusive jurisdiction by the commencement of legal proceedings in such a court; nor is he committed or detained by virtue of the final judgment or decree of a competent tribunal of civil or criminal jurisdiction, or the final order of such a tribunal, made in the special proceedings instituted, for any cause except to punish him for contempt, or by virtue of an execution or other process issued upon such a judgment, decree, or final order; that the cause or pretense of the imprisonment or restraint of said William Kemmler, otherwise called John Hort, according to the best knowledge and belief of your petitioner, is that he was indicted by a grand jury of Erie county for murder in the first degree; . . . The conclusion of the warrant, pursuing the sentence, was in these words: "Now, therefore, you are hereby ordered, commanded, and required to execute the said sentence upon him, the said William Kemmler, otherwise called John Hort, upon some day within the week commencing on Monday, the 24th day of June, in the year of our Lord one thousand eight hundred and eighty-nine, and within the walls of Auburn state-prison, or within the yard or inclosure adjoining thereto, by then and there causing to pass through the body of him the said William Kemmler, otherwise called John Hort, a current of electricity of sufficient intensity to cause death, and that the application of such current of electricity be continued until he, the said William Kemmler, otherwise called John Hort, be dead."

Upon the return of the writ before the county judge, counsel for the petitioner offered to prove that the infliction of death by the application of electricity as directed 'is a cruel and unusual punishment, within the meaning of the constitution, and that it cannot, therefore, be lawfully inflicted, and to establish the facts upon which the court can pass as to the character of the penalty.

. . . we think that the evidence is clearly in favor of the conclusion that it is within easy reach of electrical science at this day to so generate and apply to the person of the convict a current of electricity of such known and sufficient force as certainly to produce instantaneous, and therefore painless, death.'

From this judgment of the supreme court an appeal was prosecuted to the court of appeals, and the order appealed from was affirmed. It is said in the opinion by O'BRIEN, J.: "The only question involved in this appeal is whether this enactment is in conflict with the provision of the state constitution which forbids the infliction of cruel and unusual punishment. . . . If it cannot be made to appear that a law is in conflict with the constitution, by argument deduced from the language of the law itself, or from matters of which a court can take judicial notice, then the act must stand. The testimony of expert or other witnesses is not admissible to show that in carrying out a law enacted by the legislature some provision of the constitution may possibly be violated." The determination of the legislature that the use of electricity as an agency for producing death constituted a more humane method of executing the judgment of the court in capital cases was held conclusive. . . .

We find, then, the law held constitutional by the court of oyer and terminer in rendering the original judgment; by the supreme court and the court of appeals in affirming it; by the county judge in the proceedings, upon the writ of habeas corpus; by the supreme court in affirming the order of the county judge; and by the court of appeals in affirming that judgment of the supreme court. It appears that the first step which led to the enactment of the law was a statement contained in the annual message of the governor of the state of New York, transmitted to the legislature January 6, 1885, as follows: "The present mode of executing criminals by hanging has come down to us from the dark ages, and it may well be questioned whether the science of the present day cannot provide a means for taking the life of such as are condemned to die in a less barbarous manner. I commend this suggestion to the consideration of the legislature." The legislature accordingly appointed a commission to investigate and report "the most humane and practical method known to modern science of carrying into effect the sentence of death in capital cases." . . .

Kemmler was indicted for and convicted of a murder committed on the 29th day of March, 1889, and therefore came within the statute. The inhibition of the federal constitution upon the passage of ex post facto laws has no application. Section 5, art. 1, of the constitution of the state of New York provides that "excessive bail shall not be required, nor excessive fines imposed, nor shall cruel and unusual punishments be inflicted, nor shall witnesses be unreasonably detained." The eighth amendment to the federal constitution reads thus: "Excessive bail shall not be required, nor excessive fines imposed, nor cruel and unusual punishments inflicted." . . .

In *Wilkerson v. Utah*, 99 U.S. 130, 135 Mr. Justice CLIFFORD, in delivering the opinion of the court, referring to Blackstone, said: "Difficulty would attend the effort to define with exactness the extent of the constitutional provision which provides that cruel and unusual punishments shall not be inflicted; but it is safe to affirm that punishments of torture, such as those mentioned by the commentator referred to, and all others in the same line of unnecessary cruelty, are forbidden by that amendment to the constitution." Punishments are cruel when they involve torture or a lingering death; but the punishment of death is not cruel within the meaning of that word as used in the constitution. It implies there something inhuman and barbarous,-something more than the mere extinguishment of life. The courts of New York held that the mode adopted in this instance might be said to be unusual because it was new, but that it could not be assumed to be cruel in the light of that common knowledge which has stamped certain punishments as such; that it was for the legislature to say in what manner sentence of death should be executed; . . .

The enactment of this statute was, in itself, within the legitimate sphere of the legislative power of the state, and in the observance of those general rules prescribed by our systems of jurisprudence; and the legislature of the state of New York determined that it did not inflict cruel and unusual punishment, and its courts have sustained that determination. We cannot perceive that the state has thereby abridged the privileges or immunities of the petitioner, or deprived him of due process of law.

In order to reverse the judgment of the highest court of the state of New York, we should be compelled to hold that it had committed an error so gross as to amount in law to a denial by the state of due process of law to one accused of crime, or of some right secured to him by the constitution of the United States. We have no hesitation in saying that this we cannot do upon the record before us. The application for a writ of error is denied.

SOURCE: In Re Kemmler, 136 U.S. 436 (1890).

ANALYSIS

For many years, executions were primarily conducted by public hanging. Executions were the nineteenth-century equivalent of major rock concerts, as thousands upon thousands of people attended the events that often were highlighted by fiery sermons from a religious figure.

However, many believed that public hangings were a gruesome spectacle and that there needed to be a better way to execute persons. New York officials commissioned a group of officials to study and examine other possible methods of execution.

One way that showed some promise was through electricity. The term "electrocution" came from combining the words "execution" and "electricity." Two major figures vied for the dominant market share of the execution chair: Thomas Edison, the famous inventor of Menlo Park fame, and Thomas Westinghouse.

Eventually, the New York legislature passed a law mandating that the way of executions would be electrocution. William Kemmler, a man convicted of killing his girlfriend, was on death row. His lawyers filed a *habeas corpus* petition, arguing that electrocution was cruel and unusual punishment and, thus, violative of the Eighth Amendment.

However, the U.S. Supreme Court ruled that it did not violate the Eighth Amendment. The Court did not necessarily approve of electrocution but rather exercised judicial restraint and deferred to the wisdom of New York legislators.

Electrocution later became the dominant mode of executions in the United States for many decades before there was a gradual shift toward lethal injection. There have been several infamous executions where a person essentially was torched and did not immediately die. For this reason, electrocution is a relatively rarer form of execution in the United States.

However, the Court's decision in *In Re Kemmler* (1890), in the words of Professor Deborah W. Denno in her piece, "Is Electrocution an Unconstitutional Method of Execution: The Engineering of Death over the Century" (1994): "[C]ourts have continued to rely on Kemmler for the proposition that a wide range of capital punishments, most particularly electrocution, are permissible."

FURTHER READING

Banner, Stuart W. *The Death Penalty: An American History*. Cambridge, MA: Harvard University Press, 2002.

Denno, Deborah W. "Is Electrocution an Unconstitutional Method of Execution? The Engineering of Death over the Century." 35 *William & Mary Law Review* 555 (1994).

Leyden, John G. "Death in the Hot Seat: A Century of Electrocutions." *Washington Post*. August 5, 1990.

- ***Document 4:*** Supreme Court opinion in *Holden v. Minnesota*
- ***Date:*** December 8, 1890
- ***Where:*** Washington, D.C.
- ***Significance:*** The Court's decision shows the Court's deference to state legislatures when it comes to the death penalty. In this case the Court not only deferred to the state's system of execution but also confirmed the state's authority to establish execution dates and carry out other administrative function related to capital punishment. The Court also declined to interfere with the punishment of solitary confinement.

DOCUMENT

Supreme Court Approves Death by Hanging

By an indictment returned May 15, 1889, in the District Court of Redwood County, Minnesota, Clifton Holden was charged with the crime of murder in the first degree, committed in that County on the 23d day of November, 1888. Having been found guilty, and a motion for a new trial having been overruled, he prosecuted an appeal to the Supreme Court of the State. That court affirmed upon the merits the order denying the motion for a new trial, and remitted the case to the District Court. State v. Holden, 42 Minnesota, 350. In the latter Court it was adjudged, February 18, 1890, that, as a punishment for the crime of which he had been convicted, Holden be confined in the common jail of Brown County, (there being no jail in Redwood County,) and that thereafter and after the lapse of three calendar months from the date of the sentence, and at a time to be designated in the warrant of the governor of the State, he be taken to the place of execution and hanged by the neck until dead.

On the 21st of May, 1890, the governor issued a warrant to the sheriff, which, after reciting the judgment, commanded and required him to cause execution of the sentence of the law to be done upon the convict on Friday, the 27th day of June, 1890, before the hour of sunrise of the day last named, at a place in the county of Redwood, to be selected by such officer, "conformably with the provisions of section 3 of an act entitled 'An act providing for the mode of inflicting the punishment of death, the manner in which the same shall be carried into effect, and declaring a violation of any of the provisions of this act to be a misdemeanor,' approved April 24, 1889."

The accused, being in custody under the above judgment and warrant, presented to the Circuit Court of the United States for the District of Minnesota his written application for a writ of habeas corpus, based upon the ground that he was restrained of his liberty in violation of the Constitution of the United States. The writ was issued, and the officers having charge of the accused made a return to which the petitioner filed an answer. The Attorney General of Minnesota appeared on behalf of the State, insisting that the detention of the petitioner was not in violation of the supreme law of the land. . . .

The principal question before us depends upon the effect to be given to the act, referred to in the governor's warrant, of April 24, 1889. That act is as follows:

"§ 1. The mode of inflicting the punishment of death shall in all cases be hanging by the neck until the person is dead.

"§ 2. Whenever the punishment of death is inflicted upon any convict in obedience to a warrant from the governor of the State, the sheriff of the County shall be present at the execution, unless prevented by sickness or other casualty; and he may have such military guard as he may think proper. He shall return the warrant with a statement under his hand of doings thereon as soon as may be after the said execution to the governor, and shall also file in the clerk's office of the court where the conviction was had an attested copy of the warrant and statement aforesaid, and the clerk shall subjoin a brief abstract of such statement to the record of conviction and sentence.

"§ 3. The warrant of execution shall be executed before the hour of sunrise of the day designated in the warrant and within the walls of the jail in all cases where the jail is so constructed that it can be conveniently done therein; but when the jail is not so constructed, the warrant shall be executed within an enclosure which shall be higher than the gallows, and shall exclude the view of persons outside, and which shall be prepared for that purpose, under the direction of the sheriff, in the immediate vicinity of the jail, or, if there be no jail in the county, at some convenient place at the county-seat, to be selected by the sheriff.

"§ 4.After the issue of the warrant for execution by the governor, the prisoner shall be kept in solitary confinement, and the following persons shall be allowed to visit him, but none other, viz.: The sheriff and his deputies, the prisoner's counsel, any priest or clergyman the prisoner may select, and the members of his immediate family.

"§ 5. Besides the sheriff and his assistants, the following persons may be present at the execution, by none other: The clergyman or priest in attendance upon the prisoner and such other persons as the prisoner may designate, not exceeding three in number, a physician or surgeon, to be selected by the sheriff, and such other persons as the sheriff may designate, not exceeding six in number, but no person so admitted shall be a newspaper reporter or representative. No account of the details of such execution, beyond the statement of the fact that such convict was on the day in question duly executed according to law, shall be published in any newspaper.

"§ 6. Any person who shall violate or omit to comply with any of the provisions of this act shall be guilty of a misdemeanor.

. . .

. . .

We have proceeded in our examination of the case upon the ground that the prior statutes requiring the punishment of death to be inflicted by hanging, and the issuing by the governor of the warrant of execution before such punishment was inflicted, were consistent with and were not repealed by the act of 1889, and, therefore, so far as the mere imprisonment of the appellant, and his execution in conformity with prior statutes, were concerned, they could both occur without invoking the provision in the act of 1889, requiring solitary confinement after the warrant of execution was issued. . . .

The sentence against the appellant did not require that he be kept in solitary confinement. Nor did that statute cover the whole subject of murder in the first degree, or prescribe the only rules that should control in the trial and punishment for crimes of that class. It did not touch the judgments to be pronounced in such cases nor interfere with the power of the governor to issue a warrant of execution. The provisions of the previous law, as to the nature of the sentence, the particular mode of inflicting death, and the issuing by the governor of the warrant of execution before the convict was hung, were, therefore, not repealed, although some of them were reenacted or repeated in the statute of 1889, and other provisions relating merely to the time and mode of executing the warrant, but not affecting the substantial rights of the convict, were added. Indeed, as the act of 1889 does not itself prescribe the punishment of death for murder in the first degree, the authority to inflict that punishment, even for an offence committed after its passage, must be derived from the previous law. The only interpretation of that act that will give full effect to the intention of the legislature in respect to the prior unrepealed law relating to sentences of death for murder in the first degree committed before its passage, is to hold, as we do, that its fourth section, prescribing solitary confinement, is an independent provision, applicable only to future offences, not to those committed prior to its passage.

In this view, and as it does not appear that the appellant is kept in solitary confinement, there is no ground upon which it can be held that his mere imprisonment, in execution of the sentence of death, is in violation of the constitutional provision against ex post facto laws. That sentence, the subsequent imprisonment of the convict under it, without solitary confinement, and the warrant of execution, are in accordance with the law of the State as it was when the offence was committed, and do not infringe any right secured by the Constitution of the United States.

. . .

Among the assignments of error by the appellant is one to the effect that "the judgment of the State District Court that he be hanged at a time to be fixed by the governor of Minnesota was not a valid exercise of judicial authority or due process of law thus to deprive him of life at such time as the executive should arbitrarily appoint." We do not understand the counsel of the appellant to press this point. But as this assignment of error has not been formally withdrawn, and as human life is involved in our decision, it is proper to say that, under the law of Minnesota, at the time appellant committed the crime of which he was convicted, as well as when he was indicted and tried, the day on which the punishment of death should be inflicted depended upon the warrant of the governor. It is competent for the State to establish such regulations, and they are entirely consistent with due process of law. The court sentenced the convict to the punishment prescribed for the crime of murder in the first degree, leaving the precise day for inflicting the punishment to be determined by the governor. The order designating the day of execution is, strictly speaking, no part of the judgment, unless made so by statute. And the power conferred upon the governor to fix the time of infliction is no more arbitrary in its nature than the same power would be if conferred upon the court. Whether conferred upon the governor or the court, it is arbitrary in no other sense than every power is arbitrary that depends upon the discretion of the tribunal or the person authorized to exercise it. It may be, also, observed that at common law the sentence of death was generally silent as to the precise day of execution. Of course if the statute so requires, the court must, in its sentence, fix the day of execution. Equally must it forbear to do that if the statute confers upon some executive officer the power to designate the time of infliction.

Judgment affirmed.

SOURCE: *Holden v. Minnesota*, 137 U.S. 483 (1890).

ANALYSIS

The Supreme Court confronted a challenge by a convicted murderer that it was unlawful for him to be executed at some unknown date in the future inside the jail cell. The defendant also contended that it was unlawful for him to be placed in solitary confinement before his execution date.

At that time, the method of execution was hanging. New methods of execution—such as by firing squad and electrocution—had been approved by the Supreme Court in the cases of *Wilkerson v. Utah* (1879) and *In Re Kemmler* (1890), but the state of Minnesota had not changed its death penalty law—hanging was still the death method of choice.

Much of the Court's opinion in *Holden v. Minnesota* focused on whether it was an ex post facto problem for him to be subject to solitary confinement before his execution. However, it appears that often he was not placed in solitary confinement.

Another argument that Holden made was that it was unconstitutional for him to be put to death at some uncertain date in the future. Justice John Marshall Harlan I wrote the opinion for the Court and implied that deference was necessary to Minnesota authorities on this question.

Harlan explained that "at common law the sentence of death was generally silent as to the precise day of execution" and that "if the statute so requires, the court must, in its sentence, fix the day of execution."

What is also significant about the case is that the Court in dicta stated that it was proper to have the hanging conducted inside the jail without any reporters present. Today, there have been lawsuits filed on First Amendment grounds, arguing that there is a First Amendment–based right to a public execution process.

FURTHER READING

Brown, Timothy F. "Lethal Injection and the Right of Access: The Intersection of the Eighth and First Amendments." 5 *L.J. Soc. Just.* 74 (2015).

Reinert, Alexander A. "Solitary Troubles." 93 *Notre Dame Law Review* 927 (2018).

- ***Document 5:*** Supreme Court decision in *Williams v. Mississippi*
- ***Date:*** April 25, 1898
- ***Where:*** Washington, D.C.
- ***Significance:*** The Supreme Court's notorious decision in *Williams v. Mississippi* (1898) gave years of legal cover to some of the Jim Crow South's most nakedly racist laws. The *Williams* case originated with a legal challenge to the state of Mississippi's use of all-white juries in trials involving Black defendants, but the Court's decision in favor of Mississippi also upheld poll taxes, literacy tests, and other tools of disenfranchisement enshrined in Mississippi law.

DOCUMENT

Supreme Court Fails to Find Racial Discrimination in Mississippi All-White Juries

The question presented is, are the provisions of the constitution of the state of Mississippi and the laws enacted to enforce the same repugnant to the fourteenth amendment of the constitution of the United States? That amendment and its effect upon the rights of the colored race have been considered by this court in a number of cases, and it has been uniformly held that the constitution of the United States, as amended, forbids, so far as civil and political rights are concerned, discriminations by the general government or by the states against any citizen because of his race; but it has also been held, in a very recent case, to justify a removal from a state court to a federal court of a cause in which such rights are alleged to be denied, that such denial must be the result of the constitution or laws of the state, not of the administration of them. . . .

It is not asserted by plaintiff in error that either the constitution of the state or its laws discriminate in terms against the negro race, either as to the elective franchise or the privilege or duty of sitting on juries. These results, if we understand plaintiff in error, are alleged to be effected by the powers vested in certain administrative officers.

Plaintiff in error says:

"Section 241 of the constitution of 1890 prescribes the qualifications for electors; that residence in the state for two years, one year in the precinct of the applicant, must be effected; that he is twenty-one years or over of age, having paid all taxes legally due of him for two years prior to 1st day of February of the year he offers to vote, not having been convicted of theft, arson, rape, receiving money or goods under false pretenses, bigamy, embezzlement.

"Section 242 of the constitution provides the mode of registration; that the legislature shall provide by law for registration of all persons entitled to vote at any election, and that all persons offering to register shall take the oath; that they are not disqualified for voting by reason of any of the crimes named in the constitution of this state; that they will truly answer all questions propounded to them concerning their antecedents so far as they relate to the applicant's right to vote, and also as to their residence before their citizenship in the district in which such application for registration is made. The court readily sees the scheme. If the applicant swears, as he must do, that he is not disqualified by reason of the crimes specified, and that he has effected the required residence, what right has he to answer all questions as to his former residence? Section 244 of the constitution requires that the applicant for registration, after January, 1892, shall be able to read any section of the constitution, or he shall be able to understand the same (being any section of the organic law), or give a reasonable interpretation thereof. Now, we submit that these provisions vest in the administrative officers the full power, under section 242, to ask all sorts of vain, impertinent questions; and it is with that officer to say whether the questions relate to the applicant's right to vote. This officer can reject whomsoever he chooses, and register whomsoever he chooses, for he is vested by the constitution with that power. Under section 244 it is left with the administrative officer to determine whether the applicant reads, understands, or interprets the section of the constitution designated. The officer is the sole judge of the examination of the applicant, and, even though the applicant be qualified, it is left with the officer to so determine; and the said officer can refuse him registration."

To make the possible dereliction of the officers the dereliction of the constitution and laws, the remarks of the supreme court of the state are quoted by plaintiff in error as to their intent. The constitution provides for the payment of a poll tax, and by a section of the Code its payment cannot be compelled by a seizure and sale of property. We gather from the brief of counsel that its payment is a condition of the right to vote, and, in a case to test whether its payment was or was not optional, the supreme court of the state said: "Within the field of permissible action under the limitations imposed by the federal constitution, the convention swept the field of expedients, to obstruct the exercise of suffrage by the negro race." And further the court said, speaking of the negro race: "By reason of its previous condition of servitude and dependencies, this race had acquired or accentuated certain peculiarities of habit, of temperament, and of character, which clearly distinguished it as a race from the whites; a patient, docile people, but careless, landless, migratory within narrow limits, without forethought, and its criminal members given to furtive offenses, rather than the robust crimes of the whites. Restrained by the federal constitution from discriminating against the negro race, the convention discriminates against its characteristics, and the offenses to which its criminal members are prone." But nothing tangible can be deduced from this. If weakness were to be taken advantage of, it was to be done "within the field of permissible action under the limitations imposed by the federal constitution," and the means of it were the alleged characteristics of the negro race, not the administration of the law by officers of the state. Besides, the operation of the constitution and laws is not limited by their language or effects to one race. They reach weak and vicious white men as well as weak and vicious black men, and whatever is sinister in their intention, if anything, can be prevented by both races by the exertion of that duty which voluntarily pays taxes and refrains from crime.

It cannot be said, therefore, that the denial of the equal protection of the laws arises primarily from the constitution and laws of Mississippi; nor is there any sufficient allegation of an evil and discriminating administration of them. The only allegation is ". . . by granting a discretion to the said officers, as mentioned in the several sections of the constitution of the state, and the statute of the state adopted under the said constitution, the use of which discretion can be and has been used by said officers in the said Washington county to the end here complained of, to wit, the abridgment of the elective franchise of the colored voters of Washington county; that such citizens are denied the right to be selected as jurors to serve in the circuit court of the county; and that this denial to them of the right to equal protection and benefits of the laws of the state of Mississippi on account of their color and race, resulting from the exercise of the discretion partial to the white citizens, is in accordance with the purpose and intent of the framers of the present constitution of said state. . . ."

It will be observed that there is nothing direct and definite in this allegation either as to means or time as affecting the proceedings against the accused. There is no charge against the officers to whom is submitted the selection of grand or petit jurors, or those who procure the lists of the jurors. There is an allegation of the purpose of the convention to disfranchise citizens of the colored race; but with this we have no concern, unless the purpose is executed by the constitution or laws or by those who administer them. If it is done in the latter way, how or by what means should be shown. We gather from the statements of the motion that certain officers are invested with discretion in making up lists of electors, and that this discretion can be and has been exercised against the colored race, and from these lists jurors are selected. The supreme court of Mississippi, however, decided, in a case presenting the same questions as the one at bar, "that jurors are not selected from or with reference to any lists furnished by such election officers."

We do not think that this case is brought within the ruling in Yick Wo v. Hopkins. In that case the ordinances passed on discriminated against laundries conducted in wooden buildings. For the conduct of these the consent of the board of supervisors was required, and not for the conduct of laundries in brick or stone buildings. It was admitted that there were about 320 laundries in the city and county of San Francisco, of which 240 were owned and conducted by subjects of China, and, of the whole number, 310 were constructed of wood, the same material that constitutes nine-tenths of the houses of the city, and that the capital invested was not less than $200,000.

It was alleged that 150 Chinamen were arrested, and not one of the persons who were conducting the other 80 laundries, and who were not Chinamen. It was also admitted "that petitioner and 200 of his countrymen similarly situated petitioned the board of supervisors for permission to continue their business in the various houses which they had been occupying and using for laundries for more than twenty years, and such petitions were denied, and all the petitions of those who were not Chinese, with one exception of Mrs. Mary Meagles, were granted."

The ordinances were attacked as being void on their face, and as being within the prohibition of the fourteenth amendment, but, even if not so, that they were void by reason of their administration. Both contentions were sustained.

Mr. Justice Matthews said that the ordinance drawn in question "does not describe a rule and conditions for the regulation of the use of property for laundry purposes, to which all similarly situated may conform. It allows without restriction the use for such purposes of buildings of brick or stone, but as to wooden buildings, constituting all those in previous use, divides the owners or occupiers into two classes, not having respect to their personal character and qualifications for the business, nor the situation and nature and adaptation of the buildings themselves, but merely by an arbitrary line, on one side of which are those who are permitted to pursue their industry by the mere will and consent of the supervisors, and on the other those from whom that consent is withheld, at their mere will and pleasure." The ordinances, therefore, were on their face repugnant to the fourteenth amendment. The court, however, went further, and said: "This conclusion and the reasoning on which it is based are deductions from the face of the ordinance, as to its necessary tendency and ultimate actual operation."

In the present cases we are not obliged to reason from the probable to the actual, and pass upon the validity of the ordinances complained of as tried merely by the opportunities which their terms afford of unequal and unjust discrimination in their administration. For the cases present, the ordinances in actual operation, and the facts shown, establish an administration directed so exclusively against a particular class of persons as to warrant and require the conclusion that, whatever may have been the intent of the ordinances as adopted, they are applied by the public authorities charged with their administration, and thus representing the state itself, with a mind so unequal and oppressive as to amount to a practical denial by the state of that equal protection of the laws which is secured to the petitioners, as to all other persons, by the broad and benign provisions of the fourteenth amendment to the constitution of the United States. Though the law itself be fair on its face and impartial in appearance, yet, if it is applied and administered by public authority with an evil eye and an unequal hand, so as practically to make unjust and illegal discriminations between persons in similar circumstances, material to their rights, the denial of equal justice is still within the prohibition of the constitution. . . .

This comment is not applicable to the constitution of Mississippi and its statutes. They do not on their face discriminate between the races, and it has not been shown that their actual administration was evil; only that evil was possible under them.

It follows, therefore, that the judgment must be affirmed.

SOURCE: Williams v. State of Mississippi, 170 U.S. 213 (1898).

ANALYSIS

Harry Williams, an African American man, was tried and convicted of murdering a white man—a virtual automatic death sentence for the convicted. A grand jury in Washington County, Mississippi, initially indicted Williams for the murder in

June 1896. At this time, the South was beset with Jim Crow segregation laws, which mandated separation between the races in nearly all aspects of public life, including serving on juries. Often, the only Black face in a Mississippi courtroom was the person charged with a crime.

Williams contended that the Mississippi laws that excluded African Americans from jury service amounted to a violation of the Equal Protection Clause of the Fourteenth Amendment.

The Mississippi legislature established special voting requirements in its state constitution. These requirements included limiting jury duty to those who could pay a poll tax, who had no criminal record, who were literate, and who understood all the sections of the state constitution.

In 1892, the Mississippi legislature further restricted jurors based on "good intelligence, sound judgment, and fair character." These subjective requirements enabled white officials to exclude African Americans from jury service in all types of case, including Mr. Williams' trial.

By modern standards, Mississippi laws flagrantly violated the Equal Protection Clause. They were clearly designed to discriminate against African Americans. But in late nineteenth-century America, the U.S. Supreme Court nonetheless said that such laws are not in violation of the Constitution. The opinion in *Williams v. Mississippi* leaned heavily on the fact that the laws technically limited some whites from serving on juries as well as Blacks. Ultimately, however, the Court excused away its inaction with vague platitudes about how "the operation of the constitution and laws is not limited by their language or effects to one race. They reach weak and vicious white men as well as weak and vicious black men, and whatever is sinister in their intention, if anything, can be prevented by both races by the exertion of that duty which voluntarily pays taxes and refrains from crime."

Williams' attorneys had argued that the Court should apply the principles of the Court's earlier decision *Yick Wo v. Hopkins* (1886), which ruled that a San Francisco ordinance that was applied in an extremely uneven manner against Chinese-opened laundromats amounted to an Equal Protection violation. However, the Court reasoned that the *Yick Wo* decision did not apply because the Mississippi laws did not "on their face discriminate between the races."

The decision in *Williams v. Mississippi* (1898) meant that the Equal Protection Clause would not protect African American defendants facing the death penalty even if the system was very discriminatory. In blatant legal hair-splitting, the Court reasoned that the Equal Protection Clause only applied if the law itself was discriminatory but did not apply if the laws were administered in a discriminatory fashion. In other words, as long as the law itself did not use explicitly discriminatory language, it could be used in all sorts of discriminatory ways by white officials to curtail the rights of Black Americans.

FURTHER READING

Colbert, Douglas L. "Challenging the Challenge: Thirteenth Amendment as a Prohibition against the Racial Use of Peremptory Challenges." 76 *Cornell Law Review* 1 (1990).

Klarman, Michael J. "The Plessy Era." 1998 *Supreme Court Review* 303 (1998).

- ***Document 6:*** Supreme Court decision in *Davis v. Burke*
- ***Date:*** December 17, 1900
- ***Where:*** Washington, D.C.
- ***Significance:*** The Court's decision in this case showed marked deference to the independence of state and local government officials when it came to execution dates and processes.

DOCUMENT

Supreme Court Rejects Death Row Inmate's Due Process Challenge

The assignments of error, which are somewhat voluminous, are practically resolvable into two questions, first, whether the petitioner was legally prosecuted by information, and, second, whether the act of February 18, 1899, providing for executions at the state penitentiary under the direction of the warden, is as to this defendant ex post facto, and, as dependent upon this, whether he could be executed under section 8021 of the Revised Statutes as it formerly stood, after that section had been repealed by the act of February 18, 1899.

The constitution of Idaho contains the following clause: "Art. 1. Sec. 8. No person shall be held to answer for any felony or criminal offence of any grade, unless on presentment or indictment of a grand jury, or on information of the public prosecutor, after a commitment by a magistrate." Appellant's answer to this is: (a) That the provision is not self-executing. (b) That a law passed March 13, 1891, known as the Information Act, is void, because it was not passed in the manner required in the Idaho constitution, and that the journals of the legislature may be resorted to determine this question.

In reply to his first contention, it is sufficient to say that this case has been twice before the Supreme Court of Idaho, and upon neither occasion was the point made that it could not be prosecuted by information. . . .

The rule is well settled in this court that, while there may be a power on the part of the Federal courts to issue a writ of habeas corpus where the petitioner insists that he has been deprived of his liberty without due process of law, that power will not ordinarily be exercised until after an appeal made to the state courts has been denied.

. . .

This case is peculiarly one for the application of the general rule. Not only was there ample opportunity for making this defence upon the original hearing in the Supreme Court, or upon an independent application for a writ of habeas corpus; not only does the question involve the construction of the constitution and laws of the State with which the Supreme Court of the State is entirely familiar, but a ruling by this court that prosecutions by information in the courts of Idaho are invalid might result in the liberation of a large number of persons under sentence upon convictions obtained by this method of procedure. A step so important ought not to be taken without full opportunity given to the state court to pass upon the question, and without clear conviction of its necessity.

But we are also of opinion that for the purposes of this case the provision of the Idaho constitution must be deemed self-executing. . . . Thus, a constitution may very clearly require county and town government; but if it fails to indicate its range, and to provide proper machinery, it is not in this particular self-executing, and legislation is essential.

Where a constitutional provision is complete in itself it needs no further legislation to put it in force. When it lays down certain general principles, as to enact laws upon a certain subject, or for the incorporation of cities of certain population, or for uniform laws upon the subject of taxation, it may need more specific legislation to make it operative. In other words, it is self-executing only so far as it is susceptible of execution. But where a constitution asserts a certain right, or lays down a certain principle of law or procedure, it speaks for the entire people as their supreme law, and is full authority for all that is done in pursuance of its provisions. In short, if complete in itself, it executes itself. When a constitution declares that felonies may be prosecuted by information after a commitment by a magistrate, we understand exactly what is meant, since informations for the prosecution of minor offences are said by Blackstone to be as old as the common law itself, and a proceeding before magistrates for the apprehension and commitment of persons charged with crime has been the usual method of procedure since the adoption of the constitution. It is true the legislature may see fit to prescribe in detail the method of procedure, and the law enacted by it may turn out to be defective by reason of irregularity in its passage. In such case a proceeding by information might be impeached in the state court for such irregularity, but it certainly would not be void so long as it was authorized by the Constitution. For us to say that the accused had been denied due process of law would involve the absurdity of holding that what the people had declared to be the law was not the law.

(3) The question whether appellant shall be executed under the act of the legislature by the warden of the penitentiary, or under the Revised Statutes, as the law stood at the time of his trial and conviction, by the sheriff, or whether he shall escape punishment altogether, was determined adversely to him by the Supreme Court of the State, and involves no question of due process of law under the Fourteenth Amendment.

The order of the Circuit Court of the United States for the District of Idaho denying the writ of habeas corpus is, therefore,

Affirmed.

SOURCE: Davis v. Burke, 179 U.S. 399 (1900).

ANALYSIS

The case of *Davis v. Burke* (1900) is interesting for the two arguments advanced by McKenzie Davis, a convicted murderer who had received a sentence of death by hanging. He argued that it was unconstitutional for him to be prosecuted by "information" instead of by another method, such as through a grand jury (similar in respects to indictments, an "information" is a formal document prepared by prosecutors explaining the charges against the defendant). Davis's lawyers also asserted that it violated due process for him to be executed at a different location than the one that was originally stated.

Due process is arguably the most important liberty given to individuals in the U.S. Constitution. There is a due process clause in the Fifth Amendment, which limits federal government officials. There is also a due process clause in the Fourteenth Amendment, which limits state officials. Due process, at its bottom, means fundamental fairness. Both prohibit the government from infringing on "lie, liberty, or property without due process of law." There are times when a state or federal law or policy is so grossly unfair that it violates due process. There are two types of due process: (1) procedural due process and (2) substantive due process. Procedural due process means that before the government can take away or deprive a life, liberty, or property interest, that they do so by fair procedure. Substantive due process refers to the underlying substance, or lack thereof, of the law in question.

The Supreme Court rejected both contentions by the defendant. On the information argument, the Court pointed out that this argument should have been advanced in the Idaho state courts, not raised for the first time in the U.S. Supreme Court. The Supreme Court also noted that the Idaho State Constitution provided for prosecutions by information and that this provision of the state constitutional was "self-executing."

The rejection of this first argument is sometimes used by some as an early progenitor of the concept of procedural default in capital cases—that a defendant needs to argue a point at a lower court or risk waiving that issue on appeal.

On the due process argument, the Court rather cavalierly dismissed the argument that it was unconstitutional for him to be executed in a different location. The Court's response was that this argument "involves no question of due process of law under the Fourteenth Amendment."

FURTHER READING

Kovarsky, Lee. "A Constitutional Theory of Habeas Power." 99 *Virginia Law Review* 753 (2013).

2

RISING USAGE OF— AND OPPOSITION TO— THE DEATH PENALTY

During the eighteenth and nineteenth centuries, more people began to view the death penalty as an unacceptable sanctioning of state violence. The views of the eighteenth-century Enlightenment period, which called on humankind to conduct itself on a higher plane of morality, was an important element of this change.

In the mid-nineteenth century, a few states abolished the death penalty. Michigan was the first in 1846 followed by Rhode Island in 1852 and Wisconsin in 1853. Several other states abolished the death penalty in the Progressive Era before World War I—between 1907 and 1917.

The efforts in Michigan were spearheaded by leading politicians including Senator Charles P. Bush, House member Austin Blair (who later became governor of the state), and Senator Flavius Littlejohn. Legal historian Eugene G. Wanger posits that "no simple or complete explanation emerges" as to why Michigan became the first American state to abolish the death penalty. However, he notes that many Michigan politicians in this time period were likely adversely affected by the executions or near-executions of three men in three different cases—Stephen G. Simmons, Patrick Fitzpatrick, and Ebenezer M. Miller. Simmons was hanged for killing his wife in a drunken rage, but apparently, the gruesomeness of the hanging revolted many people in attendance. Fitzpatrick was executed for allegedly raping a 9-year-old girl, but substantial evidence exists that he did not commit the crime—including a confession from the actual rapist. Miller was found guilty of murder but was spared execution. Three years later, the real killer confessed to the crime on his deathbed, and Miller was finally exonerated. The net result of these tragedies and controversies was that Michigan abolished the death penalty for all crimes except treason. Eventually, in 1962, Michigan completely abolished the death penalty.

Another development occurred during the latter part of the nineteenth century—executions moved from the public square to behind closed doors. Many leaders were concerned about the spectacle of public hangings. They were not necessarily opposed to capital punishment per se; they just wanted to place it behind closed doors. This led to state legislators turning to other methods of executions to replace the public hangings, including electrocution, the gas chamber, and lethal injection.

But, several events during the early and mid-parts of the twentieth century led to a resurgence in use of the death penalty in the United States. The country experienced an upsurge in xenophobia in which many Americans of western European heritage blamed immigrants and other ethnic groups for fascism, anarchism, communism, or simply rising crime. The early to mid-twentieth century also featured a rise to prominence of organized crime. By 1935, when the United States reported nearly 200 executions across the country, capital punishment was being utilized more than ever before.

FURTHER READING

Banner, Stuart. *The Death Penalty in American History*. Cambridge, MA: Harvard University Press, 2002.

Palmer, Louis, Jr. *Encyclopedia of Capital Punishment in the United States*. Jefferson, NC: McFarland & Co., 2001.

Wanger, Eugene G. "Historical Reflections on Michigan's Abolition of the Death Penalty." 13 *Thomas M. Cooley Law Review* 755 (1996).

- ***Document 7:*** Supreme Court's decision in *Franklin v. South Carolina*
- ***Date:*** May 31, 1910
- ***Where:*** Washington, D.C.
- ***Significance:*** The Court's decision showed an unwillingness to examine or challenge racist Jim Crow laws and statutes that had been imposed by white lawmakers across the American South in the decades following the Civil War.

DOCUMENT

Supreme Court Rejects Pink Franklin's Constitutional Challenges to Jim Crow Law

The plaintiff in error, Pink Franklin, a citizen of the negro race, was convicted, in the Court of General Sessions for the county of Orangeburg, South Carolina, of the crime of murder by the shooting of one H. E. Valentine; thereupon he was sentenced to suffer the death penalty, and upon appeal to the Supreme Court of South Carolina the judgment of the Court of General Sessions was affirmed. The case is here upon a writ of error to the Supreme Court of South Carolina.

The record discloses that the homicide occurred upon the attempt of H. E. Valentine, a constable, to arrest Franklin upon a charge of "having violated and broken an agricultural contract," against the form of a statute made and provided in such cases in the State of South Carolina. The statute referred to is § 357 of the criminal code of South Carolina, which provides:

> "Any laborer working on shares of crop or for wages in money or other valuable consideration under a verbal or written contract to labor on farm lands, who shall receive advances either in money or supplies and thereafter wilfully and without just cause fail to perform the reasonable service required of him by the terms of said contract, shall be liable to prosecution for a misdemeanor, and on conviction shall be punished by imprisonment for not less than twenty days nor more than thirty days, or to be fined in the sum of not less than twenty-five dollars nor more than one hundred dollars, in the discretion of the court: Provided, The verbal contract herein referred to shall be witnessed by at least two disinterested witnesses."

Upon the filing of the complaint before a magistrate what is termed an arrest warrant was issued directed to Henry E. Valentine, as special constable, commanding him to apprehend the plaintiff in error because of the alleged violation of the agricultural contract, and to bring him before the magistrate to be dealt with according to law.

As it becomes necessary, in considering the Federal questions raised in the record, to know the facts concerning the homicide we take occasion to briefly summarize such as are pertinent. The testimony offered for the State and that offered for the plaintiff in error differed widely as to what occurred at the time the constable was shot. The record discloses that about the time of the attempted arrest Valentine, the constable, summoning one Carter to assist him, about three o'clock on the morning of the homicide proceeded to the farm of one Spires, who lived near to Franklin's house, and requested him to induce Franklin to go to his house that he might be there arrested. Accordingly, Spires went to Franklin's, and, having aroused him, asked him to do some plowing for him. Franklin replied that he would do the plowing that afternoon, but could not work for Spires that morning. Thereupon Valentine and Carter went to Franklin's house to make the arrest. For the State the testimony tended to show that the door of Franklin's house and the inner door of his bedroom were open; that Valentine rapped with a knife on the steps of the house, and called to Franklin, and received no response; that Valentine thereupon directed Carter to go around the house, which he did, and Valentine, entering the door, was instantly shot by Franklin, and Valentine's pistol was seized and wrung from his hand; that after he was shot a colored woman came in with an axe and said that she had a good will to finish up the job; that Carter, upon hearing the pistol shots, which were fired in rapid succession, ran around the house, and was caught by the leg by Franklin's son, a small boy; that upon entering the house he, too, was shot, receiving a slight wound.

On the other hand, the accused testified that he had no acquaintance with Valentine; that he did not know that he was an officer of the law and armed with a warrant for his arrest; that he heard nothing until the door was hurled open, and Valentine said to him "Hands up!" that he (Franklin) did not move; that Valentine shot him, inflicting a wound in his shoulder; that he fell down by his pallet, got his gun, and fired, intending to get out of the way, and did get out as fast as he could.

In a proceeding of this kind this court has no jurisdiction to notice other errors than those which involve alleged violations of Federal rights secured by the Constitution of the United States or Federal statutes. The States have the right to administer their own laws for the prosecution of crime, and the jurisdiction of this court extends only to the reversal of such state proceedings where fundamental rights secured by the Federal law have been denied by the proceedings in the state courts.

. . .

This change in the qualification for voters, it is said, worked a deprivation of the rights of the accused, because the qualification of grand jurors under the constitution of 1895, they being required to be electors of the State, made eligible different persons than those who were qualified to be electors under the constitution of 1868. As to this contention the South Carolina Supreme Court held that the constitution of 1895 laid no restriction on color or previous condition to entitle one to be an elector; that the act of Congress of 1868 had no reference to the selection of jurors, and that it was inapplicable to the constitution of the State in regard to juries.

If it could be held that the act of Congress restricted the State of South Carolina in fixing the qualifications for suffrage it is unnecessary to decide the point in this case, as there is nothing in the record to show that the grand jury, as actually impanelled, contained any person who was not qualified as an elector under the constitution of 1868, nor is there anything to show that the grand jury was so made up as to prevent citizens of the race of the plaintiff in error from sitting thereon. . . . It is next contended, concerning the jury law of South Carolina, that it confers arbitrary power upon the jury commissioners in selecting jurors . . .

We do not think there is anything in this provision of the statute having the effect to deny rights secured by the Federal Constitution. It gives to the jury commissioners the right to select electors of good moral character, such as they may deem qualified to serve as jurors, being persons of sound judgment and free from all legal exceptions. There is nothing in this statute which discriminates against individuals on account of race or color or previous condition, or which subjects such persons to any other or different treatment than other electors who may be qualified to serve as jurors. The statute simply provides for an exercise of judgment in attempting to secure competent jurors of proper qualifications.

Under this statute the Supreme Court of South Carolina held that the jury commissioners were only required to select men of good moral character, and that competent colored men were equally eligible with others for such service. We find no denial of Federal rights in this provision of the statute.

It is next contended that the plaintiff in error was denied due process of law in the refusal of the court to continue his case when the same was called for trial. It is elementary that he matter of continuance rests in the sound discretion of the trial court, and its action in that respect is not ordinarily reviewable. It would take an extreme case to make the action of the trial court in such a case a denial of due process of law. A continuance was asked for because, it was alleged, the counsel for the accused had not had sufficient time or opportunity to examine the notes of the testimony taken before the coroner who investigated the case. . . . He found upon examination that the testimony had not been copied into the coroner's book, and that, therefore, the counsel were not enabled to read and become familiar with the testimony "absolutely needed for contradiction on the trial of such causes." Counsel for the State stated in this connection that when the attorney for the accused came to his office and asked for the coroner's inquisition he handed to him the papers in the case, telling him at the time that he did not know whether he could read them or not, because they were written in a kind of short or running hand; that he had suppressed no record in the case, and had given the counsel all the records which he had; that the record was written in a kind of running long hand; that the young man who took the testimony was out of town at the time, and that he had so stated. Upon this showing the court declined to continue the case. Certainly there was no deprivation of due process of law in this action.

. . .

The only Federal question raised in this connection is found in this denial of the motion to direct a verdict in favor of the accused, because the statute under which he was sought to be arrested was void under the Federal Constitution, and the warrant issued for his arrest under such unconstitutional law therefore void and of no effect. . . .

It was insisted in the oral argument of this case, and an elaborate brief was filed by eminent counsel, making the contentions that the proceedings for the arrest of the accused were in violation of the Thirteenth Amendment and of § 1990 of the Revised Statutes of the United States, abolishing and prohibiting peonage, and declaring null and void the resolutions, regulations and usages of any State or Territory in that respect; and that they were in violation of § 5526 of the Revised Statutes of the United States, punishing any person who holds, arrests or returns, or causes to be held, arrested or returned, or in any way aids in the arrest or return of any person to a condition of peonage, and were in violation of the Thirteenth Amendment. This being so, and the statute and the warrant being illegal and void, the accused, it is contended, had the right to use all reasonable force to protect his person, his liberty and his habitation from such unlawful arrest, and that, therefore, the firing of the fatal shot was only a reasonable use of force for the defense of the accused under the circumstances shown.

But, as we have said, the only attempt to raise questions of a Federal character concerning the validity of the statute and the warrant under which it was issued, and the right to resist arrest under such warrant, was in the request for a peremptory instruction for an acquittal. Even upon the theory of his rights now advanced he was not entitled to a peremptory instruction taking the case from the jury.

The Supreme Court of South Carolina considered and overruled certain grounds of appeal, which embrace objections to the charge. But we do not find in these rulings any determination of Federal questions adverse to the plaintiff in error which would warrant a reversal of the judgment by this court. These rulings were upon questions of general law, concerning which no Federal right was asserted and denied as is essential to enable this court to review the judgment of a state court.

After giving this case the examination its importance deserves, in view of its gravity, we are unable to find in the record anything which worked a deprivation of Federal rights warranting this court in disturbing the judgment of the Supreme Court of South Carolina, and the judgment is affirmed.

Affirmed.

SOURCE: Franklin v. South Carolina, 218 U.S. 161 (1910).

ANALYSIS

Not much attention has been paid to the plight of Pink Franklin, an African American man sentenced to death for killing a white officer. His case deserves more attention, as it was an all-too typical example of a mistreatment of an African American man in the Jim Crow–era South.

Franklin had signed a peonage contract with a white cotton farmer. However, the terms of the arrangement were not very good, and Franklin sought to work on another farm. This decision violated South Carolina law, which prohibited a farm laborer from leaving his place of employment until he had completed the terms of his contract with the first landowner.

Constable Henry Valentine and another man, both Caucasian men, came to arrest Pink Franklin and barged into Franklin's home. In self-defense, Franklin shot and killed Valentine. This led to his arrest and conviction for murder and being sent to South Carolina's death row. His appeals in the state court system were unsuccessful.

At the U.S. Supreme Court, Franklin's attorneys argued that the peonage law violated the Thirteenth Amendment. The U.S. Supreme Court said it was not relevant whether the law was unconstitutional; that did not excuse the killing of Valentine.

His lawyers also challenged the grand jury system in Mississippi that created a system of all-white jurors convened for Franklin's case. The U.S. Supreme Court gave only cursory treatment to this issue and rejected the claim. The National Association for the Advancement of Colored People (NAACP) took up Franklin's cause and petitioned the South Carolina governor for clemency. They gathered nearly 1,000 signatures from 18 different counties.

On January 5, 1911, the governor commuted Pink Franklin's sentence to life imprisonment. It helped that one of the prosecution witnesses had recanted his testimony that Franklin had admitted to the shooting. Franklin endured chain gangs but, in 1919, was paroled by a different governor, Richard Manning. "Saving Franklin's life demonstrated that legal efforts could achieve meaningful results," wrote legal historian W. Lewis Burke. "The actions of blacks and whites from the South and from across the nation demonstrated the power of a biracial, multi-class coalition."

FURTHER READING

Burke, W. Lewis. "Pink Franklin v. South Carolina: The NAACP's First Case." 54 *American Journal of Legal History* 265 (2014).

- ***Document 8:*** *Powell v. Alabama*
- ***Date:*** November 7, 1932
- ***Where:*** Washington, D.C.
- ***Significance:*** The decision represented the first time that the U.S. Supreme Court ruled that criminal defendants in state court have the right to an attorney. The decision is also notable for its acknowledgment that racism existed in the American criminal justice system.

DOCUMENT

Supreme Court Rules Criminal Defendants Have the Constitutional Right to Counsel

These cases were argued together and submitted for decision as one case.

The petitioners, hereinafter referred to as defendants, are negroes charged with the crime of rape, committed upon the persons of two white girls. The crime is said to have been committed on March 25, 1931. The indictment was returned in a state court of first instance on March 31, and the record recites that on the same day the defendants were arraigned and entered pleas of not guilty. There is a further recital to the effect that upon the arraignment they were represented by counsel. But no counsel had been employed, and aside from a statement made by the trial judge several days later during a colloquy immediately preceding the trial, the record does not disclose when, or under what circumstances, an appointment of counsel was made, or who was appointed.

During the colloquy referred to, the trial judge, in response to a question, said that he had appointed all the members of the bar for the purpose of arraigning the defendants and then of course anticipated that the members of the bar would continue to help the defendants if no counsel appeared. Upon the argument here both sides accepted that as a correct statement of the facts concerning the matter.

There was a severance upon the request of the state, and the defendants were tried in three several groups, as indicated above. As each of the three cases was called for trial, each defendant was arraigned, and, having the indictment read to him, entered a plea of not guilty. Whether the original arraignment and pleas were regarded as ineffective is not shown.

Each of the three trials was completed within a single day. Under the Alabama statute the punishment for rape is to be fixed by the jury, and in its discretion may be from ten years imprisonment to death. The juries found defendants guilty and imposed the death penalty upon all. The trial court overruled motions for new trials and sentenced the defendants in accordance with the verdicts. The judgments were affirmed by the state supreme court. Chief Justice Anderson thought the defendants had not been accorded a fair trial and strongly dissented.

In this court the judgments are assailed upon the grounds that the defendants, and each of them, were denied due process of law and the equal protection of the laws, in contravention of the Fourteenth Amendment, specifically as follows: (1) They were not given a fair, impartial, and deliberate trial; (2) they were denied the right of counsel, with the accustomed incidents of consultation and opportunity of preparation for trial; and (3) they were tried before juries from which qualified members of their own race were systematically excluded. These questions were properly raised and saved in the courts below.

The only one of the assignments which we shall consider is the second, in respect of the denial of counsel; and it becomes unnecessary to discuss the facts of the case or the circumstances surrounding the prosecution except in so far as they reflect light upon that question.

The record shows that on the day when the offense is said to have been committed, these defendants, together with a number of other negroes, were upon a freight train on its way through Alabama. On the same train were seven white boys and the two white girls. A fight took place between the negroes and the white boys, in the course of which the white boys, with the exception of one named Gilley, were thrown off the train. A message was sent ahead, reporting the fight and asking that every negro be gotten off the train. The participants in the fight, and the two girls, were in an open gondola car. The two girls testified that each of them was assaulted by six different negroes in turn, and they identified the seven defendants as having been among the number. None of the white boys was called to testify, with the exception of Gilley, who was called in rebuttal.

Before the train reached Scottsboro, Ala., a sheriff's posse seized the defendants and two other negroes. Both girls and the negroes then were taken to Scottsboro, the county seat. Word of their coming and of the alleged assault had preceded them, and they were met at Scottsboro by a large crowd. It does not sufficiently appear that the defendants were seriously threatened with, or that they were actually in danger of, mob violence; but it does appear that the attitude of the community was one of great hostility.

The sheriff thought it necessary to call for the militia to assist in safeguarding the prisoners. Chief Justice Anderson pointed out in his opinion that every step taken from the arrest and arraignment to the sentence was accompanied by the military. Soldiers took the defendants to Gadsden for safe-keeping, brought them back to Scottsboro for arraignment, returned them to Gadsden for safe-keeping while awaiting trial, escorted them to Scottsboro for trial a few days later, and guarded the courthouse and grounds at every stage of the proceedings.

It is perfectly apparent that the proceedings, from beginning to end, took place in an atmosphere of tense, hostile, and excited public sentiment. During the entire time, the defendants were closely confined or were under military guard. The record does not disclose their ages, except that one of them was nineteen; but the record clearly indicates that most, if not all, of them were youthful, and they are constantly referred to as "the boys." They were ignorant and illiterate. All of them were residents of other states, where alone members of their families or friends resided.

However guilty defendants, upon due inquiry, might prove to have been, they were, until convicted, presumed to be innocent. It was the duty of the court having their cases in charge to see that they were denied no necessary incident of a fair trial. With any error of the state court involving alleged contravention of the state statutes or Constitution we, of course, have nothing to do. The sole inquiry which we are permitted to make is whether the federal Constitution was contravened; and as to that, we confine ourselves, as already suggested, to the inquiry whether the defendants were in substance denied the right of counsel, and if so, whether such denial infringes the due process clause of the Fourteenth Amendment.

First. The record shows that immediately upon the return of the indictment defendants were arraigned and pleaded not guilty. Apparently they were not asked whether they had, or were able to employ, counsel, or wished to have counsel appointed; or whether they had friends or relatives who might assist in that regard if communicated with. That it would not have been an idle ceremony to have given the defendants reasonable opportunity to communicate with their families and endeavor to obtain counsel is demonstrated by the fact that very soon after conviction, able counsel appeared in their behalf.

. . .

It is hardly necessary to say that the right to counsel being conceded, a defendant should be afforded a fair opportunity to secure counsel of his own choice. Not only was that not done here, but such designation of counsel as was attempted was either so indefinite or so close upon the trial as to amount to a denial of effective and substantial aid in that regard. This will be amply demonstrated by a brief review of the record.

April 6, six days after indictment, the trials began. When the first case was called, the court inquired whether the parties were ready for trial. The state's attorney replied that he was ready to proceed. No one answered for the defendants or appeared to represent or defend them. Mr. Roddy, a Tennessee lawyer not a member of the local bar, addressed the court, saying that he had not been employed, but that people who were interested had spoken to him about the case. He was asked by the court whether he intended to appear for the defendants, and answered that he would like to appear along with counsel that the court might appoint.

. . .

And in this casual fashion the matter of counsel in a capital case was disposed of.

It thus will be seen that until the very morning of the trial no lawyer had been named or definitely designated to represent the defendants. Prior to that time, the trial judge had "appointed all the members of the bar" for the limited "purpose of arraigning the defendants." Whether they would represent the defendants thereafter, if no counsel appeared in their behalf, was a matter of speculation only, or, as the judge indicated, of mere anticipation on the part of the court. Such a designation, even if made for all purposes, would, in our opinion, have fallen far short of meeting, in any proper sense, a requirement for the appointment of counsel. How many lawyers were members of the bar does not appear; but, in the very nature of things, whether many or few, they would not, thus collectively named, have been given that clear appreciation of responsibility or impressed with that individual sense of duty which should and naturally would accompany the appointment of a selected member of the bar, specifically named and assigned.

That this action of the trial judge in respect of appointment of counsel was little more than an expansive gesture, imposing no substantial or definite obligation upon any one, is borne out by the fact that prior to the calling of the case for trial on April 6, a leading member of the local bar accepted employment on the side of the prosecution and actively participated in the trial.

It is true that he said that before doing so he had understood Mr. Roddy would be employed as counsel for the defendants. This the lawyer is question, of his own accord, frankly stated to the court; and no doubt he acted with the utmost good faith

. . .

Nor do we think the situation was helped by what occurred on the morning of the trial. At that time, as appears from the colloquy printed above, Mr. Roddy stated to the court that he did not appear as counsel, but that he would like to appear along with counsel that the court might appoint; that he had not been given an opportunity to prepare the case; that he was not familiar with the procedure in Alabama, but merely came down as a friend of the people who were interested; that he thought the boys would be better off if he should step entirely out of the case.

Mr. Moody, a member of the local bar, expressed a willingness to help Mr. Roddy in anything he could do under the circumstances. To this the court responded: "All right, all the lawyers that will; of course I would not require a lawyer to appear if—." And Mr. Moody continued: "I am willing to do that for him as a member of the bar; I will go ahead and help do anything I can do."

With this dubious understanding, the trials immediately proceeded. The defendants, young, ignorant, illiterate, surrounded by hostile sentiment, haled back and forth under guard of soldiers, charged with an atrocious crime regarded with especial horror in the community where they were to be tried, were thus put in peril of their lives within a few moments after counsel for the first time charged with any degree of responsibility began to represent them.

It is not enough to assume that counsel thus precipitated into the case thought there was no defense, and exercised their best judgment in proceeding to trial without preparation. Neither they nor the court could say what a prompt and thorough-going investigation might disclose as to the facts. No attempt was made to investigate. No opportunity to do so was given. Defendants were immediately hurried to trial. Chief Justice Anderson, after disclaiming any intention to criticize harshly counsel who attempted to represent defendants at the trials, said: ". . . The record indicates that the appearance was rather pro forma than zealous and active . . ." Under the circumstances disclosed, we hold that defendants were not accorded the right of counsel in any substantial sense. To decide otherwise, would simply be to ignore actualities. . . .

It is true that great and inexcusable delay in the enforcement of our criminal law is one of the grave evils of our time. Continuances are frequently granted for unnecessarily long periods of time, and delays incident to the disposition of motions for new trial and hearings upon appeal have come in many cases to be a distinct reproach to the administration of justice. The prompt disposition of criminal cases is to be commended and encouraged. But in reaching that result a defendant, charged with a serious crime, must not be stripped of his right to have sufficient time to advise with counsel and prepare his defense. To do that is not to proceed promptly in the claim spirit of regulated justice but to go forward with the haste of the mob.

. . .

Second. The Constitution of Alabama provides that in all criminal prosecutions the accused shall enjoy the right to have the assistance of counsel; and a state statute requires the court in a capital case, where the defendant is unable to employ counsel, to appoint counsel for him. The state Supreme Court held that these provisions had not been infringed, and with that holding we are powerless to interfere. The question, however, which it is our duty, and within our power, to decide, is whether the denial of the assistance of counsel contravenes the due process clause of the Fourteenth Amendment to the Federal Constitution.

If recognition of the right of a defendant charged with a felony to have the aid of counsel depended upon the existence of a similar right at common law as it existed in England when our Constitution was adopted, there would be great difficulty in maintaining it as necessary to due process. Originally, in England, a person charged with treason or felony was denied the aid of counsel, except in respect of legal questions which the accused himself might suggest. At the same time parties in civil cases and persons accused of misdemeanors were entitled to the full assistance of counsel. After the revolution of 1688, the rule was abolished as to treason, but was otherwise steadily adhered to until 1836, when by act of Parliament the full right was granted in respect of felonies generally. 1 Cooley's Constitutional Limitations (8th Ed.) 698 et seq., and notes.

An affirmation of the right to the aid of counsel in petty offenses, and its denial in the case of crimes of the gravest character, where such aid is most needed, is so outrageous and so obviously a perversion of all sense of proportion that the rule was constantly, vigorously and sometimes passionately assailed by English statesmen and lawyers. . . .

It thus appears that in at least twelve of the thirteen colonies the rule of the English common law, in the respect now under consideration, had been definitely rejected and the right to counsel fully recognized in all criminal prosecutions, save that in one or two instances the right was limited to capital offenses or to the more serious crimes; and this court seems to have been of the opinion that this was true in all the colonies. . . .

One test which has been applied to determine whether due process of law has been accorded in given instances is to ascertain what were the settled usages and modes of proceeding under the common and statute law of England before the Declaration of Independence, subject, however, to the qualification that they be shown not to have been unsuited to the civil and political conditions of our ancestors by having been followed in this country after it became a nation. . . .

The Sixth Amendment, in terms, provides that in all criminal prosecutions the accused shall enjoy the right "to have the Assistance of Counsel for his defence." In the face of the reasoning of the Hurtado Case, if it stood alone, it would be difficult to justify the conclusion that the right to counsel, being thus specifically granted by the Sixth Amendment, was also within the intendement of the due process of law clause. But the Hurtado Case does not stand alone. . . .

. . .

It never has been doubted by this court, or any other so far as we know, that notice and hearing are preliminary steps essential to the passing of an enforceable judgment, and that they, together with a legally competent tribunal having jurisdiction of the case, constitute basic elements of the constitutional requirement of due process of law. . . .

What, then, does a hearing include? Historically and in practice, in our own country at least, it has always included the right to the aid of counsel when desired and provided by the party asserting the right. The right to be heard would be, in many cases, of little avail if it did not comprehend the right to be heard by counsel. Even the intelligent and educated layman has small and sometimes no skill in the science of law. If charged with crime, he is incapable, generally, of determining for himself whether the indictment is good or bad. He is unfamiliar with the rules of evidence. Left without the aid of counsel he may be put on trial without a proper charge, and convicted upon incompetent evidence, or evidence irrelevant to the issue or otherwise inadmissible. He lacks both the skill and knowledge adequately to prepare his defense, even though he have a perfect one. He requires the guiding hand of counsel at every step in the proceedings against him. Without it, though he be not guilty, he faces the danger of conviction because he does not know how to establish his innocence. If that be true of men of intelligence, how much more true is it of the ignorant and illiterate, or those of feeble intellect. If in any case, civil of criminal, a state or federal court were arbitrarily to refuse to hear a party by counsel, employed by and appearing for him, it reasonably may not be doubted that such a

- ***Document 9:*** U.S. Supreme Court decision in *Watts v. Indiana*
- ***Date:*** June 27, 1949
- ***Where:*** Washington, D.C.
- ***Significance:*** In this decision, the U.S. Supreme Court explained that just because a defendant is charged with capital punishment does not give police officers and interrogators free license to elicit a confession by subjecting a suspect to abuse or other mistreatment.

DOCUMENT

Supreme Court Confirms Constitutional Protections for Suspects in Capital Crimes

Although the Constitution puts protection against crime predominantly in the keeping of the States, the Fourteenth Amendment severely restricted the States in their administration of criminal justice. Thus, while the State courts have the responsibility for securing the rudimentary requirements of a civilized order, in discharging that responsibility there hangs over them the reviewing power of this Court.

Power of such delicacy and import must, of course, be exercised with the greatest forbearance. When, however, appeal is made to it, there is no escape. And so this Court once again must meet the uncongenial duty of testing the validity of a conviction by a State court for a State crime by what is to be found in the Due Process Clause of the Fourteenth Amendment.

This case is here because the Supreme Court of Indiana rejected petitioner's claim that confessions elicited from him were procured under circumstances rendering their admission as evidence against him a denial of due process of law. The grounds on which our review was sought seemed sufficiently weighty to grant the petition for certiorari.

On review here of State convictions, all those matters which are usually termed issues of fact are for conclusive determination by the State courts and are not open for reconsideration by this Court. Observance of this restriction in our review of State courts calls for the utmost scruple. But "issue of fact" is a coat of many colors. It does not cover a conclusion drawn from uncontroverted happenings, when that conclusion incorporates standards of conduct or criteria for judgment which in themselves are decisive of constitutional rights. Such standards and criteria, measured against the requirements drawn from constitutional provisions, and their proper applications, are issues for this Court's adjudication. Especially in cases arising under the Due Process Clause is it important to distinguish between issues of fact that are here foreclosed and issues which, though cast in the form of determinations of fact, are the very issues to review which this Court sits.

In the application of so embracing a constitutional concept as "due process," it would be idle to expect at all times unanimity of views. Nevertheless, in all the cases that have come here during the last decade from the courts of the various States in which it was claimed that the admission of coerced confessions vitiated convictions for murder, there has been complete agreement that a conflict in testimony as to what actually led to a contested confession is not this Court's concern. Such conflict comes here authoritatively resolved by the State's adjudication. Therefore only those elements of the events and circumstances in which a confession was involved that are unquestioned in the State's version of what happened are relevant to the constitutional issue here. But if force has been applied, this Court does not leave to local determination whether or not the confession was voluntary. There is torture of mind as well as body; the will is as much affected by fear as by force. And there comes a point where this Court should not be ignorant as judges of what we know as men.

This brings us to the undisputed circumstances which must determine the issue of due process in this case. Thanks to the forthrightness of counsel for Indiana, these circumstances may be briefly stated.

On November 12, 1947, a Wednesday, petitioner was arrested and held as the suspected perpetrator of an alleged criminal assault earlier in the day. Later the same day, in the vicinity of this occurrence, a woman was found dead under conditions suggesting murder in the course of an attempted criminal assault. Suspicion of murder quickly turned towards petitioner and the police began to question him. They took him from the county jail to State Police Headquarters, where he was questioned by officers in relays from about eleven thirty that night until sometime between 2:30 and 3 o'clock the following morning. The same procedure of persistent interrogation from about 5:30 in the afternoon until about 3 o'clock the following morning, by a relay of six to eight officers, was pursued on Thursday the 13th, Friday the 14th, Saturday the 15th, Monday the 17th. Sunday was a day of rest from interrogation. About 3 o'clock on Tuesday morning, November 18, the petitioner made an incriminating statement after continuous questioning since 6 o'clock of the preceding evening. The statement did not satisfy the prosecutor who had been called in and he then took petitioner in hand. Petitioner, questioned by an interrogator of twenty years' experience as lawyer, judge and prosecutor, yielded a more incriminating document.

Until his inculpatory statements were secured, the petitioner was a prisoner in the exclusive control of the prosecuting authorities. He was kept for the first two days in solitary confinement in a cell aptly enough called 'the hole' in view of its physical conditions as described by the State's witnesses. Apart from the five night sessions, the police intermittently interrogated Watts during the day and on three days drove him around town, hours at a time, with a view to eliciting identifications and other disclosures. Although the law of Indiana required that petitioner be given a prompt preliminary hearing before a magistrate, with all the protection a hearing was intended to give him, the petitioner was not only given no hearing during the entire period of interrogation but was without friendly or professional aid and without advice as to his constitutional rights. Disregard of rudimentary needs of life- opportunities for sleep and a decent allowance of food-are also relevant, not as aggravating elements of petitioner's treatment, but as part of the total situation out of which his confessions came and which stamped their character.

A confession by which life becomes forfeit must be the expression of free choice. A statement to be voluntary of course need not be volunteered. But if it is the product of sustained pressure by the police it does not issue from a free choice. When a suspect speaks because he is overborne, it is immaterial whether he has been subjected to a physical or a mental ordeal. Eventual yielding to questioning under such circumstances is plainly the product of the suction process of interrogation and therefore the reverse of voluntary. We would have to shut our minds to the plain significance of what here transpired to deny that this was a calculated endeavor to secure a confession through the pressure of unrelenting interrogation. The very relentlessness of such interrogation implies that it is better for the prisoner to answer than to persist in the refusal of disclosure which is his constitutional right. To turn the detention of an accused into a process of wrenching from him evidence which could not be extorted in open court with all its safeguards, is so grave an abuse of the power of arrest as to offend the procedural standards of due process.

This is so because it violates the underlying principle in our enforcement of the criminal law. Ours is the accusatorial as opposed to the inquisitorial system. Such has been the characteristic of Anglo-American criminal justice since it freed itself from practices borrowed by the Star Chamber from the Continent whereby an accused was interrogated in secret for hours on end. Under our system society carries the burden of proving its charge against the accused not out of his own mouth. It must establish its case, not by interrogation of the accused even under judicial safeguards, but by evidence independently secured through skillful investigation. . . . Protracted, systematic and uncontrolled subjection of an accused to interrogation by the police for the purpose of eliciting disclosures or confessions is subversive of the accusatorial system. It is the inquisitorial system without its safeguards. For while under that system the accused is subjected to judicial interrogation, he is protected by the disinterestedness of the judge in the presence of counsel.

In holding that the Due Process Clause bars police procedure which violates the basic notions of our accusatorial mode of prosecuting crime and vitiates a conviction based on the fruits of such procedure, we apply the Due Process Clause to its historic function of assuring appropriate procedure before liberty is curtailed or life is taken. We are deeply mindful of the anguishing problems which the incidence of crime presents to the States. But the history of the criminal law proves overwhelmingly that brutal methods of law enforcement are essentially self-defeating, whatever may be their effect in a particular case.

Law triumphs when the natural impulses aroused by a shocking crime yield to the safeguards which our civilization has evolved for an administration of criminal justice at once rational and effective.

We have examined petitioner's other contentions and do not sustain them.

Reversed

SOURCE: *Watts v. Indiana*, 338 U.S. 49 (1949).

ANALYSIS

Defendants sometimes do confess to criminal acts, and securing confessions is a common goal of police seeking to solve crimes. However, the Due Process Clause of the Fourteenth Amendment imposes limitations on the conduct of police officers. They cannot extract a confession by force or torture or other barbaric conduct. The questioning cannot be too prolonged such that it becomes questionable whether the confession truly was voluntary or the product of a defendant's free will.

In the case of *Watts v. Indiana*, the police in November 1947 arrested Robert Austin Watts, an African American, for an alleged assault. When a woman's body was found near the scene of the alleged crime for which Watts had been originally arrested, the police suspected Watts of homicide and attempted rape. They incarcerated him for seven days, interrogated him for hours on end, placed him in solitary confinement for two days, and limited his eating and sleeping. Watts finally confessed to killing the woman on the seventh day.

The prosecutor sought the death penalty against Watts. A jury convicted Watts to death. He faced death by electrocution, the method of execution at that time in Indiana. He appealed to the Indiana Supreme Court, alleging that his constitutional rights had been violated at several points. He contended that the jury pool was tainted because it was discriminatory toward African Americans, that the prosecutor made improper statements during closing argument, and that his confession was obtained through threats and coercion. The Indiana Supreme Court rejected these constitutional claims and affirmed Watts' death sentence.

Watts then sought a petition for writ of certiorari to the U.S. Supreme Court. This is the procedure by which a party appeals an adverse decision for review by the court of last resort. The U.S. Supreme Court agreed to hear the case, likely because it was appalled at the underlying circumstances in which the police extracted a confession from Watts. One of the lawyers for Watts at the U.S. Supreme Court was none other than Thurgood Marshall, a famed lawyer with the NAACP civil rights organization who later became the first African American to serve on the U.S. Supreme Court.

In considering the case, the Supreme Court expressed concern that Watts' "confession" was not the product of a free will. Writing for a plurality, Justice Felix Frankfurter explained:

> A confession by which life becomes forfeit must be the expression of free choice. A statement to be voluntary of course need not be volunteered. But if it is the product of sustained pressure by the police it does not issue from a free choice. When a suspect speaks because he is overborne, it is immaterial whether he has been subjected to a physical or a mental ordeal.

Justice Frankfurter also wrote that "brutal methods of law enforcement are essentially self-defeating."

Justice William O. Douglas offered an even more poignant condemnation of the procedure used by the police against Robert Watts, charging that it "breeds coerced confessions. It is the root of the evil. It is the procedure without which the inquisition could not flourish in the country."

FURTHER READING

Hancock, Catherine. "Due Process Before Miranda." 70 *Tulane Law Review* 2195 (1996).

Mallett, Conrad, Jr. "Tribute to Thurgood Marshall." 71 *University of Detroit Mercy Law Review* 933 (1994).

Penney, Steven. "Theories of Confession Admissibility: A Historical View." 25 *American Journal of Criminal Law* 309 (1998).

- ***Document 10:*** U.S. Supreme Court opinion in *Alcorta v. Texas*
- ***Date:*** November 12, 1957
- ***Where:*** Washington, D.C.
- ***Significance:*** The opinion establishes that death penalty defendants have a due process right not to convicted based on perjured testimony and unethical prosecutorial behavior.

DOCUMENT

Supreme Court Reverses Death Sentence on Perjury Grounds

Petitioner, Alvaro Alcorta, was indicted for murder in a Texas state court for stabbing his wife to death. He admitted the killing but claimed it occurred in a fit of passion when he discovered his wife, whom he had already suspected of marital infidelity, kissing one Castilleja late at night in a parked car. Petitioner relied on Texas statutes which treat killing under the influence of a "sudden passion arising from an adequate cause . . . as would commonly produce a degree of anger, rage, resentment, or terror in a person of ordinary temper sufficient to render the mind incapable of cool reflection" as murder without malice punishable by a maximum sentence of five years' imprisonment. The jury, however, found him guilty of murder with malice and, acting under broad statutory authority to determine the extent of punishment, sentenced him to death. The judgment and sentence were affirmed by the Texas Court of Criminal Appeals.

Castilleja, the only eye witness to the killing, testified for the State at petitioner's trial. In response to inquiries by the prosecutor about his relationship with the petitioner's wife, Castilleja said that he had simply driven her home from work a couple of times, and in substance testified that his relationship with her had been nothing more than a casual friendship. He stated that he had given her a ride on the night she was killed and was parked in front of her home with his car lights out at two o'clock in the morning because of engine trouble. The prosecutor then asked what had transpired between Castilleja and petitioner's wife in the parked car:

"Q. Did you have a conversation with Herlinda?
"A. Yes; she opened the door. She was going to get off [sic] and, then, she told me to tell my sister to come and pick her up in the morning so she could go to church.

"Q. To tell your sister, Delfina Cabrera, to come pick her up in the morning so she could go to church?
"A. Yes."

At the conclusion of Castilleja's testimony the following colloquy took place between him and the prosecutor:

"Q. Natividad [Castilleja], were you in love with Herlinda?
"A. No.

"Q. Was she in love with you?
"A. No.

"Q. Had you ever talked about love?
"A. No.

"Q. Had you ever had any dates with her other than to take her home?
"A. No. Well, just when I brought her from there.

"Q. Just when you brought her from work?
"A. Yes."

All this testimony was quite plainly inconsistent with petitioner's claim that he had come upon his wife kissing Castilleja in the parked car.

Some time after petitioner's conviction had been affirmed, Castilleja issued a sworn statement in which he declared that he had given false testimony at the trial. Relying on this statement petitioner asked the trial court to issue a writ of habeas corpus. He contended that he had been denied a fair trial in violation of State and Federal Constitutions because Castilleja had testified falsely, with the knowledge of the prosecutor, that his relationship with petitioner's wife had been only "that of a friend and neighbor, and that he had had no 'dates,' nor other relations with her, when in truth and in fact the witness had been her lover and paramour, and had had sexual intercourse with her on many occasions . . ." Petitioner further alleged that he had no knowledge of this illicit intercourse at the time of his trial.

A hearing was held on the petition for habeas corpus. Castilleja was called as a witness. He confessed having sexual intercourse with petitioner's wife on five or six occasions within a relatively brief period before her death. He testified that he had informed the prosecutor of this before trial and the prosecutor had told him he should not volunteer any information about such intercourse but if specifically asked about it to answer truthfully. The prosecutor took the stand and admitted that these statements were true. He conceded that he had not told petitioner about Castilleja's illicit intercourse with his wife. He also admitted that he had not included this information in a written statement taken from Castilleja prior to the trial but instead had noted it in a separate record. At the conclusion of the hearing the trial judge denied the petition for habeas corpus. Petitioner then applied to the Texas Court of Criminal Appeals for a writ of habeas corpus but that court, acting on the record made at the hearing before the trial court, also refused to issue the writ. We granted certiorari. Texas concedes that petitioner has exhausted all remedies available to him under state law.

Under the general principles laid down by this Court . . . petitioner was not accorded due process of law. It cannot seriously be disputed that Castilleja's testimony, taken as a whole, gave the jury the false impression that his relationship with petitioner's wife was nothing more than that of casual friendship. This testimony was elicited by the prosecutor who knew of the illicit intercourse between Castilleja and petitioner's wife. Undoubtedly Castilleja's testimony was seriously prejudicial to petitioner. It tended squarely to refute his claim that he had adequate cause for a surge of "sudden passion" in which he killed his wife. If Castilleja's relationship with petitioner's wife had been truthfully portrayed to the jury, it would have, apart from impeaching his credibility, tended to corroborate petitioner's contention that he had found his wife embracing Castilleja. If petitioner's defense had been accepted by the jury, as it might well have been if Castilleja had not been allowed to testify falsely, to the knowledge of the prosecutor, his offense would have been reduced to "murder without malice" precluding the death penalty now imposed upon him.

The judgment is reversed and the cause is remanded to the Court of Criminal Appeals of the State of Texas for further proceedings not inconsistent with this opinion.

SOURCE: Alcorta v. Texas, 355 U.S. 28 (1957).

ANALYSIS

Alvaro Alcorta admitted killing his wife but claimed he did so in a fit of passion when he saw his wife kissing another man named Castilleja. This was significant, because Texas law at the time provided for a separate penalty for "murder without malice." This applied to impulsive killings rather than ones where perpetrators carried out a premeditated plot or scheme. The maximum penalty under this "murder without malice" law was five years.

During the trial, Castilleja, the only eyewitness to the crime, testified that he was merely a friend of Alcorta's wife, nothing more. However, in a later appeal, it was revealed that Castilleja had an affair with Alcorta's wife. Castilleja had told the prosecutor in the case that he had sexual intercourse with Alcorta's wife multiple times. The prosecutor told him not to volunteer this information when called to testify but to speak truthfully about it if asked.

At the trial, Castilleja said nothing about the affair. In fact, he testified falsely that he was merely friends with Alcorta's wife and was simply offering her a ride in his car. Later, Alcorta filed a petition for habeas corpus. During this proceeding, Castilleja admitted that he had offered false testimony. At a later hearing, the prosecutor also admitted that he knew of the perjured testimony that convicted Alcorta.

The U.S. Supreme Court reasoned in *Alcorta v. Texas* that Alcorta was convicted based on false testimony and that this violated his fundamental right to due process. He was denied the right to a fair trial. Ethics prohibit a prosecutor from offering false witness testimony. In fact, prosecutors are called "ministers of justice" and are supposed to disclose any exculpatory evidence to the defendant's attorneys.

The Supreme Court in a per curiam opinion recognized that Alcorta's death sentence was a miscarriage of justice, because he was convicted based on perjured testimony.

FURTHER READING

Ferguson-Gilbert, Catherine. "It is Not Whether You Win or Lose, But How You Play the Game: Is the Win-Loss Scorekeeping Mentality Doing Justice for Prosecutors?" 38 *California Western Law Review* 283 (2001).

Miller, Colin. "The Right to Evidence of Innocence before Pleading Guilty." 53 *University of California at Davis Law Review* 271 (2019).

- ***Document 11:*** Justice Arthur Goldberg's dissent in *Rudolph v. Alabama*
- ***When:*** October 21, 1963
- ***Where:*** Washington, D.C.
- ***Significance:*** This short dissent inspired a long-standing and inspired legal effort by the NAACP Legal Defense Fund against the death penalty in the United States.

DOCUMENT

Justice Goldberg Issues Dissent Questioning the Constitutionality of the Death Penalty

I would grant certiorari in this case . . . to consider whether the Eighth and Fourteenth Amendments to the United States Constitution permit the imposition of the death penalty on a convicted rapist who has neither taken nor endangered human life.

The following questions, *inter alia*, seem relevant and worthy of argument and consideration:

(1) In light of the trend both in this country and throughout the world against punishing rape by death, does the imposition of the death penalty by those States which retain it for rape violate "evolving standards of decency that mark the progress of [our] maturing society," or "standards of decency more or less universally accepted"?

(2) Is the taking of human life to protect a value other than human life consistent with the constitutional proscription against "punishments which by their excessive . . . severity are greatly disproportioned to the offenses charged"?

(3) Can the permissible aims of punishment (*e.g.*, deterrence, isolation, rehabilitation) be achieved as effectively by punishing rape less severely than by death (*e.g.*, by life imprisonment); if so, does the imposition of the death penalty for rape constitute "cruel and unusual punishment."

SOURCE: *Rudolph v. Alabama*, 375 U.S. 889 (1963).

ANALYSIS

Justice Arthur Goldberg only served on the U.S. Supreme Court for a few years (October 1962–July 1965) before resigning to serve as the U.S. Ambassador to the United Nations in the administration of Lyndon B. Johnson. In 1963, Justice Goldberg instructed his then 24-year-old law clerk Alan Dershowitz—who later became an acclaimed criminal defense attorney and prominent legal mind—to draft a memorandum outlining objections to the death penalty.

Dershowitz's memorandum focused on racial disparities in the implementation and application of the death penalty. Dershowitz had pointed out in his research that the death penalty for rape convictions was very disproportionally applied based on race. Rudolph was a Black man convicted of raping a white woman. Goldberg later dissented in two cases—the leading one being *Rudolph v. Alabama*—in which death sentences were handed down for rape convictions.

In his short dissent, Justice Goldberg removed references to race, focusing on three questions: (1) whether imposing the death penalty for a rape conviction was too harsh a punishment; (2) whether the death penalty itself was unconstitutional; and (3) whether one could deter the crime of rape just as effectively with a long sentence, such as life imprisonment, rather than death.

It was this dissent—and the earlier Dershowitz memorandum—that launched the mission of the NAACP's Legal Defense Fund's attempt to end the death penalty in the United States. In the words of death penalty historian Evan Mandery, Goldberg instructed Dershowitz to send his memo out to various civil rights organizations. Dershowitz sent his memo to the NAACP Legal Defense Fund, and the memo "stirred the pot."

It was this memo that started the NAACP into a serious mission to end the death penalty by focusing at least initially on racial disparities in the imposition of the death penalty. It was the efforts of the NAACP Legal Defense Fund that ultimately led to the Supreme Court's invalidation of the death penalty several years later in *Furman v. Georgia* (1972).

FURTHER READING

Goldberg, Arthur J., and Alan M. Dershowitz. "Declaring the Death Penalty Unconstitutional." 83 *Harvard Law Review* 1773 (1970).

- ***Document 12:*** Supreme Court decision in *Boykin v. Alabama*
- ***Date:*** June 2, 1969
- ***Where:*** Washington, D.C.
- ***Significance:*** The U.S. Supreme Court emphasized that before a waiver of constitutional rights in a death penalty case, there must be clear evidence that the defendant intelligently and knowingly agrees to waive his or her rights.

DOCUMENT

Supreme Court Reverses Death Sentence on "Knowing Waiver of Rights" Grounds

Over the course of a few weeks in the spring of 1966 a series of armed robberies occurred in Mobile, Alabama. The victims, in each case, were local shopkeepers open at night who were forced by a gunman to hand over money. While robbing one grocery store, the assailant fired his gun once, sending a bullet through a door into the ceiling. A few days earlier in a drugstore, the robber had allowed his gun to discharge in such a way that the bullet, on ricochet from the floor, struck a customer in the leg. Shortly thereafter, a local grand jury returned five indictments against petitioner, a 27-year-old Negro, for common-law robbery - an offense punishable in Alabama by death.

Before the matter came to trial, the court determined that petitioner was indigent and appointed counsel to represent him. Three days later, at his arraignment, petitioner pleaded guilty to all five indictments. So far as the record shows, the judge asked no questions of petitioner concerning his plea, and petitioner did not address the court.

Trial strategy may of course make a plea of guilty seem the desirable course. But the record is wholly silent on that point and throws no light on it.

Alabama provides that when a defendant pleads guilty, "the court must cause the punishment to be determined by a jury" (except where it is required to be fixed by the court) and may "cause witnesses to be examined, to ascertain the character of the offense." In the present case a trial of that dimension was held, the prosecution presenting its case largely through eyewitness testimony. Although counsel for petitioner engaged in cursory cross-examination, petitioner neither testified himself nor presented testimony concerning his character and background. There was nothing to indicate that he had a prior criminal record.

In instructing the jury, the judge stressed that petitioner had pleaded guilty in five cases of robbery, defined as "the felonious taking of money . . . from another against his will . . . by violence or by putting him in fear . . . [carrying] from ten years minimum in the penitentiary to the supreme penalty of death by electrocution." The jury, upon deliberation, found petitioner guilty and sentenced him severally to die on each of the five indictments.

Taking an automatic appeal to the Alabama Supreme Court, petitioner argued that a sentence of death for common-law robbery was cruel and unusual punishment within the meaning of the Federal Constitution, a suggestion which that court unanimously rejected. On their own motion, however, four of the seven justices discussed the constitutionality of the process by which the trial judge had accepted petitioner's guilty plea.

From the order affirming the trial court, three justices dissented on the ground that the record was inadequate to show that petitioner had intelligently and knowingly pleaded guilty. The fourth member concurred separately, conceding that "a trial judge should not accept a guilty plea unless he has determined that such a plea was voluntarily and knowingly entered by the defendant," but refusing "[f]or aught appearing" "to presume that the trial judge failed to do his duty." We granted certiorari.

Respondent does not suggest that we lack jurisdiction to review the voluntary character of petitioner's guilty plea because he failed to raise that federal question below and the state court failed to pass upon it. But the question was raised on oral argument and we conclude that it is properly presented. The very Alabama statute that provides automatic appeal in capital cases also requires the reviewing court to comb the record for "any error prejudicial to the appellant, even though not called to our attention in brief of counsel." The automatic appeal statute "is the only provision under the Plain Error doctrine of which we are aware in Alabama criminal appellate review."

. . .

It was error, plain on the face of the record, for the trial judge to accept petitioner's guilty plea without an affirmative showing that it was intelligent and voluntary. That error, under Alabama procedure, was properly before the court below and considered explicitly by a majority of the justices and is properly before us on review.

A plea of guilty is more than a confession which admits that the accused did various acts; it is itself a conviction; nothing remains but to give judgment and determine punishment. Admissibility of a confession must be based on a "reliable determination on the voluntariness issue which satisfies the constitutional rights of the defendant." The requirement that the prosecution spread on the record the prerequisites of a valid waiver is no constitutional innovation. . . .

We think that the same standard must be applied to determining whether a guilty plea is voluntarily made. For, as we have said, a plea of guilty is more than an admission of conduct; it is a conviction. Ignorance, incomprehension, coercion, terror, inducements, subtle or blatant threats might be a perfect cover-up of unconstitutionality. The question of an effective waiver of a federal constitutional right in a proceeding is of course governed by federal standards.

Several federal constitutional rights are involved in a waiver that takes place when a plea of guilty is entered in a state criminal trial. First, is the privilege against compulsory self-incrimination guaranteed by the Fifth Amendment and applicable to the States by reason of the Fourteenth. Second, is the right to trial by jury. Third, is the right to confront one's accusers. We cannot presume a waiver of these three important federal rights from a silent record.

What is at stake for an accused facing death or imprisonment demands the utmost solicitude of which courts are capable in canvassing the matter with the accused to make sure he has a full understanding of what the plea connotes and of its consequence. When the judge discharges that function, he leaves a record adequate for any review that may be later sought and forestalls the spin-off of collateral proceedings that seek to probe murky memories.

The three dissenting justices in the Alabama Supreme Court stated the law accurately when they concluded that there was reversible error "because the record does not disclose that the defendant voluntarily and understandingly entered his pleas of guilty."

Reversed.

SOURCE: Boykin v. Alabama, 395 U.S. 238 (1969).

ANALYSIS

Edward Boykin Jr. was a 27-year-old African American man charged with five separate counts of armed robbery. At that time, the state of Alabama allowed for the death penalty for the conviction of robbery. In fact, at an oral argument before the U.S. Supreme Court, Boykin's attorney, E. Graham Gibbons, told the justices that his client "is the only man in America that awaits execution for the common-law crime of robbery."

Boykin's attorney challenged his death penalty conviction on three grounds: (1) it violates due process to convict a person without that person knowing and understanding the waiver, (2) a death sentence for the crime of robbery is cruel within the meaning of the Eighth Amendment, and (3) a law that gives the jury unfettered discretion to impose the death penalty also violates the Due Process.

The Alabama Supreme Court had affirmed Boykin's death sentence by a vote of 4–3. The three dissenting judges focused on the fact that there was no affirmative showing that Boykin knowingly and intelligently waived his constitutional rights when he pleaded guilty.

Gibbons told the Supreme Court at the oral argument, "That if you look at this record right here, you do not know and I do not know whether Edward Boykin entered his plea of guilty voluntarily and understandingly. And yet he is going to have to die because of the bareness of the record."

That argument obviously resonated with the U.S. Supreme Court, who reversed Boykin's conviction and held that it must be shown that a defendant willingly and knowingly pled guilty and waived his rights, particularly in a death penalty case. The Court noted that a plea of guilty like this means that a defendant is waiving several serious constitutional rights, including the Fifth Amendment privilege against self-incrimination, the right to a jury trial, and the right to confront one's accusers.

FURTHER READING

Snowdon, Marlee A. "The Boykin-Tahl Requirement." 22 *Pepperdine Law Review* 273 (1994).

3

THE SUPREME COURT ABOLISHES—AND SUBSEQUENTLY REINSTATES—CAPITAL PUNISHMENT

The 1970s were a tumultuous decade in the history of the death penalty in the United States of America. At the beginning of the decade, opponents of capital punishment rejoiced at a Supreme Court decision that seemed to outlaw the practice—only to see the Court revive capital punishment five years later in another landmark decision.

The Supreme Court, in effect, abolished the death penalty in the United States with its historic 5–4 decision in *Furman v. Georgia* (1972). Five justices ruled that death penalty statutes were unconstitutional in Georgia and Texas. Three of the five justices wrote opinions expressing profound misgivings with what they characterized as systemic problems with capital punishment. Two of these three—William Brennan and Thurgood Marshall—believed that the death penalty was unconstitutional as a practice no matter how it was implemented. In fact, for the rest of their careers on the Supreme Court—Brennan retired in 1990 and Marshall in 1993—they dissented every time the Court handed down opinions legitimizing the death penalty. Brennan called the death penalty "fatally offensive to human dignity," while Marshall described it as "morally unacceptable."

Justice William O. Douglas also attacked the death penalty, but he focused specifically on the problem of race. He wrote that the death penalty laws in Georgia and Texas were "pregnant with discrimination." Douglas warned that "the discretion of judges and juries in imposing the death penalty enables the penalty to be selectively applied, feeding prejudices against the accused if he is poor and despised, and lacking political clout, or if he is a member of a suspect or unpopular minority, and saving those who by social position may be in a more protected position."

The two other justices of the five with reservations about capital punishment—Potter Stewart and Byron White—wrote much narrower opinions. Stewart famously wrote that the death penalty laws at issue simply did not provide enough guidance to jurors: "These death sentences are cruel and unusual in the same way that being struck by lightning is cruel and unusual." White echoed similar concerns, writing that "there is no meaningful basis for distinguishing the few cases in which it is imposed from the many cases in which it is not."

The *Furman* decision ended state-sanctioned executions in the United States—but only for four and a half years, at which time the state of Utah executed Gary Gilmore by firing squad in 1977. The *Furman* decision also unleashed an unprecedented flurry of legislative activity, as 35 states passed new death penalty laws by 1976. Rising crime rates in the 1970s also fanned the flames of public discontent.

The net result was that legislatures passed new death penalty laws upon which the Supreme Court was called to pass judgment. In *Gregg v. Georgia* (1976), for example, the Supreme Court upheld Georgia's new death penalty law. Justice Stewart this time voted in favor of the law, noting that the legislators had identified a series of aggravating and mitigating factors for jurors to assess. Stewart wrote that "no longer can a jury wantonly and freakishly impose the death sentence; it is always circumscribed by the legislative guidelines."

Gregg provided a blueprint for state legislators to draft death penalty laws that would survive a constitutional challenge under the Eighth Amendment. Ever since the *Gregg* decision, the Court has never struck down the death penalty holistically, as it did in the *Furman* decision. It has, however, been receptive to efforts by death penalty opponents to exclude particular defendants (such as juveniles or those who are intellectually disabled) or further regulate particular methods of execution (challenging specific protocols for lethal injection for example).

FURTHER READING

Garland, David. *Peculiar Institution: America's Death Penalty in an Age of Abolition*. Cambridge, MA: Harvard University Press, 2012.

Mandery, Evan. *A Wild Justice: The Death and Resurrection of Capital Punishment in America*. New York: Norton & Co., 2013.

- ***Document 13:*** Justice Potter Stewart's concurring opinion in *Furman v. Georgia*
- ***Date:*** June 29, 1972
- ***Where:*** Washington, D.C.
- ***Significance:*** Justice Stewart's opinion was influential in ending the death penalty for several years in the United States—until the Court reinstated the death penalty in *Gregg v. Georgia* (1976).

DOCUMENT

Justice Stewart Questions Arbitrary Quality of Death Penalty Sentences

The penalty of death differs from all other forms of criminal punishment, not in degree but in kind. It is unique in its total irrevocability. It is unique in its rejection of rehabilitation of the convict as a basic purpose of criminal justice. And it is unique, finally, in its absolute renunciation of all that is embodied in our concept of humanity.

For these and other reasons, at least two of my Brothers have concluded that the infliction of the death penalty is constitutionally impermissible in all circumstances under the Eighth and Fourteenth Amendments. Their case is a strong one. But I find it unnecessary to reach the ultimate question they would decide.

The opinions of other Justices today have set out in admirable and thorough detail the origins and judicial history of the Eighth Amendment's guarantee against the infliction of cruel and unusual punishments, and the origin and judicial history of capital punishment. There is thus no need for me to review the historical materials here, and what I have to say can, therefore, be briefly stated.

Legislatures—state and federal—have sometimes specified that the penalty of death shall be the mandatory punishment for every person convicted of engaging in certain designated criminal conduct. Congress, for example, has provided that anyone convicted of acting as a spy for the enemy in time of war shall be put to death. The Rhode Island Legislature has ordained the death penalty for a life term prisoner who commits murder. Massachusetts has passed a law imposing the death penalty upon anyone convicted of murder in the commission of a forcible rape. An Ohio law imposes the mandatory penalty of death upon the assassin of the President of the United States or the Governor of a State.

If we were reviewing death sentences imposed under these or similar laws, we would be faced with the need to decide whether capital punishment is unconstitutional for all crimes and under all circumstances. We would need to decide whether a legislature—state or federal—could constitutionally determine that certain criminal conduct is so atrocious that society's interest in deterrence and retribution wholly outweighs any considerations of reform or rehabilitation of the perpetrator, and that, despite the inconclusive empirical evidence, only the automatic penalty of death will provide maximum deterrence.

On that score I would say only that I cannot agree that retribution is a constitutionally impermissible ingredient in the imposition of punishment. The instinct for retribution is part of the nature of man, and channeling that instinct in the administration of criminal justice serves an important purpose in promoting the stability of a society governed by law. When people begin to believe that organized society is unwilling or unable to impose upon criminal offenders the punishment they "deserve," then there are sown the seeds of anarchy—of self-help, vigilante justice, and lynch law.

The constitutionality of capital punishment in the abstract is not, however, before us in these cases. For the Georgia and Texas Legislatures have not provided that the death penalty shall be imposed upon all those who are found guilty of forcible rape. And the Georgia Legislature has not ordained that death shall be the automatic punishment for murder. In a word, neither State has made a legislative determination that forcible rape and murder can be deterred only by imposing the penalty of death upon all who perpetrate those offenses. As MR. JUSTICE WHITE so tellingly puts it, the "legislative will is not frustrated if the penalty is never imposed."

Instead, the death sentences now before us are the product of a legal system that brings them, I believe, within the very core of the Eighth Amendment's guarantee against cruel and unusual punishments, a guarantee applicable against the States through the Fourteenth Amendment. In the first place, it is clear that these sentences are "cruel" in the sense that they excessively go beyond, not in degree but in kind, the punishments that the state legislatures have determined to be necessary. In the second place, it is equally clear that these sentences are "unusual" in the sense that the penalty of death is infrequently imposed for murder, and that its imposition for rape is extraordinarily rare. But I do not rest my conclusion upon these two propositions alone.

These death sentences are cruel and unusual in the same way that being struck by lightning is cruel and unusual. For, of all the people convicted of rapes and murders in 1967 and 1968, many just as reprehensible as these, the petitioners are among a capriciously selected random handful upon whom the sentence of death has in fact been imposed. My concurring Brothers have demonstrated that, if any basis can be discerned for the selection of these few to be sentenced to die, it is the constitutionally impermissible basis of race. But racial discrimination has not been proved, and I put it to one side. I simply conclude that the Eighth and Fourteenth Amendments cannot tolerate the infliction of a sentence of death under legal systems that permit this unique penalty to be so wantonly and so freakishly imposed.

For these reasons I concur in the judgments of the Court.

SOURCE: Furman v. Georgia, 408 U.S. 238 (1972).

ANALYSIS

On June 29, 1972, the U.S. Supreme Court effectively ended capital punishment in the United States of America with its opinion in *Furman v. Georgia*. The Court was sharply divided 5–4, and all nine justices wrote separate opinions, totaling 238 pages in all. At the time, the *Furman* decision was the longest in the history of the Court (this record was later broken in the campaign finance decision *Buckley v. Valeo* in 1976).

The five justices who ended capital punishment did so for different reasons. The five justices in the majority were Justices William Brennan, Thurgood Marshall, William O. Douglas, Byron White, and Potter Stewart. Justices Brennan and Marshall wrote that the death penalty—in any form—violated the Eighth Amendment and constituted cruel and unusual punishment. For the reminder of their tenures on the Court, these two Justices registered their objections to the death penalty in every relevant case.

Justice William O. Douglas wrote that the current capital punishment scheme could not be justified because the death penalty laws were "pregnant with discrimination." He found arguments of the National Association for the Advancement of Colored People's (NAACP) Legal Defense Fund that racial discrimination pervaded the U.S. legal system to be particularly persuasive.

The other two justices in the majority were Byron White and Potter Stewart. These two justices did not object to the death penalty in all cases. Rather they objected to the particular death penalty statutes they were reviewing.

Justice Stewart's opinion emphasized that there was not sufficient guidance given to juries in determining which defendants deserved the death penalty. He famously wrote that which defendants received the death penalty was too random, "cruel and unusual in the same way that being struck by lightning is cruel and unusual." He concluded that death sentences were "wantonly and freakishly imposed."

The *Furman* decision actually was a consolidation of three separate cases from Georgia and Texas. William Furman was convicted of the murder of William Micke in Savannah, Georgia. The other two cases were *Jackson v. Georgia* and *Branch v. Texas*. Both these two defendants—Lucious Jackson and Elmer Branch—were

DID YOU KNOW?

Justice William Brennan's Concurring Opinion in *Furman v. Georgia*

Justice William Brennan—like the rest of his colleagues on the U.S. Supreme Court—wrote a separate opinion in the death penalty decision *Furman v. Georgia*. Brennan reasoned that the death penalty per se was "cruel and unusual punishment" under the Eighth Amendment.

Brennan began by noting that the "Cruel and Unusual Punishment Clause, like the other great clauses of the Constitution, is not susceptible of precise definition." But, he said the Court must determine its meaning based on the values important to the Constitution.

Brennan found the historical record from the days of the founding to be inconclusive and not determinative of the meaning of the clause. Instead, he reasoned that the Cruel and Unusual Punishment Clause forbids punishments that are "uncivilized and inhuman" and "degrading to the dignity of human beings."

Brennan concluded that "the deliberate extinguishment of human life by the State is uniquely degrading to human dignity."

Brennan—like his colleague Thurgood Marshall—dissented in death penalty cases even when his colleagues in the majority effectively reinstated the death penalty in *Gregg v. Georgia* (1976). In fact, scholar Michael Mello writes that since *Gregg*, Brennan and Marshall reiterated their view that the death penalty violated the Eighth Amendment in more than 2,100 cases.

FURTHER READING

Mello, Michael. "Adhering to Our Views: Justices Brennan and Marshall and the Relentless Dissent to Death as a Punishment." 22 *Florida State University Law Review* 592 (1995).

African American men convicted and sentenced to death for rape. All three defendants were African American.

The immediate result of *Furman v. Georgia* was that the death sentences of more than 600 inmates across the country were converted into life sentences. Death penalty opponents rejoiced at the end of the death penalty—or so they thought. However, the Court's decision in *Furman* case provoked a swift response from death penalty proponents.

Legislatures in different states passed revised death penalty statutes that purported to give jurors more guidance on whether certain defendants should be given the death penalty. These statutes contained both "aggravating" and "mitigating" factors that supposedly provided this additional guidance to jurors in capital cases. Ultimately, the Supreme Court upheld these revised death penalty statutes in *Gregg v. Georgia* (1976).

William Henry Furman himself was released from prison in 1984. For more than two decades, he managed to avoid the criminal justice system, ostensibly living peacefully in his home state of Georgia. However, in 2006, he was convicted of burglary in Macon, Georgia. He was sentenced to 20 years in prison.

FURTHER READING

Beasley, David. "Georgia Inmate in Historic Death Penalty Case Gains Perspective." *Reuters*. April 27, 2016.

Chammah, Maurice. *Let the Lord Sort Them: The Rise and Fall of the Death Penalty*. New York: Crown Publishers, 2021.

Steiker, Carol S. "Furman v. Georgia: Not an End, But a Beginning." In *Death Penalty Stories*, eds. John H. Blume and Jordan M. Steiker, pp. 94–127. St. Paul, Minnesota: Foundation Press, 2009.

- ***Document 14:*** President Nixon's State of the Union Message
- ***Date:*** March 14, 1973
- ***Where:*** Washington, D.C.
- ***Significance:*** During President Richard Nixon's first State of the Union Address after winning re-election in November 1972, he devoted considerable time to defending capital punishment, which he characterized as a "valuable deterrent" in fighting crime (relevant excerpts follow). The president's message indicated strong political support for the death penalty even after the Supreme Court struck down capital punishment as unconstitutional in *Furman v. Georgia* (1972).

DOCUMENT

President Nixon Reaffirms Support for the Death Penalty

. . . The sharp reduction in the application of the death penalty was a component of the more permissive attitude toward crime in the last decade.

I do not contend that the death penalty is a panacea that will cure crime. Crime is the product of a variety of different circumstances—sometimes social, sometimes psychological—but it is committed by human beings and at the point of commission it is the product of that individual's motivation. If the incentive not to commit crime is stronger than the incentive to commit it, then logic suggests that crime will be reduced. It is in part the entirely justified feeling of the prospective criminal that he will not suffer for his deed which, in the present circumstances, helps allow those deeds to take place.

Federal crimes are rarely "crimes of passion." Airplane hi-jacking is not done in a blind rage; it has to be carefully planned. The use of incendiary devices and bombs is not a crime of passion, nor is kidnapping; all these must be thought out in advance. At present those who plan these crimes do not have to include in. their deliberations the possibility that they will be put to death for their deeds. I believe that in making their plans, they should have to consider the fact that if a death results from their crime, they too may die.

Under those conditions, I am confident that the death penalty can be a valuable deterrent. By making the death penalty available, we will provide Federal enforcement authorities with additional leverage to dissuade those individuals who may commit a Federal crime from taking the lives of others in the course of committing that crime.

Hard experience has taught us that with due regard for the rights of all—including the right to life itself we must return to a greater concern with protecting those who might otherwise be the innocent victims of violent crime than with protecting those who have committed those crimes. The society which fails to recognize this as a reasonable ordering of its priorities must inevitably find itself, in time, at the mercy of criminals.

America was heading in that direction in the last decade, and I believe that we must not risk returning to it again. Accordingly, I am proposing the re-institution of the death penalty for war-related treason, sabotage, and espionage, and for all specifically enumerated crimes under Federal jurisdiction from which death results.

The Department of Justice has examined the constitutionality of the death penalty in the light of the Supreme Court's recent decision in *Furman v. Georgia*. It is the Department's opinion that Furman holds unconstitutional the imposition of the death penalty only insofar as it is applied arbitrarily and capriciously. I believe the best way to accommodate the reservations of the Court is to authorize the automatic imposition of the death penalty where it is warranted.

Under the proposal drafted by the Department of Justice, a hearing would be required after the trial for the purpose of determining the existence or nonexistence of certain rational standards which delineate aggravating factors or mitigating factors.

Among those mitigating factors which would preclude the imposition of a death sentence are the youth of the defendant, his or her mental capacity, or the fact that the crime was committed under duress. Aggravating factors include the creation of a grave risk of danger to the national security, or to the life of another person, or the killing of another person during the commission of one of a circumscribed list of serious offenses, such as treason, kidnapping, or aircraft piracy.

The hearing would be held before the judge who presided at the trial and before either the same jury, or, if circumstances require, a jury specially impaneled. Imposition of the death penalty by the judge would be mandatory if the jury returns a special verdict finding the existence of one or more aggravating factors and the absence of any mitigating factor. The death sentence is prohibited if the jury finds the existence of one or more mitigating factors.

Current statutes containing the death penalty would be amended to eliminate the requirement for jury recommendation, thus limiting the imposition of the death penalty to cases in which the legislative guidelines for its imposition clearly require it, and eliminating arbitrary and capricious application of the death penalty which the Supreme Court has condemned in the Furman case.

SOURCE: Nixon, Richard M. "State of the Union Message to the Congress on Law Enforcement and Drug Abuse Prevention." March 14, 1973. American Presidency Project. https://www.presidency.ucsb.edu/documents/state-the-union-message-the-congress-law-enforcement-and-drug-abuse-prevention

ANALYSIS

President Richard M. Nixon, himself an attorney who once argued a case before the U.S. Supreme Court, had campaigned as a "law and order" candidate. He railed against what he deemed to be the liberal excesses of the 1960s and of permissive attitudes toward crime.

In his March 1973 State of the Union address, President Nixon focused on law enforcement and carrying out what he described as a "War on Drugs." A part of his State of the Union address focused specifically on the death penalty.

Nixon contended that the death penalty does deter at least some level of crime. He noted the death penalty is not a "panacea" but cautioned Congress that the country must not become too permissive and soft toward crime.

Nixon advocated reinstating the death penalty for certain federal crimes. He acknowledged the U.S. Supreme Court's decision in *Furman v. Georgia* (1972), in which a sharply divided Court had ruled death penalty statutes in Georgia and Texas to be unconstitutional. The net effect of the *Furman* decision was that the death penalty was on hold in the United States.

Death penalty abolitionists had obtained a stunning victory with *Furman*, and some believed that the death penalty had been interred. However, public reaction to the *Furman* decision was negative in many parts of the country, and legislators responded with a dizzying array of new statutes.

President Nixon was prescient on this point, emphasizing that his administration's Department of Justice believed "that *Furman* holds unconstitutional the imposition of the death penalty only insofar as it is applied arbitrarily and capriciously." In other words, Nixon accurately saw that the Court did not strike down the death penalty because it was inherently unconstitutional but rather because it was applied too arbitrarily in practice.

History would prove President Nixon correct with the Supreme Court's decision a few years later in *Gregg v. Georgia* (1976). In *Gregg*, the Supreme Court examined revised death penalty laws that provided for guidance to jurors in determining whether a defendant should receive the death penalty or not.

Nixon specifically talked about aggravating and mitigating factors. This is how modern death penalty statutes read. Before a defendant can be sentenced to death, a jury must look at whether there are aggravating factors—such as the defendant committed murder while robbing someone or the crime was unusually brutal or heinous—and whether there are mitigating factors, such as the youth of the defendant.

FURTHER READING

Banner, Stuart. "The Death Penalty's Strange Career." *The Washington Quarterly*. Spring 2002.
Weaver, Warren, Jr. "Nixon's Justice." *New York Times*. March 18, 1973.

- ***Document 15:*** Supreme Court's Opinion in *Gregg v. Georgia*
- ***Date:*** July 2, 1976
- ***Where:*** Washington, D.C.
- ***Significance:*** This decision reestablished that the death penalty was constitutional and did not violate the Eighth Amendment. The decision also provided a blueprint for other state legislatures on how to craft death penalty statutes that would survive judicial review.

DOCUMENT

Supreme Court Finds Death Penalty Constitutional Four Years after *Furman*

The issue in this case is whether the imposition of the sentence of death for the crime of murder under the law of Georgia violates the Eighth and Fourteenth Amendments.

I

The petitioner, Troy Gregg, was charged with committing armed robbery and murder. In accordance with Georgia procedure in capital cases, the trial was in two stages, a guilt stage and a sentencing stage. The evidence at the guilt trial established that on November 21, 1973, the petitioner and a traveling companion, Floyd Allen, while hitchhiking north in Florida were picked up by Fred Simmons and Bob Moore. Their car broke down, but they continued north after Simmons purchased another vehicle with some of the cash he was carrying. While still in Florida, they picked up another hitchhiker, Dennis Weaver, who rode with them to Atlanta, where he was let out about 11 p. m. A short time later the four men interrupted their journey for a rest stop along the highway. The next morning the bodies of Simmons and Moore were discovered in a ditch nearby.

. . .

The trial judge submitted the murder charges to the jury on both felony-murder and nonfelony-murder theories. He also instructed on the issue of self-defense but declined to instruct on manslaughter. He submitted the robbery case to the jury on both an armed-robbery theory and on the lesser included offense of robbery by intimidation. The jury found the petitioner guilty of two counts of armed robbery and two counts of murder.

At the penalty stage, which took place before the same jury, neither the prosecutor nor the petitioner's lawyer offered any additional evidence. Both counsel, however, made lengthy arguments dealing generally with the propriety of capital punishment under the circumstances and with the weight of the evidence of guilt. The trial judge instructed the jury that it could recommend either a death sentence or a life prison sentence on each count. The judge further charged the jury that in determining what sentence was appropriate the jury was free to consider the facts and circumstances, if any, presented by the parties in mitigation or aggravation.

Finally, the judge instructed the jury that it "would not be authorized to consider [imposing] the penalty of death" unless it first found beyond a reasonable doubt one of these aggravating circumstances:

> "One—That the offense of murder was committed while the offender was engaged in the commission of two other capital felonies, to-wit the armed robbery of [Simmons and Moore].
>
> "Two—That the offender committed the offense of murder for the purpose of receiving money and the automobile described in the indictment.
>
> "Three—The offense of murder was outrageously and wantonly vile, horrible and inhuman, in that they [sic] involved the depravity of [the] mind of the defendant."

Finding the first and second of these circumstances, the jury returned verdicts of death on each count.

The Supreme Court of Georgia affirmed the convictions and the imposition of the death sentences for murder. . . .

We granted the petitioner's application for a writ of certiorari limited to his challenge to the imposition of the death sentences in this case as "cruel and unusual" punishment in violation of the Eighth and the Fourteenth Amendments.

Before considering the issues presented it is necessary to understand the Georgia statutory scheme for the imposition of the death penalty. The Georgia statute, as amended after our decision in *Furman v. Georgia* (1972), retains the death penalty for six categories of crime: murder, kidnaping for ransom or where the victim is harmed, armed robbery, rape, treason, and aircraft hijacking. The capital defendant's guilt or innocence is determined in the traditional manner, either by a trial judge or a jury, in the first stage of a bifurcated trial.

. . .

III

We address initially the basic contention that the punishment of death for the crime of murder is, under all circumstances, "cruel and unusual" in violation of the Eighth and Fourteenth Amendments of the Constitution. In Part IV of this opinion, we will consider the sentence of death imposed under the Georgia statutes at issue in this case.

The Court on a number of occasions has both assumed and asserted the constitutionality of capital punishment. In several cases that assumption provided a necessary foundation for the decision, as the Court was asked to decide whether a particular method of carrying out a capital sentence would be allowed to stand under the Eighth Amendment. But until *Furman v. Georgia* (1972), the Court never confronted squarely the fundamental claim that the punishment of death always, regardless of the enormity of the offense or the procedure followed in imposing the sentence, is cruel and unusual punishment in violation of the Constitution. . . . We now hold that the punishment of death does not invariably violate the Constitution.

A

The history of the prohibition of "cruel and unusual" punishment already has been reviewed at length. . . .

In the earliest cases raising Eighth Amendment claims, the Court focused on particular methods of execution to determine whether they were too cruel to pass constitutional muster. The constitutionality of the sentence of death itself was not at issue, and the criterion used to evaluate the mode of execution was its similarity to "torture" and other "barbarous" methods. . . .

But our cases also make clear that public perceptions of standards of decency with respect to criminal sanctions are not conclusive. A penalty also must accord with "the dignity of man," which is the "basic concept underlying the Eighth Amendment." This means, at least, that the punishment not be "excessive." . . .

B

Of course, the requirements of the Eighth Amendment must be applied with an awareness of the limited role to be played by the courts. This does not mean that judges have no role to play, for the Eighth Amendment is a restraint upon the exercise of legislative power.

. . .

Therefore, in assessing a punishment selected by a democratically elected legislature against the constitutional measure, we presume its validity. We may not require the legislature to select the least severe penalty possible so long as the penalty selected is not cruelly inhumane or disproportionate to the crime involved. And a heavy burden rests on those who would attack the judgment of the representatives of the people.

. . .

C

In the discussion to this point we have sought to identify the principles and considerations that guide a court in addressing an Eighth Amendment claim. We now consider specifically whether the sentence of death for the crime of murder is a per se violation of the Eighth and Fourteenth Amendments to the Constitution. We note first that history and precedent strongly support a negative answer to this question.

The imposition of the death penalty for the crime of murder has a long history of acceptance both in the United States and in England. . . .

As we have seen, however, the Eighth Amendment demands more than that a challenged punishment be acceptable to contemporary society. The Court also must ask whether it comports with the basic concept of human dignity at the core of the Amendment. . . .

The death penalty is said to serve two principal social purposes: retribution and deterrence of capital crimes by prospective offenders.

. . .

The value of capital punishment as a deterrent of crime is a complex factual issue the resolution of which properly rests with the legislatures, which can evaluate the results of statistical studies in terms of their own local conditions and with a flexibility of approach that is not available to the courts. . . .

In sum, we cannot say that the judgment of the Georgia Legislature that capital punishment may be necessary in some cases is clearly wrong. . . .

Finally, we must consider whether the punishment of death is disproportionate in relation to the crime for which it is imposed. There is no question that death as a punishment is unique in its severity and irrevocability. . . .

We hold that the death penalty is not a form of punishment that may never be imposed, regardless of the circumstances of the offense, regardless of the character of the offender, and regardless of the procedure followed in reaching the decision to impose it.

IV

We now consider whether Georgia may impose the death penalty on the petitioner in this case. . . .

A

While Furman did not hold that the infliction of the death penalty per se violates the Constitution's ban on cruel and unusual punishments, it did recognize that the penalty of death is different in kind from any other punishment imposed under our system of criminal justice. Because of the uniqueness of the death penalty, Furman held that it could not be imposed under sentencing procedures that created a substantial risk that it would be inflicted in an arbitrary and capricious manner. . . .

Furman mandates that where discretion is afforded a sentencing body on a matter so grave as the determination of whether a human life should be taken or spared, that discretion must be suitably directed and limited so as to minimize the risk of wholly arbitrary and capricious action.

. . .

In summary, the concerns expressed in Furman that the penalty of death not be imposed in an arbitrary or capricious manner can be met by a carefully drafted statute that ensures that the sentencing authority is given adequate information and guidance. As a general proposition these concerns are best met by a system that provides for a bifurcated proceeding at which the sentencing authority is apprised of the information relevant to the imposition of sentence and provided with standards to guide its use of the information.

. . .

B

We now turn to consideration of the constitutionality of Georgia's capital-sentencing procedures. In the wake of *Furman*, Georgia amended its capital punishment statute, but chose not to narrow the scope of its murder provisions. . . .

Georgia did act, however, to narrow the class of murderers subject to capital punishment by specifying 10 statutory aggravating circumstances, one of which must be found by the jury to exist beyond a reasonable doubt before a death sentence can ever be imposed. In addition, the jury is authorized to consider any other appropriate aggravating or mitigating circumstances. The jury is not required to find any mitigating circumstance in order to make a recommendation of mercy that is binding on the trial court, but it must find a statutory aggravating circumstance before recommending a sentence of death.

These procedures require the jury to consider the circumstances of the crime and the criminal before it recommends sentence. No longer can a Georgia jury do as Furman's jury did: reach a finding of the defendant's guilt and then, without guidance or direction, decide whether he should live or die. . . .

As an important additional safeguard against arbitrariness and caprice, the Georgia statutory scheme provides for automatic appeal of all death sentences to the State's Supreme Court. That court is required by statute to review each sentence of death and determine whether it was imposed under the influence of passion or prejudice, whether the evidence supports the jury's finding of a statutory aggravating circumstance, and whether the sentence is disproportionate compared to those sentences imposed in similar cases.

In short, Georgia's new sentencing procedures require as a prerequisite to the imposition of the death penalty, specific jury findings as to the circumstances of the crime or the character of the defendant. . . .

The petitioner contends, however, that the changes in the Georgia sentencing procedures are only cosmetic, that the arbitrariness and capriciousness condemned by Furman continue to exist in Georgia—both in traditional practices that still remain and in the new sentencing procedures adopted in response to Furman.

1

First, the petitioner focuses on the opportunities for discretionary action that are inherent in the processing of any murder case under Georgia law. He notes that the state prosecutor has unfettered authority to select those persons whom he wishes to prosecute for a capital offense and to plea bargain with them. . . .

The petitioner further contends that the capital-sentencing procedures adopted by Georgia in response to Furman do not eliminate the dangers of arbitrariness and caprice in jury sentencing that were held in Furman to be violative of the Eighth and Fourteenth Amendments. He claims that the statute is so broad and vague as to leave juries free to act as arbitrarily and capriciously as they wish in deciding whether to impose the death penalty. . . .

The petitioner next argues that the requirements of Furman are not met here because the jury has the power to decline to impose the death penalty even if it finds that one or more statutory aggravating circumstances are present in the case. . . .

3

Finally, the Georgia statute has an additional provision designed to assure that the death penalty will not be imposed on a capriciously selected group of convicted defendants. The new sentencing procedures require that the State Supreme Court review every death sentence to determine whether it was imposed under the influence of passion, prejudice, or any other arbitrary factor, whether the evidence supports the findings of a statutory aggravating circumstance, and "[w]hether the sentence of death is excessive or disproportionate to the penalty imposed in similar cases, considering both the crime and the defendant." . . .

The provision for appellate review in the Georgia capital-sentencing system serves as a check against the random or arbitrary imposition of the death penalty. In particular, the proportionality review substantially eliminates the possibility that a person will be sentenced to die by the action of an aberrant jury. If a time comes when juries generally do not impose the death sentence in a certain kind of murder case, the appellate review procedures assure that no defendant convicted under such circumstances will suffer a sentence of death.

V

The basic concern of Furman centered on those defendants who were being condemned to death capriciously and arbitrarily. Under the procedures before the Court in that case, sentencing authorities were not directed to give attention to the nature or circumstances of the crime committed or to the character or record of the defendant. Left unguided, juries imposed the death sentence in a way that could only be called freakish. The new Georgia sentencing procedures, by contrast, focus the jury's attention on the particularized nature of the crime and the particularized characteristics of the individual defendant. While the jury is permitted to consider any aggravating or mitigating circumstances, it must find and identify at least one statutory aggravating factor before it may impose a penalty of death. In this way the jury's discretion is channeled. No longer can a jury wantonly and freakishly impose the death sentence; it is always circumscribed by the legislative guidelines. In addition, the review function of the Supreme Court of Georgia affords additional assurance that the concerns that prompted our decision in Furman are not present to any significant degree in the Georgia procedure applied here.

For the reasons expressed in this opinion, we hold that the statutory system under which Gregg was sentenced to death does not violate the Constitution. Accordingly, the judgment of the Georgia Supreme Court is affirmed.

It is so ordered.

SOURCE: Gregg v. Georgia, 428 U.S. 153 (1976).

ANALYSIS

The Supreme Court's decision in *Furman v Georgia* (1972) effectively invalidated the death penalty all across the United States. It also inspired a massive legislative response, as 35 states passed new death penalty statutes by 1976. A primary concern in *Furman* was that juries did not have sufficient guidance to determine which defendants should live and which should die. As Justice Potter Stewart famously wrote in his concurring opinion in *Furman*, "These death sentences are cruel and unusual in the same way that being struck by lightning is cruel and unusual."

The new legislative model was to list a series of aggravating and mitigating factors. Before jurors could impose a sentence a death, they had to find at least one aggravating factor present. For example, a typical aggravating factor was the crime was committed in the course of another felony or whether it was committed upon a police officer. Mitigating factors might include whether the defendant suffered from mental problems, showed remorse, or experienced a particularly traumatic or abusive childhood.

In *Gregg*, the Supreme Court examined Georgia's new death penalty statute. Justice Potter Stewart, who had voted against the state's death penalty law in *Furman*, wrote the opinion finding the amended Georgia law constitutional. He noted that the new law focused the jury's attention on "the particularized nature of the crime and the particularized characteristics of the individual defendant." He also wrote that because of the consideration of the aggravating and mitigating factors, "[n]o longer can a jury wantonly and freakishly impose the death sentence; it is always circumscribed by the legislative guidelines."

The *Gregg* decision provided a blueprint for other states to tinker with their death penalty laws to make sure they provided appropriate guidance to jurors in capital cases. The Court in *Gregg* case also focused on another aspect of Georgia's law—that the state supreme court had to review every death sentence to make sure it was imposed properly.

Justice Stewart explained, "The provision for appellate review in the Georgia capital-sentencing system serves as a check against the random or arbitrary imposition of the death penalty. In particular, the proportionality review substantially eliminates the possibility that a person will be sentenced to die by the action of an aberrant jury."

Justices William Brennan and Thurgood Marshall dissented in *Gregg*. For the reminder of their careers on the High Court, they dissented in every decision that upheld a death sentence. The *Gregg* decision established that the death penalty per se does not violate the Eighth Amendment.

Since *Gregg*, the focus has turned to whether particular forms of punishment are unconstitutional or whether it is unconstitutional to apply the death penalty to particular types of defendants, such as those who are under 18 or who are intellectually disabled.

FURTHER READING

Banner, Stuart. *The Death Penalty: An American History*. Cambridge, MA: Harvard University Press, 2002.

Hudson, David L., Jr. "Does Capital Punishment Have a Future? A Resource Guide for Teachers." American Bar Association, 2004.

- ***Document 16:*** Chief Justice Warren Burger's concurring opinion in *Gilmore v. Utah*
- ***Date:*** December 13, 1976
- ***Where:*** Washington, D.C.
- ***Significance:*** The decision is significant, primarily because the death row inmate Gary Gilmore became a pop culture icon of sorts. He wanted to be executed and resisted attempts by family members and attorneys to save his life. Here, the Court ruled that Gilmore's mother did not have the legal right to argue against his wishes in court.

DOCUMENT

Supreme Court Allows Convicted Murderer to Pursue His Own Death via Capital Punishment

CONCURRING OPINION BY CHIEF JUSTICE WARREN BURGER

On December 2, 1976, Bessie Gilmore, claiming to act as "next friend" on behalf of her son, Gary Mark Gilmore, filed with this Court an application for a stay of execution of the death sentence then scheduled for December 6, 1976. Since only a limited record was then before the Court, we granted a temporary stay of execution on December 3, 1976, in order to secure a response from the State of Utah. That response was received on December 7, 1976. On December 8, 1976, a response was filed by Gary Mark Gilmore, by and through his attorneys of record, Ronald R. Stanger and Robert L. Moody, challenging the standing of Bessie Gilmore to initiate any proceedings in his behalf.

When the application for a stay was initially filed on December 2, a serious question was presented as to whether Bessie Gilmore had standing to seek the requested relief or any relief from this Court. Assuming the Court would otherwise have jurisdiction with respect to a "next friend" application, that jurisdiction would arise only if it were demonstrated that Gary Mark Gilmore is unable to seek relief in his own behalf. However, in view of Gary Mark Gilmore's response on December 8, 1976, it is now clear that the "next friend" concept is wholly inapplicable to this case. Since Gary Mark Gilmore has now filed a response and appeared in his own behalf, through his retained attorneys, any basis for the standing of Bessie Gilmore to seek relief in his behalf is necessarily eliminated. The only possible exception to this conclusion would be if the record suggested, despite the representations of Gary Mark Gilmore's attorneys, that he was incompetent to waive his right of appeal under state law and was at the present time incompetent to assert rights or to challenge Bessie Gilmore's standing to assert rights in his behalf as "next friend."

After examining with care the pertinent portions of the transcripts and reports of state proceedings, and the response of Gary Mark Gilmore filed on December 8, I am in complete agreement with the conclusion expressed in the Court's order that Gary Mark Gilmore knowingly and intelligently, with full knowledge of his right to seek an appeal in the Utah Supreme Court, has waived that right. I further agree that the State's determinations of his competence to waive his rights knowingly and intelligently were firmly grounded.

When the record establishing a knowing and intelligent waiver of Gary Mark Gilmore's right to seek appellate review is combined with the December 8 written response submitted to this Court, it is plain that the Court is without jurisdiction to entertain the "next friend" application filed by Bessie Gilmore. This Court has jurisdiction pursuant to Art. III of the Constitution only over "cases and controversies," and we can issue stays only in aid of our jurisdiction. There is no dispute, presently before us, between Gary Mark Gilmore and the State of Utah, and the application of Bessie Gilmore manifestly fails to meet the statutory requirements to invoke this Court's power to review the action of the Supreme Court of Utah. No authority to the contrary has been brought to our attention, and nothing suggested in dissent bears on the threshold question of jurisdiction.

In his dissenting opinion, MR. JUSTICE White suggests that Gary Mark Gilmore is "unable" as a matter of law to waive the right to state appellate review. Whatever may be said as to the merits of this suggestion, the question simply is not before us.

Gilmore, duly found to be competent by the Utah courts, has had available meaningful access to this Court and has declined expressly to assert any claim here other than his explicit repudiation of Bessie Gilmore's effort to speak for him as next friend.

It follows, therefore, that the Court is without jurisdiction to consider the question posed by the dissent.

SOURCE: Gilmore v. Utah, 429 U.S. 1012, 97 S. Ct. 436 (1976).

ANALYSIS

Law professor John Blume explains that "Gary Gilmore is probably the most famous death row inmate in American History." He was profiled by the famed writer Norman Mailer in the book *The Executioner's Song*, and an English punk rock band named one of its songs "Gary Gilmore's Eyes."

Gary Gilmore's notoriety stemmed from his decision to waive all appeals of the capital punishment sentence he received and instead willingly face death by firing squad in Utah. Indeed, on January 17, 1977, he was shot to death by firing squad. His famous last words were "Let's do it." He also wrote a letter to the Utah Supreme Court that read: "Let's do it and to hell with all the bullshit." Those words inspired Dan Wieden, an ad executive, to use a play on those words as the slogan for Nike, the iconic shoe company.

Gilmore's life story was a sad one. He dropped out of high school at age 14 and began a life of crime that included armed robbery, car theft, and various other charges. He served prison time in Oregon state prisons on multiple occasions, at one point attempting suicide.

Upon his last release, he traveled to Utah to live with his cousin, Brenda, and work for his uncle, Vern Damico, at his shoe business. However, Gilmore took to drinking and taking drugs and cavorting with a 19-year-old woman named Nicole Barrett. After breaking up with Barrett, he became even more unstable and violent.

On June 19, 1976, Gilmore robbed and killed gas station attendant Max Jenson in the town of Orem. The next night, he shot and killed hotel manager Ben Bushnell in Provo, Utah. Gilmore was convicted of first degree murder on October 7, 1976. At some point after his convictions, Gilmore decided to waive all his appeals. He even retained California lawyer Dennis Bonz, a former prosecutor, to help him in his quest to die.

Gilmore told the Supreme Court of Utah: "I believe I was given a fair trial and I think the sentence is proper and I am willing to accept it like a man. I don't wish to appeal. . . . I desire to be executed on schedule, and I just wish to accept that with the grace and dignity of a man and I hope you will allow me to do that." Later that day, the state high court vacated the stay.

Bessie Gilmore, Gary's mother, tried to file an appeal with the U.S. Supreme Court as his "next friend." The U.S. Supreme Court took the case but determined that Gilmore had validly waived his appeal and that his mother did not have legal standing to file an appeal on his behalf anyway.

Some scholars have criticized the Court's decision in *Gilmore v. Utah*, because Gilmore was never evaluated by mental health experts at any evidentiary hearing in any court, despite years of erratic behavior and his known suicide attempt.

FURTHER READING

Blume, John H. "Gilmore v. Utah: The Persistent Problem of Volunteers." In *Death Penalty Stories*, eds. John H. Blume and Jordan M. Steiker, pp. 203–228. St. Paul, Minnesota: Foundation Press, 2009.

Gilmore, Mikal. *Shot in the Heart*. New York: Anchor Books, 1995.

Mailer, Norman. *The Executioner's Song*. New York: Little, Brown, and Company, 1979.

Reed, Christopher. "Gary Gilmore Gets His Death Wish: Archive." *Guardian* (US). January 18, 2022. https://www.theguardian.com/world/2022/jan/18/gary-gilmore-gets-his-death-wish-1977

- ***Document 17:*** Plurality Opinion in *Coker v. Georgia*
- ***Date:*** June 29, 1977
- ***Where:*** Washington, D.C.
- ***Significance:*** The Court ruled that the death penalty could no longer be sought for the crime of rape. This decision started a trend in which the Court started limiting the death penalty with respect to certain types of defendants.

DOCUMENT

Supreme Court Rules Defendant Convicted of Rape Cannot Be Executed

Georgia Code Ann. § 26-2001 (1972) provides that

> "[a] person convicted of rape shall be punished by death or by imprisonment for life, or by imprisonment for not less than one nor more than 20 years."

Punishment is determined by a jury in a separate sentencing proceeding in which at least one of the statutory aggravating circumstances must be found before the death penalty may be imposed. Petitioner Coker was convicted of rape and sentenced to death. Both the conviction and the sentence were affirmed by the Georgia Supreme Court. Coker was granted a writ of certiorari, limited to the single claim, rejected by the Georgia court, that the punishment of death for rape violates the Eighth Amendment, which proscribes "cruel and unusual punishments" and which must be observed by the States as well as the Federal Government.

While serving various sentences for murder, rape, kidnaping, and aggravated assault, petitioner escaped from the Ware Correctional Institution near Waycross, Ga. on September 2, 1974. At approximately 11 o'clock that night, petitioner entered the house of Allen and Elnita Carver through an unlocked kitchen door. Threatening the couple with a "board," he tied up Mr. Carver in the bathroom, obtained a knife from the kitchen, and took Mr. Carver's money and the keys to the family car. Brandishing the knife and saying "you know what's going to happen to you if you try anything, don't you," Coker then raped Mrs. Carver. Soon thereafter, petitioner drove away in the Carver car, taking Mrs. Carver with him. Mr. Carver, freeing himself, notified the police; and not long thereafter petitioner was apprehended. Mrs. Carver was unharmed.

Petitioner was charged with escape, armed robbery, motor vehicle theft, kidnaping, and rape. Counsel was appointed to represent him. Having been found competent to stand trial, he was tried. The jury returned a verdict of guilty, rejecting his general plea of insanity. A sentencing hearing was then conducted in accordance with the procedures dealt with at length in *Gregg v. Georgia* (1976), where this Court sustained the death penalty for murder when imposed pursuant to the statutory procedures.

The jury was instructed that it could consider as aggravating circumstances whether the rape had been committed by a person with a prior record of conviction for a capital felony and whether the rape had been committed in the course of committing another capital felony, namely, the armed robbery of Allen Carver. The court also instructed, pursuant to statute, that, even if aggravating circumstances were present, the death penalty need not be imposed if the jury found they were outweighed by mitigating circumstance, that is, circumstances not constituting justification or excuse for the offense in question, "but which, in fairness and mercy, may be considered as extenuating or reducing the degree" of moral culpability or punishment. The jury's verdict on the rape count was death by electrocution. Both aggravating circumstances on which the court instructed were found to be present by the jury.

II

... It is now settled that the death penalty is not invariably cruel and unusual punishment within the meaning of the Eighth Amendment; it is not inherently barbaric or an unacceptable mode of punishment for crime; neither is it always disproportionate to the crime for which it is imposed. It is also established that imposing capital punishment, at least for murder, in accordance with the procedures provided under the Georgia statutes saves the sentence from the infirmities which led the Court to invalidate the prior Georgia capital punishment statute in *Furman v. Georgia.*

In sustaining the imposition of the death penalty in *Gregg*, however, the Court firmly embraced the holdings and dicta from prior cases, to the effect that the Eighth Amendment bars not only those punishments that are "barbaric," but also those that are "excessive" in relation to the crime committed. Under *Gregg*, a punishment is "excessive" and unconstitutional if it (1) makes no measurable contribution to acceptable goals of punishment, and hence is nothing more than the purposeless and needless imposition of pain and suffering; or (2) is grossly out of proportion to the severity of the crime. A punishment might fail the test on either ground. . . .

III

That question, with respect to rape of an adult woman, is now before us. We have concluded that a sentence of death is grossly disproportionate and excessive punishment for the crime of rape, and is therefore forbidden by the Eighth Amendment as cruel and unusual punishment.

A

As advised by recent cases, we seek guidance in history and from the objective evidence of the country's present judgment concerning the acceptability of death as a penalty for rape of an adult woman. At no time in the last 50 years have a majority of the States authorized death as a punishment for rape. In 1925, 18 States, the District of Columbia, and the Federal Government authorized capital punishment for the rape of an adult female. By 1971, just prior to the decision in *Furman v. Georgia*, that number had declined, but not substantially, to 16 States plus the Federal Government. *Furman* then invalidated most of the capital punishment statutes in this country, including the rape statutes, because, among other reasons, of the manner in which the death penalty was imposed and utilized under those laws.

With their death penalty statutes for the most part invalidated, the States were faced with the choice of enacting modified capital punishment laws in an attempt to satisfy the requirements of *Furman* or of being satisfied with life imprisonment as the ultimate punishment for any offense. Thirty-five States immediately reinstituted the death penalty for at least limited kinds of crime. *Gregg v. Georgia*. This public judgment as to the acceptability of capital punishment, evidenced by the immediate, post-*Furman* legislative reaction in a large majority of the States, heavily influenced the Court to sustain the death penalty for murder in *Gregg v. Georgia*.

But if the "most marked indication of society's endorsement of the death penalty for murder is the legislative response to *Furman*," it should also be a telling datum that the public judgment with respect to rape, as reflected in the statutes providing the punishment for that crime, has been dramatically different. In reviving death penalty laws to satisfy *Furman's* mandate, none of the States that had not previously authorized death for rape chose to include rape among capital felonies. Of the 16 States in which rape had been a capital offense, only three provided the death penalty for rape of an adult woman in their revised statute—Georgia, North Carolina, and Louisiana. In the latter two States, the death penalty was mandatory for those found guilty, and those laws were invalidated by *Woodson* and *Roberts*. When Louisiana and North Carolina, responding to those decisions, again revised their capital punishment laws, they reenacted the death penalty for murder but not for rape; none of the seven other legislatures that to our knowledge have amended or replaced their death penalty statutes since July 2, 1976, including four States (in addition to Louisiana and North Carolina) that had authorized the death sentence for rape prior to 1972 and had reacted to *Furman* with mandatory statutes, included rape among the crimes for which death was an authorized punishment.

Georgia argues that 11 of the 16 States that authorized death for rape in 1972 attempted to comply with *Furman* by enacting arguably mandatory death penalty legislation, and that it is very likely that, aside from Louisiana and North Carolina, these States simply chose to eliminate rape as a capital offense rather than to require death for each and every instance of rape. The argument is not without force, but 4 of the 16 States did not take the mandatory course, and also did not continue rape of an adult woman as a capital offense. Further, as we have indicated, the legislatures of 6 of the 11 arguably mandatory States have revised their death penalty laws since *Woodson* and *Roberts* without enacting a new death penalty for rape. And this is to say nothing of 19 other States that enacted nonmandatory, post-*Furman* statutes and chose not to sentence rapists to death.

It should be noted that Florida, Mississippi, and Tennessee also authorized the death penalty in some rape cases, but only where the victim was a child and the rapist an adult. The Tennessee statute has since been invalidated because the death sentence was mandatory. The upshot is that Georgia is the sole jurisdiction in the United States at the present time that authorizes a sentence of death when the rape victim is an adult woman, and only two other jurisdictions provide capital punishment when the victim is a child.

The current judgment with respect to the death penalty for rape is not wholly unanimous among state legislatures, but it obviously weighs very heavily on the side of rejecting capital punishment as a suitable penalty for raping an adult woman.

B

It was also observed in *Gregg* that "[t]he jury . . . is a significant and reliable objective index of contemporary values because it is so directly involved," and that it is thus important to look to the sentencing decisions that juries have made in the course of assessing whether capital punishment is an appropriate penalty for the crime being tried. Of course, the jury's judgment is meaningful only where the jury has an appropriate measure of choice as to whether the death penalty is to be imposed. As far as execution for rape is concerned, this is now true only in Georgia and in Florida; and in the latter State, capital punishment is authorized only for the rape of children.

According to the factual submissions in this Court, out of all rape convictions in Georgia since 1973—and that total number has not been tendered—63 cases had been reviewed by the Georgia Supreme Court as of the time of oral argument; and of these, 6 involved a death sentence, 1 of which was set aside, leaving 5 convicted rapists now under sentence of death in the State of Georgia. Georgia juries have thus sentenced rapists to death six times since 1973.

This obviously is not a negligible number; and the State argues that, as a practical matter, juries simply reserve the extreme sanction for extreme cases of rape, and that recent experience surely does not prove that jurors consider the death penalty to be a disproportionate punishment for every conceivable instance of rape, no matter how aggravated. Nevertheless, it is true that, in the vast majority of cases, at least 9 out of 10, juries have not imposed the death sentence.

IV

These recent events evidencing the attitude of state legislatures and sentencing juries do not wholly determine this controversy, for the Constitution contemplates that, in the end, our own judgment will be brought to bear on the question of the acceptability of the death penalty under the Eighth Amendment. Nevertheless, the legislative rejection of capital punishment for rape strongly confirms our own judgment, which is that death is indeed a disproportionate penalty for the crime of raping an adult woman.

We do not discount the seriousness of rape as a crime. It is highly reprehensible, both in a moral sense and in its almost total contempt for the personal integrity and autonomy of the female victim and for the latter's privilege of choosing those with whom intimate relationships are to be established. Short of homicide, it is the "ultimate violation of self." It is also a violent crime because it normally involves force, or the threat of force or intimidation, to overcome the will and the capacity of the victim to resist. Rape is very often accompanied by physical injury to the female and can also inflict mental and psychological damage. Because it undermines the community's sense of security, there is public injury as well.

Rape is without doubt deserving of serious punishment; but in terms of moral depravity and of the injury to the person and to the public, it does not compare with murder, which does involve the unjustified taking of human life. Although it may be accompanied by another crime, rape, by definition, does not include the death of or even the serious injury to another person. The murderer kills; the rapist, if no more than that, does not. Life is over for the victim of the murderer; for the rape victim, life may not be nearly so happy as it was, but it is not over, and normally is not beyond repair. We have the abiding conviction that the death penalty, which "is unique in its severity and irrevocability," is an excessive penalty for the rapist who, as such, does not take human life.

This does not end the matter, for, under Georgia law, death may not be imposed for any capital offense, including rape, unless the jury or judge finds one of the statutory aggravating circumstances and then elects to impose that sentence. For the rapist to be executed in Georgia, it must therefore be found not only that he committed rape, but also that one or more of the following aggravating circumstances were present: (1) that the rape was committed by a person with a prior record of conviction for a capital felony; (2) that the rape was committed while the offender was engaged in the commission of another capital felony, or aggravated battery; or (3) the rape "was outrageously or wantonly vile, horrible or inhuman in that it involved torture, depravity of mind, or aggravated battery to the victim."

Here, the first two of these aggravating circumstances were alleged and found by the jury. Neither of these circumstances, nor both of them together, change our conclusion that the death sentence imposed on Coker is a disproportionate punishment for rape. Coker had prior convictions for capital felonies—rape, murder, and kidnaping—but these prior convictions do not change the fact that the instant crime being punished is a rape not involving the taking of life.

It is also true that the present rape occurred while Coker was committing armed robbery, a felony for which the Georgia statutes authorize the death penalty. But Coker was tried for the robbery offense as well as for rape, and received a separate life sentence for this crime; the jury did not deem the robbery itself deserving of the death penalty, even though accompanied by the aggravating circumstance, which was stipulated, that Coker had been convicted of a prior capital crime.

We note finally that, in Georgia, a person commits murder when he unlawfully and with malice aforethought, either express or implied, causes the death of another human being. He also commits that crime when, in the commission of a felony, he causes the death of another human being, irrespective of malice. But even where the killing is deliberate, it is not punishable by death absent proof of aggravating circumstances. It is difficult to accept the notion, and we do not, that the rapist, with or without aggravating circumstances, should be punished more heavily than the deliberate killer as long as the rapist does not himself take the life of his victim. The judgment of the Georgia Supreme Court upholding the death sentence is reversed, and the case is remanded to that court for further proceedings not inconsistent with this opinion.

So ordered.

SOURCE: Coker v. Georgia, 433 U.S. 584 (1977).

ANALYSIS

Ehrlich Anthony Coker was an extremely unsympathetic defendant. He raped and killed a woman in December 1971 and then kidnapped, raped, and beat another woman nearly to death. He was sentenced to three life terms for these crimes, but in 1974, he escaped from a prison in Waycross, Georgia. He went on another crime spree after his escape. He broke into the home of Allen and Elnita Carver. He tied up the husband and raped the wife *and* then kidnapped the wife in a stolen vehicle. He was apprehended by authorities, however, and convicted of rape. He ultimately was sentenced to death under a Georgia law that allowed for jurors to sentence defendants to the death penalty if there were sufficient aggravating circumstances. Coker had such aggravating circumstances in the form of prior convictions for rape and violence.

The NAACP Legal Defense Fund agreed to represent Coker in his appeal of his sentence, because they viewed the Georgia statute as a remnant of racism. Indeed, the law traditionally was used to target African American men who had allegedly raped white women. Coker, however, was a Caucasian male. David E. Kendall argued the cause for Coker before the U.S. Supreme Court. Kendall went on to have a distinguished legal career, representing the likes of Hillary Clinton, the *Washington Post*, and the *National Enquirer* in American courts.

Ironically, before taking a position with the NAACP Legal Defense Fund, Kendall clerked for U.S. Supreme Court justice Byron White. The plurality opinion in *Coker v. Georgia* was authored by Justice White.

In *Coker*, the U.S. Supreme Court emphasized that very few states—16 in the 1970s—had statutes that allowed a jury to sentence a defendant to be sentenced to death for rape.

After the Supreme Court outlawed the death penalty in *Furman v. Georgia* (1972), many states recrafted their death penalty statutes. However, only Georgia and Tennessee sanctioned capital punishment for the crime of

DID YOU KNOW?

Attorney David E. Kendall

David E. Kendall is one of the most prominent attorneys in modern American history. His list of clients includes then president Bill Clinton, then secretary of state Hilary Clinton, *Washington Post*, and General David Petraeus. But Kendall is also known for representing convicted rapist Ehrlich Anthony Coker before the U.S. Supreme Court in *Coker v. Georgia* (1977). Working under the auspices of the NAACP Legal Defense and Educational Fund, Kendall convinced the justices that the death penalty for the crime of rape was an excessive punishment under the Eighth Amendment.

Kendall earned his law degree from Yale Law School in 1971—which is where he met both Bill and Hillary Clinton. After law school, he clerked for U.S. Supreme Court justice Byron White.

FURTHER READING

Amidon, Jim. "30 Minutes with David Kendall." *Wabash Magazine*. Fall/Winter 2001.

rape, and the Tennessee Supreme Court ultimately invalidated the Tennessee law. A couple *of* other states allowed death sentences for rape but only if the victim was a child. "The current judgment with respect to the death penalty for rape is not wholly unanimous among state legislatures, but it obviously weighs very heavily on the side of rejecting capital punishment as a suitable penalty for raping an adult woman," Justice White wrote in his plurality opinion.

Ultimately, a majority of the Court ruled that the statute was unconstitutional because it imposed a disproportionate punishment. Justice White wrote:

> Rape is without doubt deserving of serious punishment; but in terms of moral depravity and of the injury to the person and to the public, it does not compare with murder, which does involve the unjustified taking of human life. Although it may be accompanied by another crime, rape, by definition, does not include the death of or even the serious injury to another person.

The Court's decision in *Coker* started a trend in which the Court carved out exceptions to the death penalty for certain types of defendants. In later decisions, the Court ruled that those who are insane, intellectually disabled, juveniles, or child rapists could not be executed.

FURTHER READING

Karp, David J. "Coker v. Georgia: Disproportionate Punishment and the Death Penalty for Rape." 78 *Columbia Law Review* 1714 (1978).

Lesage, C. R. "Death Penalty for Rape: Cruel and Unusual Punishment?" 38 *Louisiana Law Review* 868 (1978).

Mintz, Morton. "High Court Bars Execution for Rape of Woman." *Washington Post*. June 30, 1977.

- ***Document 18:*** Supreme Court decision in *Lockett v. Ohio*
- ***Date:*** July 3, 1978
- ***Where:*** Washington, D.C.
- ***Significance:*** The *Lockett* decision established that juries and judges in death penalty cases must take into account the specific circumstances of individual defendants. Specifically, they must consider so-called mitigating evidence.

DOCUMENT

Supreme Court Invalidates Ohio's Death Penalty Law on "Mitigating Evidence" Grounds

We granted certiorari in this case to consider, among other questions, whether Ohio violated the Eighth and Fourteenth Amendments by sentencing Sandra Lockett to death pursuant to a statute that narrowly limits the sentencer's discretion to consider the circumstances of the crime and the record and character of the offender as mitigating factors.

I

Lockett was charged with aggravated murder with the aggravating specifications (1) that the murder was "committed for the purpose of escaping detection, apprehension, trial, or punishment" for aggravated robbery, and (2) that the murder was "committed while . . . committing, attempting to commit, or fleeing immediately after committing or attempting to commit . . . aggravated robbery." That offense was punishable by death in Ohio. She was also charged with aggravated robbery.

The State's case against her depended largely upon the testimony of a coparticipant, one Al Parker, who gave the following account of her participation in the robbery and murder.

Lockett became acquainted with Parker and Nathan Earl Dew while she and a friend, Joanne Baxter, were in New Jersey. Parker and Dew then accompanied Lockett, Baxter, and Lockett's brother back to Akron, Ohio, Lockett's hometown. After they arrived in Akron, Parker and Dew needed money for the trip back to New Jersey. Dew suggested that he pawn his ring. Lockett overheard his suggestion, but felt that the ring was too beautiful to pawn, and suggested instead that they could get some money by robbing a grocery store and a furniture store in the area. She warned that the grocery store's operator was a "big guy" who carried a "45" and that they would have "to get him real quick." She also volunteered to get a gun from her father's basement to aid in carrying out the robberies, but by that time, the two stores had closed and it was too late to proceed with the plan to rob them.

Someone, apparently Lockett's brother, suggested a plan for robbing a pawnshop. He and Dew would enter the shop and pretend to pawn a ring. Next Parker, who had some bullets, would enter the shop, ask to see a gun, load it, and use it to rob the shop. No one planned to kill the pawnshop operator in the course of the robbery. Because she knew the owner, Lockett was not to be among those entering the pawnshop, though she did guide the others to the shop that night.

The next day Parker, Dew, Lockett, and her brother gathered at Baxter's apartment. Lockett's brother asked if they were "still going to do it," and everyone, including Lockett, agreed to proceed. The four then drove by the pawnshop several times and parked the car. Lockett's brother and Dew entered the shop. Parker then left the car and told Lockett to start it again in two minutes. The robbery proceeded according to plan until the pawnbroker grabbed the gun when Parker announced the "stickup." The gun went off with Parker's finger on the trigger, firing a fatal shot into the pawnbroker.

Parker went back to the car where Lockett waited with the engine running. While driving away from the pawnshop, Parker told Lockett what had happened. She took the gun from the pawnshop and put it into her purse. Lockett and Parker drove to Lockett's aunt's house and called a taxicab. Shortly thereafter, while riding away in a taxicab, they were stopped by the police, but by this time Lockett had placed the gun under the front seat. Lockett told the police that Parker rented a room from her mother and lived with her family. After verifying this story with Lockett's parents, the police released Lockett and Parker. Lockett hid Dew and Parker in the attic when the police arrived at the Lockett household later that evening.

Parker was subsequently apprehended and charged with aggravated murder with specifications, an offense punishable by death, and aggravated robbery. Prior to trial, he pleaded guilty to the murder charge and agreed to testify against Lockett, her brother, and Dew. In return, the prosecutor dropped the aggravated robbery charge and the specifications to the murder charge, thereby eliminating the possibility that Parker could receive the death penalty.

Lockett's brother and Dew were later convicted of aggravated murder with specifications. Lockett's brother was sentenced to death, but Dew received a lesser penalty because it was determined that his offense was "primarily the product of mental deficiency," one of the three mitigating circumstances specified in the Ohio death penalty statute.

Two weeks before Lockett's separate trial, the prosecutor offered to permit her to plead guilty to voluntary manslaughter and aggravated robbery (offenses which each carried a maximum penalty of 25 years' imprisonment and a maximum fine of $10,000, if she would cooperate with the State, but she rejected the offer. Just prior to her trial, the prosecutor offered to permit her to plead guilty to aggravated murder without specifications, an offense carrying a mandatory life penalty, with the understanding that the aggravated robbery charge and an outstanding forgery charge would be dismissed. Again she rejected the offer.

At trial, the opening argument of Lockett's defense counsel summarized what appears to have been Lockett's version of the events leading to the killing. He asserted the evidence would show that, as far as Lockett knew, Dew and her brother had planned to pawn Dew's ring for $100 to obtain money for the trip back to New Jersey. Lockett had not waited in the car while the men went into the pawnshop but had gone to a restaurant for lunch and had joined Parker, thinking the ring had been pawned, after she saw him walking back to the car. Lockett's counsel asserted that the evidence would show further that Parker had placed the gun under the seat in the taxicab and that Lockett had voluntarily gone to the police station when she learned that the police were looking for the pawnbroker's killers.

Parker was the State's first witness. His testimony related his version of the robbery and shooting, and he admitted to a prior criminal record of breaking and entering, larceny, and receiving stolen goods, as well as bond jumping. He also acknowledged that his plea to aggravated murder had eliminated the possibility of the death penalty, and that he had agreed to testify against Lockett, her brother, and Dew as part of his plea agreement with the prosecutor.

At the end of the major portion of Parker's testimony, the prosecutor renewed his offer to permit Lockett to plead guilty to aggravated murder without specifications and to drop the other charges against her. For the third time Lockett refused the option of pleading guilty to a lesser offense.

Lockett called Dew and her brother as defense witnesses, but they invoked their Fifth Amendment rights and refused to testify. In the course of the defense presentation, Lockett's counsel informed the court, in the presence of the jury, that he believed Lockett was to be the next witness and requested a short recess. After the recess, Lockett's counsel told the judge that Lockett wished to testify but had decided to accept her mother's advice to remain silent, despite her counsel's warning that, if she followed that advice, she would have no defense except the cross-examination of the State's witnesses. Thus, the defense did not introduce any evidence to rebut the prosecutor's case.

The court instructed the jury that, before it could find Lockett guilty, it had to find that she purposely had killed the pawnbroker while committing or attempting to commit aggravated robbery. The jury was further charged that one who

> "purposely aids, helps, associates himself or herself with another for the purpose of committing a crime is regarded as if he or she were the principal offender and is just as guilty as if the person performed every act constituting the offense. . . ."

Regarding the intent requirement, the court instructed:

> "A person engaged in a common design with others to rob by force and violence an individual or individuals of their property is presumed to acquiesce in whatever may reasonably be necessary to accomplish the object of their enterprise. . . .
>
> "If the conspired robbery and the manner of its accomplishment would be reasonably likely to produce death, each plotter is equally guilty with the principal offender as an aider and abettor in the homicide . . . An intent to kill by an aider and abettor may be found to exist beyond a reasonable doubt under such circumstances."

The jury found Lockett guilty as charged.

Once a verdict of aggravated murder with specifications had been returned, the Ohio death penalty statute required the trial judge to impose a death sentence unless, after "considering the nature and circumstances of the offense" and Lockett's "history, character, and condition," he found by a preponderance of the evidence that (1) the victim had induced or facilitated the offense, (2) it was unlikely that Lockett would have committed the offense but for the fact that she "was under duress, coercion, or strong provocation," or (3) the offense was "primarily the product of [Lockett's] psychosis or mental deficiency."

In accord with the Ohio statute, the trial judge requested a presentence report as well as psychiatric and psychological reports. The reports contained detailed information about Lockett's intelligence, character, and background. The psychiatric and psychological reports described her as a 21-year-old with low-average or average intelligence, and not suffering from a mental deficiency. One of the psychologists reported that "her prognosis for rehabilitation" if returned to society was favorable. The presentence report showed that Lockett had committed no major offenses although she had a record of several minor ones as a juvenile and two minor offenses as an adult. It also showed that she had once used heroin but was receiving treatment at a drug abuse clinic and seemed to be "on the road to success" as far as her drug problem was concerned.

It concluded that Lockett suffered no psychosis and was not mentally deficient.

After considering the reports and hearing argument on the penalty issue, the trial judge concluded that the offense had not been primarily the product of psychosis or mental deficiency. Without specifically addressing the other two statutory mitigating factors, the judge said that he had "no alternative, whether [he] like[d] the law or not" but to impose the death penalty. He then sentenced Lockett to death.

II

A

At the outset, we address Lockett's various challenges to the validity of her conviction. Her first contention is that the prosecutor's repeated references in his closing remarks to the State's evidence as "unrefuted" and "uncontradicted" constituted a comment on her failure to testify and violated her Fifth and Fourteenth Amendment rights. See Griffin v. California (1965). We conclude, however, that the prosecutor's closing comments in this case did not violate constitutional prohibitions. . . .

III

Lockett challenges the constitutionality of Ohio's death penalty statute on a number of grounds. We find it necessary to consider only her contention that her death sentence is invalid because the statute under which it was imposed did not permit the sentencing judge to consider, as mitigating factors, her character, prior record, age, lack of specific intent to cause death, and her relatively minor part in the crime. To address her contention from the proper perspective, it is helpful to review the developments in our recent cases where we have applied the Eighth and Fourteenth Amendments to death penalty statutes. We do not write on a "clean slate."

. . .

B

With that obligation in mind we turn to Lockett's attack on the Ohio statute. Essentially she contends that the Eighth and Fourteenth Amendments require that the sentencer be given a full opportunity to consider mitigating circumstances in capital cases and that the Ohio statute does not comply with that requirement. . . .

We begin by recognizing that the concept of individualized sentencing in criminal cases generally, although not constitutionally required, has long been accepted in this country. Consistent with that concept, sentencing judges traditionally have taken a wide range of factors into account. That States have authority to make aiders and abettors equally responsible, as a matter of law, with principals, or to enact felony-murder statutes is beyond constitutional challenge. But the definition of crimes generally has not been thought automatically to dictate what should be the proper penalty.

. . .

We are now faced with those questions and we conclude that the Eighth and Fourteenth Amendments require that the sentencer, in all but the rarest kind of capital case, not be precluded from considering, as a mitigating factor, any aspect of a defendant's character or record and any of the circumstances of the offense that the defendant proffers as a basis for a sentence less than death. We recognize that, in noncapital cases, the established practice of individualized sentences rests not on constitutional commands, but on public policy enacted into statutes. The considerations that account for the wide acceptance of individualization of sentences in noncapital cases surely cannot be thought less important in capital cases. Given that the imposition of death by public authority is so profoundly different from all other penalties, we cannot avoid the conclusion that an individualized decision is essential in capital cases. The need for treating each defendant in a capital case with that degree of respect due the uniqueness of the individual is far more important than in noncapital cases. . . .

There is no perfect procedure for deciding in which cases governmental authority should be used to impose death. But a statute that prevents the sentencer in all capital cases from giving independent mitigating weight to aspects of the defendant's character and record and to circumstances of the offense proffered in mitigation creates the risk that the death penalty will be imposed in spite of factors which may call for a less severe penalty. When the choice is between life and death, that risk is unacceptable and incompatible with the commands of the Eighth and Fourteenth Amendments.

C

The Ohio death penalty statute does not permit the type of individualized consideration of mitigating factors we now hold to be required by the Eighth and Fourteenth Amendments in capital cases.

. . .

The limited range of mitigating circumstances which may be considered by the sentencer under the Ohio statute is incompatible with the Eighth and Fourteenth Amendments. To meet constitutional requirements, a death penalty statute must not preclude consideration of relevant mitigating factors.

Accordingly, the judgment under review is reversed to the extent that it sustains the imposition of the death penalty, and the case is remanded for further proceedings.

So ordered.

SOURCE: Lockett v. Ohio, 438 U.S. 586 (1978).

ANALYSIS

Lockett v. Ohio is one of the most significant death penalty cases in the modern era. It established that in a death penalty case, a defendant's individual mitigating evidence must be considered. Ohio had a statute at the time that mandated the imposition of the death penalty upon conviction in a capital case unless one of three conditions took place: (1) the victim had induced or facilitated the offense; (2) it was unlikely the convicted individual would have committed the offense but for the fact that he or she "was under duress, coercion, or strong provocation"; or (3) the offense was "primarily the product of psychosis or mental deficiency."

Lockett was a 21-year-old female who was the driver of the getaway car in a robbery of a pawnshop. The Supreme Court reasoned that the Ohio statute was unconstitutional, because it failed to adhere to the principle that a death sentence can be imposed only if there is a consideration of the particular circumstances of the case and the defendant. The Court explained, in oft-cited language, that jury or judge in a capital case may "not be precluded from considering, as a mitigating factor, any aspect of a defendant's character or record and any of the circumstances of the offense that the defendant proffers as a basis for a sentence less than death."

Lockett's sentence of death seemed quite disproportionate given her alleged role in the robbery. Al Parker, the triggerman in the robbery, testified against Lockett and Lockett's brother in order to save his own life. Ultimately, the Supreme Court decision in *Lockett v. Ohio* implicitly recognized the potential unfairness in her being punished more than the triggerman.

Her death sentence invalidated, Lockett was resentenced to a life sentence with the possibility of parole for her role in the robbery plan that led to a murder. She was paroled in 1993 and frequently spoke against the death penalty for her remaining years. She died in March 2020 at the age of 65.

One of Lockett's appellate lawyers, Peggy Cooper Davis wrote about Lockett in 2018 at a law school symposium recognizing the 40th anniversary of the decision: "The story of Sandra Lockett reminds us that the law should moderate those responses and give each criminal defendant the equal respect that her life commands."

FURTHER READING

Amsterdam, Anthony. "For Sandra Lockett." 10 *ConLawNOW* 117 (2018).
Davis, Peggy C. "*Reflections on the Sandra Lockett Case*." 10 *ConLawNOW* 29 (2018).
"Sandra Lockett-Young, Whose Case Established a Capital Defendant's Right to Present Mitigating Evidence, Has Died." Death Penalty Information Center. March 3, 2020.

- ***Document 19:*** Supreme Court decision in *Eddings v. Oklahoma*
- ***Date:*** January 19, 1982
- ***Where:*** Washington, D.C.
- ***Significance:*** The Court's decision established that judges must consider mitigating evidence in death penalty cases, including violence and abuse in the defendant's childhood.

DOCUMENT

Supreme Court Strikes Down Death Sentence of 16-Year-Old on Mitigating Evidence Grounds

Petitioner Monty Lee Eddings was convicted of first degree murder, and sentenced to death. Because this sentence was imposed without "the type of individualized consideration of mitigating factors . . . required by the Eighth and Fourteenth Amendments in capital cases," we reverse.

I

On April 4, 1977, Eddings, a 16-year-old youth, and several younger companions ran away from their Missouri homes. They traveled in a car owned by Eddings' brother, and drove without destination or purpose in a southwesterly direction, eventually reaching the Oklahoma Turnpike. Eddings had in the car a shotgun and several rifles he had taken from his father. After he momentarily lost control of the car, he was signalled to pull over by Officer Crabtree of the Oklahoma Highway Patrol. Eddings did so, and when the officer approached the car, Eddings stuck a loaded shotgun out of the window and fired, killing the officer.

Because Eddings was a juvenile, the State moved to have him certified to stand trial as an adult. Finding that there was prosecutive merit to the complaint and that Eddings was not amenable to rehabilitation within the juvenile system, the trial court granted the motion. The ruling was affirmed on appeal. Eddings was then charged with murder in the first degree, and the District Court of Creek County found him guilty upon his plea of *nolo contendere*.

The Oklahoma death penalty statute provides in pertinent part:

> "Upon conviction . . . of guilt of a defendant of murder in the first degree, the court shall conduct a separate sentencing proceeding to determine whether

> the defendant should be sentenced to death or life imprisonment. . . . In the sentencing proceeding, evidence may be presented as to *any mitigating circumstances* or as to any of the aggravating circumstances enumerated in this act."

[the law] lists seven separate aggravating circumstances; the statute nowhere defines what is meant by "any mitigating circumstances."

At the sentencing hearing, the State alleged three of the aggravating circumstances enumerated in the statute: that the murder was especially heinous, atrocious, or cruel, that the crime was committed for the purpose of avoiding or preventing a lawful arrest, and that there was a probability that the defendant would commit criminal acts of violence that would constitute a continuing threat to society.

In mitigation, Eddings presented substantial evidence at the hearing of his troubled youth. The testimony of his supervising Juvenile Officer indicated that Eddings had been raised without proper guidance. His parents were divorced when he was 5 years old, and until he was 14, Eddings lived with his mother without rules or supervision. There is the suggestion that Eddings' mother was an alcoholic, and possibly a prostitute. By the time Eddings was 14, he no longer could be controlled, and his mother sent him to live with his father. But neither could the father control the boy. Attempts to reason and talk gave way to physical punishment. The Juvenile Officer testified that Eddings was frightened and bitter, that his father overreacted and used excessive physical punishment:

> "Mr. Eddings found the only thing that he thought was effectful with the boy was actual punishment, or physical violence—hitting with a strap or something like this."

Testimony from other witnesses indicated that Eddings was emotionally disturbed in general and at the time of the crime, and that his mental and emotional development were at a level several years below his age. A state psychologist stated that Eddings had a sociopathic or antisocial personality and that approximately 30% of youths suffering from such a disorder grew out of it as they aged. A sociologist specializing in juvenile offenders testified that Eddings was treatable. A psychiatrist testified that Eddings could be rehabilitated by intensive therapy over a 15- to 20-year period.

He testified further that Eddings "did pull the trigger, he did kill someone, but I don't even think he knew that he was doing it." The psychiatrist suggested that, if treated, Eddings would no longer pose a serious threat to society.

At the conclusion of all the evidence, the trial judge weighed the evidence of aggravating and mitigating circumstances. He found that the State had proved each of the three alleged aggravating circumstances beyond a reasonable doubt. Turning to the evidence of mitigating circumstances, the judge found that Eddings' youth was a mitigating factor of great weight:

> "I have given very serious consideration to the youth of the Defendant when this particular crime was committed. Should I fail to do this, I think I would not be carrying out my duty." But he would not consider in mitigation the circumstances of Eddings' unhappy upbringing and emotional disturbance:

> "[T]he Court cannot be persuaded entirely by the . . . fact that the youth was sixteen years old when this heinous crime was committed. *Nor can the Court, in following the law, in my opinion, consider the fact of this young man's violent background.*"

Finding that the only mitigating circumstance was Eddings' youth, and finding further that this circumstance could not outweigh the aggravating circumstances present, the judge sentenced Eddings to death.

The Court of Criminal Appeals affirmed the sentence of death. It found that each of the aggravating circumstances alleged by the State had been present. It recited the mitigating evidence presented by Eddings in some detail, but, in the end, it agreed with the trial court that only the fact of Eddings' youth was properly considered as a mitigating circumstance:

> "[Eddings] also argues his mental state at the time of the murder. He stresses his family history in saying he was suffering from severe psychological and emotional disorders, and that the killing was, in actuality, an inevitable product of the way he was raised. There is no doubt that the petitioner has a personality disorder. But all the evidence tends to show that he knew the difference between right and wrong at the time he pulled the trigger, and that is the test of criminal responsibility in this State. For the same reason, the petitioner's family history is useful in explaining why he behaved the way he did, but it does not excuse his behavior."

II

In *Lockett v. Ohio* (1978), CHIEF JUSTICE BURGER, writing for the plurality, stated the rule that we apply today:

> "[W]e conclude that the Eighth and Fourteenth Amendments require that the sentencer . . . not be precluded from considering, *as a mitigating factor*, any aspect of a defendant's character or record and any of the circumstances of the offense that the defendant proffers as a basis for a sentence less than death."

. . .

Similarly, in *Woodson v. North Carolina* (1976), the plurality held that mandatory death sentencing was not a permissible response to the problem of arbitrary jury discretion. As the history of capital punishment had shown, such an approach to the problem of discretion could not succeed while the Eighth Amendment required that the individual be given his due:

. . .

Thus, the rule in *Lockett* followed from the earlier decisions of the Court and from the Court's insistence that capital punishment be imposed fairly, and with reasonable consistency, or not at all. By requiring that the sentencer be permitted to focus "on the characteristics of the person who committed the crime," the rule in *Lockett* recognizes that "justice . . . requires . . . that there be taken into account the circumstances of the offense, together with the character and propensities of the offender."

By holding that the sentencer in capital cases must be permitted to consider any relevant mitigating factor, the rule in *Lockett* recognizes that a consistency produced by ignoring individual differences is a false consistency.

III

We now apply the rule in *Lockett* to the circumstances of this case. The trial judge stated that, "in following the law," he could not "consider the fact of this young man's violent background." There is no dispute that, by "violent background," the trial judge was referring to the mitigating evidence of Eddings' family history. From this statement, it is clear that the trial judge did not evaluate the evidence in mitigation and find it wanting as a matter of fact; rather, he found that, *as a matter of law*, he was unable even to consider the evidence.

The Court of Criminal Appeals took the same approach. It found that the evidence in mitigation was not relevant because it did not tend to provide a legal excuse from criminal responsibility. Thus, the court conceded that Eddings had a "personality disorder," but cast this evidence aside on the basis that "he knew the difference between right and wrong . . ., and that is the test of criminal responsibility." Similarly, the evidence of Eddings' family history was "useful in explaining" his behavior, but it did not "excuse" the behavior. From these statements, it appears that the Court of Criminal Appeals also considered only that evidence to be mitigating which would tend to support a legal excuse from criminal liability.

We find that the limitations placed by these courts upon the mitigating evidence they would consider violated the rule in *Lockett*. . . .

Nor do we doubt that the evidence Eddings offered was relevant mitigating evidence. Eddings was a youth of 16 years at the time of the murder. Evidence of a difficult family history and of emotional disturbance is typically introduced by defendants in mitigation. In some cases, such evidence properly may be given little weight. But when the defendant was 16 years old at the time of the offense, there can be no doubt that evidence of a turbulent family history, of beatings by a harsh father, and of severe emotional disturbance is particularly relevant.

The trial judge recognized that youth must be considered a relevant mitigating factor. But youth is more than a chronological fact. It is a time and condition of life when a person may be most susceptible to influence and to psychological damage. Our history is replete with laws and judicial recognition that minors, especially in their earlier years, generally are less mature and responsible than adults. Particularly "during the formative years of childhood and adolescence, minors often lack the experience, perspective, and judgment" expected of adults.

Even the normal 16-year-old customarily lacks the maturity of an adult. In this case, Eddings was not a normal 16-year-old; he had been deprived of the care, concern, and paternal attention that children deserve. On the contrary, it is not disputed that he was a juvenile with serious emotional problems, and had been raised in a neglectful, sometimes even violent, family background. In addition, there was testimony that Eddings' mental and emotional development were at a level several years below his chronological age. All of this does not suggest an absence of responsibility for the crime of murder, deliberately committed in this case. Rather, it is to say that, just as the chronological age of a minor is itself a relevant mitigating factor of great weight, so must the background and mental and emotional development of a youthful defendant be duly considered in sentencing.

We are not unaware of the extent to which minors engage increasingly in violent crime. Nor do we suggest an absence of legal responsibility where crime is committed by a minor. We are concerned here only with the manner of the imposition of the ultimate penalty: the death sentence imposed for the crime of murder upon an emotionally disturbed youth with a disturbed child's immaturity.

On remand, the state courts must consider all relevant mitigating evidence and weigh it against the evidence of the aggravating circumstances. We do not weigh the evidence for them. Accordingly, the judgment is reversed to the extent that it sustains the imposition of the death penalty, and the case is remanded for further proceedings not inconsistent with this opinion.

So ordered.

SOURCE: Eddings v. Oklahoma, 455 U.S. 104 (1982).

ANALYSIS

The U.S. Supreme Court originally granted review in Monty Lee Eddings' case in order to address whether executing a person who had committed the crime under the age of 18 was an unconstitutional violation of the Eighth Amendment's "cruel and unusual punishment" provisions. Eddings certainly fit the bill, as he was only 16 years old when he shot and killed Oklahoma Highway Trooper Larry Crabtree on April 4, 1977.

However, the U.S. Supreme Court declined to address the issue of juveniles and the death penalty. Instead, the Court focused on another aspect of Eddings' case: the fact that the trial court judge refused to consider as mitigating evidence Eddings' violent and troubled childhood, which was marked by frequent beatings from his father. Eddings allegedly said to an arresting officer that he would have rather shot the officer than go back to his home. Furthermore, Eddings was developmentally delayed to a significant degree. However, the trial judge only considered Eddings' youth as a mitigating factor.

The U.S. Supreme Court applied the rule from *Lockett v. Ohio* (1978) that a court in reviewing a death sentence must consider the mitigating evidence from a particular defendant. The Court emphasized, however, that such mitigating evidence does not excuse the horrible crime committed. As the Court explained:

> In addition, there was testimony that Eddings' mental and emotional development were at a level several years below his chronological age. All of this does not suggest an absence of responsibility for the crime of murder, deliberately committed in this case. Rather, it is to say that, just as the chronological age of a minor is itself a relevant mitigating factor of great weight, so must the

background and mental and emotional development of a youthful defendant be duly considered in sentencing.

The *Eddings* decision is a significant one in death penalty litigation, as defense attorneys often introduce evidence of a defendant's abusive and violent childhood in the hopes that such mitigating evidence might lead to a life sentence rather than a sentence of death.

For his part, Monty Lee Eddings remains incarcerated. He was denied clemency in 2019.

FURTHER READING

Gohara, Miriam S. "In Defense of the Injured: How Trauma-Informed Criminal Defense Can Reform Sentencing." 45 *American Journal of Criminal Law* 1 (2018).

Greenwald, Helene B. "Supreme Court Review: Eighth Amendment—Minors and the Death Penalty: Decision and Avoidance: Eddings v. Oklahoma (1982)." 73 *Journal of Criminal Law & Criminology* 1525 (1982).

Stott, Kim. "Slain Trooper's Family Upset at Overturning of His Killer's Death Penalty." *Oklahoman*. August 1, 1984.

- ***Document 20:*** Supreme Court majority opinion in *Strickland v. Washington*
- ***Date:*** May 14, 1984
- ***Where:*** Washington, D.C.
- ***Significance:*** The Supreme Court established a standard for determining whether an attorney provided effective or ineffective assistance of counsel within the meaning of the Sixth Amendment of the U.S. Constitution. It remains the leading standard by which quality of legal representation in capital punishment and other criminal law cases is measured.

DOCUMENT

Supreme Court Sets Standard for Ineffective Assistance of Counsel Claims in Death Penalty Cases

This case requires us to consider the proper standards for judging a criminal defendant's contention that the Constitution requires a conviction or death sentence to be set aside because counsel's assistance at the trial or sentencing was ineffective.

I

A

During a 10-day period in September 1976, respondent planned and committed three groups of crimes, which included three brutal stabbing murders, torture, kidnaping, severe assaults, attempted murders, attempted extortion, and theft. After his two accomplices were arrested, respondent surrendered to police and voluntarily gave a lengthy statement confessing to the third of the criminal episodes. The State of Florida indicted respondent for kidnaping and murder and appointed an experienced criminal lawyer to represent him.

. . .

Counsel advised respondent to invoke his right under Florida law to an advisory jury at his capital sentencing hearing. Respondent rejected the advice and waived the right. He chose instead to be sentenced by the trial judge without a jury recommendation.

In preparing for the sentencing hearing, counsel spoke with respondent about his background. He also spoke on the telephone with respondent's wife and mother, though he did not follow up on the one unsuccessful effort to meet with them. He did not otherwise seek out character witnesses for respondent. Nor did he request a psychiatric examination, since his conversations with his client gave no indication that respondent had psychological problems.

. . .

At the sentencing hearing, counsel's strategy was based primarily on the trial judge's remarks at the plea colloquy as well as on his reputation as a sentencing judge who thought it important for a convicted defendant to own up to his crime. . . .

The trial judge found several aggravating circumstances with respect to each of the three murders. He found that all three murders were especially heinous, atrocious, and cruel, all involving repeated stabbings. . . .

With respect to mitigating circumstances, the trial judge made the same findings for all three capital murders. . . .

In short, the trial judge found numerous aggravating circumstances and no (or a single comparatively insignificant) mitigating circumstance. . . . The Florida Supreme Court upheld the convictions and sentences on direct appeal.

B

Respondent subsequently sought collateral relief in state court on numerous grounds, among them that counsel had rendered ineffective assistance at the sentencing proceeding. . . .

The trial court denied relief without an evidentiary hearing, finding that the record evidence conclusively showed that the ineffectiveness claim was meritless.

. . .

Applying the standard for ineffectiveness claims articulated by the Florida Supreme Court in *Knight v. State*, the trial court concluded that respondent had not shown that counsel's assistance reflected any substantial and serious deficiency measurably below that of competent counsel that was likely to have affected the outcome of the sentencing proceeding.

. . .

The Florida Supreme Court affirmed the denial of relief. . . .

C

Respondent next filed a petition for a writ of habeas corpus in the United States District Court for the Southern District of Florida. . . .

On appeal, a panel of the United States Court of Appeals for the Fifth Circuit affirmed in part, vacated in part, and remanded with instructions to apply to the particular facts the framework for analyzing ineffectiveness claims that it developed in its opinion. . . .

D

Petitioners, who are officials of the State of Florida, filed a petition for a writ of certiorari seeking review of the decision of the Court of Appeals. . . .

For these reasons, we granted certiorari to consider the standards by which to judge a contention that the Constitution requires that a criminal judgment be overturned because of the actual ineffective assistance of counsel. We agree with the Court of Appeals that the exhaustion rule requiring dismissal of mixed petitions, though to be strictly enforced, is not jurisdictional. We therefore address the merits of the constitutional issue.

. . .

II

In a long line of cases . . . this Court has recognized that the Sixth Amendment right to counsel exists, and is needed, in order to protect the fundamental right to a fair trial. . . .

Because of the vital importance of counsel's assistance, this Court has held that, with certain exceptions, a person accused of a federal or state crime has the right to have counsel appointed if retained counsel cannot be obtained. . . .

The Court has not elaborated on the meaning of the constitutional requirement of effective assistance in the latter class of cases—that is, those presenting claims of "actual ineffectiveness." In giving meaning to the requirement, however, we must take its purpose—to ensure a fair trial—as the guide. The benchmark for judging any claim of ineffectiveness must be whether counsel's conduct so undermined the proper functioning of the adversarial process that the trial cannot be relied on as having produced a just result.

III

A convicted defendant's claim that counsel's assistance was so defective as to require reversal of a conviction or death sentence has two components. First, the defendant must show that counsel's performance was deficient. This requires showing that counsel made errors so serious that counsel was not functioning as the "counsel" guaranteed the defendant by the Sixth Amendment. Second, the defendant must show that the deficient performance prejudiced the defense. This requires showing that counsel's errors were so serious as to deprive the defendant of a fair trial, a trial whose result is reliable. Unless a defendant makes both showings, it cannot be said that the conviction or death sentence resulted from a breakdown in the adversary process that renders the result unreliable.

A

As all the Federal Courts of Appeals have now held, the proper standard for attorney performance is that of reasonably effective assistance. . . .

More specific guidelines are not appropriate. The Sixth Amendment refers simply to "counsel," not specifying particular requirements of effective assistance. It relies instead on the legal profession's maintenance of standards sufficient to justify the law's presumption that counsel will fulfill the role in the adversary process that the Amendment envisions. The proper measure of attorney performance remains simply reasonableness under prevailing professional norms.

Representation of a criminal defendant entails certain basic duties. Counsel's function is to assist the defendant, and hence counsel owes the client a duty of loyalty, a duty to avoid conflicts of interest. From counsel's function as assistant to the defendant derive the overarching duty to advocate the defendant's cause and the more particular duties to consult with the defendant on important decisions and to keep the defendant informed of important developments in the course of the prosecution. Counsel also has a duty to bring to bear such skill and knowledge as will render the trial a reliable adversarial testing process.

These basic duties neither exhaustively define the obligations of counsel nor form a checklist for judicial evaluation of attorney performance. In any case presenting an ineffectiveness claim, the performance inquiry must be whether counsel's assistance was reasonable considering all the circumstances. . . .

Judicial scrutiny of counsel's performance must be highly deferential. It is all too tempting for a defendant to second-guess counsel's assistance after conviction or adverse sentence, and it is all too easy for a court, examining counsel's defense after it has proved unsuccessful, to conclude that a particular act or omission of counsel was unreasonable. . . .

Thus, a court deciding an actual ineffectiveness claim must judge the reasonableness of counsel's challenged conduct on the facts of the particular case, viewed as of the time of counsel's conduct.

A convicted defendant making a claim of ineffective assistance must identify the acts or omissions of counsel that are alleged not to have been the result of reasonable professional judgment. The court must then determine whether, in light of all the circumstances, the identified acts or omissions were outside the wide range of professionally competent assistance. In making that determination, the court should keep in mind that counsel's function, as elaborated in prevailing professional norms, is to make the adversarial testing process work in the particular case. At the same time, the court should recognize that counsel is strongly presumed to have rendered adequate assistance and made all significant decisions in the exercise of reasonable professional judgment.

. . .

The reasonableness of counsel's actions may be determined or substantially influenced by the defendant's own statements or actions. Counsel's actions are usually based, quite properly, on informed strategic choices made by the defendant and on information supplied by the defendant. In particular, what investigation decisions are reasonable depends critically on such information.

. . .

B

An error by counsel, even if professionally unreasonable, does not warrant setting aside the judgment of a criminal proceeding if the error had no effect on the judgment. The purpose of the Sixth Amendment guarantee of counsel is to ensure that a defendant has the assistance necessary to justify reliance on the outcome of the proceeding. Accordingly, any deficiencies in counsel's performance must be prejudicial to the defense in order to constitute ineffective assistance under the Constitution.

In certain Sixth Amendment contexts, prejudice is presumed. Actual or constructive denial of the assistance of counsel altogether is legally presumed to result in prejudice. . . .

Representation is an art, and an act or omission that is unprofessional in one case may be sound or even brilliant in another. Even if a defendant shows that particular errors of counsel were unreasonable, therefore, the defendant must show that they actually had an adverse effect on the defense.

It is not enough for the defendant to show that the errors had some conceivable effect on the outcome of the proceeding. Virtually every act or omission of counsel would meet that test and not every error that conceivably could have influenced the outcome undermines the reliability of the result of the proceeding. . . .

On the other hand, we believe that a defendant need not show that counsel's deficient conduct more likely than not altered the outcome in the case. This outcome-determinative standard has several strengths. It defines the relevant inquiry in a way familiar to courts, though the inquiry, as is inevitable, is anything but precise. The standard also reflects the profound importance of finality in criminal proceedings. Moreover, it comports with the widely used standard for assessing motions for new trial based on newly discovered evidence. Nevertheless, the standard is not quite appropriate.

Even when the specified attorney error results in the omission of certain evidence, the newly discovered evidence standard is not an apt source from which to draw a prejudice standard for ineffectiveness claims. The high standard for newly discovered evidence claims presupposes that all the essential elements of a presumptively accurate and fair proceeding were present in the proceeding whose result is challenged. An ineffective assistance claim asserts the absence of one of the crucial assurances that the result of the proceeding is reliable, so finality concerns are somewhat weaker and the appropriate standard of prejudice should be somewhat lower.

The result of a proceeding can be rendered unreliable, and hence the proceeding itself unfair, even if the errors of counsel cannot be shown by a preponderance of the evidence to have determined the outcome.

Accordingly, the appropriate test for prejudice finds its roots in the test for materiality of exculpatory information not disclosed to the defense by the prosecution, and in the test for materiality of testimony made unavailable to the defense by Government deportation of a witness. The defendant must show that there is a reasonable probability that, but for counsel's unprofessional errors, the result of the proceeding would have been different. A reasonable probability is a probability sufficient to undermine confidence in the outcome.

In making the determination whether the specified errors resulted in the required prejudice, a court should presume, absent challenge to the judgment on grounds of evidentiary insufficiency, that the judge or jury acted according to law. . . .

The governing legal standard plays a critical role in defining the question to be asked in assessing the prejudice from counsel's errors. When a defendant challenges a conviction, the question is whether there is a reasonable probability that, absent the errors, the factfinder would have had a reasonable doubt respecting guilt. . . .

In making this determination, a court hearing an ineffectiveness claim must consider the totality of the evidence before the judge or jury. Some of the factual findings will have been unaffected by the errors, and factual findings that were affected will have been affected in different ways.

. . .

IV

A number of practical considerations are important for the application of the standards we have outlined. Most important, in adjudicating a claim of actual ineffectiveness of counsel, a court should keep in mind that the principles we have stated do not establish mechanical rules. Although those principles should guide the process of decision, the ultimate focus of inquiry must be on the fundamental fairness of the proceeding whose result is being challenged. In every case the court should be concerned with whether, despite the strong presumption of reliability, the result of the particular proceeding is unreliable because of a breakdown in the adversarial process that our system counts on to produce just results.

. . .

The principles governing ineffectiveness claims should apply in federal collateral proceedings as they do on direct appeal or in motions for a new trial. As indicated by the "cause and prejudice" test for overcoming procedural waivers of claims of error, the presumption that a criminal judgment is final is at its strongest in collateral attacks on that judgment. An ineffectiveness claim, however, as our articulation of the standards that govern decision of such claims makes clear, is an attack on the fundamental fairness of the proceeding whose result is challenged. Since fundamental fairness is the central concern of the writ of habeas corpus, no special standards ought to apply to ineffectiveness claims made in habeas proceedings.

. . .

V

Having articulated general standards for judging ineffectiveness claims, we think it useful to apply those standards to the facts of this case in order to illustrate the meaning of the general principles. The record makes it possible to do so. There are no conflicts between the state and federal courts over findings of fact, and the principles we have articulated are sufficiently close to the principles applied both in the Florida courts and in the District Court that it is clear that the factfinding was not affected by erroneous legal principles.

Application of the governing principles is not difficult in this case. The facts as described above make clear that the conduct of respondent's counsel at and before respondent's sentencing proceeding cannot be found unreasonable. They also make clear that, even assuming the challenged conduct of counsel was unreasonable, respondent suffered insufficient prejudice to warrant setting aside his death sentence.

With respect to the performance component, the record shows that respondent's counsel made a strategic choice to argue for the extreme emotional distress mitigating circumstance and to rely as fully as possible on respondent's acceptance of responsibility for his crimes. Although counsel understandably felt hopeless about respondent's prospects, nothing in the record indicates, as one possible reading of the District Court's opinion suggests, that counsel's sense of hopelessness distorted his professional judgment. Counsel's strategy choice was well within the range of professionally reasonable judgments, and the decision not to seek more character or psychological evidence than was already in hand was likewise reasonable.

The trial judge's views on the importance of owning up to one's crimes were well known to counsel. The aggravating circumstances were utterly overwhelming. Trial counsel could reasonably surmise from his conversations with respondent that character and psychological evidence would be of little help. Respondent had already been able to mention at the plea colloquy the substance of what there was to know about his financial and emotional troubles. Restricting testimony on respondent's character to what had come in at the plea colloquy ensured that contrary character and psychological evidence and respondent's criminal history, which counsel had successfully moved to exclude, would not come in. On these facts, there can be little question, even without application of the presumption of adequate performance, that trial counsel's defense, though unsuccessful, was the result of reasonable professional judgment.

With respect to the prejudice component, the lack of merit of respondent's claim is even more stark. The evidence that respondent says his trial counsel should have offered at the sentencing hearing would barely have altered the sentencing profile presented to the sentencing judge. . . . Given the overwhelming aggravating factors, there is no reasonable probability that the omitted evidence would have changed the conclusion that the aggravating circumstances outweighed the mitigating circumstances and, hence, the sentence imposed. Indeed, admission of the evidence respondent now offers might even have been harmful to his case: his "rap sheet" would probably have been admitted into evidence, and the psychological reports would have directly contradicted respondent's claim that the mitigating circumstance of extreme emotional disturbance applied to his case.

Our conclusions on both the prejudice and performance components of the ineffectiveness inquiry do not depend on the trial judge's testimony at the District Court hearing. We therefore need not consider the general admissibility of that testimony, although that testimony is irrelevant to the prejudice inquiry. Moreover, the prejudice question is resolvable, and hence the ineffectiveness claim can be rejected, without regard to the evidence presented at the District Court hearing. The state courts properly concluded that the ineffectiveness claim was meritless without holding an evidentiary hearing.

Failure to make the required showing of either deficient performance or sufficient prejudice defeats the ineffectiveness claim. Here there is a double failure. More generally, respondent has made no showing that the justice of his sentence was rendered unreliable by a breakdown in the adversary process caused by deficiencies in counsel's assistance. Respondent's sentencing proceeding was not fundamentally unfair.

We conclude, therefore, that the District Court properly declined to issue a writ of habeas corpus. The judgment of the Court of Appeals is accordingly

SOURCE: Strickland v. Washington, 466 U.S. 668 (1984).

ANALYSIS

The last "freedom" explicitly stipulated in the Sixth Amendment of the U.S. Constitution provides for the "assistance of counsel" for those facing criminal charges. The U.S. Supreme Court determined in *McMann v. Richardson* (1970) that the right to counsel means the right to reasonably effective assistance of counsel.

However, the Court did not set a clear standard for a line between effective assistance of counsel and ineffective assistance of counsel. Some lower courts applied what was known as the "farce and mockery" standard, meaning that a defendant had "assistance of counsel" as long as his trial was not a "farce and mockery." Other lower courts proclaimed that the applicable standard was that of a reasonably competent attorney.

The determination was vitally important, because defendants who challenged their convictions in state post-conviction proceedings or federal habeas corpus proceedings often argued that their convictions should be set aside because they received so-called ineffective assistance of counsel. In other words, these defendants argued they were deprived of their Sixth Amendment right to assistance of counsel.

In 1984, the Supreme Court finally set the standard for ineffective assistance of counsel in *Strickland v. Washington*, a decision involving the death sentence of inmate David Washington. Washington had committed a string of murders and kidnappings, allegedly to obtain money for his family.

Washington waived his right to a jury trial and admitted his involvement in the murders. He pleaded guilty and hoped for leniency from the trial judge. Washington's attorney offered little to nothing in the way of mitigating evidence, and the trial judge sentenced Washington to death.

Later, Washington filed a petition for habeas corpus relief in federal court, contending that his trial counsel committed ineffective assistance of counsel. A federal district court ruled against Washington, but a federal appeals court ruled in his favor. Thus, the state of Florida—through then prison superintendent Mark Strickland—sought review in the U.S. Supreme Court.

The U.S. Supreme Court established a two-part test for determining ineffective assistance of counsel. The first prong was deficiency—the inmate had to show that his trial attorney was deficient in his representation. This meant far below that of a reasonably competent attorney. In her majority opinion, Justice Sandra Day O'Connor wrote that "a fair assessment of attorney performance requires that every effort be made to eliminate the distorting effects of hindsight, to reconstruct the circumstances of counsel's challenged conduct, and to evaluate the conduct from counsel's perspective at the time."

The next prong is prejudice. The challenging inmate must show that the attorney's deficient performance prejudiced the defendant. "The defendant must show that there is a reasonable probability that, but for counsel's unprofessional errors, the result of the proceeding would have been different," O'Connor wrote. "A reasonable probability is a probability sufficient to undermine confidence in the outcome."

Applying this new standard, the majority reasoned that David Washington received the effective assistance of counsel. The majority reasoned that the trial counsel followed a reasonably strategic choice in having his client accept responsibility for his crimes in the hope that his guilty plea might cause the judge to refrain from imposing the death penalty.

With regard to prejudice, the majority also reasoned that the attorney's failure to offer mitigating evidence did not change the outcome of the proceeding. Justice O'Connor wrote, "Given the overwhelming aggravating factors, there is no reasonable probability that the omitted evidence would have changed the conclusion that the aggravating circumstances outweighed the mitigating circumstances and, hence, the sentence imposed."

Justice Thurgood Marshall dissented, reasoning that if an attorney's performance was deficient, there was no need to show prejudice. Marshall also differed in his assessment of the facts of the case. He reasoned that Washington's trial attorney was deficient in failing to offer mitigating evidence and to have psychological testing of his client. "If counsel had investigated the availability of mitigating evidence, he might well have decided to present some such material at the hearing," Marshall wrote. "If he had done so, there is a significant chance that [Washington] would have been given a life sentence."

FURTHER READING

Gabriel, Richard L. "The Strickland Standard for Claims of Ineffective Assistance of Counsel: Emasculating the Sixth Amendment in the Guise of Due Process." 134 *University of Pennsylvania Law Review* 1259 (1986).

Klein, Richard. "The Constitutionalizing of Ineffective Assistance of Counsel." 58 *Maryland Law Review* 1433 (1999).

- ***Document 21:*** Supreme Court decision in *Darden v. Wainwright*
- ***Date:*** June 23, 1986
- ***Where:*** Washington, D.C.
- ***Significance:*** The decision is significant because it shows the Court willing to uphold a death sentence despite improper prosecutorial conduct; to this day many believe that Willie Darden was innocent of the crimes for which he was convicted and put to death.

DOCUMENT

Supreme Court Upholds Death Sentence despite Improper Prosecutorial Conduct

This case presents three questions concerning the validity of petitioner's criminal conviction and death sentence: (i) whether the exclusion for cause of a member of the venire violated the principles announced in Wainwright v. Witt (1985); (ii) whether the prosecution's closing argument during the guilt phase of a bifurcated trial rendered the trial fundamentally unfair and deprived the sentencing determination of the reliability required by the Eighth Amendment; and (iii) whether petitioner was denied effective assistance of counsel at the sentencing phase of his trial.

I

Petitioner was tried and found guilty of murder, robbery, and assault with intent to kill in the Circuit Court for Citrus County, Florida, in January 1974. Pursuant to Florida's capital sentencing statute, the same jury that convicted petitioner heard further testimony and argument in order to make a nonbinding recommendation as to whether a death sentence should be imposed. The jury recommended a death sentence, and the trial judge followed that recommendation. On direct appeal, the Florida Supreme Court affirmed the conviction and the sentence. . . .

Petitioner then sought federal habeas corpus relief, raising the same claims he raises here. The District Court denied the petition. A divided panel of the Court of Appeals for the Eleventh Circuit affirmed. The Court of Appeals granted rehearing en banc, and affirmed the District Court by an equally divided court. Following a second rehearing en banc the Court of Appeals reversed on the claim of improper excusal of a member of the venire. This Court granted the State's petition for certiorari on that claim, vacated the Court of Appeals' judgment, and remanded for reconsideration . . . On remand, the en banc court denied relief Petitioner filed an application for a stay of his execution that this Court treated as a petition for certiorari and granted, at the same time staying his execution. 473 U.S. 928 (1985). We now affirm.

II

Because of the nature of petitioner's claims, the facts of this case will be stated in more detail than is normally necessary in this Court. On September 8, 1973, at about 5:30 p.m., a black adult male entered Carl's Furniture Store near Lakeland, Florida. The only other person in the store was the proprietor, Mrs. Turman, who lived with her husband in a house behind the store. Mr. Turman, who worked nights at a juvenile home, had awakened at about 5 p.m., had a cup of coffee at the store with his wife, and returned home to let their dogs out for a run. Mrs. Turman showed the man around the store. He stated that he was interested in purchasing about $ 600 worth of furniture for a rental unit, and asked to see several different items. He left the store briefly, stating that his wife would be back to look at some of the items.

The same man returned just a few minutes later asking to see some stoves, and inquiring about the price. When Mrs. Turman turned toward the adding machine, he grabbed her and pressed a gun to her back, saying "Do as I say and you won't get hurt." He took her to the rear of the store and told her to open the cash register. He took the money, then ordered her to the part of the store where some box springs and mattresses were stacked against the wall. At that time Mr. Turman appeared at the back door. Mrs. Turman screamed while the man reached across her right shoulder and shot Mr. Turman between the eyes. Mr. Turman fell backwards, with one foot partially in the building. Ordering Mrs. Turman not to move, the man tried to pull Mr. Turman into the building and close the door, but could not do so because one of Mr. Turman's feet was caught in the door. The man left Mr. Turman faceup in the rain, and told Mrs. Turman to get down on the floor approximately five feet from where her husband lay dying. While she begged to go to her husband, he told her to remove her false teeth. He unzipped his pants, unbuckled his belt, and demanded that Mrs. Turman perform oral sex on him. She began to cry "Lord, have mercy." He told her to get up and go towards the front of the store.

Meanwhile, a neighbor family, the Arnolds, became aware that something had happened to Mr. Turman. The mother sent her 16-year-old son Phillip, a part-time employee at the furniture store, to help. When Phillip reached the back door he saw Mr. Turman lying partially in the building. When Phillip opened the door to take Turman's body inside, Mrs. Turman shouted "Phillip, no, go back." Phillip did not know what she meant and asked the man to help get Turman inside. He replied, "Sure, buddy, I will help you." As Phillip looked up, the man was pointing a gun in his face. He pulled the trigger and the gun misfired; he pulled the trigger again and shot Phillip in the mouth. Phillip started to run away, and was shot in the neck. While he was still running, he was shot a third time in the side. Despite these wounds, Phillip managed to stumble to the home of a neighbor, Mrs. Edith Hill. She had her husband call an ambulance while she tried to stop Phillip's bleeding. While she was helping Phillip, she saw a late model green Chevrolet leave the store and head towards Tampa on State Highway 92. Phillip survived the incident; Mr. Turman, who never regained consciousness, died later that night.

Minutes after the murder petitioner was driving towards Tampa on Highway 92, just a few miles away from the furniture store. He was out on furlough from a Florida prison, and was driving a car borrowed from his girl friend in Tampa. He was driving fast on a wet road. Petitioner testified that as he came up on a line of cars in his lane, he was unable to slow down. He attempted to pass, but was forced off the road to avoid a head-on collision with an oncoming car. Petitioner crashed into a telephone pole. The driver of the oncoming car, John Stone, stopped his car and went to petitioner to see if he could help. Stone testified that as he approached the car, petitioner was zipping up his pants and buckling his belt. Police at the crash site later identified petitioner's car as a 1969 Chevrolet Impala of greenish golden brown color. Petitioner paid a bystander to give him a ride to Tampa. Petitioner later returned with a wrecker, only to find that the car had been towed away by the police.

By the time the police arrived at the scene of the accident, petitioner had left. The fact that the car matched the description of the car leaving the scene of the murder, and that the accident had occurred within three and one-half miles of the furniture store and within minutes of the murder, led police to suspect that the car was driven by the murderer. They searched the area. An officer found a pistol—a revolver—about 40 feet from the crash site. The arrangement of shells within the chambers exactly matched the pattern that should have been found in the murder weapon: one shot, one misfire, followed by three shots, with a live shell remaining in the next chamber to be fired. A specialist for the Federal Bureau of Investigation examined the pistol and testified that it was a Smith & Wesson .38 special revolver. It had been manufactured as a standard .38; it later was sent to England to be rebored, making it a much rarer type of gun than the standard .38. An examination of the bullet that killed Mr. Turman revealed that it came from a .38 Smith & Wesson special.

On the day following the murder petitioner was arrested at his girl friend's house in Tampa. A few days later Mrs. Turman identified him at a preliminary hearing as her husband's murderer. Phillip Arnold selected petitioner's picture out of a spread of six photographs as the man who had shot him. By that time, a Public Defender had been appointed to represent petitioner.

As petitioner's arguments all relate to incidents in the course of his trial, they will be taken up, together with the relevant facts, in chronological order.

III

Petitioner contends that one member of the venire, Mr. Murphy, was excluded improperly under the test enunciated in Wainwright v. Witt (1985).That case modified this Court's opinion in Witherspoon v. Illinois (1968). Witherspoon had held that potential jurors may be excused for cause when their opposition to the death penalty is such that they automatically would vote against a sentence of death or would be impaired in the task of determining defendant's guilt. Witt held that the proper test is whether the juror's views on capital punishment would "prevent or substantially impair the performance of his duties as a juror in accordance with his instructions and his oath." Witt also made clear that the trial judge's determination that a potential juror is impermissibly biased is a factual finding entitled to a presumption of correctness under 28 U.S.C. § 2254.

Petitioner's argument on this issue relies solely on the wording of a question the trial court asked Murphy before excluding him. The court asked: "Do you have any moral or religious, conscientious moral or religious principles in opposition to the death penalty so strong that you would be unable without violating your own principles to vote to recommend a death penalty regardless of the facts?" Petitioner argues that this question does not correctly state the relevant legal standard. As Witt makes clear, however, our inquiry does not end with a mechanical recitation of a single question and answer. We therefore examine the context surrounding Murphy's exclusion to determine whether the trial court's decision that Murphy's beliefs would "substantially impair the performance of his duties as a juror" was fairly supported by the record.

During voir dire, but prior to individual questioning on this point, the trial court spoke to the entire venire, including Murphy, saying:

> "Now I am going to ask each of you individually the same question so listen to me carefully, I want to know if any of you have such strong religious, moral or conscientious principles in opposition to the death penalty that you would be unwilling to vote to return an advisory sentence recommending the death sentence even though the facts presented to you should be such as under the law would require that recommendation? Do you understand my question?"

The court then proceeded to question the members of the venire individually, but did so while the entire venire was present in the courtroom. Thus, throughout the individual questioning, all the veniremen could hear the questions and answers. In fact, the prosecution frequently incorporated prior questioning of other veniremen by reference, each time with the assurance from the individual being questioned that he or she had heard and understood the previous questions.

The court repeatedly stated the correct standard when questioning individual members of the venire. Murphy was present and heard the court ask the proper Witherspoon question over and over again. After many instances of such questioning, Murphy was seated in the jury box. The court first asked Murphy his occupation, and learned that he was retired, but had spent the eight years before retirement working in the administration office of St. Pios Seminary. As previously noted, the court then asked: "Do you have any moral or religious, conscientious moral or religious principles in opposition to the death penalty so strong that you would be unable without violating your own principles to vote to recommend a death penalty regardless of the facts?" After Murphy responded "Yes, I have" he was excused.

The precise wording of the question asked of Murphy, and the answer he gave, do not by themselves compel the conclusion that he could not under any circumstance recommend the death penalty. . . . Viewing the record of voir dire in its entirety, we agree with the reasoning of the Court of Appeals that the trial court's decision to exclude this juror was proper.

IV

Petitioner next contends that the prosecution's closing argument at the guilt-innocence stage of the trial rendered his conviction fundamentally unfair and deprived the sentencing determination of the reliability that the Eighth Amendment requires.

It is helpful as an initial matter to place these remarks in context. Closing argument came at the end of several days of trial. Because of a state procedural rule petitioner's counsel had the opportunity to present the initial summation as well as a rebuttal to the prosecutors' closing arguments. The prosecutors' comments must be evaluated in light of the defense argument that preceded it, which blamed the Polk County Sheriff's Office for a lack of evidence, alluded to the death penalty, characterized the perpetrator of the crimes as an "animal," and contained counsel's personal opinion of the strength of the State's evidence.

The prosecutors then made their closing argument. That argument deserves the condemnation it has received from every court to review it, although no court has held that the argument rendered the trial unfair. Several comments attempted to place some of the blame for the crime on the Division of Corrections, because Darden was on weekend furlough from a prison sentence when the crime occurred. Some comments implied that the death penalty would be the only guarantee against a future similar act. Others incorporated the defense's use of the word "animal." Prosecutor McDaniel made several offensive comments reflecting an emotional reaction to the case. These comments undoubtedly were improper. . . . The relevant question is whether the prosecutors' comments "so infected the trial with unfairness as to make the resulting conviction a denial of due process." Moreover, the appropriate standard of review for such a claim on writ of habeas corpus is "the narrow one of due process, and not the broad exercise of supervisory power."

Under this standard of review, we agree with the reasoning of every court to consider these comments that they did not deprive petitioner of a fair trial. The prosecutors' argument did not manipulate or misstate the evidence, nor did it implicate other specific rights of the accused such as the right to counsel or the right to remain silent. . . .

Petitioner contends that he was denied effective assistance of counsel at the sentencing phase of trial. That claim must be evaluated against the two-part test announced in *Strickland v. Washington* (1984). First, petitioner must show that "counsel's representation fell below an objective standard of reasonableness." Second, petitioner must show that "there is a reasonable probability that, but for counsel's unprofessional errors, the result of the proceeding would have been different." Petitioner argues that his trial counsel did not delve sufficiently into his background, and as a result were unprepared to present mitigating evidence at the sentencing hearing.

As an initial matter, petitioner contends that trial counsel devoted only the time between the close of the guilt phase of trial and the start of the penalty phase—approximately one-half hour—to preparing the case in mitigation. That argument is without merit. Defense counsel engaged in extensive preparation prior to trial, in a manner that included preparation for sentencing. . . .

Petitioner also claims that his trial counsel interpreted Fla. Stat. § 921.141(6) (1985), a statutory list of mitigating factors, as an exclusive list. He contends that their failure to introduce any evidence in mitigation was the result of this interpretation of the statute, and that he was thereby deprived of effective assistance of counsel. We express no view about the reasonableness of that interpretation of Florida law, because in this case the trial court specifically informed petitioner and his counsel just prior to the sentencing phase of trial that they could "go into any other factors that might really be pertinent to full consideration of your case and the analysis of you and your family situation, your causes, or anything else that might be pertinent to what is the appropriate sentence." At that point, even if counsel previously believed the list to be exclusive, they knew they were free to offer nonstatutory mitigating evidence, and chose not to do so.

As we recognized in Strickland "Judicial scrutiny of counsel's performance must be highly deferential". . . .

Petitioner has failed to satisfy the first part of the Strickland test, that his trial counsels' performance fell below an objective standard of reasonableness. We agree with both the District Court and the Court of Appeals that petitioner was not deprived of the effective assistance of counsel.

VI

The judgment of the Court of Appeals is affirmed, and the case is remanded for proceedings consistent with this opinion.

It is so ordered.

SOURCE: Darden v. Wainwright, 477 U.S. 168 (1986).

ANALYSIS

The *Willie Darden* case is one that remains controversial even decades later. Darden, an African American man, was convicted and sentenced to death for killing a white man. An important factor in his conviction was that the murder victim's widow identified Darden as the assailant—but she initially told police she could not identify the man who assaulted her and shot her husband. A neighbor identified

Darden after being presented with pictures of six men—but Darden's photo was the only one that contained a label "Sheriff's Department, Bartow, Florida."

Furthermore, a woman named Christine Bass said that Darden was at her house from 4:00 p.m. until 5:30 p.m. on September 8, 1973, the day of the murder. The actual crime was committed at about 6:00 p.m. If Bass was telling the truth, there was simply not time for Darden to have committed the crime. However, Darden's attorney never called Christine Bass to the witness stand. For his part, Willie Darden constantly maintained his innocent for all of his 14 years on death row.

The Supreme Court decision in *Darden v. Wainwright* did not consider any of these troubling elements of Darden's prosecution. Instead, the Court's sole concern in this case was whether the prosecutors in Darden's trial made such improper comments that the prosecutorial misconduct mandated that Darden should receive a new trial. Prosecutors called Darden "an animal" that he was "an animal who ought to be placed on a leash." A prosecutor also said that he wished he could see Darden's face "blown away by a shotgun."

The Supreme Court, however, ruled against Darden by a 5–4 vote. The majority, in an opinion by Justice Lewis Powell, acknowledged that the prosecutors' comments "undoubtedly" were "improper." However, Powell reasoned that these comments, however regretful, did not deprive Darden of a fair trial. Powell reasoned that the prosecutors did not misstate or manipulate the evidence.

The Court also rejected two other claims by Darden—that a prospective juror was improperly dismissed from the jury pool and that Darden's trial attorneys were ineffective and deprived Darden of his Sixth Amendment's right to the effective assistance of counsel. The Court rejected both of those arguments.

Justice Harry Blackmun wrote a passionate dissent. "I believe this Court must do more than wring its hands when a state uses improper legal standards to select juries in capital cases and permits prosecutors to pervert the adversary process."

Darden's case attracted worldwide attention. Evening network television programs broadcast stories on the controversy, and Amnesty International launched a worldwide campaign to try to urge clemency for Darden. Many celebrities advocated for his cause, including Jesse Jackson, Margot Kidder, and others, but their efforts were not successful. The state of Florida executed Willie Darden on March 15, 1988.

FURTHER READING

Associated Press. "Florida Executes Celebrated Killer." *New York Times*. March 16, 1988.

Ingle, Joseph B. *Last Rights: 13 Fatal Encounters with the State's Justice*. Nashville, TN: Abingdon Press, 1990.

- ***Document 22:*** Court decision in *Ford v. Wainwright*
- ***Date:*** June 26, 1986
- ***Where:*** Washington, D.C.
- ***Significance:*** The Court ruled that inmates who were legally insane could not be executed. The decision signified the Court's willingness to find that the death penalty cannot constitutionally be applied to certain types of defendants.

DOCUMENT

Supreme Court Rules the Insane Cannot Be Executed

For centuries, no jurisdiction has countenanced the execution of the insane, yet this Court has never decided whether the Constitution forbids the practice. Today we keep faith with our common law heritage in holding that it does.

I

Alyin Bernard Ford was convicted of murder in 1974 and sentenced to death. There is no suggestion that he was incompetent at the time of his offense, at trial, or at sentencing.

In early 1982, however, Ford began to manifest gradual changes in behavior. They began as an occasional peculiar idea or confused perception, but became more serious over time. After reading in the newspaper that the Ku Klux Klan had held a rally in nearby Jacksonville, Florida, Ford developed an obsession focused upon the Klan. His letters to various people reveal endless brooding about his "Klan work," and an increasingly pervasive delusion that he had become the target of a complex conspiracy, involving the Klan and assorted others, designed to force him to commit suicide. He believed that the prison guards, part of the conspiracy, had been killing people and putting the bodies in the concrete enclosures used for beds. Later, he began to believe that his women relatives were being tortured and sexually abused somewhere in the prison. This notion developed into a delusion that the people who were tormenting him at the prison had taken members of Ford's family hostage. The hostage delusion took firm hold and expanded, until Ford was reporting that 135 of his friends and family were being held hostage in the prison, and that only he could help them. By "day 287" of the "hostage crisis," the list of hostages had expanded to include "senators, Senator Kennedy, and many other leaders." In a letter to the Attorney General of Florida, written in 1983, Ford appeared to assume authority for ending the "crisis," claiming to have fired a number of prison officials. He began to refer to himself as "Pope John Paul, III," and reported having appointed nine new justices to the Florida Supreme Court.

Counsel for Ford asked a psychiatrist who had examined Ford earlier, Dr. Jamal Amin, to continue seeing him and to recommend appropriate treatment. On the basis of roughly 14 months of evaluation, taped conversations between Ford and his attorneys, letters written by Ford, interviews with Ford's acquaintances, and various medical records, Dr. Amin concluded in 1983 that Ford suffered from "a severe, uncontrollable, mental disease which closely resembles *Paranoid Schizophrenia With Suicide Potential' "—a "major mental disorder . . . severe enough to substantially affect Mr. Ford's present ability to assist in the defense of his life.*"

Ford subsequently refused to see Dr. Amin again, believing him to have joined the conspiracy against him, and Ford's counsel sought assistance from Dr. Harold Kaufman, who interviewed Ford in November, 1983. Ford told Dr. Kaufman that "I know there is some sort of death penalty, but I'm free to go whenever I want, because it would be illegal and the executioner would be executed." When asked if he would be executed, Ford replied: "I can't be executed because of the landmark case. I won. Ford v. State will prevent executions all over." These statements appeared amidst long streams of seemingly unrelated thoughts in rapid succession. Dr. Kaufman concluded that Ford had no understanding of why he was being executed, made no connection between the homicide of which he had been convicted and the death penalty, and indeed sincerely believed that he would not be executed because he owned the prisons and could control the Governor through mind waves. Dr. Kaufman found that there was "no reasonable possibility that Mr. Ford was dissembling, malingering or otherwise putting on a performance . . ." The following month, in an interview with his attorneys, Ford regressed further into nearly complete incomprehensibility, speaking only in a code characterized by intermittent use of the word "one," making statements such as "Hands one, face one. Mafia one. God one, father one, Pope one. Pope one. Leader one."

Counsel for Ford invoked the procedures of Florida law governing the determination of competency of a condemned inmate, Fla.Stat. § 922.07 (1985). Following the procedures set forth in the statute, the Governor of Florida appointed a panel of three psychiatrists to evaluate whether, under § 922.07(2), Ford had "the mental capacity to understand the nature of the death penalty and the reasons why it was imposed upon him." At a single meeting, the three psychiatrists together interviewed Ford for approximately 30 minutes. Each doctor then filed a separate two- or three-page report with the Governor, to whom the statute delegates the final decision. One doctor concluded that Ford suffered from "psychosis with paranoia," but had "enough cognitive functioning to understand the nature and the effects of the death penalty, and why it is to be imposed on him." Another found that, although Ford was "psychotic," he did "know fully what can happen to him." The third concluded that Ford had a "severe adaptational disorder," but did "comprehend his total situation including being sentenced to death, and all of the implications of that penalty." He believed that Ford's disorder, "although severe, seem[ed] contrived and recently learned." Thus, the interview produced three different diagnoses, but accord on the question of sanity as defined by state law.

The Governor's decision was announced on April 30, 1984, when, without explanation or statement, he signed a death warrant for Ford's execution. Ford's attorneys unsuccessfully sought a hearing in state court to determine anew Ford's competency to suffer execution. Counsel then filed a petition for habeas corpus in the United States District Court for the Southern District of Florida, seeking an evidentiary hearing on the question of Ford's sanity, proffering the conflicting findings of the Governor-appointed commission and subsequent challenges to their methods by other psychiatrists. The District Court denied the petition without a hearing. The Court of Appeals granted a certificate of probable cause and stayed Ford's execution. . . . This Court granted Ford's petition for certiorari in order to resolve the important issue whether the Eighth Amendment prohibits the execution of the insane and, if so, whether the District Court should have held a hearing on petitioner's claim.

II

Since this Court last had occasion to consider the infliction of the death penalty upon the insane, our interpretations of the Due Process Clause and the Eighth Amendment have evolved substantially. . . . Now that the Eighth Amendment has been recognized to affect significantly both the procedural and the substantive aspects of the death penalty, the question of executing the insane takes on a wholly different complexion. The adequacy of the procedures chosen by a State to determine sanity, therefore, will depend upon an issue that this Court has never addressed: whether the Constitution places a substantive restriction on the State's power to take the life of an insane prisoner.

There is now little room for doubt that the Eighth Amendment's ban on cruel and unusual punishment embraces, at a minimum, those modes or acts of punishment that had been considered cruel and unusual at the time that the Bill of Rights was adopted. . . .

Moreover, the Eighth Amendment's proscriptions are not limited to those practices condemned by the common law in 1789. Not bound by the sparing humanitarian concessions of our forebears, the Amendment also recognizes the "evolving standards of decency that mark the progress of a maturing society." In addition to considering the barbarous methods generally outlawed in the 18th century, therefore, this Court takes into account objective evidence of contemporary values before determining whether a particular punishment comports with the fundamental human dignity that the Amendment protects.

A

We begin, then, with the common law. The bar against executing a prisoner who has lost his sanity bears impressive historical credentials; the practice consistently has been branded "savage and inhuman." . . .

As is often true of common law principles, the reasons for the rule are less sure and less uniform than the rule itself. One explanation is that the execution of an insane person simply offends humanity,; another, that it provides no example to others, and thus contributes nothing to whatever deterrence value is intended to be served by capital punishment. Other commentators postulate religious underpinnings: that it is uncharitable to dispatch an offender "into another world, when he is not of a capacity to fit". . . . We know of virtually no authority condoning the execution of the insane at English common law.

Further indications suggest that this solid proscription was carried to America, where it was early observed that "the judge is bound" to stay the execution upon insanity of the prisoner.

B

This ancestral legacy has not outlived its time. Today, no State in the Union permits the execution of the insane. It is clear that the ancient and humane limitation upon the State's ability to execute its sentences has as firm a hold upon the jurisprudence of today as it had centuries ago in England. The various reasons put forth in support of the common law restriction have no less logical, moral, and practical force than they did when first voiced. For today, no less than before, we may seriously question the retributive value of executing a person who has no comprehension of why he has been singled out and stripped of his fundamental right to life. Similarly, the natural abhorrence civilized societies feel at killing one who has no capacity to come to grips with his own conscience or deity is still vivid today. And the intuition that such an execution simply offends humanity is evidently shared across this Nation. Faced with such widespread evidence of a restriction upon sovereign power, this Court is compelled to conclude that the Eighth Amendment prohibits a State from carrying out a sentence of death upon a prisoner who is insane. Whether its aim be to protect the condemned from fear and pain without comfort of understanding, or to protect the dignity of society itself from the barbarity of exacting mindless vengeance, the restriction finds enforcement in the Eighth Amendment.

III

The Eighth Amendment prohibits the State from inflicting the penalty of death upon a prisoner who is insane. Petitioner's allegation of insanity in his habeas corpus petition, if proved, therefore, would bar his execution. The question before us is whether the District Court was under an obligation to hold an evidentiary hearing on the question of Ford's sanity. In answering that question, we bear in mind that, while the underlying social values encompassed by the Eighth Amendment are rooted in historical traditions, the manner in which our judicial system protects those values is purely a matter of contemporary law. Once a substantive right or restriction is recognized in the Constitution, therefore, its enforcement is in no way confined to the rudimentary process deemed adequate in ages past.

A

In a habeas corpus proceeding, "a federal evidentiary hearing is required unless the state court trier of fact has after a full hearing reliably found the relevant facts."

. . .

B

The adequacy of a state court procedure under *Townsend* is largely a function of the circumstances and the interests at stake. In capital proceedings generally, this Court has demanded that factfinding procedures aspire to a heightened standard of reliability. This especial concern is a natural consequence of the knowledge that execution is the most irremediable and unfathomable of penalties; that death is different.

Although the condemned prisoner does not enjoy the same presumptions accorded a defendant who has yet to be convicted or sentenced, he has not lost the protection of the Constitution altogether; if the Constitution renders the fact or timing of his execution contingent upon establishment of a further fact, then that fact must be determined with the high regard for truth that befits a decision affecting the life or death of a human being. Thus, the ascertainment of a prisoner's sanity as a predicate to lawful execution calls for no less stringent standards than those demanded in any other aspect of a capital proceeding. Indeed, a particularly acute need for guarding against error inheres in a determination that "in the present state of the mental sciences is at best a hazardous guess however conscientious." That need is greater still because the ultimate decision will turn on the finding of a single fact, not on a range of equitable considerations. In light of these concerns, the procedures employed in petitioner's case do not fare well.

C

Florida law directs the Governor, when informed that a person under sentence of death may be insane, to stay the execution and appoint a commission of three psychiatrists to examine the prisoner. Fla.Stat. § 922.07. "The examination of the convicted person shall take place with all three psychiatrists present at the same time." *Ibid.* After receiving the report of the commission, the Governor must determine whether "the convicted person has the mental capacity to understand the nature of the death penalty and the reasons why it was imposed on him." If the Governor finds that the prisoner has that capacity, then a death warrant is issued; if not, then the prisoner is committed to a mental health facility. The procedure is conducted wholly within the executive branch, *ex parte*, and provides the exclusive means for determining sanity.

Petitioner received the statutory process. The Governor selected three psychiatrists, who together interviewed Ford for a total of 30 minutes, in the presence of eight other people, including Ford's counsel, the State's attorneys, and correctional officials. The Governor's order specifically directed that the attorneys should not participate in the examination in any adversarial manner. This order was consistent with the present Governor's "publicly announced policy of excluding all advocacy on the part of the condemned from the process of determining whether a person under a sentence of death is insane."

After submission of the reports of the three examining psychiatrists, reaching conflicting diagnoses but agreeing on the ultimate issue of competency, Ford's counsel attempted to submit to the Governor some other written materials, including the reports of the two other psychiatrists who had examined Ford at greater length, one of whom had concluded that the prisoner was not competent to suffer execution. The Governor's office refused to inform counsel whether the submission would be considered. The Governor subsequently issued his decision in the form of a death warrant. That this most cursory form of procedural review fails to achieve even the minimal degree of reliability required for the protection of any constitutional interest, and thus falls short of adequacy under *Townsend*, is self-evident.

IV

The first deficiency in Florida's procedure lies in its failure to include the prisoner in the truth-seeking process. . . . It would be odd were we now to abandon our insistence upon unfettered presentation of relevant information, before the final fact antecedent to execution has been found.

Rather, consistent with the heightened concern for fairness and accuracy that has characterized our review of the process requisite to the taking of a human life, we believe that any procedure that precludes the prisoner or his counsel from presenting material relevant to his sanity or bars consideration of that material by the factfinder is necessarily inadequate.

. . .

We recently had occasion to underscore the value to be derived from a factfinder's consideration of differing psychiatric opinions when resolving contested issues of mental state. . . .

B

A related flaw in the Florida procedure is the denial of any opportunity to challenge or impeach the state-appointed psychiatrists' opinions. . . . The failure of the Florida procedure to afford the prisoner's representative any opportunity to clarify or challenge the state experts' opinions or methods creates a significant possibility that the ultimate decision made in reliance on those experts will be distorted.

C

Perhaps the most striking defect in the procedures of Fla.Stat. § 922.07, as noted earlier, is the State's placement of the decision wholly within the executive branch. Under this procedure, the person who appoints the experts and ultimately decides whether the State will be able to carry out the sentence that it has long sought is the Governor, whose subordinates have been responsible for initiating every stage of the prosecution of the condemned, from arrest through sentencing. The commander of the State's corps of prosecutors cannot be said to have the neutrality that is necessary for reliability in the factfinding proceeding.

Historically, delay of execution on account of insanity was not a matter of executive clemency (*ex mandato regis*) or judicial discretion (*ex arbitrio judicis*); rather, it was required by law (*ex necessitate legis*). 1 N. Walker, Crime and Insanity in England 196 (1968). Thus, history affords no better basis than does logic for placing the final determination of a fact, critical to the trigger of a constitutional limitation upon the State's power, in the hands of the State's own chief executive. In no other circumstance of which we are aware is the vindication of a constitutional right entrusted to the unreviewable discretion of an administrative tribunal.

Having identified various failings of the Florida scheme, we must conclude that the State's procedures for determining sanity are inadequate to preclude federal redetermination of the constitutional issue. We do not here suggest that only a full trial on the issue of sanity will suffice to protect the federal interests; we leave to the State the task of developing appropriate ways to enforce the constitutional restriction upon its execution of sentences. It may be that some high threshold showing on behalf of the prisoner will be found a necessary means to control the number of nonmeritorious or repetitive claims of insanity. Other legitimate pragmatic considerations may also supply the boundaries of the procedural safeguards that feasibly can be provided.

Yet the lodestar of any effort to devise a procedure must be the overriding dual imperative of providing redress for those with substantial claims and of encouraging accuracy in the factfinding determination. The stakes are high, and the "evidence" will always be imprecise. It is all the more important that the adversary presentation of relevant information be as unrestricted as possible. Also essential is that the manner of selecting and using the experts responsible for producing that "evidence" be conducive to the formation of neutral, sound, and professional judgments as to the prisoner's ability to comprehend the nature of the penalty. Fidelity to these principles is the solemn obligation of a civilized society.

B

Today we have explicitly recognized in our law a principle that has long resided there. It is no less abhorrent today than it has been for centuries to exact in penance the life of one whose mental illness prevents him from comprehending the reasons for the penalty or its implications. . . . petitioner is entitled to an evidentiary hearing in the District Court, *de novo*, on the question of his competence to be executed.

The judgment of the Court of Appeals is reversed, and the case is remanded for further proceedings consistent with this opinion.

It is so ordered.

SOURCE: Ford v. Wainwright, 477 U.S. 399 (1986).

ANALYSIS

Defendant Alvin Bernard Ford was convicted in 1974 of murder and sentenced to death. At the time, there was no indication that he was insane. However, Ford's behavior grew increasingly bizarre in prison. He referred to himself as the Pope, began speaking in code, and became obsessed with a delusion that the Ku Klux Klan and numerous guards were conspiring against him.

His attorneys had Ford evaluated by a psychiatrist who determined that Ford suffered from paranoid schizophrenia and delusional thinking. Florida law, at the time, required the Florida governor to appoint three psychological experts to evaluate the inmate to determine the sanity of the inmate.

The three state experts all determined that Ford was competent and not insane. However, none of the three experts evaluated him for a significant period of time. Ford's attorneys managed to obtain an evidentiary hearing to determine Ford's sanity. A federal district court ruled against Ford, but a federal appeals court reversed.

On further appeal, the U.S. Supreme Court unanimously ruled that the state of Florida could not execute Ford, because it violates the Eighth Amendment to execute someone like Ford. Marshall identified considerable evidence that Ford was insane. Writing for the Court, Justice Thurgood Marshall noted that there was a long-standing history in English common law against executing the insane.

Justice Marshall also noted that the Florida statute that provided for the appointment of the three Florida experts was not constitutionally sound. For one, the statute did not allow any cross-examination of the three experts. Even worse, the Florida statute allowed the state governor, whose decisions might reflect political considerations, to appoint the experts instead of individuals who might be more naturally impartial.

In sum, the Court found the Florida law did not provide enough safeguards to ensure that the evaluation of the inmate would be an accurate fact-finding mission: "Consistent with the heightened concern for fairness and accuracy that has characterized our review of the process requisite to the taking of a human life, we believe that any procedure that precludes the prisoner or his counsel from presenting material relevant to his sanity or bars consideration of that material by the factfinder is necessarily inadequate."

Aside from the defects in the specific Florida procedure, Justice Marshall also emphasized that it offended humanity to execute an inmate who was insane. "Similarly, the natural abhorrence civilized societies feel at killing one who has no capacity to come to grips with his own conscience or deity is still vivid today," he wrote. "And the intuition that such an execution simply offends humanity is evidently shared across this Nation. Faced with such widespread evidence of a restriction upon sovereign power, this Court is compelled to conclude that the Eighth Amendment prohibits a State from carrying out a sentence of death upon a prisoner who is insane."

FURTHER READING

Cox, Kevin E. "Execution of the Insane Criminal: Ford v. Wainwright." 41 *Southwestern Law Journal* 745 (1987).

Radelet, Michael, and Kent Miller. "The Aftermath of Ford v. Wainwright." *Behavioral Sciences and the Law*. Summer 1992.

Sullivan, Shannon S. "Ford v. Wainwright: States Cannot Execute Insane—But How Is Insanity Determined." 20 *John Marshall Law Review* 549 (1987).

- ***Document 23:*** Justice Lewis Powell's majority opinion in *McCleskey v. Kemp*
- ***Date:*** April 22, 1987
- ***Where:*** Washington, D.C.
- ***Significance:*** This decision established that a defendant alleging racial discrimination has to show *purposeful* discrimination on the part of his or her individual prosecutors to have a guilty verdict in a death penalty case overturned. Powell's majority opinion ignored clear evidence that in Georgia the race of the victim was a significant factor in whether prosecutors sought the death penalty.

DOCUMENT

Supreme Court Upholds Death Sentence despite Evidence of Racial Discrimination in Capital Punishment Sentencing

This case presents the question whether a complex statistical study that indicates a risk that racial considerations enter into capital sentencing determinations proves that petitioner McCleskey's capital sentence is unconstitutional under the Eighth or Fourteenth Amendment.

I

McCleskey, a black man, was convicted of two counts of armed robbery and one count of murder in the Superior Court of Fulton County, Georgia, on October 12, 1978. McCleskey's convictions arose out of the robbery of a furniture store and the killing of a white police officer during the course of the robbery. The evidence at trial indicated that McCleskey and three accomplices planned and carried out the robbery. All four were armed. McCleskey entered the front of the store while the other three entered the rear. McCleskey secured the front of the store by rounding up the customers and forcing them to lie face down on the floor. The other three rounded up the employees in the rear and tied them up with tape. The manager was forced at gunpoint to turn over the store receipts, his watch, and $6. During the course of the robbery, a police officer, answering a silent alarm, entered the store through the front door. As he was walking down the center aisle of the store, two shots were fired. Both struck the officer. One hit him in the face and killed him.

Several weeks later, McCleskey was arrested in connection with an unrelated offense. He confessed that he had participated in the furniture store robbery, but denied that he had shot the police officer. At trial, the State introduced evidence that at least one of the bullets that struck the officer was fired from a .38 caliber Rossi revolver. This description matched the description of the gun that McCleskey had carried during the robbery. The State also introduced the testimony of two witnesses who had heard McCleskey admit to the shooting.

The jury convicted McCleskey of murder. At the penalty hearing, the jury heard arguments as to the appropriate sentence. Under Georgia law, the jury could not consider imposing the death penalty unless it found beyond a reasonable doubt that the murder was accompanied by one of the statutory aggravating circumstances. The jury in this case found two aggravating circumstances to exist beyond a reasonable doubt: the murder was committed during the course of an armed robbery; and the murder was committed upon a peace officer engaged in the performance of his duties. In making its decision whether to impose the death sentence, the jury considered the mitigating and aggravating circumstances of McCleskey's conduct. McCleskey offered no mitigating evidence. The jury recommended that he be sentenced to death on the murder charge and to consecutive life sentences on the armed robbery charges. The court followed the jury's recommendation and sentenced McCleskey to death.

On appeal, the Supreme Court of Georgia affirmed the convictions and the sentences. . . .

McCleskey next filed a petition for a writ of habeas corpus in the Federal District Court for the Northern District of Georgia. His petition raised 18 claims, one of which was that the Georgia capital sentencing process is administered in a racially discriminatory manner in violation of the Eighth and Fourteenth Amendments to the United States Constitution. In support of his claim, McCleskey proffered a statistical study performed by Professors David C. Baldus, Charles Pulaski, and George Woodworth (the Baldus study) that purports to show a disparity in the imposition of the death sentence in Georgia based on the race of the murder victim and, to a lesser extent, the race of the defendant. The Baldus study is actually two sophisticated statistical studies that examine over 2,000 murder cases that occurred in Georgia during the 1970's. The raw numbers collected by Professor Baldus indicate that defendants charged with killing white persons received the death penalty in 11% of the cases, but defendants charged with killing blacks received the death penalty in only 1% of the cases. The raw numbers also indicate a reverse racial disparity according to the race of the defendant: 4% of the black defendants received the death penalty, as opposed to 7% of the white defendants.

Baldus also divided the cases according to the combination of the race of the defendant and the race of the victim. He found that the death penalty was assessed in 22% of the cases involving black defendants and white victims; 8% of the cases involving white defendants and white victims; 1% of the cases involving black defendants and black victims; and 3% of the cases involving white defendants and black victims. Similarly, Baldus found that prosecutors sought the death penalty in 70% of the cases involving black defendants and white victims; 32% of the cases involving white defendants and white victims; 15% of the cases involving black defendants and black victims; and 19% of the cases involving white defendants and black victims.

Baldus subjected his data to an extensive analysis, taking account of 230 variables that could have explained the disparities on nonracial grounds. One of his models concludes that, even after taking account of 39 nonracial variables, defendants charged with killing white victims were 4.3 times as likely to receive a death sentence as defendants charged with killing blacks. According to this model, black defendants were 1.1 times as likely to receive a death sentence as other defendants. Thus, the Baldus study indicates that black defendants, such as McCleskey, who kill white victims have the greatest likelihood of receiving the death penalty.

The District Court held an extensive evidentiary hearing on McCleskey's petition. . . . [T]he court denied the petition insofar as it was based upon the Baldus study.

The Court of Appeals for the Eleventh Circuit, sitting en banc, carefully reviewed the District Court's decision on McCleskey's claim. It assumed the validity of the study itself and addressed the merits of McCleskey's Eighth and Fourteenth Amendment claims.

. . .

The Court of Appeals affirmed the denial by the District Court of McCleskey's petition for a writ of habeas corpus insofar as the petition was based upon the Baldus study, with three judges dissenting as to McCleskey's claims based on the Baldus study. We granted certiorari, and now affirm.

II

McCleskey's first claim is that the Georgia capital punishment statute violates the Equal Protection Clause of the Fourteenth Amendment. He argues that race has infected the administration of Georgia's statute in two ways: persons who murder whites are more likely to be sentenced to death than persons who murder blacks, and black murderers are more likely to be sentenced to death than white murderers. As a black defendant who killed a white victim, McCleskey claims that the Baldus study demonstrates that he was discriminated against because of his race and because of the race of his victim. In its broadest form, McCleskey's claim of discrimination extends to every actor in the Georgia capital sentencing process, from the prosecutor who sought the death penalty and the jury that imposed the sentence, to the State itself that enacted the capital punishment statute and allows it to remain in effect despite its allegedly discriminatory application. We agree with the Court of Appeals, and every other court that has considered such a challenge, that this claim must fail.

A

Our analysis begins with the basic principle that a defendant who alleges an equal protection violation has the burden of proving "the existence of purposeful discrimination." A corollary to this principle is that a criminal defendant must prove that the purposeful discrimination "had a discriminatory effect" on him. Thus, to prevail under the Equal Protection Clause, McCleskey must prove that the decisionmakers in his case acted with discriminatory purpose. He offers no evidence specific to his own case that would support an inference that racial considerations played a part in his sentence. Instead, he relies solely on the Baldus study. McCleskey argues that the Baldus study compels an inference that his sentence rests on purposeful discrimination. McCleskey's claim that these statistics are sufficient proof of discrimination, without regard to the facts of a particular case, would extend to all capital cases in Georgia, at least where the victim was white and the defendant is black.

The Court has accepted statistics as proof of intent to discriminate in certain limited contexts. First, this Court has accepted statistical disparities as proof of an equal protection violation in the selection of the jury venire in a particular district. . . .

But the nature of the capital sentencing decision, and the relationship of the statistics to that decision, are fundamentally different from the corresponding elements in the venire-selection or Title VII cases. Most importantly, each particular decision to impose the death penalty is made by a petit jury selected from a properly constituted venire. Each jury is unique in its composition, and the Constitution requires that its decision rest on consideration of innumerable factors that vary according to the characteristics of the individual defendant and the facts of the particular capital offense. Thus, the application of an inference drawn from the general statistics to a specific decision in a trial and sentencing simply is not comparable to the application of an inference drawn from general statistics to a specific venire-selection or Title VII case. In those cases, the statistics relate to fewer entities, and fewer variables are relevant to the challenged decisions.

. . .

B

McCleskey also suggests that the Baldus study proves that the State as a whole has acted with a discriminatory purpose. He appears to argue that the State has violated the Equal Protection Clause by adopting the capital punishment statute and allowing it to remain in force despite its allegedly discriminatory application. But "'[d]iscriminatory purpose' . . . implies more than intent as volition or intent as awareness of consequences. It implies that the decisionmaker, in this case a state legislature, selected or reaffirmed a particular course of action at least in part 'because of,' not merely 'in spite of,' its adverse effects upon an identifiable group." For this claim to prevail, McCleskey would have to prove that the Georgia Legislature enacted or maintained the death penalty statute because of an anticipated racially discriminatory effect. In Gregg v. Georgia, supra, this Court found that the Georgia capital sentencing system could operate in a fair and neutral manner. There was no evidence then, and there is none now, that the Georgia Legislature enacted the capital punishment statute to further a racially discriminatory purpose.

Nor has McCleskey demonstrated that the legislature maintains the capital punishment statute because of the racially disproportionate impact suggested by the Baldus study. As legislatures necessarily have wide discretion in the choice of criminal laws and penalties, and as there were legitimate reasons for the Georgia Legislature to adopt and maintain capital punishment, we will not infer a discriminatory purpose on the part of the State of Georgia. Accordingly, we reject McCleskey's equal protection claims.

III

McCleskey also argues that the Baldus study demonstrates that the Georgia capital sentencing system violates the Eighth Amendment. We begin our analysis of this claim by reviewing the restrictions on death sentences established by our prior decisions under that Amendment.

A

The Eighth Amendment prohibits infliction of "cruel and unusual punishments." This Court's early Eighth Amendment cases examined only the "particular methods of execution to determine whether they were too cruel to pass constitutional muster." . . .

B

Two principal decisions guide our resolution of McCleskey's Eighth Amendment claim. In Furman v. Georgia, the Court concluded that the death penalty was so irrationally imposed that any particular death sentence could be presumed excessive. Under the statutes at issue in Furman, there was no basis for determining in any particular case whether the penalty was proportionate to the crime: "[T]he death penalty [was] exacted with great infrequency even for the most atrocious crimes and . . . there [was] no meaningful basis for distinguishing the few cases in which it [was] imposed from the many cases in which it [was] not."

In *Gregg*, the Court specifically addressed the question left open in *Furman*—whether the punishment of death for murder is "under all circumstances, 'cruel and unusual' in violation of the Eighth and Fourteenth Amendments of the Constitution."

. . .

C

. . .

In contrast to the carefully defined standards that must narrow a sentencer's discretion to impose the death sentence, the Constitution limits a State's ability to narrow a sentencer's discretion to consider relevant evidence that might cause it to decline to impose the death sentence. "[T]he sentencer . . . [cannot] be precluded from considering, as a mitigating factor, any aspect of a defendant's character or record and any of the circumstances of the offense that the defendant proffers as a basis for a sentence less than death." Any exclusion of the "compassionate or mitigating factors stemming from the diverse frailties of humankind" that are relevant to the sentencer's decision would fail to treat all persons as "uniquely individual human beings."

Although our constitutional inquiry has centered on the procedures by which a death sentence is imposed, we have not stopped at the face of a statute, but have probed the application of statutes to particular cases. . . .

D

In sum, our decisions since *Furman* have identified a constitutionally permissible range of discretion in imposing the death penalty. First, there is a required threshold below which the death penalty cannot be imposed. In this context, the State must establish rational criteria that narrow the decisionmaker's judgment as to whether the circumstances of a particular defendant's case meet the threshold. Moreover, a societal consensus that the death penalty is disproportionate to a particular offense prevents a State from imposing the death penalty for that offense. Second, States cannot limit the sentencer's consideration of any relevant circumstance that could cause it to decline to impose the penalty. In this respect, the State cannot channel the sentencer's discretion, but must allow it to consider any relevant information offered by the defendant.

IV

A

In light of our precedents under the Eighth Amendment, McCleskey cannot argue successfully that his sentence is "disproportionate to the crime in the traditional sense."

. . .

B

Although our decision in *Gregg* as to the facial validity of the Georgia capital punishment statute appears to foreclose McCleskey's disproportionality argument, he further contends that the Georgia capital punishment system is arbitrary and capricious in application, and therefore his sentence is excessive, because racial considerations may influence capital sentencing decisions in Georgia. We now address this claim.

To evaluate McCleskey's challenge, we must examine exactly what the Baldus study may show. Even Professor Baldus does not contend that his statistics prove that race enters into any capital sentencing decisions or that race was a factor in McCleskey's particular case. Statistics at most may show only a likelihood that a particular factor entered into some decisions. There is, of course, some risk of racial prejudice influencing a jury's decision in a criminal case. There are similar risks that other kinds of prejudice will influence other criminal trials.

. . .

Individual jurors bring to their deliberations "qualities of human nature and varieties of human experience, the range of which is unknown and perhaps unknowable." The capital sentencing decision requires the individual jurors to focus their collective judgment on the unique characteristics of a particular criminal defendant. It is not surprising that such collective judgments often are difficult to explain. But the inherent lack of predictability of jury decisions does not justify their condemnation. . . .

C

At most, the Baldus study indicates a discrepancy that appears to correlate with race. Apparent disparities in sentencing are an inevitable part of our criminal justice system. The discrepancy indicated by the Baldus study is "a far cry from the major systemic defects identified in *Furman*," . . . Where the discretion that is fundamental to our criminal process is involved, we decline to assume that what is unexplained is invidious. In light of the safeguards designed to minimize racial bias in the process, the fundamental value of jury trial in our criminal justice system, and the benefits that discretion provides to criminal defendants, we hold that the Baldus study does not demonstrate a constitutionally significant risk of racial bias affecting the Georgia capital sentencing process.

V

Two additional concerns inform our decision in this case. First, McCleskey's claim, taken to its logical conclusion, throws into serious question the principles that underlie our entire criminal justice system. The Eighth Amendment is not limited in application to capital punishment, but applies to all penalties. . . . Similarly, since McCleskey's claim relates to the race of his victim, other claims could apply with equally logical force to statistical disparities that correlate with the race or sex of other actors in the criminal justice system, such as defense attorneys or judges. Also, there is no logical reason that such a claim need be limited to racial or sexual bias. If arbitrary and capricious punishment is the touchstone under the Eighth Amendment, such a claim could—at least in theory—be based upon any arbitrary variable, such as the defendant's facial characteristics, or the physical attractiveness of the defendant or the victim, that some statistical study indicates may be influential in jury decisionmaking. As these examples illustrate, there is no limiting principle to the type of challenge brought by McCleskey. The Constitution does not require that a State eliminate any demonstrable disparity that correlates with a potentially irrelevant factor in order to operate a criminal justice system that includes capital punishment.

. . .

VI

Accordingly, we affirm the judgment of the Court of Appeals for the Eleventh Circuit.

It is so ordered.

SOURCE: McCleskey v. Kemp, 481 U.S. 279 (1987).

ANALYSIS

One of the most controversial death penalty cases is *McCleskey v. Kemp* (1987), a case involving an African American man, Warren McCleskey, who was convicted and sentenced to death for the killing of police officer Frank Schatt in Atlanta, Georgia. McCleskey and three other men robbed a furniture store in October 1978, and Schatt, while off duty, entered the store and confronted the armed robbers.

After McCleskey's conviction and death sentence in 1978, his attorneys presented a complex statistical study known as "the Baldus study" that showed a disturbing correlation between the death penalty and race. The study was named after lead author David C. Baldus, who conducted it with colleagues George Woodworth and Charles A. Pulaski.

The study examined 128 death sentences in more than 2,000 murder and manslaughter cases in the state of Georgia from 1973 to 1979. The study's most notable finding was that those defendants who killed a white victim were 4.3 times more likely to be sentenced to death for committing a capital crime than defendants convicted of killing non-white victims.

The study also found that prosecutors in Georgia sought the death penalty in 70% of the cases involving Black defendants and white victims; 32% of the cases involving white defendants and white victims; only 15% of the cases involving Black defendants and Black victims; and 19% of the cases involving white defendants and Black victims. Thus, the farmost likely scenario for prosecutors to seek the death penalty was when an African American defendant killed a Caucasian victim.

McCleskey's attorneys argued that his death sentence violated the Equal Protection Clause of both the Fourteenth Amendment and the Eighth Amendment, which prohibits cruel and unusual punishment. However, the U.S. Supreme Court found that the Baldus

DID YOU KNOW?

Attorney John Charles Boger

John Charles Boger argued on behalf of Warren McCleskey before the U.S. Supreme Court in *McCleskey v. Kemp*. Boger worked at the NAACP Legal Defense and Education Fund when he represented McCleskey. Twenty-five years after the Court's fateful decision ruling against Warren McCleskey, Boger delivered a keynote address at a symposium created to address the impact of the Court's decision. According to Boger, "*McCleskey* effectively closed the book, not only on further racial challenges in capital sentencing but, far more broadly, on empirical racial challenges in other kinds of criminal cases."

Boger also noted that the Supreme Court seemed quite hesitant to fully accept statistical proof of racial discrimination in capital sentencing. He also said that the Court majority in *McCleskey v. Kemp* seemed reluctant to fully appreciate the race-of-the-victim discrimination identified by Professor David Baldus and colleagues in the so-called Baldus study. In 1990, Boger joined the faculty at the University of North Carolina School of Law. He became dean of the law school in 2006.

FURTHER READING

Boger, John C. "A Fear of Too Much Justice? Equal Protection and the Social Sciences Thirty Years after *McCleskey v. Kemp* Symposium: Keynote Address." 112 *Northwestern University Law Review* 1637 (2018).

study did not prove the purposeful discrimination necessary to establish a violation of the Equal Protection Clause or the Eighth Amendment. Writing for the majority, Justice Lewis Powell reasoned that "to prevail under the Equal Protection Clause, McCleskey must prove that the decisionmakers in his case acted with discriminatory purpose."

The U.S. Supreme Court—even the majority justices—did not question the findings of the Baldus study. Powell noted that "the Baldus study indicates a discrepancy that appears to correlate with race." However, he recognized that "[a]pparent disparities in sentencing are an inevitable part of our criminal justice system."

Justice William Brennan wrote the dissent for the four dissenters. He explained that "[c]lose analysis of the Baldus study . . . in light of both statistical principles and human experience, reveals that the risk that race influenced McCleskey's sentence is intolerable by any imaginable standard."

Subsequent studies also have found disturbing correlations between race and the death penalty. Many opponents of the death penalty have cited these findings of racial discrimination as showing why the death penalty is an immoral institution.

In 2009, Professor Baldus wrote that "McCleskey has effectively legitimized racial discrimination in the administration of the death penalty by placing it beyond the reach of the courts."

For his part, Warren McCleskey was executed on September 25, 1991. That same year, Justice Lewis Powell—now retired from the U.S. Supreme Court—told his biographer John C. Jeffries that the one decision he regretted was *McCleskey v. Kemp*.

FURTHER READING

Baldus, David C., George Woodworth, and Charles Pulaski. *Equal Justice and the Death Penalty: A Legal and Empirical Analysis*. Boston: Northeastern University Press, 1990.

Baldus, David C., George Woodworth, John C. Boger, and Charles A. Pulaski. "McCleskey v. Kemp (1987): Denial, Avoidance, and the Legitimization of Racial Discrimination in the Administration of the Death Penalty." In *Death Penalty Stories*, eds. John Blume and Jordan Steiker, pp. 229–275. St. Paul, MN: Foundation Press, 2009.

Banner, Stuart A. *The Death Penalty: An American History*. Boston, MA: Harvard University Press, 2002.

- ***Document 24:*** Supreme Court decision in *Whitmore v. Arkansas*
- ***When:*** April 27, 1990
- ***Where:*** Washington, D.C.
- ***Significance:*** The decision emphasizes the importance of standing in death penalty cases. This means that third parties often cannot litigate a death penalty challenge in the place of the actual defendant.

DOCUMENT

One Death Row Inmate Can't Appeal on Behalf of Another Death Row Inmate, Supreme Court Finds

This case presents the question whether a third party has standing to challenge the validity of a death sentence imposed on a capital defendant who has elected to forgo his right of appeal to the State Supreme Court. Petitioner Jonas Whitmore contends that the Eighth and Fourteenth Amendments prevent the State of Arkansas from carrying out the death sentence imposed on Ronald Gene Simmons without first conducting a mandatory appellate review of Simmons' conviction and sentence. We hold that petitioner lacks standing, and therefore dismiss the writ of certiorari.

I

On December 28, 1987, Ronald Gene Simmons shot and killed two people and wounded three others in the course of a rampage through the town of Russellville, Arkansas. After police apprehended Simmons, they searched his home in nearby Dover, Arkansas, and discovered the bodies of 14 members of Simmons' family, all of whom had been murdered. The State filed two sets of criminal charges against Simmons, one based on the two Russellville murders and the other covering the deaths of his family members.

Simmons was first tried for the Russellville crimes, and a jury convicted him of capital murder and sentenced him to death. After being sentenced, Simmons made this statement under oath: "'I, Ronald Gene Simmons, Sr., want it to be known that it is my wish and my desire that absolutely no action by anybody be taken to appeal or in any way change this sentence. It is further respectfully requested that this sentence be carried out expeditiously.'" . . . The trial court conducted a hearing concerning Simmons' competence to waive further proceedings, and concluded that his decision was knowing and intelligent.

As Simmons' execution date approached Louis J. Franz, a Catholic priest who counsels inmates at the Arkansas Department of Corrections, petitioned the Supreme Court of Arkansas for permission to proceed as Simmons' "next friend" and to prosecute an appeal on his behalf. The court held that Franz did not have standing as "next friend," because he had not alleged facts showing that he had ever met Simmons, much less that he had a close relationship with the defendant. It also rejected both his argument for standing under the Arkansas Constitution as an aggrieved taxpayer and his assertion that he should have standing as a concerned citizen to prevent an important legal issue from going unresolved at the appellate level.

In dicta, the court went on to state that Arkansas law does not require a mandatory appeal in all death penalty cases. . . . After reviewing the record of the trial court's competency hearing, the Supreme Court held that Simmons had made a knowing and intelligent waiver of his right to appeal. Franz and another Arkansas death row inmate, Darrel Wayne Hill, then applied in Federal District Court for a writ of habeas corpus to prevent Simmons' execution, but the petition was denied on the ground that Franz and Hill did not have standing.

The State subsequently tried Simmons for the murder of his 14 family members, and on February 10, 1989, a jury convicted him of capital murder and imposed a sentence of death by lethal injection. Simmons again notified the trial court of his desire to waive his right to direct appeal, and after a hearing, the court found Simmons competent to do so. . . .

Three days later, petitioner Jonas Whitmore, another death row inmate in Arkansas, sought permission from the Supreme Court of Arkansas to intervene in Simmons' proceeding both individually and "as next friend of Ronald Gene Simmons." The court concluded that Whitmore had failed to show he had standing to intervene, and it denied the motion. Whitmore then asked this Court to stay Simmons' execution, which was scheduled for March 16, 1989. We granted a stay pending the filing and disposition of a petition for certiorari, and later granted Whitmore's petition for certiorari.

II

A

This is not the first time we have encountered a third party seeking to prevent the execution of a capital defendant who has decided to forgo further judicial proceedings. In *Gilmore v. Utah* (1976), we considered an application for a stay of the execution of Gary Mark Gilmore, filed by his mother Bessie Gilmore after the defendant declined to request relief. A majority of the Court concluded that Gilmore had made a knowing and intelligent waiver of any federal rights available to him and, accordingly, allowed the execution to go forward. . . .

Petitioner Whitmore asks this Court to hold that despite Simmons' failure to appeal, the Eighth and Fourteenth Amendments require the State of Arkansas to conduct an appellate review of his conviction and sentence before it can proceed to execute him. It is well established, however, that before a federal court can consider the merits of a legal claim, the person seeking to invoke the jurisdiction of the court must establish the requisite standing to sue. . . .

B

As we understand Whitmore's claim of standing in his individual capacity, he alleges that the State has infringed rights that the Eighth Amendment grants to him personally and to the subject of the impending execution, Simmons. He therefore rests his claim to relief both on his own asserted legal right to a system of mandatory appellate review and on Simmons' similar right. . . .

Whitmore's principal claim of injury in fact is that Arkansas has established a system of comparative review in death penalty cases, and that he has "a direct and substantial interest in having the data base against which his crime is compared to be complete and to not be arbitrarily skewed by the omission of any other capital case." . . .

Petitioner's alleged injury is too speculative to invoke the jurisdiction of an Art. III court. Whitmore's conviction and death sentence are final, and his claim that he may eventually secure federal habeas relief from his conviction is obviously problematic. Nor, although the odds may well be better, can petitioner prove that if he were to obtain habeas relief, he would be retried, convicted, and again sentenced to death. . . .

Whitmore's theory of injury is at least as speculative as others we have found insufficient to establish Art. III injury in fact. . . .

Whitmore also contends that as a citizen of Arkansas, he is "entitled to the public interest protections of the Eighth Amendment," and has a right to invoke this Court's jurisdiction to insure that an execution is not carried out in Arkansas without appellate review. This allegation raises only the "generalized interest of all citizens in constitutional governance," and is an inadequate basis on which to grant petitioner standing to proceed. . . .

Perhaps recognizing the weakness of his claim for standing, petitioner argues next that the Court should create an exception to traditional standing doctrine for this case. The uniqueness of the death penalty and society's interest in its proper imposition, he maintains, justify a relaxed application of standing principles. . . .

As an alternative basis for standing to maintain this action, petitioner purports to proceed as "next friend of Ronald Gene Simmons." Although we have never discussed the concept of "next friend" standing at length, it has long been an accepted basis for jurisdiction in certain circumstances. Most frequently, "next friends" appear in court on behalf of detained prisoners who are unable, usually because of mental incompetence or inaccessibility, to seek relief themselves. . . .

A "next friend" does not himself become a party to the habeas corpus action in which he participates, but simply pursues the cause on behalf of the detained person, who remains the real party in interest. . . .

Whitmore, of course, does not seek a writ of habeas corpus on behalf of Simmons. He desires to intervene in a state-court proceeding to appeal Simmons' conviction and death sentence. Under these circumstances, there is no federal statute authorizing the participation of "next friends." The Supreme Court of Arkansas recognizes, apparently as a matter of common law, the availability of "next friend" standing in the Arkansas courts, but declined to grant it to Whitmore. Without deciding whether a "next friend" may ever invoke the jurisdiction of a federal court absent congressional authorization, we think the scope of any federal doctrine of "next friend" standing is no broader than what is permitted by the habeas corpus statute, which codified the historical practice. And in keeping with the ancient tradition of the doctrine, we conclude that one necessary condition for "next friend" standing in federal court is a showing by the proposed "next friend" that the real party in interest is unable to litigate his own cause due to mental incapacity, lack of access to court, or other similar disability.

That prerequisite for "next friend" standing is not satisfied where an evidentiary hearing shows that the defendant has given a knowing, intelligent, and voluntary waiver of his right to proceed, and his access to court is otherwise unimpeded. Although we are not here faced with the question whether a hearing on mental competency is required by the United States Constitution whenever a capital defendant desires to terminate further proceedings, such a hearing will obviously bear on whether the defendant is able to proceed on his own behalf. The Supreme Court of Arkansas requires a competency hearing as a matter of state law, and in this case it affirmed the trial court's finding that Simmons had "the capacity to understand the choice between life and death and to knowingly and intelligently waive any and all rights to appeal his sentence." At oral argument, Whitmore's counsel questioned the validity of the waiver, but we find no reason to disturb the judgment of the Supreme Court of Arkansas on this point.

Simmons was questioned by counsel and the trial court concerning his choice to accept the death sentence, and his answers demonstrate that he appreciated the consequences of that decision. He indicated that he understood several possible grounds for appeal, which had been explained to him by counsel, but informed the court that he was "not seeking any technicalities.". . . We therefore hold that Whitmore, having failed to establish that Simmons is unable to proceed on his own behalf, does not have standing to proceed as "next friend" of Ronald Gene Simmons.

* * *

. . . Jonas Whitmore lacks standing to proceed in this Court, and the writ of certiorari is dismissed for want of jurisdiction.

It is so ordered.

SOURCE: Whitmore v. Arkansas, 495 U.S. 149 (1990).

ANALYSIS

One of the most important concepts in constitutional law is *standing*: a litigant has a sufficient stake in the litigation to proceed with the lawsuit. In other words, a litigant has standing when she can show that she has suffered an injury or harm. Standing is traced to the actual language in the U.S. Constitution that courts have power over actual cases and controversies.

In 1976, the U.S. Supreme Court ruled that Bessie Gilmore, the mother of death row inmate Gary Gilmore, did not have standing to appeal on behalf of her son, who had waived his right to an appeal of his imminent execution. Similarly, in *Whitmore v. Arkansas* (1990), the Court ruled one death row inmate, Jonas Whitmore, lacked standing to appeal on behalf of another death row inmate, Ronald Gene Simmons.

Both Gary Gilmore and Ronald Gene Simmons emphatically told the court that they wished to be executed and did not want to appeal their convictions. The question in each case was whether someone could step in the place of these inmates and advocate on their behalf.

A litigant has standing when she can show that she has suffered an injury or harm. Otherwise, the litigant's claim is a generalized grievance and not special to the actual litigant. Whitmore argued that he had standing, because as a death row inmate, he could perhaps challenge his sentence in a later proceeding based on the concept of proportionality or comparative review—that his death sentence was disproportionate to the other types of cases in Arkansas that actually merited the death penalty.

The Supreme Court rejected this argument by a 7–2 vote with Chief Justice William Rehnquist writing the Court's majority opinion. Rehnquist reasoned that Whitmore's invocation of the concept of comparative review was too speculative.

Whitmore also argued that there should be a special rule allowing standing for a "next friend" in death penalty cases, because the death penalty is a unique, ultimate punishment. This builds on the idea of what the Court wrote in *Gregg v. Georgia* (1976) that "death is different." However, Rehnquist rejected this and said that there was no reason to create an exception for death penalty cases.

Justice Thurgood Marshall—joined by Justice William Brennan—dissented. Marshall emphasized that an appellate court had never analyzed the merits of Simmons' conviction and death sentence.

Simmons was executed on June 25, 1990. Whitmore was executed a few years later on May 11, 1994.

FURTHER READING

Casey, Anthony J. "Maintaining the Integrity of Death: An Argument for Restricting a Defendant's Right to Volunteer for Execution at Certain Stages in Capital Proceedings." 30 *American Journal of Criminal Law* 75 (2002).

McClellan, Jane L. "Stopping the Rush to the Death House: Third-Party Standing in Death-Row Volunteer Cases." 26 *Arizona State Law Journal* 201 (1994).

4

VICTIMS' RIGHTS, MORATORIUMS, AND OTHER ISSUES

In the early 1990s, a new movement took root across the United States concerning criminal justice. That movement became known as the "victims' rights" movement. Many states actually amended their state constitutions to even add a "victims' rights amendment." In the death penalty context, the victims' rights question became whether family members of slain victims could testify at capital defendants' sentencing hearings.

Initially, the U.S. Supreme Court reasoned in *Booth v. Maryland* (1987) that the introduction of a so-called victim impact statement at a capital defendant's criminal sentencing was problematic and could more likely persuade the jury to adopt the death penalty. In the *Booth* case, defendant John Booth was convicted of murdering his elderly neighbors, Irvin and Rose Bronstein.

The state of Maryland sought the death penalty against Booth. At the sentencing phase of Booth's trial, the judge allowed the state to read to the jury a victim impact statement from Bronstein's son, daughter, son-in-law, and granddaughter. All talked about the traumatic impact the murder of their parents or grandparents had.

Booth's attorney argued to no avail that the victim impact statements were inflammatory and unduly prejudicial to Booth. The jury sentenced Booth to death.

The case was appealed all the way to the U.S. Supreme Court, which reversed Booth's death sentence. Writing for the majority, Justice Lewis Powell reasoned that the victim impact evidence was "irrelevant to a capital sentencing decision, and that its admission creates a constitutionally unacceptable risk that the jury may impose the death penalty in an arbitrary and capricious manner."

This ruling upset the victims' rights community. Only four years later, the Court reexamined this issue in the case of *Payne v. Tennessee* (1991). In this chapter, you will read about the victim impact case of Pervis Payne. This chapter also includes testimony from law professor Paul Cassell, a noted supporter of victims' rights.

However, at the same time that the victims' rights movement was gaining traction, there continued to be disturbing questions about the way the death penalty operated in at least certain jurisdictions. Some religious leaders called for a stop to the death penalty, as did the largest professional organization of lawyers—the

American Bar Association. Still other entries come from individual states where a governor considers a moratorium. The idea behind a moratorium is that there are enough problems with the death penalty and that the process has to be halted.

FURTHER READING

Cassell, Paul. "In Defense of Victim Impact Statements." 6 *Ohio State Journal of Criminal Law* 611 (2009).

Dolliver, J. M. "Victims' Rights Constitutional Amendment: A Bad Idea Whose Time Should Not Come." 34 *Wayne Law Review* 87 (1987).

- ***Document 25:*** Majority Opinion in *Payne v. Tennessee*
- ***Date:*** June 27, 1991
- ***Where:*** Washington, D.C.
- ***Significance:*** The decision enables prosecutors to introduce victim impact evidence at the sentencing phase of death penalty cases. This means that victims can testify at a defendant's sentencing hearing.

DOCUMENT

Supreme Court Rules Victim Impact Evidence Is Permissible in Sentencing Phase of Death Penalty Case

In this case we reconsider our holdings in *Booth v. Maryland*, 482 U.S. 496 (1987), and *South Carolina v. Gathers*, 490 U.S. 805 (1989), that the Eighth Amendment bars the admission of victim impact evidence during the penalty phase of a capital trial.

Petitioner, Pervis Tyrone Payne, was convicted by a jury on two counts of first-degree murder and one count of assault with intent to commit murder in the first degree. He was sentenced to death for each of the murders and to 30 years in prison for the assault.

The victims of Payne's offenses were 28-year-old Charisse Christopher, her 2-year-old daughter Lacie, and her 3-year-old son Nicholas. The three lived together in an apartment in Millington, Tennessee, across the hall from Payne's girlfriend, Bobbie Thomas. On Saturday, June 27, 1987, Payne visited Thomas' apartment several times in expectation of her return from her mother's house in Arkansas, but found no one at home. On one visit, he left his overnight bag, containing clothes and other items for his weekend stay, in the hallway outside Thomas' apartment. With the bag were three cans of malt liquor.

Payne passed the morning and early afternoon injecting cocaine and drinking beer. Later, he drove around the town with a friend in the friend's car, each of them taking turns reading a pornographic magazine. Sometime around 3 p.m., Payne returned to the apartment complex, entered the Christophers' apartment, and began making sexual advances towards Charisse. Charisse resisted and Payne became violent. A neighbor who resided in the apartment directly beneath the Christophers heard Charisse screaming, "'Get out, get out,' as if she were telling the children to leave." The noise briefly subsided and then began, "'horribly loud.'" The neighbor called the police after she heard a "blood curdling scream" from the Christophers' apartment.

When the first police officer arrived at the scene, he immediately encountered Payne, who was leaving the apartment building, so covered with blood that he appeared to be "'sweating blood.'" The officer confronted Payne, who responded, "'I'm the complainant.'" When the officer asked, "'What's going on up there?'" Payne struck the officer with the overnight bag, dropped his tennis shoes, and fled.

Inside the apartment, the police encountered a horrifying scene. Blood covered the walls and floor throughout the unit. Charisse and her children were lying on the floor in the kitchen. Nicholas, despite several wounds inflicted by a butcher knife that completely penetrated through his body from front to back, was still breathing. Miraculously, he survived, but not until after undergoing seven hours of surgery and a transfusion of 1,700 cc's of blood–400 to 500 cc's more than his estimated normal blood volume. Charisse and Lacie were dead.

Charisse's body was found on the kitchen floor on her back, her legs fully extended. She had sustained 42 direct knife wounds and 42 defensive wounds on her arms and hands. The wounds were caused by 41 separate thrusts of a butcher knife. None of the 84 wounds inflicted by Payne were individually fatal; rather, the cause of death was most likely bleeding from all of the wounds.

Lacie's body was on the kitchen floor near her mother. She had suffered stab wounds to the chest, abdomen, back, and head. The murder weapon, a butcher knife, was found at her feet. Payne's baseball cap was snapped on her arm near her elbow. Three cans of malt liquor bearing Payne's fingerprints were found on a table near her body, and a fourth empty one was on the landing outside the apartment door.

Payne was apprehended later that day hiding in the attic of the home of a former girlfriend. As he descended the stairs of the attic, he stated to the arresting officers, "'Man, I ain't killed no woman.'" According to one of the officers, Payne had "'a wild look about him. His pupils were contracted. He was foaming at the mouth, saliva. He appeared to be very nervous. He was breathing real rapid.'" He had blood on his body and clothes and several scratches across his chest. It was later determined that the blood stains matched the victims' blood types. A search of his pockets revealed a packet containing cocaine residue, a hypodermic syringe wrapper, and a cap from a hypodermic syringe. His overnight bag, containing a bloody white shirt, was found in a nearby dumpster.

At trial, Payne took the stand and, despite the overwhelming and relatively uncontroverted evidence against him, testified that he had not harmed any of the Christophers. Rather, he asserted that another man had raced by him as he was walking up the stairs to the floor where the Christophers lived. He stated that he had gotten blood on himself when, after hearing moans from the Christophers' apartment, he had tried to help the victims. According to his testimony, he panicked and fled when he heard police sirens and noticed the blood on his clothes. The jury returned guilty verdicts against Payne on all counts.

During the sentencing phase of the trial, Payne presented the testimony of four witnesses: his mother and father, Bobbie Thomas, and Dr. John T. Hutson, a clinical psychologist specializing in criminal court evaluation work. Bobbie Thomas testified that she met Payne at church, during a time when she was being abused by her husband. She stated that Payne was a very caring person, and that he devoted much time and attention to her three children, who were being affected by her marital difficulties. She said that the children had come to love him very much and would miss him, and that he "behaved just like a father that loved his kids." She asserted that he did not drink, nor did he use drugs, and that it was generally inconsistent with Payne's character to have committed these crimes.

Dr. Hutson testified that based on Payne's low score on an IQ test, Payne was "mentally handicapped." Hutson also said that Payne was neither psychotic nor schizophrenic, and that Payne was the most polite prisoner he had ever met. Payne's parents testified that their son had no prior criminal record and had never been arrested. They also stated that Payne had no history of alcohol or drug abuse, he worked with his father as a painter, he was good with children, and he was a good son.

The State presented the testimony of Charisse's mother, Mary Zvolanek. When asked how Nicholas had been affected by the murders of his mother and sister, she responded:

"He cries for his mom. He doesn't seem to understand why she doesn't come home. And he cries for his sister Lacie. He comes to me many times during the week and asks me, Grandmama, do you miss my Lacie. And I tell him yes. He says, I'm worried about my Lacie."

In arguing for the death penalty during closing argument, the prosecutor commented on the continuing effects of Nicholas' experience, stating:

> "But we do know that Nicholas was alive. And Nicholas was in the same room. Nicholas was still conscious. His eyes were open. He responded to the paramedics. He was able to follow their directions. He was able to hold his intestines in as he was carried to the ambulance. So he knew what happened to his mother and baby sister."

. . .

The jury sentenced Payne to death on each of the murder counts.

The Supreme Court of Tennessee affirmed the conviction and sentence. The court rejected Payne's contention that the admission of the grandmother's testimony and the State's closing argument constituted prejudicial violations of his rights under the Eighth Amendment as applied in *Booth v. Maryland*, 482 U.S. 496 (1987), and *South Carolina v. Gathers*, 490 U.S. 805 (1989).

. . .

The court determined that the prosecutor's comments during closing argument were "relevant to [Payne's] personal responsibility and moral guilt." The court explained that "[w]hen a person deliberately picks a butcher knife out of a kitchen drawer and proceeds to stab to death a twenty-eight-year-old mother, her two and one-half year old daughter and her three and one-half year old son, in the same room, the physical and mental condition of the boy he left for dead is surely relevant in determining his 'blameworthiness.'" The court concluded that any violation of Payne's rights under *Booth and Gathers* "was harmless beyond a reasonable doubt."

We granted certiorari to reconsider our holdings in Booth and Gathers that the Eighth Amendment prohibits a capital sentencing jury from considering "victim impact" evidence relating to the personal characteristics of the victim and the emotional impact of the crimes on the victim's family.

In *Booth*, the defendant robbed and murdered an elderly couple. As required by a state statute, a victim impact statement was prepared based on interviews with the victims' son, daughter, son-in-law, and granddaughter. The statement, which described the personal characteristics of the victims, the emotional impact of the crimes on the family, and set forth the family members' opinions and characterizations of the crimes and the defendant, was submitted to the jury at sentencing. The jury imposed the death penalty. The conviction and sentence were affirmed on appeal by the State's highest court.

This Court held by a 5-to-4 vote that the Eighth Amendment prohibits a jury from considering a victim impact statement at the sentencing phase of a capital trial. The Court made clear that the admissibility of victim impact evidence was not to be determined on a case-by-case basis, but that such evidence was per se inadmissible in the sentencing phase of a capital case except to the extent that it "relate[d] directly to the circumstances of the crime." In *Gathers*, decided two years later, the Court extended the rule announced in Booth to statements made by a prosecutor to the sentencing jury regarding the personal qualities of the victim.

. . .

Booth and Gathers were based on two premises: that evidence relating to a particular victim or to the harm that a capital defendant causes a victim's family do not in general reflect on the defendant's "blameworthiness," and that only evidence relating to "blameworthiness" is relevant to the capital sentencing decision. However, the assessment of harm caused by the defendant as a result of the crime charged has understandably been an important concern of the criminal law, both in determining the elements of the offense and in determining the appropriate punishment. Thus, two equally blameworthy criminal defendants may be guilty of different offenses solely because their acts cause differing amounts of harm. . . .

Wherever judges in recent years have had discretion to impose sentence, the consideration of the harm caused by the crime has been an important factor in the exercise of that discretion:

> "The first significance of harm in Anglo-American jurisprudence is, then, as a prerequisite to the criminal sanction. The second significance of harm—one no less important to judges—is as a measure of the seriousness of the offense and therefore as a standard for determining the severity of the sentence that will be meted out."

. . .

We have held that a State cannot preclude the sentence from considering "any relevant mitigating evidence" that the defendant proffers in support of a sentence less than death. . . . But it was never held or even suggested in any of our cases preceding

Booth that the defendant, entitled as he was to individualized consideration, was to receive that consideration wholly apart from the crime which he had committed.

. . .

Payne echoes the concern voiced in Booth's case that the admission of victim impact evidence permits a jury to find that defendants whose victims were assets to their community are more deserving of punishment than those whose victims are perceived to be less worthy. As a general matter, however, victim impact evidence is not offered to encourage comparative judgments of this kind—for instance, that the killer of a hardworking, devoted parent deserves the death penalty, but that the murderer of a reprobate does not. It is designed to show instead each victim's "uniqueness as an individual human being," whatever the jury might think the loss to the community resulting from his death might be. . . .

Under our constitutional system, the primary responsibility for defining crimes against state law, fixing punishments for the commission of these crimes, and establishing procedures for criminal trials rests with the States. The state laws respecting crimes, punishments, and criminal procedure are, of course, subject to the overriding provisions of the United States Constitution.

. . .

Victim impact evidence is simply another form or method of informing the sentencing authority about the specific harm caused by the crime in question, evidence of a general type long considered by sentencing authorities. We think the Booth Court was wrong in stating that this kind of evidence leads to the arbitrary imposition of the death penalty. In the majority of cases, and in this case, victim impact evidence serves entirely legitimate purposes. In the event that evidence is introduced that is so unduly prejudicial that it renders the trial fundamentally unfair, the Due Process Clause of the Fourteenth Amendment provides a mechanism for relief.

. . .

We are now of the view that a State may properly conclude that for the jury to assess meaningfully the defendant's moral culpability and blameworthiness, it should have before it at the sentencing phase evidence of the specific harm caused by the defendant. . . .

The present case is an example of the potential for such unfairness. The capital sentencing jury heard testimony Payne's girlfriend that they met at church; that he was affectionate, caring, and kind to her children; that he was not an abuser of drugs or alcohol; and that it was inconsistent with his character to have committed the murders. Payne's parents testified that he was a good son, and a clinical psychologist testified that Payne was an extremely polite prisoner and suffered from a low IQ. None of this testimony was related to the circumstances of Payne's brutal crimes. In contrast, the only evidence of the impact of Payne's offenses during the sentencing phase was Nicholas' grandmother's description—in response to a single question—that the child misses his mother and baby sister. Payne argues that the Eighth Amendment commands that the jury's death sentence must be set aside because the jury heard this testimony. But the testimony illustrated quite poignantly some of the harm that Payne's killing had caused; there is nothing unfair about allowing the jury to bear in mind that harm at the same time as it considers the mitigating evidence introduced by the defendant. . . .

We thus hold that if the State chooses to permit the admission of victim impact evidence and prosecutorial argument on that subject, the Eighth Amendment erects no per se bar. A State may legitimately conclude that evidence about the victim and about the impact of the murder on the victim's family is relevant to the jury's decision as to whether or not the death penalty should be imposed. There is no reason to treat such evidence differently than other relevant evidence is treated.

. . .

Applying these general principles, the Court has during the past 20 Terms overruled in whole or in part 33 of its previous constitutional decisions. Booth and Gathers were decided by the narrowest of margins, over spirited dissents challenging the basic underpinnings of those decisions. They have been questioned by Members of the Court in later decisions and have defied consistent application by the lower courts. . . . Reconsidering these decisions now, we conclude, for the reasons heretofore stated, that they were wrongly decided and should be, and now are, overruled. We accordingly affirm the judgment of the Supreme Court of Tennessee.

It is so ordered.

SOURCE: Payne v. Tennessee, 501 U.S. 808 (1991).

ANALYSIS

Death penalty cases are bifurcated, meaning they are split into two parts. The first part is the so-called guilt/innocence phase. If the jury acquits the defendant, the case ends. However, if the jury convicts the defendant, then there is a need for the second part of the proceeding called the sentencing phase. At the sentencing phase, the jury considers whether to impose the death penalty or perhaps a life sentence.

Victim impact evidence refers to evidence presented by the prosecution about the harms suffered by the victims in the case. It serves to inform the jury about the egregiousness and lasting harm caused by the defendant. In 1987, the U.S. Supreme Court had ruled in *Booth v. Maryland* that such victim impact evidence was prejudicial to the defendant and, therefore, unconstitutional under the Eighth Amendment.

Pervis Tyrone Payne was convicted of murdering a mother and her young daughter. At his trial, both the grandmothers of the deceased child spoke about the impact of the deaths upon the surviving son, who was stabbed repeatedly but survived. Also, the prosecutor talked about the impact on the victims during the closing argument.

In *Payne v. Tennessee*, the U.S. Supreme Court, by a vote of 6–3, overruled *Booth* and another later decision and determined that victim impact evidence at the sentencing proceeding was constitutional.

Many scholars have objected to *Payne* ruling, finding that victim impact statements are troublesome, because they have nothing to do with the culpability of the defendant. They also argue that it leads to arbitrary, inconsistent sentences and makes it difficult for defendants to rebut such evidence.

Justice Thurgood Marshall wrote a dissenting opinion in which he bitterly disagreed with his colleagues in the majority. "Cast aside today are those condemned to face society's ultimate penalty," Marshall wrote. "Tomorrow's victims may be minorities, women, or the indigent."

Marshall resigned from the Supreme Court only two hours after reading his dissent in the *Payne* case from the bench.

For his part, Pervis Tyrone Payne remains incarcerated but is no longer on death row. His attorneys argued that Payne is intellectually disabled and, thus, cannot be executed. In November 2021, he was removed from death row.

However, he remains incarcerated. He consistently has maintained his innocence of the crimes for which he was convicted. The Innocence Project continues to support Payne and has called for a fundamental reevaluation of his case. DNA testing on the murder weapon, a knife, included DNA from an unknown third party. The Innocence Project contends that this supports Payne's long-standing claims of innocence.

FURTHER READING

Dow, David R. "When Law Bows to Politics: Explaining Payne v. Tennessee." 26 *University of California Davis Law Review* 157 (1992).

Frankel, Joe. "Payne, Victim Impact Statements, and Nearly Two Decades of Devolving Standards of Decency." 12 *New York City Law Review* 87 (2008).

Selby, Danielle. "8 Things You Need to Know about Pervis Payne Who Is Facing Execution." Innocence Project. July 22, 2020.

- ***Document 26:*** Congressional Testimony of Law Professor Paul G. Cassell
- ***Date:*** April 1, 1993
- ***Where:*** Washington, D.C.
- ***Significance:*** Professor Cassell's testimony advocates that innocent persons have not been executed in recent years, thus proving that the sentence is being justly carried out. He also asserts that the failure to implement the death penalty is bad policy and dangerous.

DOCUMENT

Law Professor Testifies in Support of the Death Penalty

TESTIMONY OF LAW PROFESSOR PAUL G. CASSELL

Thanks very much, Mr. Chairman. I would like to thank you for inviting me here today to testify, and to Senator Hatch for his kind remarks earlier. I will do my best to meet the 5-minute limit. I know how anxious my students get when that red light goes on in the classroom clock, and I certainly won't indulge more than the time you have allotted.

The committee, of course, has heard today very moving statements from Mr. McMillian and Mr. Adams. I think we just heard an equally moving statement from Ms. Shehane, and the question has, of course, then is one of balancing these competing concerns.

What I would like to suggest today is a way to put these statements in context and a way to balance these concerns, and to do that I think the committee might consider a hypothetical proposal to reduce the speed limit on our Nation's highways to 5 miles per hour. After all, it might be argued we know with some certainty that perhaps an innocent person will be killed every week in a traffic accident and if we reduce the speeds, that risk would be avoided.

Yet, I take it we would all be against such a proposal, and the reason, of course, is that efficient use of our Nation's highways is very important to our country's welfare. By the same token, any fair-minded and balanced assessment of our country's capital sentencing system leads to the same type of conclusion that efficient use of capital punishment is a critical part of our country's welfare.

Now, this morning we heard testimony about the possibility that an innocent person might be executed, but unlike the undeniable deaths that occur on our Nation's highways, the best evidence is that no innocent person has been executed in this country for at least the last 50 years. And while the death penalty in recent history has a perfect record in punishing only guilty murderers, it is also equally clear that innocent lives will be put at risk from the failure to carry out capital sentences in a timely fashion where those sentences have been affirmed by the courts and reviewed by the governors for possible executive clemency.

If passed, S. 221 would substantially increase the risk of this kind of error, this risk to innocent lives, by unduly interfering with the imposition of death sentences throughout the country.

Now, it is first important to understand that S. 221 does nothing to change the risk of convicting an innocent person. Instead, it simply creates procedures designed to reduce the risk of executing an innocent person. Thus, much of today's testimony may be beside the point when considering this bill.

The Senate Judiciary Committee has previously found the risk of executing an innocent person to be minimal, and I reached the same conclusion in a 1989 article published in the Stanford Law Review with then Assistant Attorney General Stephen Markman.

We reviewed all claims of erroneous executions that had been offered by Professors Bedau and Radelet, and this morning, I believe, Mr. Chairman, you referred to their book, "In Spite of Innocence," in your opening statement.

I think it is important for the committee to be aware of some of the abuses that we located in that so-called study. Now, to give you an example, they claim-to take an example from Senator Hatch's home State and my home State of Utah, they claim that Joseph Hillstrom was innocent of murdering a shopkeeper, but was nonetheless executed by Utah in 1915. Well, I have today with me once of the courses they cite. It is entitled "Joe Hill, A Biographical Novel," and if you read the Forward-of that book, the Forward says very clearly this is fiction, with fiction's prerogatives and none of history's limiting obligations.

Now, they go on to say—and I hope I don't give away the ending of the novel for the Senators that haven't had a chance to read it, but they go on to say that—the book goes on to have its protagonist, in fact, be a guilty murderer-. Now, this isn't surprising because the Pulitzer Prize-winning author of this book, Wallace Stegner, had written a nonfiction article in which he said that Joe Hill was, in fact, a guilty murderer.

Now, this is not the only example. I have some other books with me. There is one entitled "Meet the Murderer," a rather unlikely title for a book that would be describing innocent people and, in fact, when one looks there, sure enough, they cite this book to prove that Mr. Appelgate is innocent. When you read the book it says, frankly, I do not doubt the culpability of Mr. Appelgate. And I could go through some other examples; we go through those in our articles.

But the important point is it is very easy for opponents of the death penalty to claim that an innocent person has been executed and when, in fact, you look at the court records and actual documents, as I have done, you find that these claims are not substantiated, at least back through the last 50 years.

Time Magazine did a similar thing last year where they put on their cover Roger Keith Coleman, claiming that he was innocent and, in fact, it was quite clear that a Federal district court judge reviewed all the evidence, including the newly discovered evidence that Time Magazine referred to, and found that he was guilty.

So on the one hand, no innocent person has ever been executed, at least in recently history. On the other hand, failing to carry out capital sentences in a timely fashion undeniably poses a risk to innocent persons. The death penalty, of course, when carried out, can incapacitate murderers, prevent them from killing again. It also has a very powerful deterrent effect. In my article and in my testimony today, I cite studies suggesting that perhaps as many as 125,000 innocent lives have been saved through the use of capital punishment in this century.

The relative risk—the balance that has to be struck in this area is obvious. While no innocent person has been executed in recent memory, each year more than 20,000 of the nation's citizens will be the victims of murder. The death penalty is the most visible deterrent to such crimes. Small reductions in the deterrent value of capital punishment will clearly affect many innocent lives.

Senate bill 221 would place these lives in jeopardy by making it extraordinarily difficult to execute even the most' dangerous murderers.

SOURCE: Cassell, Paul G. Testimony. Innocence and the Death Penalty: Hearing before the Committee on the Judiciary. U.S. Senate. April 1, 1993.

ANALYSIS

Law professor Paul G. Cassell, who later served as a federal district court judge between 2002 and 2007, testified before Congress in 1993 against proposed legislation that would allow inmates on death row to present evidence of newly discovered evidence of innocence.

The bill came in response to the U.S. Supreme Court's decision in *Herrera v. Collins* (1993), in which the Court ruled that an inmate did not have a right to a habeas corpus hearing to introduce evidence of actual innocence. Chief Justice William Rehnquist wrote that "[f]ew rulings would be more disruptive of our federal system than to provide for federal *habeas* review of freestanding claims of actual innocence." Rehnquist reasoned that a death row inmate must show a constitutional violation in order to have an evidentiary hearing.

Professor Cassell is primarily known as a major proponent of victims' rights, and his 1993 testimony in favor of capital punishment reflected that. Cassell cited his own study, a response to Professors Hugo Bedau and Michael Radelet's claim that some actually innocent inmates had been executed in the United States.

Cassell and co-author Stephen J. Markman examined some of these cases and came to the opposite conclusion—that these individuals likely were guilty of their convicted crimes. Cassell testified to Congress that while no inmate was executed who was innocent in recent years, "each year more than 20,000 of the nation's citizens will be the victims of murder."

Cassell also mentioned the case of Roger Keith Coleman, a Virginia inmate who was executed. The U.S. Supreme Court had denied his appeal in *Coleman v. Thompson* (1991). Many believed that Coleman was actually innocent of the crime for which he had been convicted. However, Coleman allegedly failed a polygraph when then Virginia governor Douglas Wilder was considering giving him clemency.

Years later, DNA testing showed that Coleman was guilty of the crime. Cassell mentions the *Coleman* case as an example of anti-death penalty advocates taking up causes of those who are not actually innocent. However, Cassell did acknowledge the compelling testimony earlier in the hearings of both Walter McMillan and Randall Dale Adams, two men who served time on death row for crimes they did not commit.

DID YOU KNOW?

Anti-Capital Punishment Scholar Hugo Bedau

Hugo Bedau (1926–2012) was a prominent scholar on capital punishment in the United States. Bedau's seminal text, *The Death Penalty in America*, was first published in 1964. According to fellow scholar Michael Radelet, "Bedau was the first guy to put it all together and the first to make the general empirical argument against the death penalty—that is, a little race, a little deterrent, a little innocence." Other notable works by Bedau included *Debating the Death Penalty* (2005), which he coauthored with pro-capital punishment scholar Paul Cassell.

Bedau graduated from college at the University of the Redlands in Southern California and then did graduate work at Boston University and Harvard University. He taught at several universities, but he was best known for teaching philosophy at Tufts University.

FURTHER READING

Bedau, Hugo A. *The Death Penalty in America: Current Controversies*. London: Oxford University Press, 1998.

Bedau, Hugo A., and Paul Cassell. *Debating the Death Penalty*. London: Oxford University Press, 2005.

Yardley, William. "Hugo Bedau, Philosopher Who Opposed Death Penalty, Dies at 85." *New York Times*. August 16, 2012.

FURTHER READING

Cassell, Paul G. "Overstating America's Wrongful Conviction Rate? Reassessing Conventional Wisdom about the Incidence of Wrongful Convictions." 60 *Arizona Law Review* 815 (2018).

Cassell, Paul G., and Stephen J. Markman. "Protecting the Innocent: A Response to the Bedau-Radelet Study." 41 *Stanford Law Review* 121 (1988).

- ***Document 27:*** Congressional testimony of Randall Adams
- ***Date:*** April 1, 1993
- ***Where:*** Washington, D.C.
- ***Significance:*** Randall Adams' harrowing story—told beautifully in *The Thin Blue Line*—was important for members of Congress to hear. Adams was wrongfully convicted of killing a police officer.

DOCUMENT

The Subject of the Death Row Documentary *Thin Blue Line* Tells His Story to Congress

TESTIMONY OF RANDALL ADAMS

Thank you, Senator Metzenbaum and the rest of the Senators that have gathered here together, because I believe this is a very important issue and I have listened very intently to each of you that have made an opening statement. You know, I think everyone can understand the opinions and the thoughts that you have on the issues, and that is one reason, again, I am happy to be here.

My name, of course, is Randall Adams. My story was depicted in the film "The Thin Blue Line" which was released in 1988 across the country. I am from Ohio; as Senator Metzenbaum stated, from Columbus, OH. I had gone to Dallas to try to find work and was in the Dallas area less than 2 months when I was picked up at my job site, arrested, and charged with the killing of a Dallas police officer, was indicted for capital murder. Within a few months—in fact, in April 1977, I was taken to trial. Ultimately, I was convicted and sentenced to death.

The trial lasted around 4 days, I believe it was. I took the witness stand in my own behalf and at the end of my testimony my attorney and I felt at the end of that trial-we felt that we had won the case. On the last afternoon of what we thought would be the last day of trial, the State reopened its case and introduced three witnesses that they stated had passed the scene of the crime and, you know, could positively identify me. Under oath, they, of course, testified for the State basically that they had passed the scene, and one witness testified that she had picked me out of a lineup.

Until that time, I had never been in trouble. I had never been convicted of anything other than one OMVI when I was in high school and had just learned to drive. You know, having never gone to a courtroom, having never needed an attorney, my family and I altogether was completely baffled by the system. We trusted in the system. We hoped the system, and believed in the system, that the system would work in the end.

All the way up until my conviction, we, of course, had that belief and trust that the American legal system was fair. Little did we know that the prosecutor was hiding evidence from us. Little did we know that the three witnesses now, of course, have committed perjury. We knew that at the time, but at the time of a trial if witnesses are sprung on you as surprise witnesses, how are you supposed to defend yourself? You can't do it at that point, and that is basically the time you must do it. If you cannot defend yourself at that point, you get convicted.

I understand and I believe that most prosecutors in America are honest, are ethical, but as many of you Senators have mentioned, mistakes do happen. If they are honest and ethical mistakes, it is understandable and maybe we can correct these mistakes. But when they are not honest, when they are unethical, what do we do?

Do we shut our courts down?

We have a limit now for 90 days of shutting down habeas. We did not have some of the evidence that finally caused my release for close to 9 years. I came 72 hours from execution in 1979.

Thankfully, the Supreme Court stayed my execution. Thankfully, the Supreme Court in an 8 to 1 decision overturned my case. Yes, some people in America may say it was a technicality. I have the right to a fair trial. I have the right for justice, and when that justice is used by a prosecutor to hide evidence, to pay witnesses, I think we are in a sorry state, and I am not just talking about Texas, which is where this happened. I think it happens everywhere at some point at some time, and because of that we really need to watch what we are doing.

Again, I want to thank you for allowing me to be here. I will kind of brief through this very quickly here. In December 1988, a new judge in the Dallas criminal—well, the Texas Court of Criminal Appeals made a ruling and in that ruling he stated that my hearing—well, anyway, I do believe you have this statement in front of you and you can read a lot of this.

But my conviction was originally upheld by the Texas Court of Criminal Appeals. My death sentence went to the Supreme Court in a Federal appeal. Of course, the Supreme Court removed my death sentence in 1980. I was given an automatic life sentence through the governor's office, a commuted sentence, and had to begin appealing a life sentence. It took my attorney, Randy Schaffer, and my family and myself another 8 years to finally get that life sentence removed.

It took, of course, very good legal assistance. It took the film "The Thin Blue Line." It took an investigation by Errol Morris. It took even cooperation from the

State, unknowingly. The district attorney turned over my file to the filmmaker, Errol Morris, because he thought he was doing a favorable film at the time, and there was no way my attorney could have had that file at that time, but he turned it over to a film producer, which allowed us new evidence to present back into court. In 1988, we were given evidentiary hearings and, of course, my case was overturned at that point.

Again, I thank you.

SOURCE: Adams, Randall. Testimony. Innocence and the Death Penalty: Hearing Before the Committee on the Judiciary. U.S. Senate. April 1, 1993.

ANALYSIS

The story of Randall Dale Adams is an American nightmare. He was an innocent man who was charged and convicted of killing a Dallas police officer named Robert Wood. The real culprit—a juvenile named David Harris—had spent time with Adams earlier on the day of the murder. Harris, who bragged to others that he had shot a police officer, told investigating police that Adams had committed the crime. Harris and other witnesses all gave perjured testimony that Adams had committed the crime. Adams was convicted and sentenced to death. He served more than three years on death row but then had his sentence commuted to life.

Adams spent another eight years in prison until his story was told in the powerful 1988 documentary film *The Thin Blue Line*. The documentary, written and directed by Errol Morris, included powerful evidence showing that Adams was innocent. The film even contained what seemed like an actual confession to the crime from Harris, who by then was incarcerated on death row for another offense.

A prosecutor in the case withheld exculpatory evidence in Adams' case. That is why Adams told Congress in his testimony what do we do when prosecutors act unethically and unlawfully. Adams' testimony was something he would do for much of his life after his release, when he became an anti-death penalty activist. Adams died in 2010 at the age of 61. David Harris was executed in June 2004 for another murder unrelated to the killing of the Dallas police officer.

The Thin Blue Line continues to be regarded as a classic film about the fairness of the death penalty and the criminal justice system. In 2001, it was entered into the Library of Congress' National Film Registry of "culturally, historically, or aesthetically significant" films.

FURTHER READING

Adams, Randall, with William Hoffer and Marilyn Mona Hoffer. *Adams v. Texas*. New York: St. Martin's Press, 1991.

Morris, Errol. *The Thin Blue Line* (documentary). 1988.

- ***Document 28:*** Justice Blackmun's Dissenting Opinion in U.S. Supreme Court case *Callins v. Collins*
- ***Date:*** February 22, 1994
- ***Where:*** Washington, D.C.
- ***Significance:*** Justice Harry Blackmun's dissent provided a spark of hope for opponents of the death penalty—a renewed belief that one day the Court might invalidate the death penalty, as it did years earlier in *Furman v. Georgia* (1972). They were particularly heartened by the fact that Justice Blackmun, who supported the death penalty in his dissenting opinion in *Furman*, had changed his mind about the issue.

DOCUMENT

Justice Blackmun Reverses Course, Says Capital Punishment Is Unconstitutional

On February 23, 1994, at approximately 1:00 a.m., Bruce Edwin Callins will be executed by the State of Texas. Intravenous tubes attached to his arms will carry the instrument of death, a toxic fluid designed specifically for the purpose of killing human beings. The witnesses, standing a few feet away, will behold Callins, no longer a defendant, an appellant, or a petitioner, but a man, strapped to a gurney, and seconds away from extinction.

Within days, or perhaps hours, the memory of Callins will begin to fade. The wheels of justice will churn again, and somewhere, another jury or another judge will have the unenviable task of determining whether some human being is to live or die. We hope, of course, that the defendant whose life is at risk will be represented by competent counsel—someone who is inspired by the awareness that a less-than-vigorous defense truly could have fatal consequences for the defendant. We hope that the attorney will investigate all aspects of the case, follow all evidentiary and procedural rules, and appear before a judge who is still committed to the protection of defendants' rights—even now, as the prospect of meaningful judicial oversight has diminished. In the same vein, we hope that the prosecution, in urging the penalty of death, will have exercised its discretion wisely, free from bias, prejudice, or political motive, and will be humbled, rather than emboldened, by the awesome authority conferred by the State.

But even if we can feel confident that these actors will fulfill their roles to the best of their human ability, our collective conscience will remain uneasy. Twenty years have passed since this Court declared that the death penalty must be imposed fairly, and with reasonable consistency, or not at all, and, despite the effort of the States and courts to devise legal formulas and procedural rules to meet this daunting challenge, the death penalty remains fraught with arbitrariness, discrimination, caprice, and mistake. This is not to say that the problems with the death penalty today are identical to those that were present 20 years ago. Rather, the problems that were pursued down one hole with procedural rules and verbal formulas have come to the surface somewhere else, just as virulent and pernicious as they were in their original form. Experience has taught us that the constitutional goal of eliminating arbitrariness and discrimination from the administration of death can never be achieved without compromising an equally essential component of fundamental fairness—individualized sentencing.

It is tempting, when faced with conflicting constitutional commands, to sacrifice one for the other or to assume that an acceptable balance between them already has been struck. In the context of the death penalty, however, such jurisprudential maneuvers are wholly inappropriate. The death penalty must be imposed "fairly, and with reasonable consistency, or not at all."

. . .

Reasonable consistency, on the other hand, requires that the death penalty be inflicted evenhandedly, in accordance with reason and objective standards, rather than by whim, caprice, or prejudice. Finally, because human error is inevitable, and because our criminal justice system is less than perfect, searching appellate review of death sentences and their underlying convictions is a prerequisite to a constitutional death penalty scheme.

. . .

From this day forward, I no longer shall tinker with the machinery of death. For more than 20 years I have endeavored—indeed, I have struggled—along with a majority of this Court, to develop procedural and substantive rules that would lend more than the mere appearance of fairness to the death penalty endeavor. Rather than continue to coddle the Court's delusion that the desired level of fairness has been achieved and the need for regulation eviscerated, I feel morally and intellectually obligated simply to concede that the death penalty experiment has failed. It is virtually self-evident to me now that no combination of procedural rules or substantive regulations ever can save the death penalty from its inherent constitutional deficiencies. The basic question—does the system accurately and consistently determine which defendants "deserve" to die?—cannot be answered in the affirmative. . . .

I dissented in Furman. . . . Four years after Furman was decided, I concurred in the judgment in *Gregg v. Georgia*, 428 U.S. 153 (1976), and its companion cases which upheld death sentences rendered under statutes passed after Furman was decided. . . .

There is little doubt now that Furman's essential holding was correct. Although most of the public seems to desire, and the Constitution appears to permit, the penalty of death, it surely is beyond dispute that if the death penalty cannot be administered consistently and rationally, it may not be administered at all. . . .

Delivering on the *Furman* promise, however, has proved to be another matter. *Furman* aspired to eliminate the vestiges of racism and the effects of poverty in capital sentencing; it deplored the "wanton" and "random" infliction of death by a government with constitutionally limited power. *Furman* demanded that the sentencer's discretion be directed and limited by procedural rules and objective standards in order to minimize the risk of arbitrary and capricious sentences of death.

. . .

This development in the American conscience would have presented no constitutional dilemma if fairness to the individual could be achieved without sacrificing the consistency and rationality promised in Furman. But over the past two decades, efforts to balance these competing constitutional commands have been to no avail. Experience has shown that the consistency and rationality promised in Furman are inversely related to the fairness owed the individual when considering a sentence of death. A step toward consistency is a step away from fairness.

B

There is a heightened need for fairness in the administration of death. This unique level of fairness is born of the appreciation that death truly is different from all other punishments a society inflicts upon its citizens. . . .

Over time, I have come to conclude that even this approach is unacceptable: It simply reduces, rather than eliminates, the number of people subject to arbitrary sentencing. It is the decision to sentence a defendant to death—not merely the decision to make a defendant eligible for death—that may not be arbitrary. While one might hope that providing the sentencer with as much relevant mitigating evidence as possible will lead to more rational and consistent sentences, experience has taught otherwise. It seems that the decision whether a human being should live or die is so inherently subjective—rife with all of life's understandings, experiences, prejudices, and passions—that it inevitably defies the rationality and consistency required by the Constitution.

E

The arbitrariness inherent in the sentencer's discretion to afford mercy is exacerbated by the problem of race. Even under the most sophisticated death penalty statutes, race continues to play a major role in determining who shall live and who shall die. Perhaps it should not be surprising that the biases and prejudices that infect society generally would influence the determination of who is sentenced to death, even within the narrower pool of death-eligible defendants selected according to objective standards. . . .

A renowned example of racism infecting a capital-sentencing scheme is documented in *McCleskey v. Kemp*, 481 U.S. 279 (1987). . . .

Despite this staggering evidence of racial prejudice infecting Georgia's capital-sentencing scheme, the majority turned its back on McCleskey's claims, apparently troubled by the fact that Georgia had instituted more procedural and substantive safeguards than most other States since *Furman*, but was still unable to stamp out the virus of racism. . . .

F

In the years since McCleskey, I have come to wonder whether there was truth in the majority's suggestion that discrimination and arbitrariness could not be purged from the administration of capital punishment without sacrificing the equally essential component of fairness—individualized sentencing. Viewed in this way, the consistency promised in Furman and the fairness to the individual demanded in Lockett are not only inversely related, but irreconcilable in the context of capital punishment. . . .

Perhaps one day this Court will develop procedural rules or verbal formulas that actually will provide consistency, fairness, and reliability in a capital-sentencing scheme. I am not optimistic that such a day will come. I am more optimistic, though, that this Court eventually will conclude that the effort to eliminate arbitrariness while preserving fairness "in the infliction of [death] is so plainly doomed to failure that it—and the death penalty—must be abandoned altogether." I may not live to see that day, but I have faith that eventually it will arrive. The path the Court has chosen lessens us all. I dissent.

SOURCE: Callins v. Collins, 510 U.S. 1141 (1994).

ANALYSIS

In *Callins v. Collins* (1994), the U.S. Supreme Court declined to review Bruce Edwin Callins' death penalty appeal. In June 1980, a then 20-year-old Callins entered a Dallas bar armed and robbed the place and its customers. He apparently believed that one customer, Allen Huckleberry, did not hand over all his money and shot him in the neck, killing him.

A jury convicted him of murder and sentenced him to death two years later. His case then worked its way through, first, the Texas state court system and then the federal courts. His last chance at appeal was the U.S. Supreme Court, sometimes known as "the court of last resort." But it takes four justices to vote for the Court to hear an appeal. Instead, the Court denied certiorari, a legal term meaning it decided not to hear Callins' appeal. He was executed in May 1997.

Justice Harry Blackmun dissented with the majority's 1994 decision to deny certiorari, holding that the Court should have heard Callins' appeal. Blackmun used the dissenting opinion to take aim at the death penalty system in the United States. It was a remarkable change of heart for the justice, who came on the Court back in 1971. In 1972, as he acknowledges in his *Callins* dissent, Blackmun had dissented in *Furman v. Georgia* (1972). That decision had effectively banned the death penalty in the United States for several years.

In the intervening years, Blackmun had come to believe that the death penalty system was broken and that it was infected with discrimination and other problems. "Even under the most sophisticated death penalty statutes, race continues to play a major role in determining who shall live and who shall die," he wrote.

But, the most oft-quoted line of his dissent was the following: "From this day forward, I shall no longer tinker with the machinery of death." It was Blackmun's formal denunciation of the death penalty and what one newspaper reporter called the end of a "tortuous personal odyssey" for Blackmun.

Justice Antonin Scalia wrote a separate concurring opinion taking aim at Justice Blackmun's dissent. Scalia emphasized the text of the Fifth Amendment: "[N]o person shall be held to answer for a capital . . . crime, unless on a presentment or indictment of a Grand Jury, . . . nor be deprived of life . . . without due process of law." Scalia focused on the fact that the Fifth Amendment, part of the text of the Constitution, surely thought that capital punishment was proper, as it speaks of a "capital" crime. He accused Blackmun of bringing to bear his moral and personal opposition to the death penalty in his opinion rather than on "the text and tradition of the Constitution."

But, many in the abolitionist community applauded Justice Blackmun's dissenting opinion. The *New York Times*' Supreme Court reporter Linda Greenhouse called Blackmun's 7,000-word dissenting opinion "remarkable."

FURTHER READING

Greenhouse, Linda. "Death Penalty Is Renounced by Blackmun." *New York Times*. February 23, 1994.

Smith, Stephen F. "Has the 'Machinery of Death' Become a Clunker?" 49 *University of Richmond Law Review* 845 (2015).

Stewart, Malcolm L. "Justice Blackmun's Capital Punishment Jurisprudence." 26 *Hastings Constitutional Law Quarterly* 271 (1998–1999).

- ***Document 29:*** Death Penalty Moratorium Resolution from the American Bar Association
- ***Date:*** February 3, 1997
- ***Where:*** Chicago
- ***Significance:*** The American Bar Association (ABA) is the largest association of attorneys in the United States, and its influence on the legal community is significant. When the ABA called for a stop to the death penalty, the organization's stand garnered considerable attention from the legal community and the general public alike.

DOCUMENT

American Bar Association Calls for a Moratorium on the Death Penalty

RECOMMENDATION

RESOLVED, That the American Bar Association calls upon each jurisdiction that imposes capital punishment not to carry out the death penalty until the jurisdiction implements policies and procedures that are consistent with the following longstanding American Bar Association policies intended to (1) ensure that death penalty cases are administered fairly and impartially, in accordance with due process, and (2) minimize the risk that innocent persons may be executed:

(i) Implementing ABA "Guidelines for the Appointment and Performance of Counsel in Death Penalty Cases" (adopted Feb. 1989) and Association policies intended to encourage competency of counsel in capital cases (adopted Feb. 1979, Feb. 1988, Feb. 1990, Aug. 1996);

(ii) Preserving, enhancing, and streamlining state and federal courts' authority and responsibility to exercise independent judgment on the merits of constitutional claims in state post-conviction and federal *habeas corpus* proceedings (adopted Aug. 1982, Feb. 1990);

(iii) Striving to eliminate discrimination in capital sentencing on the basis of the race of either the victim or the defendant (adopted Aug. 1988, Aug. 1991); and

(iv) Preventing execution of mentally retarded persons (adopted Feb. 1989) and persons who were under the age of 18 at the time of their offenses (adopted Aug. 1983).

FURTHER RESOLVED, That in adopting this recommendation, apart from existing Association policies relating to offenders who are mentally retarded or under the age of 18 at the time of the commission of the offenses, the Association takes no position on the death penalty.

American Bar Association. Death Penalty Moratorium Resolution. 1997. https://www.americanbar.org/groups/committees/death_penalty_representation/resources/dp-policy/moratorium-1997/

ANALYSIS

The ABA, the largest association of lawyers in the United States, is a prominent organization in the legal profession. When the ABA acts, many states and federal government officials at the very least listen and pay attention.

In its accompanying report to this February 1997 resolution, the ABA said that it was time for the organization to take "additional decisive action with regard to the death penalty." The ABA believed that since the reinstitution of the death penalty with the Supreme Court's decision in *Gregg v. Georgia* (1976), the death penalty has not been implemented with a sufficient level of fairness. Moreover, the organization's leadership pointed out that too many persons on death row had been exonerated only on the eve of execution.

The American Civil Liberties Union wrote about the significant impact of the ABA's death penalty moratorium: "ABA's previous Moratorium Resolution of February 3, 1997 identifying flaws in the death penalty has had a profound impact on how the nation, including the Supreme Court, views the constitutionality of the administration of the death penalty."

For example, the ABA resolution called for an end to the execution of inmates who are intellectually disabled (the ABA resolution uses common terminology of the period that has since fallen into disfavor). After this resolution, many states passed laws that forbade the execution of intellectually disabled inmates. The U.S. Supreme Court followed suit in *Atkins v. Virginia* (2002), ruling that it violated the Eighth Amendment to execute intellectually disabled inmates.

Similarly, the ABA resolution calls for an end to the execution of inmates who committed murder when they were juveniles. Many states also banned that practice, and the U.S. Supreme Court ruled in *Roper v. Simmons* (2005) that such a practice constitutes cruel and unusual punishment.

The ABA resolution also called for better training of attorneys who handle death penalty cases. Unfortunately, many inmates who are convicted in death penalty cases were represented by attorneys who did not show effective assistance of counsel. In its accompanying report, the ABA writes that it "is especially well positioned to identify the professional legal services that should be available to capital defendants and death row inmates." The ABA warns that many grossly incompetent and underpaid attorneys are handling death penalty cases.

The resolution also emphasizes the need to reduce, if not eliminate, the ugly specter of racial discrimination and racial biases in the criminal justice system and specifically capital cases. The ABA warns of the "corrosive effects" of racial discrimination in capital cases.

FURTHER READING

Associated Press. "Bar Association Leaders Urge Moratorium on Death Penalty." *New York Times*. February 4, 1997.

Coleman, James E., Jr. "Foreword." 61 *Law & Contemporary Problems* 1 (1998).

Editorial Board. "A Lawyerly Cry of Conscience." *New York Times*. February 22, 1997.

Thompson, Kara. "ABA's Resolution Calling for a Moratorium on Executions: What Jurisdictions Can Do to Ensure That the Death Penalty Is Imposed Responsibly." 40 *Arizona Law Review* 1515 (1998).

- ***Document 30:*** Dr. Pat Robertson's Speech at William & Mary
- ***Date:*** April 7, 2000
- ***Where:*** William & Mary College in Williamsburg, Virginia
- ***Significance:*** Dr. Pat Robertson, a popular conservative televangelist and personality, criticized the death penalty in his 2000 speech that he delivered at William and Mary College in Virginia. His remarks vividly underscored the fact that opposition to capital punishment can span the political spectrum. He talked about the possibility of human redemption.

DOCUMENT

Televangelist Pat Robertson Calls for "Justice Tempered with Mercy"

I'm very honored and delighted to discuss this important topic with you today. I want to talk a little bit about the role of religion and the death penalty, and I'd like to share some personal experiences because they have touched my heart, perhaps more than just a cold understanding of what the Bible says or what Christian ethics say.

About fifteen years ago, I was in the maximum-security prison in Raiford, Florida, and after I had spoken to the inmates, and had several interviews for our television program, I was permitted to go back into death row. It was a very sobering sight because the electric chair was just down the hall from where I was, and you could see that rather grim room. There were two men that they had asked me to talk to. One was a young man, in his mid-twenties who had been a contract killer for organized crime. He had dispatched at least twenty people to the next world as a cold-blooded killer. He was there on death row awaiting execution.

The other man was a rather simple soul who had discovered his wife having an affair with another man, at least that's my understanding, and in a fit of rage, he killed her. In the subsequent trial, he had received the death penalty for his action.

Both of these men had had profound religious conversions. I know the difference between some jailhouse conversions—and there are plenty of them out there—and something that's sincere from the heart. Both of these men, in my opinion, had been spiritually transformed.

I went into that prison, not so much as a sociologist, or lawyer, or professor, but as a minister to minister to them. I carried with me a clear knowledge of what the Bible had to say about the death penalty. If you go back into the 20th chapter of Leviticus, for example, it chronicles the list of offenses that brought death. Among them were bestiality, adultery, incest, offering children to Molech and the pagan gods, and so on. It was a rather comprehensive list and each one of them involved the death penalty. The one who recorded that was Moses, the same one who recorded the Ten Commandments. People say, the commandment says "Thou shall not kill" and it says "Thou shall not commit murder," and these were offenses.

I knew in the Old Testament it says when blood is shed on the ground, the earth is to be cleansed by the shedding of blood I also was familiar with the New Testament, where in the trial of Jesus, the Jewish leaders said, "We have a law, and by our law, he needs to die." I'm also aware of what happened with the first martyr, Stephen—who was stoned to death because of his religious beliefs—who said, "I saw Jesus, I saw God," and they stopped their ears. They said he was a heretic and they stoned him to death. The apostle Paul wrote in his letter to the Romans, "The civil authority wields the sword and he doesn't do so in vain, but he's a minister of God to bring vengeance on the malefactors." I was aware of all that when I went in to talk to these men.

I went in as strongly pro-capital punishment. Now, I'm going to pray with two men who are facing death in a week. Both of them have had religious conversions and are now my brothers in Christ. So what am I going to do with them? I could pray a prayer, "Oh God, give them grace to be launched into the next world," or I could say, "Oh God, please commute their sentences so that they won't face this terrible fate." I didn't know how to pray. They were in adjoining cells. I took the hand of one in this cell, took the hand of the other, put their hands through the bars and I held both of their hands, and I said, "Oh God, I don't know what to ask for, but I ask for a miracle. Amen." I told them "God bless you and I'll see you later."

The next day, the Florida Supreme Court reversed both of their sentences of execution. They were released into the prison population, and the death sentences had effectively been commuted. The One, who in my opinion stands above all the courts in this world, had ruled that in their cases there would be no death penalty.

It was certainly not up to me to argue with God, because I didn't ask Him for anything except a miracle and it was up to Him to decide what to do. I didn't say to the Lord, "If you just read Leviticus, here's what it says," or "here's what the apostle Paul wrote in the book of Romans." I didn't tell Him all those things, because I presume He knows the Bible a whole lot better than I do. I merely asked for a miracle, and that was what He did.

Well, I had another very profound experience some years later, fairly recently, that dealt with a woman whose name was Karla Faye Tucker. Now, Karla Faye, as a young girl-I presume she was a teenager or just into her very early twenties-had been involved in a hippie lifestyle, a heavy user of drugs, and had taken up with a boyfriend who himself had been a drug dealer.

While in a drug-crazed state, the boyfriend said, "Karla Faye, there's a man in an apartment who has cheated me in a drug deal and we need to take vengeance on him." So they planned to go and take severe vengeance. They took with them a pick-ax to punish this person, and I presume, kill him. Well, it just so happened that this man, this reputed drug dealer, was now in bed with the wife of a citizen of Dallas who had been put out of her house. Her husband, a rather brutish gentleman, had rejected her entreaties to let her return to her home, and he literally threw her out of the house. He wouldn't let her come back even though she asked her children to ask daddy to let her come home; he wouldn't do it. So, through his actions, and perhaps through her will, she was now in harm's way.

Karla Faye and her boyfriend broke the door down to the apartment, came upon this couple in bed and brutally murdered them with a pick-ax. There was blood all over the place. It was just an absolutely heinous crime that was committed by these people, as I say, under the influence of drugs. They were tried—duly tried—the evidence was clear. They were guilty of the crime, there was no question about it, and they were sentenced to the death penalty.

In the process, there were thirteen years of appeals for Karla Faye to get her sentence commuted in some fashion. During that period, she had a profound conversion experience, and when we sent a reporter down to talk to her, we didn't find some wild-eyed hippie, we found the most beautiful Christian woman we had encountered . . . sublime, if I can use that term, a lovely spirit. The person who had committed those crimes really wasn't there anymore. She was like a different person, and when we interviewed her and showed her testimony on television, and others did the same thing, they found a person who was absolutely radiant. It was so impressive, actually, that during her time of incarceration, she married the assistant chaplain of the prison. Even though they couldn't have any physical contact with each other, they got married anyhow, because there was a bond of love between them.

We did everything we could to see if there wasn't a possibility of mercy in that case. What we were dealing with was not justice; it was vengeance. We said, "Is there some way that her sentence can be commuted?" Well, Texas has a rather unique prison system in terms of the pardon and parole board. They are supposed to be a deliberating body, but they don't ever meet to deliberate. As a matter of fact, we found that up to that time, they had never had a meeting where they all got together in one place. They communicated by mail with each other. They sent reports when somebody was coming up for the possible commutation of sentence or pardon and they decided by mail. Up to that time, they had never commuted anybody's sentence for anything. So, it was very difficult.

We also put a great deal of pressure on Governor George W. Bush, and he said, basically, "My hands are tied; I can't do anything about this." We said, "But there's got to be an escape valve in the law for some type of mercy." He said, "The law is clear in Texas. The governor cannot commute a sentence unless it's on the recommendation of the pardon and parole board, and this board has voted not to commute Karla Faye's sentence. She was duly tried and they did not determine that there was going to be any mercy." So the execution went forward. The brutish individual who had thrown his wife out of the house and put her in harm's way was quoted as saying, "[k]ill the bitch," talking about Karla Faye. Outside the prison, it was like a Roman circus. There was bloodthirstiness out there, they were cursing and cheering and chanting for her to be executed-this beautiful person that we had grown to love. When we showed her on our show the day before her execution, there wasn't a dry eye in our place, but there wasn't a thing anybody could do about it except through that particular board.

Just for your edification or information, there are twelve states in the U.S. that do not have a death penalty. Fifteen states have unilateral clemency power given to the governor who can pardon who he or she sees fit. Virginia is one of the states that gives the governor that power. Some states have a clemency board whose decisions are not binding on the governor. In nine states, the governor can commute a death sentence only on the recommendation of the clemency board. That is the case in Texas, as in Arizona, Delaware, Florida, Indiana, Louisiana, Montana, Oklahoma, and Pennsylvania. Three states have only a clemency board, cutting the governor out entirely: Connecticut, Georgia, and Idaho, and then there are three others that have the governor as a member of the pardoning board-Nebraska, Nevada, and Utah.

Apparently, in most states there is some kind of relief from the death penalty. In Illinois, they've suspended the death penalty because there have been so many people, apparently a large proportion of whom are poor blacks, or African- Americans, who have been unjustly accused and unjustly tried and who have been sentenced to death on charges that are not supported.

In the last ten or twenty years, politicians were concerned with what seemed to be a rising crime wave in America. They passed a sentencing bill which itself has become a nightmare. The United States has perhaps as high a percentage of its population incarcerated as any other country, with the possible exception of Communist China. It is a shocking fact that in certain federal prisons some prisoners spend thirty years, even forty years in prison. In Virginia, we've passed a law that takes away the privilege of parole, so except in rare occasions, there's no parole opportunity.' When politicians go before the voters, the voters say, "[w]e're sick of this crime wave, we want something done about it." The next push, of course, was not just to lock people up for a long time. They said in order to show harshness against crime we have to put a barrier against crime, and this is the death penalty.

In 1976, the Supreme Court brought down what is called the *Gregg* decision, and they re-instituted the death penalty for capital crimes so long as there was a dual track system of justice and some other appropriate safeguards. In 1972, the Supreme Court had banned capital punishment entirely, saying it was cruel and unjust punishment. Now, they came back and changed their mind. Since that *Gregg* decision in the United States, we've had over five hundred executions since 1976, including sixty-eight in one year a couple years ago. Thirty-one states, most in the South, conducted executions. Texas topped the list with twenty in 1998 and thirty-seven in 1997. Nationwide, we now have 3,517 people—that was as of last year—awaiting execution. So, there's been a dramatic increase in people who have been convicted and sentenced to death.

I'm under the impression that in Ohio alone, there are over one hundred people who are now awaiting sentences of death. I don't think that really speaks well for our society because we're looking at vengeance, or we're looking at capital punishment, as a way to mitigate against the fact that we have taken many of our moral standards away from our young people. We have an epidemic of drugs and broken homes and out-of-wedlock births, and young people are growing up without proper influences in their lives. The stopgap is that if people don't conform, we're going to put them in prison or we're going to execute them.

I think we're going at it the wrong way. From a religious standpoint, what we need is to bring moral values back into the schools and into the home. What we need to do is to strengthen families, and particularly to make sure young people have some kind of an intact family where they can identify their fathers. Young boys in particular need fathers—they need a parental influence. When they don't have that, they're going to tend to move into gangs and crime.

In many of the inner cities-I've worked a great deal in the inner cities of America—I have found that there's a sense of hopelessness among many of these young men. They don't have enough education—we're not teaching them how to read and write properly in the schools. They can't succeed in a high-tech society because they don't have the learning skills that they need, so they tend to be bored in school, then they drop out of school at an early age, and they hang around on street corners. Crime and drugs are major opportunities because, after all, if you can make $100 a day selling drugs, why should you take a job at minimum wage doing some unpleasant task? So many people are moving in that direction, and they're the ones who are arrested, and they're the ones who often commit the violent crime.

We have in our society the need for something far, far more profound than merely executing three thousand people. That's not going to solve society's problems. And if the death penalty is going to be effective at all, it needs to be swift and certain. But it's not swift and it's not certain. In the case of Karla Faye Tucker, she waited thirteen years on death row in the anguish and agony of not knowing what's going to happen tomorrow, through endless appeals, where there was absolutely no certainty and there certainly were no deterrents to crime. It does not seem to have deterred any crime whatsoever from what we can gather, in this era. The only thing we can say about the death penalty, as it's currently being applied, is that it does keep society from having to pay for hardened criminals for the rest of their lives, and a year in prison costs about what an education at Harvard would cost. Having gone to Yale, I'm not sure if they're comparable in their value or not, but nevertheless, it's very expensive to incarcerate people.

Perhaps you don't realize the religious roots of the term "penitentiary," but the early Puritans and others thought that if somebody had broken the law, then by putting him in some kind of confinement that he would become penitent—that he would become sorry for his sins and he would ask God's forgiveness. That's where the word penitentiary comes from.

I don't think that there are many people locked up in penitentiaries today who are exactly sorry for their sins, and who are in their cells praying. I think there's a great deal more training now in violence, and they've become hardened and skillful criminals when they come out.

But there's something else, and I want to commend His Holiness John Paul II on his stand in relation to life. I think it's very important. I do believe, from Protestants and Catholics alike, that we must recognize that life is a seamless whole. It is very hard for those who are of the liberal political persuasion to say, "Well, we oppose the death penalty of hardened criminals because this is a barbaric act, and yet we applaud the slaughter of-now it's almost forty million unborn babies-through abortion." We can't have it both ways. We can't have [Dr. Jack] Kevorkian and people like him advocating euthanasia of the elderly and creating a culture of death, while we say, in this one particular discreet segment of our population, those who really have done things that are wrong should be let go and kept at society's expense for the rest of their lives.

I think that if we're going to deal with this matter, we've got a much, much larger scene that we need to address. And, that is the question, are we going to be for life? The Pope is for life, and so he says, "I'm opposed to the death penalty." That's fine, because he's also opposed to the killing of innocent unborn babies. So, it's a seamless whole, and I believe that we need to address that if we're going to grapple with the whole question of the dignity of life. I, frankly, stand before you as one who is in favor of the death penalty. I'm not opposed to the death penalty as such for somebody like Charles Manson who's a vicious killer, who has brutally murdered people, who apparently is crazed enough that if he's let back on the streets he would kill again. I'm not sure society needs to be burdened with somebody like that. I don't think there's anything morally wrong, there's certainly nothing biblically wrong about an execution. I'm not opposed to it personally, and I don't think the Old Testament, which is the rule of faith and practice of most of the Christian denominations and the Jewish faith as well, opposes it. We can say that there's a moral biblical basis for just doing away with the death penalty and not having it. I think people can come to the point, as I have, that we must temper justice with mercy.

There has to be the concept of mercy. There has to be the ability of legislators, governors, judges, to determine when mercy is applicable and not be bound that certain things have to be done—that there has to be a sentence of death, or that there has to be this killing. The last thing that we need in our society is the Roman orgy and spectacle of an execution where people are cheering and applauding the killing of somebody. We don't need that sort of thing in our society. We need to have a society based on love, a society based on compassion, a society based on mercy. Having said that, I also want to say that hardened killers and career criminals and those who would use the system to continue lives of crime, are not necessarily candidates for a great deal of mercy in society. In a state like Virginia, where we just had an execution, I talked to the governor about it. The condemned man, Lonnie Weeks, had shot a Virginia state patrolman. He asked for one basic thing: he wanted to be able to speak to the relatives of that patrolman, to ask forgiveness because he had taken the life of their loved one, and he was being prevented from doing that by the prison system. I interceded with the governor, and I think he said, "I don't want to get into a big public relations battle," and I don't blame him for that. They did arrange for Lonnie to call the patrolman's sister living in California. They didn't want to arrange a visit because they didn't want a circus and these things become circuses if they're not careful. In that case, again, Lonnie Weeks said, "I have made peace with God, I have done something wrong, and I just want to ask forgiveness of those that I offended." I think he died at peace with God. I think that all of us in our society are somewhat ambivalent about how to deal with the raging crime wave. We have organized crime pushing crack-cocaine, heroin, amphetamines, barbiturates, and designer drugs on the young. They're destroying the lives of millions of people, ruining the futures of young people, and

I think society wants to deal with that. At the same time, I believe that the sentencing guidelines that are currently in effect, that have been passed by Congress under this anti-crime wave fervor, need to be amended. The law just has to be changed to give judges discretion again. We don't want people to get slaps on the wrists if they've done something terrible, but at the same time, judges have to have discretion so that he just doesn't put someone in jail for ten years or twenty years, or thirty years or forty years, for a relatively minor offense.

On a broader basis for our society, we need, in my opinion, a vast public relations campaign to change the hearts of our nation toward mercy, toward a respect for life, toward a culture of compassion, and not a culture of death. The root cause of the crime wave is not just a few miscreants. I think we have a problem throughout our society. We had it in Columbine. We had it in other areas where young people have felt alienated from society. They have gone out and committed terrible acts. They have killed their fellow students, have gone on shooting rampages, and there has to be something that touches their hearts. They have to be changed from within.

I believe that in this nation, we need to return to some of the basic biblical values: the Ten Commandments, the Sermon on the Mount, some of the things that would show respect for God, that we should honor Him and love Him. Our society cannot exist strictly on a materialistic basis, because when we give ourselves over strictly to humanism, and strictly to materialism, we find the situation that we're in. I believe that what society is doing to stop it is really not the right way. I would argue for more mercy. I would certainly argue that in the state legislatures, in the laws that are currently on the books, that something be done to ameliorate the harsh edge of justice and bring about-as in the case of Karla Faye Tucker and others-the mercy that this situation cries out for so desperately.

SOURCE: © M. G. Robertson

Robertson, Pat. Transcript of Address on Religion's Role in the Administration of the Death Penalty, College of William and Mary. *William and Mary Bill of Rights Journal* 9, no. 1 (April 7, 2000). https://scholarship.law.wm.edu/cgi/viewcontent.cgi?article=1378&context=wmborj

ANALYSIS

Few people ever thought they would hear conservative religious televangelist and social commentator Pat Robertson ever criticize the death penalty, but that is exactly what he did in a speech at the College of William and Mary in April 2000. Robertson notes in his speech that he is not morally opposed to the death penalty itself, citing various passages in the Bible that support the ultimate punishment. However, Robertson expressed grave concerns about the administration of the death penalty, noting that it often was imposed on poor and minority criminal defendants.

Robertson also was moved by the religious conversions of several inmates that he met on death row. He especially emphasized the story of Karla Faye Tucker, who was convicted of murdering two persons in 1983 with a pickax. However, while awaiting trial and during her time on death row, Tucker—who had been exposed to drugs and sex at an early age—had a widely publicized conversion to Christianity.

Tucker's conversion impressed many as completely sincere, and Pat Robertson was one of her most vocal supporters. He pleaded with Texas governor (and future president) George W. Bush to commute her sentence to life in prison, but Governor Bush claimed that his hands were tied by the state parole board.

The efforts of Robertson and countless other high-profile individuals failed to change the fate of Tucker, who was executed by lethal injection in Texas in 1998 after spending 13 years on death row. Robertson mentioned her long stay on death row as one of his complaints about the death penalty.

Robertson also devoted much of his address to the need for mercy—what he termed "justice tempered with mercy." He criticized politicians' tendency to demand "tough-on-crime" bills and laws that take discretion out of judge's hands to mitigate sentences when appropriate.

Robertson also talked about visiting with other death row inmates, including two men in Florida who had their sentences commuted. Robertson related to the audience his feeling that their religious conversions were sincere and heartfelt, as he believed to be the case with Karla Faye Tucker.

Robertson also reiterated a frequent criticism of the death penalty—that it fails to deter crime. Essentially, Robertson's view is that certain hardened criminals do not stop to think about whether or not they will be executed if they are caught and convicted.

Another theme of Robertson's speech was providing greater educational opportunities for youth, particularly in the inner cities. These juveniles often lack two-parent families and the resources to avoid trouble and problems.

During the question-and-answer session after his prepared remarks, Robertson said he was not opposed to a moratorium on executions in the United States until the system was improved and much more fair.

FURTHER READING

Masters, Brooke A. "Pat Robertson Urges Moratorium on U.S. Executions." *Washington Post*. April 8, 2000.

Strom, Linda. *Karla Faye Tucker Set Free: Life and Faith on Death Row*. Wheaton, IL: Shaw Books, 2000.

- ***Document 31:*** Statement by President Bill Clinton on Temporarily Staying Execution of Federal Death Row Inmate
- ***Date:*** December 7, 2000
- ***Where:*** Washington, D.C.
- ***Significance:*** The decision showed that President Clinton was attuned to the reality of concerns over racial disparities in the death penalty—a persistent criticism of the U.S. system of capital punishment.

DOCUMENT

President Clinton Issues a Stay of Execution, Citing Racial Disparities in Capital Punishment Cases

Today I have decided to stay the execution of Juan Raul Garza, an inmate on Federal death row, for 6 months, until June, 2001, to allow the Justice Department time to gather and properly analyze more information about racial and geographic disparities in the Federal death penalty system.

I believe that the death penalty is appropriate for the most heinous crimes. As President, I have signed Federal legislation that authorizes it under certain circumstances. It is clearly, however, an issue of the most serious weight. The penalty of death, as Justice Potter Stewart and Justice Sandra Day O'Connor have reminded us, is "qualitatively different" from other punishments we impose. Whether one supports the death penalty or opposes it, there should be no question that the gravity and finality of the penalty demand that we be certain that when it is imposed, it is imposed fairly.

As I have said before, supporters of capital punishment bear a special responsibility to ensure the fairness of this irreversible punishment. Further, Article II of the Constitution vests in the President the sole authority to grant pardons and reprieves for Federal crimes. Therefore, I have approached this matter with great deliberation.

This fall the Department of Justice released the results of a statistical survey of the Federal death penalty. It found that minority defendants and certain geographic districts are disproportionately represented in Federal death penalty prosecutions. As the Deputy Attorney General said at the time the survey was released, no one confronted with those statistics can help but be troubled by those disparities. We do not, however, fully understand what lies behind those statistics. The Attorney General has said that more information and a broader analysis are needed to better interpret the data we now have and to determine whether the disparities that are evident reflect any bias in our system. She has undertaken an effort to gather and analyze the relevant information so that an appropriate decision can be made on the question of bias.

After a close and careful review of this issue and after conferring with the Attorney General and the Deputy Attorney General, I am not satisfied that, given the uncertainty that exists, it is appropriate to go forward with an execution in a case that may implicate the very issues at the center of that uncertainty.

In issuing this stay, I have not decided that the death penalty should not be imposed in this case, in which heinous crimes were proved. Nor have I decided to halt all executions in the Federal system. I have simply concluded that the examination of possible racial and regional bias should be completed before the United States goes forward with an execution in a case that may implicate the very questions raised by the Justice Department's continuing study. In this area, there is no room for error.

I have asked that the Attorney General report to the President by the end of April, 2001, on the Justice Department's analysis of the racial and geographic disparities in Federal death penalty prosecutions.

SOURCE: Clinton, Bill. Statement on the Decision to Stay the Execution of Juan Raul Garza. December 7, 2000. American Presidency Project. https://www.presidency.ucsb.edu/documents/statement-the-decision-stay-the-execution-juan-raul-garza

ANALYSIS

Juan Raul Garza was convicted and sentenced to death in 1993 in Brownsville, Texas, for killing three men. He ran a drug distribution network that had imported tons of marijuana into the United States from Mexico. Garza filed a series of appeals in the federal court to no avail.

His conviction was deemed controversial by some in that prosecutors in his trial introduced evidence that Garza was suspected of killing four people in Mexico. Defense attorneys argued that the introduction of this evidence was prejudicial and inflamed the passions of the jury against Garza. Garza's attorneys filed a petition with the Inter-American Commission on Human Rights. That commission found that Garza's death penalty conviction violated international norms.

However, federal courts are not bound by such findings from an international commission. In fact, the 7th U.S. Circuit Court of Appeals ruled in *Garza v. Lappin* (2001)—only five days before Garza's ultimate execution—that "the American Declaration of the Rights and Duties of Man, on which the Inter-American Commission relied, is merely an aspirational document that, in itself, creates no directly enforceable rights." The federal appeals court added that "as a general rule, international agreements, even those benefitting private parties, do not create private rights enforceable in domestic courts."

Garza had pleaded with President Clinton to grant him clemency, even putting forth a videotape asking for clemency. Clinton did not grant Garza clemency, but as his statement indicates, he delayed the execution after a study of the death penalty in federal cases showed that there were possible racial and regional disparities in the death penalty.

Garza's execution was delayed by this action. However, Clinton left office after serving two terms. Garza was executed on June 19, 2001, by lethal injection at a federal facility in Terre Haute, Indiana.

He was the second federal inmate executed after 1963. The first was convicted bomber Timothy McVeigh, who bombed a federal building in Oklahoma City, killing 168 people.

DID YOU KNOW?

Governor Bill Clinton and the Case of Ricky Ray Rector

In 1992, Arkansas governor Bill Clinton was running to become president of the United States. On the campaign trail, he identified himself as tough on crime and in favor of the death penalty. In fact, in January 1992, Clinton denied clemency to death row inmate Ricky Ray Rector, who was intellectually disabled.

Rector had been sentenced to death for killing Officer Robert Martin. After he shot Officer Martin, Rector then shot himself in the head—but survived. His attorneys argued that his head injuries made him incompetent to stand trial, but a judge ruled him competent.

During his presidential campaign, Clinton flew back to Arkansas to oversee the execution of Rector. Critics charged that Clinton's actions in the Rector case were motivated by the political goal of convincing the public he was tough on crime, but others defended Clinton's decisions as necessary and appropriate.

FURTHER READING

Frady, Marshall. "Death in Arkansas." *New Yorker*. February 14, 1993.

clearly documented geographic and regional disparities in the administration of the death penalty. This is extremely misleading. The patterns that need to be studied are differences between regions in the rates at which death sentences are (a) sought by United State's Attorneys, (b) approved by the Attorney General, and (c) imposed by juries.

The September 2000 report clearly shows that in practice the federal death sentencing system is largely a Southern program. Twelve of the 19 men on federal death row as of September were sentenced in the South, including 6 from Texas and 4 from Virginia. The new report focuses on regional differences in the racial composition of the pools of potential capital cases that the districts have generated. This has nothing to do with regional disparities in the rates at which death eligible defendants in the system are capitally charged and sentenced to death.

3. THE REPORT PRESENTS NO DATA OR OTHER COMPELLING REASONS TO DISPEL CONCERNS ABOUT THE EXERCISE OF DISCRETION BY U.S. ATTORNEYS IN THE POST-AUTHORIZATION STAGE OF THE PROCESS

One the most striking findings of the September 2000 report is that in the period after the AG has approved a capital prosecution, 48% of white defendants avoid the risk of a death penalty by entering a plea agreement to a non-capital charge, while the rates that blacks and Hispanics enter such agreements are 25% and 28% respectively. The department is obviously concerned about this issue because it plans to limit the power of U.S. Attorneys to enter such agreements without AG approval.

The report seeks to dispel concerns created by these data by pointing out first that it "takes two to make a plea agreement" and the data do not reflect racial differences in the rates at which the government offered post-authorization plea agreements. This argument raises an empirical question about the 62 cases (as of the September 2000 report) in which a post-authorization plea agreement was not reached. Was a plea bargain offered by the prosecution in these cases and rejected by the defense, or was none offered? It would have been easy for the DOJ to ask its own prosecutors whether they offered plea agreements in these cases. Apparently, it was not done.

The report further argues that even if differential acceptance rates by white and minority defendants did not explain the race disparities in the post-authorization guilty pleas, the September 2000 report's findings on this issue "would not be suggestive of bias by the U.S. Attorney's offices." (p. 20) The argument is that the detection of discrimination by U.S. Attorneys must rest on an analysis of "what happens in the process as a whole" and that decisions taken "at the final plea stage are uninformative as possible indications of bias by the U.S. Attorney offices." Certainly it is important to view the system as a whole, but prior research demonstrates that race disparities may operate at discrete stages in a decision making process that overall appears to be evenhanded. There is serious cause for worry here, and the report makes no attempt to address it.

The claim that no differential treatment exists in the post-authorization plea stage is a mere assertion with no evidence whatever to support it. Without data on the comparative culpability of the offenders (and the race of the victims) in the cases affected by these post-authorization pleas bargaining decisions, one has no idea the extent to which similarly situated defendants were in fact treated comparably.

4. THE REPORT PROVIDES NO COMPELLING REASON FOR THE DOJ'S FAILURE TO AUTHORIZE A COMPREHENSIVE STATE OF THE ART STUDY OF FAIRNESS IN THE ADMINISTRATION OF THE FEDERAL DEATH PENALTY SYSTEM

The report notes a meeting of "researchers and practitioners on January 10, 2001" in Washington D.C. to consider the feasibility of conducting a comprehensive empirical study and evaluation of fairness in the administration of the federal system. I was one of the researchers at that meeting.

The report correctly states that there was general agreement at the January meeting that the conduct of such a study would entail a "multi-year research initiative." Two years would be the likely time line. In the meantime, half a year has passed since that meeting, and nine months since the release of the initial report, and neither the NIJ nor any other agency of the Department of Justice has taken any visible step to begin to make such a study possible. Quite the opposite. Attorney General Ashcroft's testimony last week suggested that he believes that the idea should be abandoned.

The report also states that "discussion" at the January 10 meeting "indicated," that such a study "could not be expected to yield definitive answers concerning the reasons for disparities in federal death penalty cases." This was certainly not the consensus of the researchers at the January 10 meeting. On the contrary, the consensus was that such a study would provide the best possible evidence on the question. Certainly the results of such a study would yield far more definitive answers to the issue of racial fairness in the system than the arguments presented in the department's latest report.

The new report offers no reason at all why such a study should not be conducted even if it would require up to two years to complete. It also offers no reason why the DOJ appears unwilling to identify by defendant name and docket number the more than 700 death-eligible cases that make up the database for its latest study. With this information independent researchers could collect data on the cases in the DOJ database and conduct the kind of study that would provide the best evidence available on the question of fairness in the federal death sentencing system.

5. THE REPORT MISCONCEIVES THE NATURE OF RACE DISCRIMINATION IN THE ADMINISTRATION OF THE FEDERAL DEATH PENALTY

A main theme of the report is that the core issue of racial fairness is whether U.S. Attorneys are consciously engaged in "favoritism towards White defendants." In other words, are their decisions based on "invidious" racial reasons or motivated by "bias" or a "particular desire to secure the death penalty for minority defendants." This states the issue far too crudely. No one with an understanding of the system suggests that it is driven by such a conscious and blatant animus against minority defendants or defendants whose victims are white.

The concern about racial unfairness in the system is whether defendants with similar levels of criminal culpability and deathworthiness are treated comparably or differently because of their race or the race of their victims. The reasons for differential treatment by U.S. Attorneys—and by agents of the FBI, the DEA and other are federal law enforcement agencies—are almost certainly nonconscious. More importantly, the reasons for the differential treatment of similarly situated offenders on the basis of their race or the race of the victim are irrelevant. It is the fact that differential treatment cannot be explained by legitimate case characteristics that makes it morally and legally objectionable, when it exists. Without a systematic study based on full information concerning the criminal culpability and the race of the victims of all of the death eligible offenders, we will remain in the dark about whether unexplained differential treatment based on the race of the defendant and victim exists in the federal death penalty system, and if so, what causes it.

SOURCE: Baldus, David C. Statement before Senate Committee on the Judiciary. June 11, 2001. Death Penalty Information Center. https://deathpenaltyinfo.org/stories/statement-of-david-c-baldus

ANALYSIS

David C. Baldus (1935—2011) was a leading expert on the role of race in the administration of the death penalty. He is best known for his pioneering work as lead author of the Baldus study, a research study that found significant race-of-the-victim discrimination in the implementation of the death penalty in the state of Georgia. The Baldus study was used by attorneys for African American defendant Warren McCleskey who was convicted and sentenced to die for killing a white police officer.

The U.S. Supreme Court did not refute the findings of the Baldus study but held that it was not sufficient to overturn McCleskey's death sentence.

In light of his pioneering work on race and the death penalty, he was asked to offer his testimony to the Senate Judiciary Committee on the death penalty in the federal system. Baldus critiqued a federal report that found there was not significant racial discrimination in the implementation of the federal death penalty system.

Baldus noted in his testimony that the federal study failed to focus on the key type of discrimination uncovered by the Baldus study—race-of-the-victim discrimination. In other words, a key determinant in who gets the death penalty is the race of the victim. As Baldus stated to the Senate Judiciary Committee, "The concern about racial unfairness in the system is whether defendants with similar levels of criminal culpability and deathworthiness are treated comparably or differently because of their race or the race of their victims."

FURTHER READING

Baldus, David, Charles Pulaski, and George Woodworth. "Comparative Review of Death Sentences: An Empirical Study of the Georgia Experience." 74 *Journal of Criminal Law & Criminology* 661 (1983).

Kennedy, Randall L. "McCleskey v. Kemp: Race, Capital Punishment, and the Supreme Court." 101 *Harvard Law Review* 1388 (1988).

Liptak, Adam. "David C. Baldus, 75, Dies; Studied Race and the Law." *New York Times*. June 14, 2011.

U.S. Department of Justice. "The Federal Death Penalty System: Supplementary Data, Analysis and Revised Protocols for Capital Case Review." June 6, 2001.

5

THE CAPITAL PUNISHMENT DEBATE INTENSIFIES AS COURTS NARROW ITS APPLICATION

Since *Gregg v. Georgia* (1976), the death penalty has remained a fixture in the American criminal justice system. However, there have been several significant developments that have caused some to question what capital punishment will look like in the future: (1) the Supreme Court has eliminated the death penalty for particular defendants and crimes, and (2) several states have abolished the death penalty.

A prominent feature of modern death penalty jurisprudence has been the elimination of the death penalty for particular types of defendants and crimes due to Supreme Court rulings, especially in the first decade of the twenty-first century. Consider that in the following decisions—all of which are analyzed in this book—the Supreme Court has eliminated the death penalty:

Coker v. Georgia (1977)—no death penalty for the crime of rape of an adult victim;

Ford v. Wainwright (1986)—no death penalty for defendants who are insane;

Atkins v. Virginia (2002)—no death penalty for defendants who are intellectually disabled;

Roper v. Simmons (2005)—no death penalty for defendants who committed murder as juveniles;

Kennedy v. Louisiana (2008)—no death penalty for the crime of child rape.

A majority of the Supreme Court reasoned that under the governing Eighth Amendment standard of "evolving standards of decency" that mark society's progress, such punishments would constitute cruel and unusual punishment.

FURTHER READING

Goldstone, Adam S. "The Death Penalty: How America's Highest Court Is Narrowing Its Application." 4 *American University Criminal Law Brief* 23 (2009).

Hughes, Jamie. "For Mice or Men or Children—Will the Expansion of the Eighth Amendment in Atkins v. Virginia Force the Supreme Court to Re-Examine the Minimum Age for the Death Penalty." 93 *Journal of Criminal Law & Criminology* 973 (2003).

Sundby, Scott E. "*The True Legacy of Atkins and Roper: The Unreliability Principle, Mentally Ill Defendants, and the Death Penalty's Unraveling.*" 23 *William & Mary Bill of Rights Journal* 487 (2014).

- ***Document 33:*** U.S. Supreme Court Decision in *Atkins v. Virginia*
- ***Date:*** June 20, 2002
- ***Where:*** Washington, D.C.
- ***Significance:*** The Supreme Court starts a trend of eliminating the death penalty for certain types of defendants. In this instance, the Court reasoned that inmates who were intellectually disabled could not be executed because they could not appreciate the gravity of the harm their actions caused to the extent of normally functioning defendants.

DOCUMENT

Supreme Court Rules Intellectually Disabled Defendants Cannot Be Executed

Those mentally retarded persons who meet the law's requirements for criminal responsibility should be tried and punished when they commit crimes. Because of their disabilities in areas of reasoning, judgment, and control of their impulses, however, they do not act with the level of moral culpability that characterizes the most serious adult criminal conduct. Moreover, their impairments can jeopardize the reliability and fairness of capital proceedings against mentally retarded defendants. Presumably for these reasons, in the 13 years since we decided *Penry* v. *Lynaugh*, 492 U.S. 302 (1989), the American public, legislators, scholars, and judges have deliberated over the question whether the death penalty should ever be imposed on a mentally retarded criminal. The consensus reflected in those deliberations informs our answer to the question presented by this case: whether such executions are "cruel and unusual punishments" prohibited by the Eighth Amendment to the Federal Constitution.

Petitioner, Daryl Renard Atkins, was convicted of abduction, armed robbery, and capital murder, and sentenced to death. At approximately midnight on August 16, 1996, Atkins and William Jones, armed with a semiautomatic handgun, abducted Eric Nesbitt, robbed him of the money on his person, drove him to an automated teller machine in his pickup truck where cameras recorded their withdrawal of additional cash, then took him to an isolated location where he was shot eight times and killed.

Jones and Atkins both testified in the guilt phase of Atkins' trial. Each confirmed most of the details in the other's account of the incident, with the important exception that each stated that the other had actually shot and killed Nesbitt. Jones' testimony, which was both more coherent and credible than Atkins', was obviously credited by the jury and was sufficient to establish Atkins' guilt. At the penalty phase of the trial, the State introduced victim impact evidence and proved two aggravating circumstances: future dangerousness and "vileness of the offense." To prove future dangerousness, the State relied on Atkins' prior felony convictions as well as the testimony of four victims of earlier robberies and assaults. To prove the second aggravator, the prosecution relied upon the trial record, including pictures of the deceased's body and the autopsy report.

In the penalty phase, the defense relied on one witness, Dr. Evan Nelson, a forensic psychologist who had evaluated Atkins before trial and concluded that he was "mildly mentally retarded." His conclusion was based on interviews with people who knew Atkins, a review of school and court records, and the administration of a standard intelligence test which indicated that Atkins had a full scale IQ of 59.

The jury sentenced Atkins to death, but the Virginia Supreme Court ordered a second sentencing hearing because the trial court had used a misleading verdict form. At the resentencing, Dr. Nelson again testified. The State presented an expert rebuttal witness, Dr. Stanton Samenow, who expressed the opinion that Atkins was not mentally retarded, but rather was of "average intelligence, at least," and diagnosable as having antisocial personality disorder. The jury again sentenced Atkins to death.

The Supreme Court of Virginia affirmed the imposition of the death penalty. Atkins did not argue before the Virginia Supreme Court that his sentence was disproportionate to penalties imposed for similar crimes in Virginia, but he did contend "that he is mentally retarded and thus cannot be sentenced to death." The majority of the state court rejected this contention, relying on our holding in *Penry*. . . .

Because of the gravity of the concerns expressed by the dissenters, and in light of the dramatic shift in the state legislative landscape that has occurred in the past 13 years, we granted certiorari to revisit the issue that we first addressed in the *Penry* case.

. . .

The parties have not called our attention to any state legislative consideration of the suitability of imposing the death penalty on mentally retarded offenders prior to 1986. In that year, the public reaction to the execution of a mentally retarded murderer in Georgia apparently led to the enactment of the first state statute prohibiting such executions. In 1988, when Congress enacted legislation reinstating the federal death penalty, it expressly provided that a "sentence of death shall not be carried out upon a person who is mentally retarded." In 1989, Maryland enacted a similar prohibition. It was in that year that we decided *Penry*, and concluded that those two state enactments, "even when added to the 14 States that have rejected capital punishment completely, do not provide sufficient evidence at present of a national consensus."

Much has changed since then. Responding to the national attention received by the Bowden execution and our decision in *Penry*, state legislatures across the country began to address the issue. In 1990 Kentucky and Tennessee enacted statutes similar to those in Georgia and Maryland, as did New Mexico in 1991, and Arkansas, Colorado, Washington, Indiana, and Kansas in 1993 and 1994. In 1995, when New

York reinstated its death penalty, it emulated the Federal Government by expressly exempting the mentally retarded. Nebraska followed suit in 1998. There appear to have been no similar enactments during the next two years, but in 2000 and 2001 six more States—South Dakota, Arizona, Connecticut, Florida, Missouri, and North Carolina—joined the procession. The Texas Legislature unanimously adopted a similar bill, and bills have passed at least one house in other States, including Virginia and Nevada.

It is not so much the number of these States that is significant, but the consistency of the direction of change. Given the well-known fact that anticrime legislation is far more popular than legislation providing protections for persons guilty of violent crime, the large number of States prohibiting the execution of mentally retarded persons (and the complete absence of States passing legislation reinstating the power to conduct such executions) provides powerful evidence that today our society views mentally retarded offenders as categorically less culpable than the average criminal. The evidence carries even greater force when it is noted that the legislatures that have addressed the issue have voted overwhelmingly in favor of the prohibition. Moreover, even in those States that allow the execution of mentally retarded offenders, the practice is uncommon. Some States, for example New Hampshire and New Jersey, continue to authorize executions, but none have been carried out in decades. Thus there is little need to pursue legislation barring the execution of the mentally retarded in those States. And it appears that even among those States that regularly execute offenders and that have no prohibition with regard to the mentally retarded, only five have executed offenders possessing a known IQ less than 70 since we decided *Penry*. The practice, therefore, has become truly unusual, and it is fair to say that a national consensus has developed against it.

. . .

This consensus unquestionably reflects widespread judgment about the relative culpability of mentally retarded offenders, and the relationship between mental retardation and the penological purposes served by the death penalty. Additionally, it suggests that some characteristics of mental retardation undermine the strength of the procedural protections that our capital jurisprudence steadfastly guards.

. . .

In light of these deficiencies, our death penalty jurisprudence provides two reasons consistent with the legislative consensus that the mentally retarded should be categorically excluded from execution. First, there is a serious question as to whether either justification that we have recognized as a basis for the death penalty applies to mentally retarded offenders. . . .

The reduced capacity of mentally retarded offenders provides a second justification for a categorical rule making such offenders ineligible for the death penalty. The risk "that the death penalty will be imposed in spite of factors which may call for a less severe penalty," is enhanced, not only by the possibility of false confessions, but also by the lesser ability of mentally retarded defendants to make a persuasive showing of mitigation in the face of prosecutorial evidence of one or more aggravating factors. Mentally retarded defendants may be less able to give meaningful assistance to their counsel and are typically poor witnesses, and their demeanor may create an unwarranted impression of lack of remorse for their crimes . . . Mentally retarded defendants in the aggregate face a special risk of wrongful execution. . . .

Our independent evaluation of the issue reveals no reason to disagree with the judgment of "the legislatures that have recently addressed the matter" and concluded that death is not a suitable punishment for a mentally retarded criminal. We are not persuaded that the execution of mentally retarded criminals will measurably advance the deterrent or the retributive purpose of the death penalty. Construing and applying the Eighth Amendment in the light of our "evolving standards of decency," we therefore conclude that such punishment is excessive and that the Constitution "places a substantive restriction on the State's power to take the life" of a mentally retarded offender.

The judgment of the Virginia Supreme Court is reversed and the case is remanded for further proceedings not inconsistent with this opinion.

SOURCE: Atkins v. Virginia, 536 U.S. 304 (2002).

DID YOU KNOW?

Justice Scalia's Dissent in *Atkins v. Virginia*

The Court's 6–3 decision in *Atkins v. Virginia* aroused the ire of Justice Antonin Scalia, long a supporter of capital punishment. Scalia wrote a dissenting opinion that was very critical of the reasoning of his colleagues in the majority:

> Today's decision is the pinnacle of our Eighth Amendment death-is-different jurisprudence. Not only does it, like all of that jurisprudence, find no support in the text or history of the Eighth Amendment; it does not even have support in current social attitudes regarding the conditions that render an otherwise just death penalty inappropriate. Seldom has an opinion of this Court rested so obviously upon nothing but the personal views of its members.

He questioned the Court majority's conclusion that there was a "national conclusion" that executing intellectually disabled inmates was unconstitutional, pointing out that fewer than half of the states—18 at the time—had laws that forbade sentences of capital punishment for intellectually disabled people. Scalia also criticized the majority for relying on the views of other countries, the so-called world community. He emphasized that the justices' job is to interpret the U.S. Constitution, not focus on laws from other countries.

FURTHER READING

Totenberg, Nina. "Justice Scalia and the Death Penalty." NPR.org. June 24, 2002.

ANALYSIS

The Court's decision in *Atkins* was a significant one that started a trend in the first part of the twenty-first century in death penalty jurisprudence. While the death penalty has remained a fixture since its reinstatement in *Gregg v. Georgia* (1976), the Court began to limit the death penalty for particular types of defendants.

The Court had already prohibited the execution of defendants who are insane in *Ford v. Wainwright* (1986). But, in 1989, the Court ruled in *Penry v. Lynaugh* that it did not violate the Eighth Amendment to execute an inmate who was mentally retarded. A word is in order on the terminology. In the *Penry* and *Atkins* decisions, the U.S. Supreme Court uses the term "mentally retarded," a term now considered disrespectful and offensive. Instead, the term sanctioned and used by the National Disability Authority (NDA) is "intellectual disability."

Generally, an inmate with IQ of 70 or less is considered intellectually disabled. In the *Atkins* case, Defendant Daryl Renard Atkins allegedly had an IQ of 59—a very low score. His lawyers did not argue that his low level of intellectual functioning justified his criminal actions. Rather, they argued that his low IQ should prohibit the state of Virginia from executing him.

The Supreme Court agreed, ruling 6–3, that it violates the Eighth Amendment to execute those who truly are intellectually disabled. In his majority opinion, Justice John Paul Stevens reasoned that there was an emerging legislative trend in the states to prohibit the execution of those who are intellectually disabled. Since the Court's decision in *Penry* in 1989, at least 16 different states had amended their death penalty laws to prohibit such executions.

To Justice Stevens and his colleagues in the majority, it was not just the number of states that had abolished the death penalty for intellectually disabled inmates; rather, it was the "consistency of the direction of the change." In other words, virtually every single state that had examined this issue and had passed legislation had done so limiting the imposition of the death penalty.

Thus, Stevens reasoned that there was a national consensus developing against the execution of inmates who are intellectually disabled.

In his opinion, Stevens explained that those who are intellectually disabled are less able to appreciate the gravity of harm their criminal actions cause. He also explained that intellectually disabled defendants are less able to assist their attorneys, express remorse for their actions, understand the court proceedings, and, in sum, are more likely to be subject to wrongful executions.

The Court's decision ultimately led to Daryl Atkins' death sentence to be commuted to a life sentence. The Court's decision also spawned a new array of litigation over whether inmates truly are intellectually disabled. Obviously, after the Court's decision in *Atkins*, a host of other inmates filed petitions arguing that they also should be removed from death row because they are intellectually disabled.

As a result of the Court's decision, the fate of Daryl Renard Atkins remained undetermined. Prosecutors, defense attorneys, and experts disagreed over what his IQ score was. In 2005, Atkins' IQ score was tested at 74—which is above the cutoff at 70. Prosecutors claimed that his IQ score was even higher at 76. The *New York Times*' Supreme Court reporter Adam Liptak covered these developments in an article entitled "Inmate's Rising IQ Scores Could Mean His Death."

However, Atkins was not executed. His sentence was commuted to a life sentence after it was revealed that prosecutors may have committed misconduct in their treatment of Atkins' codefendant in his case. Controversy remained over whether the triggerman in Atkins' crime was Atkins or his codefendant William Jones.

Atkins remains incarcerated in a Virginia state prison as of May 2022.

FURTHER READING

Koocher, Gerald P. "IQ Testing: A Matter of Life or Death." 13 *Ethics & Behavior* 1 (2003).

Liptak, Adam. "Inmate's Rising IQ Scores Could Mean His Death." *New York Times*. February 6, 2005.

Olive, Mark E. "The Daryl Atkins Story." 23 *William & Mary Bill of Rights Journal* 363 (2014).

Patton, James R., and Denis W. Keyes. "Death Penalty Issues Following Atkins." 14 *Exceptionality* 237 (2006).

"Prosecutorial Misconduct Leads to Life Sentence for Daryl Atkins." Death Penalty Information Center. January 18, 2008.

Weithern, Lois A. "Conceptual Hurdles to the Application of Atkins v. Virginia." 59 *Hastings Law Journal* (2008).

- ***Document 34:*** Written Testimony of Barry Scheck
- ***Date:*** June 18, 2002
- ***Where:*** Washington, D.C.
- ***Significance:*** Noted criminal defense attorney Barry Scheck, a cofounder of the Innocence Project, testifies on Capitol Hill about the importance of DNA testing in criminal cases, including capital cases. Scheck and his colleagues at the Innocence Project have called for DNA testing in cases where they suspect the inmate is actually innocent.

DOCUMENT

Attorney Barry Scheck Calls for More DNA Testing in Death Penalty Cases

Our procedure has always been haunted by the ghost of the innocent man of the innocent man convicted. It is an unreal dream.

Judge Learned Hand, 1923.

Today those ghosts walk the land.

There are now 108 Americans who have been exonerated by post-conviction DNA testing.

Thirteen of the exonerated had at one time been sentenced to death. Thirty-two of the exonerated were convicted of murder, and many of them would have almost certainly faced execution if the death penalty had been available in the jurisdictions where they were tried.

The pace of post-conviction DNA exonerations has accelerated because states have begun to pass statutes that permit those claiming innocence a chance to gain their freedom and thirty-five law schools have started a network "innocence projects" on shoe string budgets to prevent, as best they can, these DNA statutes from becoming unfunded, unrealized mandates.

There can be no doubt the number of wrongly convicted freed by DNA testing would dramatically increase if the post-conviction DNA legislation were passed by this Congress—the number of exonerations would at least double within five years—just as apprehension of the real perpetrators of these crimes through DNA databank "hits" would impressively proliferate.

This is a "win-win" proposition for law enforcement, innocents who rot in America's prisons and death rows, crime victims, families of all involved, and anyone who loves justice.

Accordingly, we who toil in the trenches trying to harness the enormous power of this technology for the public good are grateful to Senators Specter, Feingold, and Feinstein for convening these hearings and recognizing critical importance of moving this legislation now, just as we owe an enormous debt to Chairman Leahy, Senator Gordon Smith, and all the co-sponsors of the Innocence Protection Act (IPA).

DNA testing is not a panacea for what ails the administration of the death penalty in America or the rest of the criminal justice system. The vast majority (probably 80%) of felony cases do not involve biological evidence that can be subjected to DNA testing.

DNA technology is no substitute for competent counsel, and nothing guarantees the conviction of the innocent more than incompetent, ill-trained, or ineffective defense counsel.

That is why the counsel provisions of the legislation before you is so critical.

But it would be a terrible mistake to overlook the unique importance of these post-conviction DNA exoneration cases. They have created a great "learning moment" in the history of our criminal justice system and surely constitute the most remarkable and instructive data set criminal justice researchers have ever possessed. It permits us to identify as never before the causes of wrongful convictions and their remedies for the good of the entire system.

In our book, Actual Innocence: When Justice Goes Wrong and How to Make it Right, by Scheck, Neufeld, and Dwyer (Penguin 2001), we took a first step in this direction, but the 85 recommendations recently outlined by Governor Ryan's Commission on Capital Punishment, based on a study of wrongful capital convictions in Illinois, take the agenda of "innocence reforms" much further, and help create a blue print for a new kind of civil rights movement in the criminal justice system that benefits both the accused and victims.

Every time an innocent person is arrested, convicted, or sent to death row, the real offender is at large, free to commit more crimes. There is no better illustration of how the legislation you are considering today will produce these benefits than the case of Ray Krone, who is here with us today. Mr. Krone was convicted of murder and sentenced to death in Arizona principally on the basis of bite-mark analysis, one of many longstanding forensic assays that DNA testing is helping reveal to be junk science.

Using the new Arizona post-conviction DNA statute, legislation that tracked verbatim the model bill produced by the Commission on the Future of DNA Evidence of the National Institute of Justice (the same model followed by the Innocence Protection Act), Ray Krone was able to get testing of blood and saliva stains, originally thought to have been left by the murderer, that were found on the pant leg and tank top of the victim. An STR (Short Tandem Repeat) DNA test performed on the stains showed Krone was not the source, yet that new evidence alone might not have been enough to vacate his conviction.

The stains, it could be argued, might not have come from the murderer after all; unlike semen in a sexual assault (the evidence invariably involved in the first 74 DNA exonerations), where samples can be taken from any possible prior consensual partners, getting "elimination samples" for small blood and saliva stains could prove more difficult.

Luckily, however, the STR profile from the stains could be run through the national DNA databank (STR technology is the technique used in forensic DNA databanks throughout the world), and it generated a "hit," a sex offender who had committed similar crimes (he bit his rape victims) in the Phoenix area.

But we are in a race against time and every day counts. In 75% of the cases where the Innocence Project has determined that a DNA test on some piece of biological evidence would be determinative of guilt of innocence, the evidence is reported either lost or destroyed, and without laws specifically to prevent it, precious DNA evidence is surely being thrown away, wittingly or unwittingly, every day. As these post-conviction cases get older, even when the evidence is found, the likelihood grows that bacterial degradation could make successful testing impossible.

On the other hand, reporter Laurie Cohen of the Wall Street Journal has documented that at least 40% of the post-conviction DNA tests performed by private and public laboratories generate evidence favorable to the inmate claiming innocence and demanding the test.

SPECIFIC COMMENTS ON PROPOSED LEGISLATION

A. MAKING ACCESS TO DNA TESTING TO PROVE ACTUAL INNOCENCE INMATES A CONSTITUTIONAL RIGHT

For All Inmates under Section 5 of the Fourteenth Amendment. Senator Specter's bill represents the best approach to this issue which has extremely significant short and long term implications. Although in Herrera v. Collins (1993), there undoubtedly were six United States Supreme Court Justices who believed that it would violate due process and the Eighth Amendment's prohibition against cruel and unusual punishment to execute or imprison an inmate who could prove that he or she was actually innocent, and there are almost certainly at least six votes on today's Supreme Court for the same proposition, there are still some federal and state courts who resist the proposition that even irrefutable post-conviction proof of actual innocence based on DNA evidence, standing alone, would raise a federal constitutional claim. Some even believe only inmates on death row are entitled to such relief, not those who are serving life sentences or substantial prison terms.

. . .

B. TIME LIMITS

One of the strongest arguments supporting statutes of limitations for post-conviction motions claiming newly discovered evidence of innocence is skepticism that a re-trial many years after the crime was committed, even with new evidence of innocence, would be a more reliable factfinding than the original proceeding, given the fading of memories and disappearance of witnesses.

Post-conviction DNA testing provides a unique rebuttal to this concern because it invariably results in a more accurate and reliable fact-finding with respect to crucial items of biological evidence. Consequently, the principal "finality" concern behind time limits for new evidence of innocence motions has much less force when it comes to post-conviction DNA testing and is substantially outweighed not just by considerations of justice for the wrongly convicted but also the additional unique capacity of DNA testing to identify the real offender through databank "hits."

But there are even more significant practical problems that make time limits a profoundly bad idea. Based on close to ten years of experience assessing and litigating more post-conviction DNA applications than any other office in the country, the Innocence Project has found that it takes an average of between three to five years to evaluate and perfect a post-conviction application from the time an inmate's letter arrives in our office until the time an adequately documented motion can be filed. The difficulties are legion: The inmates are indigent. They have no lawyers and their lawyers from trial or appeal have often been disbarred, died, or disappeared. They do not have complete copies of their transcripts and neither does anyone else.

Important police and laboratory reports relating to key items of biological evidence cannot be found. And most importantly, no one can find the evidence. It might be in the court house as an exhibit, at the crime laboratory, in the prosecutor's safe, with the court reporter, at a hospital or medical examiner's office, or different items could be at a variety of these locations.

. . .

The decision not to include time limits in the Leahy-Smith bill was the right one. At the Innocence Project, we regard the issue of time limits as the most critical difference between the bills.

Out of the twenty-five states that have passed post-conviction DNA statutes, a number have imposed time limits that we know will deny testing to inmates claiming innocence who cannot possibly make the deadlines. . . .

SOURCE: Scheck, Barry. Statement. Senate Committee on the Judiciary. June 18, 2002. https://www.judiciary.senate.gov/imo/media/doc/scheck_testimony_06_18_02.pdf

ANALYSIS

Barry Scheck cofounded the Innocence Project in 1992 with fellow attorney Peter Neufeld to free inmates who were wrongfully imprisoned for crimes they did not commit and to reform the criminal justice system. The results have been extraordinary, exonerating hundreds of innocent people.

Scheck has also gained fame for many of his high-profile criminal cases. He was one of the attorneys for the so-called Dream Team, a collection of prominent criminal defense attorneys who obtained a not guilty verdict for former football great O. J. Simpson in a 1994 murder trial concerning the deaths of his wife, Nicole Brown Simpson, and her friend Ron Goldman. Scheck has also earned plaudits for his defense work in several other high-profile cases.

A primary way that the Innocence Project has exonerated individuals has been through the use of DNA testing. DNA testing has been a type of truth serum in cases. At times, it has shown that the individual convicted could not possibly have been the perpetrator.

In 2002, Scheck testified before Congress about a proposed federal bill that would mandate DNA testing in capital cases. It would not put up roadblocks for those trying to get the DNA testing of key biological matter.

According to the Innocence Project, 375 people have been exonerated through DNA evidence, the first one being in 1989. Scheck talks about the case of Ray Krone, a man falsely accused and convicted of murdering a 35-year-old woman based on faulty evidence—what Scheck calls in his congressional testimony "junk science." The state's expert in Krone's case testified that bite marks found on the victim matched Krone's teeth, leading to his nickname in the press as the "Snaggletooth Killer."

DNA testing showed that Krone was not the killer and actually identified the real killer, a man named Kenneth Phillips.

In his congressional testimony, Scheck emphasized that DNA testing has provided a great "learning moment" for those concerned about the unfairness in the criminal justice system. Scheck emphasizes that there needs to be funding for DNA testing and that there does not need to be restrictive time limits imposed, barring an inmate from having DNA testing after a certain point.

Scheck urged the members of the subcommittee to support the bill being discussed, the Innocence Protection Act, because that type of legislation could lead to even more exonerations. And freeing the innocent has been the primary goal of the Innocence Project all along.

FURTHER READING

Innocence Project Website. innocenceproject.org

Scheck, Barry, Peter Neufeld, and Jim Dwyer. *Actual Innocence*. New York: Doubleday, 2000.

Scheck, Barry, Peter Neufeld, and Taryn Simon. *The Innocents*. New York: Umbrage Editions, 2003.

- ***Document* 35:** Text of Governor George Ryan's Speech Issuing a Blanket Commutation
- ***Date:*** January 11, 2003
- ***Where:*** Northwestern University in Chicago, Illinois
- ***Significance:*** Ryan's startling action, taken only two days before the end of his term, was one of the most important events in modern history of the death penalty. His commutation order for more than 160 death row inmates across Illinois—and the reasons he gave for issuing it—ignited a national debate over the constitutionality and morality of the death penalty.

DOCUMENT

Illinois Governor Ryan Commutes Sentences of Death Row Inmates to Life in Prison

Four years ago I was sworn in as the 39th Governor of Illinois. That was just four short years ago; that's when I was a firm believer in the American System of Justice and the death penalty. I believed that the ultimate penalty for the taking of a life was administrated in a just and fair manner.

Today, 3 days before I end my term as Governor, I stand before you to explain my frustrations and deep concerns about both the administration and the penalty of death. It is fitting that we are gathered here today at Northwestern University with the students, teachers, lawyers and investigators who first shed light on the sorrowful condition of Illinois' death penalty system. Professors Larry Marshall, Dave Protess have and their students along with investigators Paul Ciolino have gone above the call. They freed the falsely accused Ford Heights Four, they saved Anthony Porter's life, they fought for Rolando Cruz and Alex Hernandez. They devoted time and effort on behalf of Aaron Patterson, a young man who lost 15 years of his youth sitting among the condemned, and LeRoy Orange, who lost 17 of the best years of his life on death row.

It is also proper that we are together with dedicated people like Andrea Lyon who has labored on the front lines trying capital cases for many years and who is now devoting her passion to creating an innocence center at De Paul University. You saved Madison Hobley's life.

Together you spared the lives and secured the freedom of 17 men who were wrongfully convicted and rotting in the condemned units of our state prisons. What you have achieved is of the highest calling. Thank You!

Yes, it is right that I am here with you, where, in a manner of speaking, my journey from staunch supporters of capital punishment to reformer all began. But I must tell you since the beginning of our journey my thoughts and feelings about the death penalty have changed many, many times. I realize that over the course of my reviews I had said that I would not do blanket commutation. I have also said it was an option that was there and I would consider all options.

During my time in public office I have always reserved my right to change my mind if I believed it to be in the best public interest, whether it be about taxes, abortions or the death penalty. But I must confess that the debate with myself has been the toughest concerning the death penalty. I suppose the reason the death penalty has been the toughest is because it is so final the only public policy that determines who lives and who dies. In addition it is the only issue that attracts most of the legal minds across the country. I have received more advice on this issue than any other policy issue I have dealt with in my 35 years of public service. I have kept an open mind on both sides of the issues of commutation for life or death.

I have read, listened to and discussed the issue with the families of the victims as well as the families of the condemned. I know that any decision I make will not be accepted by one side or the other. I know that my decision will be just that—my decision based on all the facts I could gather over the past 3 years. I may never be comfortable with my final decision, but I will know in my heart, that I did my very best to do the right thing.

. . .

My responsibilities and obligations are more than my neighbors and my family. I represent all the people of Illinois, like it or not. The decision I make about our criminal justice system is felt not only here, but the world over.

The other day, I received a call from former South African President Nelson Mandela who reminded me that the United States sets the example for justice and fairness for the rest of the world. Today the United States is not in league with most of our major allies: Europe, Canada, Mexico, most of South and Central America. These countries rejected the death penalty. We are partners in death with several third world countries. Even Russia has called a moratorium.

The death penalty has been abolished in 12 states. In none of these states has the homicide rate increased. In Illinois last year we had about 1000 murders, only 2 percent of that 1000 were sentenced to death. Where is the fairness and equality in that? The death penalty in Illinois is not imposed fairly or uniformly because of the absence of standards for the 102 Illinois State Attorneys, who must decide whether to request the death sentence. Should geography be a factor in determining who gets the death sentence? I don't think so but in Illinois it makes a difference. You are 5 times more likely to get a death sentence for first degree murder in the rural area of Illinois than you are in Cook County. Where is the justice and fairness in that ? Where is the proportionality?

. . .

I never intended to be an activist on this issue. I watched in surprise as freed death row inmate Anthony Porter was released from jail. A free man, he ran into the arms of Northwestern University Professor Dave Protess who poured his heart and soul into proving Porter's innocence with his journalism students.

He was 48 hours away from being wheeled into the execution chamber where the state would kill him.

It would all be so antiseptic and most of us would not have even paused, except that Anthony Porter was innocent of the double murder for which he had been condemned to die.

After Mr. Porter's case there was the report by Chicago Tribune reporters Steve Mills and Ken Armstrong documenting the systemic failures of our capital punishment system. Half of the nearly 300 capital cases in Illinois had been reversed for a new trial or resentencing.

Nearly Half!

33 of the death row inmates were represented at trial by an attorney who had later been disbarred or at some point suspended from practicing law.

Of the more than 160 death row inmates, 35 were African American defendants who had been convicted or condemned to die by all-white juries.

More than two-thirds of the inmates on death row were African American.

46 inmates were convicted on the basis of testimony from jailhouse informants.

I can recall looking at these cases and the information from the Mills/Armstrong series and asking my staff: How does that happen? How in God's name does that happen? I'm not a lawyer, so somebody explain it to me.

But no one could. Not to this day.

Then over the next few months. There were three more exonerated men, freed because their sentence hinged on a jailhouse informant or new DNA technology proved beyond a shadow of doubt their innocence.

We then had the dubious distinction of exonerating more men than we had executed. 13 men found innocent, 12 executed.

As I reported yesterday, there is not a doubt in my mind that the number of innocent men freed from our Death Row stands at 17, with the pardons of Aaron Patterson, Madison Hobley, Stanley Howard and Leroy Orange.

That is an absolute embarrassment. 17 exonerated death row inmates is nothing short of a catastrophic failure. . . .

How many more cases of wrongful conviction have to occur before we can all agree that the system is broken?

. . .

My commission and my staff had been reviewing each and every case for three years. But, I redoubled my effort to review each case personally in order to respond to the concerns of prosecutors and victims' families. This individual review also naturally resulted in a collective examination of our entire death penalty system.

. . .

But I had to ask myself? could I send another man's son to death under the deeply flawed system of capital punishment we have in Illinois? A troubled young man, with a history of mental illness? Could I rely on the system of justice we have in Illinois not to make another horrible mistake? Could I rely on a fair sentencing?

In the United States the overwhelming majority of those executed are psychotic, alcoholic, drug addicted or mentally unstable. The frequently are raised in an impoverished and abusive environment.

Seldom are people with money or prestige convicted of capital offenses, even more seldom are they executed.

. . .

At stake throughout the clemency process, was whether some, all or none of these inmates on death row would have their sentences commuted from death to life without the possibility parole.

. . .

Earlier this year, the U.S. Supreme Court held that it is unconstitutional and cruel and unusual punishment to execute the mentally retarded. It is now the law of the land. How many people have we already executed who were mentally retarded and are now dead and buried? Although we now know that they have been killed by the state unconstitutionally and illegally. Is that fair? Is that right?

This court decision was last spring. The General Assembly failed to pass any measure defining what constitutes mental retardation. We are a rudderless ship because they failed to act.

This is even after the Illinois Supreme Court also told lawmakers that it is their job and it must be done.

I started with this issue concerned about innocence. But once I studied, once I pondered what had become of our justice system, I came to care above all about fairness. Fairness is fundamental to the American system of justice and our way of life.

The facts I have seen in reviewing each and every one of these cases raised questions not only about the innocence of people on death row, but about the fairness of the death penalty system as a whole.

If the system was making so many errors in determining whether someone was guilty in the first place, how fairly and accurately was it determining which guilty defendants deserved to live and which deserved to die? What effect was race having? What effect was poverty having?

And in almost every one of the exonerated 17, we not only have breakdowns in the system with police, prosecutors and judges, we have terrible cases of shabby defense lawyers. There is just no way to sugar coat it. There are defense attorneys that did not consult with their clients, did not investigate the case and were completely unqualified to handle complex death penalty cases. They often didn't put much effort into fighting a death sentence. If your life is on the line, your lawyer ought to be fighting for you. As I have said before, there is more than enough blame to go around.

I had more questions.

In Illinois, I have learned, we have 102 decision makers. Each of them are politically elected, each beholden to the demands of their community and, in some cases, to the media or especially vocal victims' families. In cases that have the attention of the media and the public, are decisions to seek the death penalty more likely to occur? What standards are these prosecutors using?

Some people have assailed my power to commute sentences, a power that literally hundreds of legal scholars from across the country have defended. But prosecutors in Illinois have the ultimate commutation power, a power that is exercised every day. They decide who will be subject to the death penalty, who will get a plea deal or even who may get a complete pass on prosecution. By what objective standards do they make these decisions? We do not know, they are not public. There were more than 1000 murders last year in Illinois. There is no doubt that all murders are horrific and cruel. Yet, less than 2 percent of those murder defendants will receive the death penalty. That means more than 98% of victims families do not get, and will not receive whatever satisfaction can be derived from the execution of the murderer. Moreover, if you look at the cases, as I have done? both individually and collectively—a killing with the same circumstances might get 40 years in one county and death in another county. I have also seen where co-defendants who are equally or even more culpable get sentenced to a term of years, while another less culpable defendant ends up on death row.

. . .

Supreme Court Justice Potter Stewart has said that the imposition of the death penalty on defendants in this country is as freakish and arbitrary as who gets hit by a bolt of lightning.

For years the criminal justice system defended and upheld the imposition of the death penalty for the 17 exonerated inmates from Illinois Death row. Yet when the real killers are charged, prosecutors have often sought sentences of less than death. In the Ford Heights Four Case, Verneal Jimerson and Dennis Williams fought the death sentences imposed upon them for 18 years before they were exonerated. Later, Cook County prosecutors sought life in prison for two of the real killers and a sentence of 80 years for a third.

What made the murder for which the Ford Heights Four were sentenced to die less heinous and worthy of the death penalty twenty years later with a new set of defendants?

. . .

I spent a good deal of time reviewing these death row cases. My staff, many of whom are lawyers, spent busy days and many sleepless nights answering my questions, providing me with information, giving me advice. It became clear to me that whatever decision I made, I would be criticized. It also became clear to me that it was impossible to make reliable choices about whether our capital punishment system had really done its job.

As I came closer to my decision, I knew that I was going to have to face the question of whether I believed so completely in the choice I wanted to make that I could face the prospect of even commuting the death sentence of Daniel Edwards? the man who had killed a close family friend of mine. I discussed it with my wife, Lura Lynn, who has stood by me all these years. She was angry and disappointed at my decision like many of the families of other victims will be.

I was struck by the anger of the families of murder victims. To a family they talked about closure. They pleaded with me to allow the state to kill an inmate in its name to provide the families with closure. But is that the purpose of capital punishment? Is it to soothe the families? And is that truly what the families experience.

I cannot imagine losing a family member to murder. Nor can I imagine spending every waking day for 20 years with a single minded focus to execute the killer. The system of death in Illinois is so unsure that it is not unusual for cases to take 20 years before they are resolved. And thank God. If it had moved any faster, then Anthony Porter, the Ford Heights Four, Ronald Jones, Madison Hobley and the other innocent men we've exonerated might be dead and buried.

But it is cruel and unusual punishment for family members to go through this pain, this legal limbo for 20 years. Perhaps it would be less cruel if we sentenced the killers to TAMS to life, and used our resources to better serve victims.

. . .

I have had to consider not only the horrible nature of the crimes that put men on death row in the first place, the terrible suffering of the surviving family members of the victims, the despair of the family members of the inmates, but I have also had to watch in frustration as members of the Illinois General Assembly failed to pass even one substantive death penalty reform. Not one. They couldn't even agree on ONE. How much more evidence is needed before the General Assembly will take its responsibility in this area seriously?

The fact is that the failure of the General Assembly to act is merely a symptom of the larger problem. Many people express the desire to have capital punishment. Few, however, seem prepared to address the tough questions that arise when the system fails. It is easier and more comfortable for politicians to be tough on crime and support the death penalty. It wins votes. But when it comes to admitting that we have a problem, most run for cover. Prosecutors across our state continue to deny that our death penalty system is broken ? or they say if there is a problem, it is really a small one and we can fix it somehow. It is difficult to see how the system can be fixed when not a single one of the reforms proposed by my Capital Punishment Commission has been adopted. Even the reforms the prosecutors agree with haven't been adopted.

So when will the system be fixed? How much more risk can we afford? Will we actually have to execute an innocent person before the tragedy that is our capital punishment system in Illinois is really understood? This summer, a United States District court judge held the federal death penalty was unconstitutional and noted that with the number of recent exonerations based on DNA and new scientific technology we undoubtedly executed innocent people before this technology emerged.

As I prepare to leave office, I had to ask myself whether I could really live with the prospect of knowing that I had the opportunity to act, but that I failed to do so because I might be criticized. Could I take the chance that our capital punishment system might be reformed, that wrongful convictions might not occur, that enterprising journalism students might free more men from death row? A system that's so fragile that it depends on young journalism students is seriously flawed.

. . .

Our own study showed that juries were more likely to sentence to death if the victim were white than if the victim were black—three-and-a-half times more likely to be exact. We are not alone. Just this month Maryland released a study of their death penalty system and racial disparities exist there too.

This week, Mamie Till died. Her son Emmett was lynched in Mississippi in the 1950s. She was a strong advocate for civil rights and reconciliation. In fact just three weeks ago, she was the keynote speaker at the Murder Victims' Families for Reconciliation Event in Chicago. This group, many of whom I've met, opposes the death penalty even though their family members have been lost to senseless killing.

Mamie's strength and grace not only ignited the civil rights movement—including inspiring Rosa Parks to refuse to go to the back of the bus—but inspired murder victims' families until her dying day.

Is our system fair to all? Is justice blind? These are important human rights issues.

. . .

In 1994, near the end of his distinguished career on the Supreme Court of the United States, Justice Harry Blackmun wrote an influential dissent in the body of law on capital punishment. 20 years earlier he was part of the court that issued the landmark *Furman* decision. The Court decided that the death penalty statutes in use throughout the country were fraught with severe flaws that rendered them unconstitutional. Quite frankly, they were the same problems we see here in Illinois. To many, it looked like the Furman decision meant the end of the death penalty in the United States.

This was not the case. Many states responded to *Furman* by developing and enacting new and improved death penalty statutes. In 1976, four years after it had decided Furman, Justice Blackmun joined the majority of the United States Supreme Court in deciding to give the States a chance with these new and improved death penalty statutes. There was great optimism in the air.

This was the climate in 1977, when the Illinois legislature was faced with the momentous decision of whether to reinstate the death penalty in Illinois. I was a member of the General Assembly at that time and when I pushed the green button in favor of reinstating the death penalty in this great State, I did so with the belief that whatever problems had plagued the capital punishment system in the past were now being cured. I am sure that most of my colleagues who voted with me that day shared that view.

But 20 years later, after affirming hundreds of death penalty decisions, Justice Blackmun came to the realization, in the twilight of his distinguished career that the death penalty "remains fraught with arbitrariness, discrimination, caprice and mistake." He expressed frustration with a 20-year struggle to develop procedural and substantive safeguards. In a now famous dissent he wrote in 1994, "From this day forward, I no longer shall tinker with the machinery of death."

One of the few disappointments of my legislative and executive career is that the General Assembly failed to work with me to reform our deeply flawed system.

I don't know why legislators could not heed the rising voices of reform. I don't know how many more systemic flaws we needed to uncover before they would be spurred to action.

. . .

The Governor has the constitutional role in our state of acting in the interest of justice and fairness. Our state constitution provides broad power to the Governor to issue reprieves, pardons and commutations. Our Supreme Court has reminded inmates petitioning them that the last resort for relief is the governor.

At times the executive clemency power has perhaps been a crutch for courts to avoid making the kind of major change that I believe our system needs.

Our systemic case-by-case review has found more cases of innocent men wrongfully sentenced to death row. Because our three year study has found only more questions about the fairness of the sentencing; because of the spectacular failure to reform the system; because we have seen justice delayed for countless death row inmates with potentially meritorious claims; because the Illinois death penalty system is arbitrary and capricious—and therefore immoral—I no longer shall tinker with the machinery of death.

I cannot say it more eloquently than Justice Blackmun.

The legislature couldn't reform it.

Lawmakers won't repeal it.

But I will not stand for it.

I must act.

Our capital system is haunted by the demon of error, error in determining guilt, and error in determining who among the guilty deserves to die. Because of all of these reasons today I am commuting the sentences of all death row inmates.

This is a blanket commutation. I realize it will draw ridicule, scorn and anger from many who oppose this decision. They will say I am usurping the decisions of judges and juries and state legislators. But as I have said, the people of our state have vested in me to act in the interest of justice. Even if the exercise of my power becomes my burden I will bear it. Our constitution compels it. I sought this office, and even in my final days of holding it I cannot shrink from the obligations to justice and fairness that it demands.

There have been many nights where my staff and I have been deprived of sleep in order to conduct our exhaustive review of the system. But I can tell you this: I will sleep well knowing I made the right decision.

. . .

To say it plainly one more time—the Illinois capital punishment system is broken. It has taken innocent men to a hair's breadth escape from their unjust execution. Legislatures past have refused to fix it. Our new legislature and our new Governor must act to rid our state of the shame of threatening the innocent with execution and the guilty with unfairness.

In the days ahead, I will pray that we can open our hearts and provide something for victims' families other than the hope of revenge. Lincoln once said: "I have always found that mercy bears richer fruits than strict justice." I can only hope that will be so. God bless you. And God bless the people of Illinois.

SOURCE: Ryan, George. Death Penalty Commutation Remarks. January 11, 2003. https://deathpenaltyinfo.org/stories/in-ryans-words-i-must-act

ANALYSIS

Republican Illinois governor George Ryan—the 39th governor in Illinois history—is best known for his actions related to the death penalty. In January 2000, Governor Ryan had issued a moratorium on the death penalty after a series of high-profile exonerations of death row inmates. In some of the cases, the death row inmates were weeks or even days before their scheduled executions before their innocence was discovered and recognized.

For example, four men convicted of a double murder—Verneal Jimerson, Dennis Williams, Kenneth Adams, and Willie Rainge—they did not commit were facing the death penalty or life in prison until northwestern investigative journalism professor David Protess and several of his students in the Medill Innocent Project investigated the case. Protess and his students' work on the so-called Ford Heights Four case found that the men's convictions were based in part on false forensic testimony and witness perjury.

There were numerous other death row inmates in Illinois who were freed—some just days before their executions. Another example was Anthony Porter, who served 17 years on death row and was intellectually disabled. Students in the Medill program were instrumental in Porter's exoneration.

Because of the sheer number of these exonerations, Governor Ryan came to view the capital punishment system in Illinois as broken. As he stated in his famous speech, "To say it plainly one more time—the Illinois capital punishment system is broken. It has taken innocent men to a hair's breadth escape from their unjust execution."

Ryan's actions in issuing the blanket commutation meant that all 167 inmates on death row in Illinois had their sentences commuted to life sentences. Many considered Ryan's historic action as the most significant blow against the death penalty since the U.S. Supreme Court's historic decision in *Furman v. Georgia* (1972). Sister Helen Prejean, the nun who devoted her life to fighting the death penalty, called Ryan's actions as a "pure beacon of life in a dark era of our nation."

Ryan soon faced federal corruption charges related to alleged bribery and racketeering charges. He later served several years in federal prison. However, Ryan was released in 2013 and later coauthored a book that detailed his historic decision to stop the death penalty in Illinois. "I still believe it was the right thing to do," he said in an interview in 2020.

FURTHER READING

Armstrong, Ken, and Steve Mills. "Ryan Suspends Death Penalty." *Chicago Tribune*. January 31, 2000.

Ryan, George H., Sr., and Maurice Possley. *Until I Could Be Sure: How I Stopped the Death Penalty in Illinois*. Lanham, MD: Rowman & Littlefield Publishers, 2020.

Wilgoren, Jodi. "Citing Issues of Fairness, Governor Clears Out Death Row in Illinois." *New York Times*. January 12, 2003.

- ***Document 36:*** Supreme Court majority opinion in *Miller-El v. Dretke*
- ***Date:*** June 13, 2005
- ***Where:*** Washington, D.C.
- ***Significance:*** The Court struck down a death sentence handed down against an African American defendant on constitutional grounds, finding that prosecutors in his trial had a clear, discernable pattern of striking African American jurors from consideration during the process of jury selection.

DOCUMENT

Supreme Court Reverses Death Sentence, Citing Prosecutor's Racially Discriminatory Use of Jury Strikes

Two years ago, we ordered that a certificate of appealability, under 28 U.S.C. §2253(c), be issued to habeas petitioner Miller-El, affording review of the District Court's rejection of the claim that prosecutors in his capital murder trial made peremptory strikes of potential jurors based on race. Today we find Miller-El entitled to prevail on that claim and order relief under §2254.

I

In the course of robbing a Holiday Inn in Dallas, Texas in late 1985, Miller-El and his accomplices bound and gagged two hotel employees, whom Miller-El then shot, killing one and severely injuring the other. During jury selection in Miller-El's trial for capital murder, prosecutors used peremptory strikes against 10 qualified black venire members. Miller-El objected that the strikes were based on race and could not be presumed legitimate, given a history of excluding black members from criminal juries by the Dallas County District Attorney's Office. The trial court received evidence of the practice alleged but found no "systematic exclusion of blacks as a matter of policy" by that office, and therefore no entitlement to relief under *Swain* v. *Alabama*, 380 U.S. 202 (1965), the case then defining and marking the limits of relief from racially biased jury selection. The court denied Miller-El's request to pick a new jury, and the trial ended with his death sentence for capital murder.

While an appeal was pending, this Court decided *Batson* v. *Kentucky*, 476 U.S. 79 (1986), which replaced *Swain*'s threshold requirement to prove systemic discrimination under a Fourteenth Amendment jury claim, with the rule that discrimination by the prosecutor in selecting the defendant's jury sufficed to establish the constitutional violation. The Texas Court of Criminal Appeals then remanded the matter to the trial court to determine whether Miller-El could show that prosecutors in his case peremptorily struck prospective black jurors because of race.

The trial court found no such demonstration. After reviewing the *voir dire* record of the explanations given for some of the challenged strikes, and after hearing one of the prosecutors, Paul Macaluso, give his justification for those previously unexplained, the trial court accepted the stated race-neutral reasons for the strikes, which the judge called "completely credible [and] sufficient" as the grounds for a finding of "no purposeful discrimination." . . .

Miller-El then sought habeas relief under 28 U.S.C. §2254, again pressing his *Batson* claim, among others not now before us. The District Court denied relief, and the Court of Appeals for the Fifth Circuit precluded appeal by denying a certificate of appealability, We granted certiorari to consider whether Miller-El was entitled to review on the *Batson* claim, and reversed the Court of Appeals. After examining the record of Miller-El's extensive evidence of purposeful discrimination by the Dallas County District Attorney's Office before and during his trial, we found an appeal was in order, since the merits of the *Batson* claim were, at the least, debatable by jurists of reason. After granting a certificate of appealability, the Fifth Circuit rejected Miller-El's *Batson* claim on the merits. We again granted certiorari, and again we reverse.

II

A

. . . Defendants are harmed, of course, when racial discrimination in jury selection compromises the right of trial by impartial jury, but racial minorities are harmed more generally, for prosecutors drawing racial lines in picking juries establish "state-sponsored group stereotypes rooted in, and reflective of, historical prejudice."

Nor is the harm confined to minorities. When the government's choice of jurors is tainted with racial bias, that "overt wrong . . . casts doubt over the obligation of the parties, the jury, and indeed the court to adhere to the law throughout the trial . . . ." That is, the very integrity of the courts is jeopardized when a prosecutor's discrimination "invites cynicism respecting the jury's neutrality," and undermines public confidence in adjudication . . .

The rub has been the practical difficulty of ferreting out discrimination in selections discretionary by nature, and choices subject to myriad legitimate influences, whatever the race of the individuals on the panel from which jurors are selected. . . .

Swain's demand to make out a continuity of discrimination over time, however, turned out to be difficult to the point of unworkable, and in *Batson* v. *Kentucky*, we recognized that this requirement to show an extended pattern imposed a "crippling burden of proof" that left prosecutors' use of peremptories "largely immune from constitutional scrutiny," and we accordingly held that a defendant could make out a prima facie case of discriminatory jury selection by "the totality of the relevant facts" about a prosecutor's conduct during the defendant's own trial. "Once the defendant makes a prima facie showing, the burden shifts to the State to come forward with a neutral explanation for challenging . . . jurors" within an arguably targeted class. Although there may be "any number of bases on which a prosecutor reasonably [might] believe that it is desirable to strike a juror who is not excusable for cause . . ., the prosecutor must give a clear and reasonably specific explanation of his legitimate reasons for exercising the challeng[e]." The trial court then will have the duty to determine if the defendant has established "purposeful discrimination."

Although the move from *Swain* to *Batson* left a defendant free to challenge the prosecution without having to cast *Swain*'s wide net, the net was not entirely consigned to history, for *Batson*'s individualized focus came with a weakness of its own owing to its very emphasis on the particular reasons a prosecutor might give. If any facially neutral reason sufficed to answer a *Batson* challenge, then *Batson* would not amount to much more than *Swain*. Some stated reasons are false, and although some false reasons are shown up within the four corners of a given case, sometimes a court may not be sure unless it looks beyond the case at hand. Hence *Batson*'s explanation that a defendant may rely on "all relevant circumstances" to raise an inference of purposeful discrimination.

B

This case comes to us on review of a denial of habeas relief sought under 28 U. S. C. §2254, following the Texas trial court's prior determination of fact that the State's race-neutral explanations were true.

Under the Antiterrorism and Effective Death Penalty Act of 1996, Miller-El may obtain relief only by showing the Texas conclusion to be "an unreasonable determination of the facts in light of the evidence presented in the State court proceeding." Thus we presume the Texas court's factual findings to be sound unless Miller-El rebuts the "presumption of correctness by clear and convincing evidence." The standard is demanding but not insatiable; as we said the last time this case was here, "[d]eference does not by definition preclude relief."

III

A

The numbers describing the prosecution's use of peremptories are remarkable. Out of 20 black members of the 108-person venire panel for Miller-El's trial, only 1 served. Although 9 were excused for cause or by agreement, 10 were peremptorily struck by the prosecution. "The prosecutors used their peremptory strikes to exclude 91% of the eligible African-American venire members . . . . Happenstance is unlikely to produce this disparity."

More powerful than these bare statistics, however, are side-by-side comparisons of some black venire panelists who were struck and white panelists allowed to serve. If a prosecutor's proffered reason for striking a black panelist applies just as well to an otherwise-similar nonblack who is permitted to serve, that is evidence tending to prove purposeful discrimination to be considered at *Batson*'s third step. . . .

The prosecution used its second peremptory strike to exclude Billy Jean Fields, a black man who expressed unwavering support for the death penalty. . . .

Although at one point in the questioning, Fields indicated that the possibility of rehabilitation might be relevant to the likelihood that a defendant would commit future acts of violence, he responded to ensuing questions by saying that although he believed anyone could be rehabilitated, this belief would not stand in the way of a decision to impose the death penalty:

. . .

Fields was struck peremptorily by the prosecution, with prosecutor James Nelson offering a race-neutral reason:

. . .

Thus, Nelson simply mischaracterized Fields's testimony. He represented that Fields said he would not vote for death if rehabilitation was possible, whereas Fields unequivocally stated that he could impose the death penalty regardless of the possibility of rehabilitation. Perhaps Nelson misunderstood, but unless he had an ulterior reason for keeping Fields off the jury we think he would have proceeded differently. In light of Fields's outspoken support for the death penalty, we expect the prosecutor would have cleared up any misunderstanding by asking further questions before getting to the point of exercising a strike.

. . .

In sum, when we look for nonblack jurors similarly situated to Fields, we find strong similarities as well as some differences. But the differences seem far from significant, particularly when we read Fields's *voir dire* testimony in its entirety. Upon that reading, Fields should have been an ideal juror in the eyes of a prosecutor seeking a death sentence, and the prosecutors' explanations for the strike cannot reasonably be accepted. . . .

The prosecution's proffered reasons for striking Joe Warren, another black venireman, are comparably unlikely. Warren gave this answer when he was asked what the death penalty accomplished:

> "I don't know. It's really hard to say because I know sometimes you feel that it might help to deter crime and then you feel that the person is not really suffering. You're taking the suffering away from him. So it's like I said, sometimes you have mixed feelings about whether or not this is punishment or, you know, you're relieving personal punishment."

The prosecution said nothing about these remarks when it struck Warren from the panel, but prosecutor Paul Macaluso referred to this answer as the first of his reasons when he testified at the later *Batson* hearing:

> "I thought [Warren's statements on *voir dire*] were inconsistent responses. At one point he says, you know, on a case-by-case basis and at another point he said, well, I think—I got the impression, at least, that he suggested that the death penalty was an easy way out, that they should be made to suffer more."

On the face of it, the explanation is reasonable from the State's point of view, but its plausibility is severely undercut by the prosecution's failure to object to other panel members who expressed views much like Warren's. . . .

As for law, the rule in *Batson* provides an opportunity to the prosecutor to give the reason for striking the juror, and it requires the judge to assess the plausibility of that reason in light of all evidence with a bearing on it. It is true that peremptories are often the subjects of instinct, and it can sometimes be hard to say what the reason is. But when illegitimate grounds like race are in issue, a prosecutor simply has got to state his reasons as best he can and stand or fall on the plausibility of the reasons he gives. A *Batson* challenge does not call for a mere exercise in thinking up any rational basis. If the stated reason does not hold up, its pretextual significance does not fade because a trial judge, or an appeals court, can imagine a reason that might not have been shown up as false. The Court of Appeals's and the dissent's substitution of a reason for eliminating Warren does nothing to satisfy the prosecutors' burden of stating a racially neutral explanation for their own actions.

The whole of the *voir dire* testimony subject to consideration casts the prosecution's reasons for striking Warren in an implausible light. Comparing his strike with the treatment of panel members who expressed similar views supports a conclusion that race was significant in determining who was challenged and who was not.

B

The case for discrimination goes beyond these comparisons to include broader patterns of practice during the jury selection. The prosecution's shuffling of the venire panel, its enquiry into views on the death penalty, its questioning about minimum acceptable sentences: all indicate decisions probably based on race. Finally, the appearance of discrimination is confirmed by widely known evidence of the general policy of the Dallas County District Attorney's Office to exclude black venire members from juries at the time Miller-El's jury was selected.

The first clue to the prosecutors' intentions, distinct from the peremptory challenges themselves, is their resort during *voir dire* to a procedure known in Texas as the jury shuffle. In the State's criminal practice, either side may literally reshuffle the cards bearing panel members' names, thus rearranging the order in which members of a venire panel are seated and reached for questioning. Once the order is established, the panel members seated at the back are likely to escape *voir dire* altogether, for those not questioned by the end of the week are dismissed. As we previously explained,

> "the prosecution's decision to seek a jury shuffle when a predominant number of African-Americans were seated in the front of the panel, along with its decision to delay a formal objection to the defense's shuffle until after the new racial composition was revealed, raise a suspicion that the State sought to exclude African-Americans from the jury. Our concerns are amplified by the fact that the state court also had before it, and apparently ignored, testimony demonstrating that the Dallas County District Attorney's Office had, by its

own admission, used this process to manipulate the racial composition of the jury in the past."

. . .

The next body of evidence that the State was trying to avoid black jurors is the contrasting *voir dire* questions posed respectively to black and nonblack panel members, on two different subjects. First, there were the prosecutors' statements preceding questions about a potential juror's thoughts on capital punishment. Some of these prefatory statements were cast in general terms, but some followed the so-called graphic script, describing the method of execution in rhetorical and clinical detail. It is intended, Miller-El contends, to prompt some expression of hesitation to consider the death penalty and thus to elicit plausibly neutral grounds for a peremptory strike of a potential juror subjected to it, if not a strike for cause. If the graphic script is given to a higher proportion of blacks than whites, this is evidence that prosecutors more often wanted blacks off the jury, absent some neutral and extenuating explanation.

. . .

Only 6% of white venire panelists, but 53% of those who were black, heard a different description of the death penalty before being asked their feelings about it. This is an example of the graphic script:

. . .

> The State concedes that this disparate questioning did occur but argues that use of the graphic script turned not on a panelist's race but on expressed ambivalence about the death penalty in the preliminary questionnaire. Prosecutors were trying, the argument goes, to weed out noncommittal or uncertain jurors, not black jurors. And while some white venire members expressed opposition to the death penalty on their questionnaires, they were not read the graphic script because their feelings were already clear. The State says that giving the graphic script to these panel members would only have antagonized them.

. . .

The State's attempt at a race-neutral rationalization thus simply fails to explain what the prosecutors did. But if we posit instead that the prosecutors' first object was to use the graphic script to make a case for excluding black panel members opposed to or ambivalent about the death penalty, there is a much tighter fit of fact and explanation.

. . .

There is a final body of evidence that confirms this conclusion. We know that for decades leading up to the time this case was tried prosecutors in the Dallas County office had followed a specific policy of systematically excluding blacks from juries, as we explained the last time the case was here.

"Although most of the witnesses [presented at the *Swain* hearing in 1986] denied the existence of a systematic policy to exclude African-Americans, others disagreed. A Dallas County district judge testified that, when he had served in the District

Attorney's Office from the late-1950's to early-1960's, his superior warned him that he would be fired if he permitted any African-Americans to serve on a jury. Similarly, another Dallas County district judge and former assistant district attorney from 1976 to 1978 testified that he believed the office had a systematic policy of excluding African-Americans from juries.

. . .

In the course of drawing a jury to try a black defendant, 10 of the 11 qualified black venire panel members were peremptorily struck. At least two of them, Fields and Warren, were ostensibly acceptable to prosecutors seeking a death verdict, and Fields was ideal. The prosecutors' chosen race-neutral reasons for the strikes do not hold up and are so far at odds with the evidence that pretext is the fair conclusion, indicating the very discrimination the explanations were meant to deny.

. . .

If anything more is needed for an undeniable explanation of what was going on, history supplies it. The prosecutors took their cues from a 20-year old manual of tips on jury selection, as shown by their notes of the race of each potential juror. By the time a jury was chosen, the State had peremptorily challenged 12% of qualified nonblack panel members, but eliminated 91% of the black ones.

It blinks reality to deny that the State struck Fields and Warren, included in that 91%, because they were black. The strikes correlate with no fact as well as they correlate with race, and they occurred during a selection infected by shuffling and disparate questioning that race explains better than any race-neutral reason advanced by the State. The State's pretextual positions confirm Miller-El's claim, and the prosecutors' own notes proclaim that the Sparling Manual's emphasis on race was on their minds when they considered every potential juror.

The state court's conclusion that the prosecutors' strikes of Fields and Warren were not racially determined is shown up as wrong to a clear and convincing degree; the state court's conclusion was unreasonable as well as erroneous. The judgment of the Court of Appeals is reversed, and the case is remanded for entry of judgment for petitioner together with orders of appropriate relief.

It is so ordered.

SOURCE: Miller-El v. Dretke, 545 U.S. 231 (2005).

ANALYSIS

African American defendant Thomas Miller-El was sentenced to death by a jury for killing two individuals in the course of a hotel robbery in Dallas, Texas, in 1985. However, the jury selection process in his case was infected with racial bias. Prosecutors used 10 of their 11 peremptory challenges—rejections of prospective jurors they could make without "cause" (giving a reason for their decision)—on African American jurors.

The jury selection process is known as *voir dire*. In this process, attorneys on each side get to question prospective jurors on a wide range of subjects. They can challenge jurors in two ways: for-cause challenges and peremptory challenges. A for-cause challenge exists if a juror clearly is biased and could not be impartial. But, peremptory challenges are different. These allow attorneys to strike prospective jurors for any reason.

However, the U.S. Supreme Court has established that there are certain constitutional limitations on the exercise of peremptory challenges. The most important limitation is that attorneys may not use their peremptory challenges in a racially discriminatory way.

Furthermore, prosecutors in Miller-El's case used a process known as "the jury shuffle." This process allowed the prosecution to start the jury selection process over from scratch once they saw a large pool of potential African American jurors enter the jury box.

Furthermore, the Dallas District Attorney General's Office had a significant history of racial discrimination in jury selection. One former district attorney testified that he was told he would be fired in the 1960s if he left an African American on the jury.

In 1985—when Miller-El committed his crimes—it was very difficult to show racial bias during the jury selection process. The legal standard that a defendant had to meet was set out in the Supreme Court's decision in *Swain v. Alabama* (1965). In *Swain*, a defendant had to show a pattern of a purposeful system of unlawful exclusion of juror members based on race. It was not enough to show that prosecutors acted with racial bias in an individual defendant's case.

However, the U.S. Supreme Court changed the legal rule in *Batson v. Kentucky* (1986). In *Batson*, the Court ruled that a defendant could establish racial discrimination based on the conduct of the prosecutor in his or her individual case. The Court ruled that a prosecutor violates the Equal Protection Clause of the Fourteenth Amendment if he or she strikes jurors on the basis of race.

Miller-El and his attorneys then asserted what is known as a Batson claim—that prosecutors struck jurors in a racially discriminatory manner. A Batson challenge requires a defendant to point out that prosecutors struck jurors of a particular race. The burden then shifts to the prosecutor to establish an allegedly race-neutral reason for striking the juror. A legitimate race-neutral reason might be that the prospective juror was evasive in his or her answers or did not look at the prosecutor during questioning. If the prosecutor puts forth a legitimate race-neutral reason, then the defendant has the burden of showing that the allegedly race-neutral reason was pretextual or not really the truth.

Miller-El had a case under Batson, according to the U.S. Supreme Court. At his trial, prosecutors had 11 peremptory challenges—which are challenges of prospective jurors for any reason—and they used 10 of those 11 peremptory challenges to strike African American jurors.

Furthermore, the prosecutors in Miller-El's case had some suspect reasons for striking some of these African Americans from the jury. They struck an African American man from the jury even though he said he was a supporter of the death penalty. Furthermore, prosecutors struck African Americans from the jury but kept white persons on the jury who gave nearly identical answers.

As a result of the Supreme Court's ruling, Miller-El was eligible for a new trial. In 2008, he pleaded guilty to the murders and received a life sentence.

FURTHER READING

"After Two Supreme Court Reversals, Texas Man Sentenced to Life." Death Penalty Information Center. March 24, 2008.

Garguilo, Diana L. "The Batson Standard Remains the Applicable Test for Stating a Claim of Jury Discrimination under the Fourteenth Amendment." 44 *Duquesne Law Review* 771 (2006).

Johnson, Sherri L. "Race and Recalcitrance: The Miller-El Remands." 5 *Ohio State Journal of Criminal Law* 131 (2007).

- ***Document 37:*** U.S. Supreme Court decision in *Roper v. Simmons*
- ***Date:*** March 1, 2005
- ***Where:*** Washington, D.C.
- ***Significance:*** In this decision, the U.S. Supreme Court recognized that juveniles are fundamentally different than adults in several ways. The Court overruled its decision in *Stanford v. Kentucky* (1989), which held it did not violate the Eighth Amendment to execute a person who committed murder at age 17. But, in the intervening years, the Court changed its mind and noted that there was a discernible trend in the states away from such executions.

DOCUMENT

Supreme Court Rules Those Who Commit Murder as Juveniles Cannot Be Executed

This case requires us to address, for the second time in a decade and a half, whether it is permissible under the Eighth and Fourteenth Amendments to the Constitution of the United States to execute a juvenile offender who was older than 15 but younger than 18 when he committed a capital crime. In *Stanford* v. *Kentucky*, 492 U.S. 361 (1989), a divided Court rejected the proposition that the Constitution bars capital punishment for juvenile offenders in this age group. We reconsider the question.

I

At the age of 17, when he was still a junior in high school, Christopher Simmons, the respondent here, committed murder. About nine months later, after he had turned 18, he was tried and sentenced to death. There is little doubt that Simmons was the instigator of the crime. Before its commission Simmons said he wanted to murder someone. In chilling, callous terms he talked about his plan, discussing it for the most part with two friends, Charles Benjamin and John Tessmer, then aged 15 and 16 respectively. Simmons proposed to commit burglary and murder by breaking and entering, tying up a victim, and throwing the victim off a bridge. Simmons assured his friends they could "get away with it" because they were minors.

The three met at about 2 a.m. on the night of the murder, but Tessmer left before the other two set out. (The State later charged Tessmer with conspiracy, but dropped the charge in exchange for his testimony against Simmons.) Simmons and Benjamin entered the home of the victim, Shirley Crook, after reaching through an open window and unlocking the back door. Simmons turned on a hallway light. Awakened, Mrs. Crook called out, "Who's there?" In response Simmons entered Mrs. Crook's bedroom, where he recognized her from a previous car accident involving them both. Simmons later admitted this confirmed his resolve to murder her.

Using duct tape to cover her eyes and mouth and bind her hands, the two perpetrators put Mrs. Crook in her minivan and drove to a state park. They reinforced the bindings, covered her head with a towel, and walked her to a railroad trestle spanning the Meramec River. There they tied her hands and feet together with electrical wire, wrapped her whole face in duct tape and threw her from the bridge, drowning her in the waters below.

. . .

The jury recommended the death penalty after finding the State had proved each of the three aggravating factors submitted to it. Accepting the jury's recommendation, the trial judge imposed the death penalty.

. . .

The evidence of national consensus against the death penalty for juveniles is similar, and in some respects parallel, to the evidence *Atkins* held sufficient to demonstrate a national consensus against the death penalty for the mentally retarded. When *Atkins* was decided, 30 States prohibited the death penalty for the mentally retarded. This number comprised 12 that had abandoned the death penalty altogether, and 18 that maintained it but excluded the mentally retarded from its reach. By a similar calculation in this case, 30 States prohibit the juvenile death penalty, comprising 12 that have rejected the death penalty altogether and 18 that maintain it but, by express provision or judicial interpretation, exclude juveniles from its reach. See Appendix A, *infra*. *Atkins* emphasized that even in the 20 States without formal prohibition, the practice of executing the mentally retarded was infrequent. Since *Penry*, only five States had executed offenders known to have an IQ under 70. In the present case, too, even in the 20 States without a formal prohibition on executing juveniles, the practice is infrequent. Since *Stanford*, six States have executed prisoners for crimes committed as juveniles. In the past 10 years, only three have done so: Oklahoma, Texas, and Virginia.

. . .

As in *Atkins*, the objective indicia of consensus in this case—the rejection of the juvenile death penalty in the majority of States; the infrequency of its use even where it remains on the books; and the consistency in the trend toward abolition of the practice—provide sufficient evidence that today our society views juveniles, in the words *Atkins* used respecting the mentally retarded, as "categorically less culpable than the average criminal."

. . .

Three general differences between juveniles under 18 and adults demonstrate that juvenile offenders cannot with reliability be classified among the worst offenders. First, as any parent knows and as the scientific and sociological studies respondent and his *amici* cite tend to confirm, "[a] lack of maturity and an underdeveloped sense of responsibility are found in youth more often than in adults and are more understandable among the young. These qualities often result in impetuous and ill-considered actions and decisions". . . .

The second area of difference is that juveniles are more vulnerable or susceptible to negative influences and outside pressures, including peer pressure. . . .

The third broad difference is that the character of a juvenile is not as well formed as that of an adult. The personality traits of juveniles are more transitory, less fixed. . . .

The differences between juvenile and adult offenders are too marked and well understood to risk allowing a youthful person to receive the death penalty despite insufficient culpability. An unacceptable likelihood exists that the brutality or cold-blooded nature of any particular crime would overpower mitigating arguments based on youth as a matter of course, even where the juvenile offender's objective immaturity, vulnerability, and lack of true depravity should require a sentence less severe than death. . . .

Our determination that the death penalty is disproportionate punishment for offenders under 18 finds confirmation in the stark reality that the United States is the only country in the world that continues to give official sanction to the juvenile death penalty. . . .

The Eighth and Fourteenth Amendments forbid imposition of the death penalty on offenders who were under the age of 18 when their crimes were committed. The judgment of the Missouri Supreme Court setting aside the sentence of death imposed upon Christopher Simmons is affirmed.

SOURCE: Roper v. Simmons, 543 U.S. 551 (2005).

ANALYSIS

There was no doubt that Christopher Simmons committed the brutal murder of Shirley Crook, a woman with whom he had been involved in a car accident. Simmons was obsessed with revenge and targeted Crook. Simmons, then 17, and a younger juvenile went to Crook's home, tied her up and kidnapped her, and then took her to a bridge and dumped her into the water on September 9, 1993. Prosecutors sought the death penalty for Simmons' horrific crime.

At the time of the murder, the Eighth Amendment did not consider the execution of a juvenile to be "cruel and unusual punishment." In fact, the U.S. Supreme Court had specifically rejected the argument that executing someone who committed murder while 17 years old violated the Eighth Amendment in *Stanford v. Kentucky* (1989).

A jury sentenced Simmons to death in 1994. His attorneys filed a variety of appeals through the years. The one argument that ultimately spared his life, resonating with both the Missouri Supreme Court and then the U.S. Supreme Court, was that juveniles should not be executed, no matter how heinous their offenses

The U.S. Supreme Court agreed with this position in its decision in *Roper v. Simmons*. Writing for the majority, Justice Anthony Kennedy noted that juveniles were different than adults in three significant ways: (1) juveniles are less mature than adults, (2) juveniles are more susceptible to peer pressure than adults, and (3) the character of juveniles is not as well developed as adults.

Kennedy also focused on the fact that very few executions of juvenile murders took place in the United States. The far more common penalty was life imprisonment. Kennedy identified a clear trend in the states disfavoring the imposition of the death penalty on those who committed murder before the age of 18. In other words, Kennedy sought something approaching a national consensus emerging against such executions. This was similar to what the Court had found a few years earlier with regard to the execution of intellectually disabled inmates in *Atkins v. Virginia* (2002).

Finally, and somewhat more controversially to some (including Justice Scalia in dissent), Kennedy emphasized that the United States was about the only country in the world that regularly executed those who committed murder as juveniles. Kennedy wrote that since 1990, only seven other countries—Iran, Pakistan, Saudi Arabia, Yemen, Nigeria, the Democratic Republic of Congo, and China—have executed defendants who were juveniles at the time of their crime. Kennedy's ruling clearly implied this was not the sort of company the United States wanted to be keeping.

Kennedy acknowledged that the line at age 18 might seem arbitrary to some. Why not draw the line at 17, 16, 19, or 20? But Kennedy explained that the age 18 is a familiar line-drawing age in American society: "The age of 18 is the point where society draws the line for many purposes between childhood and adulthood. It is, we conclude, the age at which the line for death eligibility ought to rest."

After the Supreme Court's ruling, the Missouri Supreme Court resentenced Simmons to a life sentence without the possibility of parole on August 26, 2003.

FURTHER READING

Alford, Roger P. "Roper v. Simmons and Our Constitution in International Equipoise." 53 *UCLA Law Review* 1 (2005).

Benekos, Peter J., and Alida V. Merlo. "A Decade of Change: Roper v. Simmons, Defending Childhood, and Juvenile Justice Policy." 30 *Criminal Journal Policy Review* 102 (2019).

Myers, Wayne. "Roper v. Simmons: The Collision of National Consensus and Proportionality Review." 96 *Journal of Crime & Criminology Review* 947 (2006).

- ***Document 38:*** Text of Speech by Richard C. Dieter
- ***Date:*** December 6, 2005
- ***Where:*** Tokyo, Japan
- ***Significance:*** Richard Dieter was the head of the Death Penalty Information Center, which advocates against the death penalty and provides copious research on the topic. Dieter's speech identified a series of trends in the area of capital punishment that signify the decline of the ultimate punishment.

DOCUMENT

Opponent of Death Penalty Discusses Cultural Aspects of Capital Punishment

I would like to thank the European Commission, the American Bar Association and the Japan Federation of Bar Associations for inviting me to speak about the death penalty in the United States. I first want to say that our Japanese hosts have been especially gracious—I immediately felt welcomed here, and I want to thank you for that.

Today we are addressing the cultural aspects of the death penalty, and the United States is certainly a complex culture, made up of many different strands. It is difficult to define exactly what motivates the death penalty in our society, or why this punishment for crime is given a special importance by many people. What I would like to talk about today are some of the facts that illustrate a dramatic change in the death penalty (and perhaps even in our culture) that has been occurring over the past few years.

To understand this change, it is helpful to review the recent history of the death penalty. Ten years ago, in the mid-1990s, the death penalty in the United States was finally "succeeding" at what it had been formulated to do. The death penalty had been stopped by the United States Supreme Court in 1972 because it was being arbitrarily applied. Many states, wishing to preserve the death penalty, then re-wrote their laws to meet the Court's requirements. The new laws were supposed to be carefully channeled so that only the worst offenders would be eligible for the death penalty, thereby eliminating its arbitrary quality. The death penalty resumed in 1976, though executions did not escalate quickly. There was one execution in 1977. The process was slow, there were many appeals, and some state laws were overturned.

In the 1990s, the United States began to experience a death penalty similar to that of the 1930s when nearly 200 people a year were executed. The number of executions went steadily up, reaching almost 100 executions in 1999. The number of people on death row kept rising as more and more people were sentenced to death. New states, such as Kansas and New York, added the death penalty to their statutes. In 1994, the federal government, which affects all 50 states but which had not been a significant participant in the death penalty, expanded its capital punishment statute so that 60 offenses were eligible for the death penalty, instead of just one offense previously.

Much of the public wanted the death penalty applied more often and more quickly. Moreover, we had just experienced a terrible act of terrorism in 1995 by one of our own citizens in the Oklahoma City bombing. In the wake of that, Congress passed the Antiterrorism and Effective Death Penalty Act of 1996 to speed up the death penalty, and the number of executions continued to rise.

The death penalty was supported by 80% of the American public in the 1990s. But surprisingly, a dramatic period of change began around the time of the new millennium. This would seem to be a very unlikely time for the death penalty to change in the U.S., given the cultural events taking place. In 2000, the U.S. elected a president, George Bush, who as governor of Texas presided over the most executions of any modern governor, 152 executions. He was not elected because of those executions or because of his death penalty position, but the election certainly symbolized that the U.S. was a country that had no problem with the death penalty.

We also experienced another act of terrorism in 2001—the attacks in New York and Washington, DC. These actions created a tremendous anger and resulted in many proposals to expand the death penalty. But despite these events, and despite the rise in the executions in the 1990s, the increase in the size of death row, the high level of public support for the death penalty and its affirmation through the electoral process, the death penalty has been in a sharp decline since 2000. Executions are down about 40%. Last year there were 59 executions compared to almost 100 in the 1999. The number of death sentences—and I think this is the most important measure of the death penalty because new sentences mean more executions and a larger death row—are down by over 60% since 1999. There were 300 death sentences a year throughout the 1990s. Last year there were 125 death sentences. That may sound like a lot, but it is far less than it had been.

This year, we are projecting that the number of sentences will remain low, the lowest they have been in 30 years since the death penalty was reinstated in the United States. Not all of the change is positive and in one direction. But the change is significant, and I think it is attributable to two causes: first, and Mr. Greco of the ABA pointed this out earlier, as the number of executions rose, lawyers from bar associations and law firms, journalism students, and concerned individuals from around the country started looking at these cases more closely, especially as executions neared. What they found in case after case was that the defendant had been wrongly convicted.

Thirteen people in Illinois, alone, were wrongly convicted and sentenced to death, many of them having come close to execution. One of them, Anthony Porter, had his case investigated by journalism students. They happened to review this case because their class met at a time when he had received a stay of execution based on his mental capacity, not because of his possible innocence. This was not an instance of the criminal justice system working well. This case illustrated how independent influences from outside the justice system could expose the problems in the death penalty. The students discovered that Porter could not have committed the crime that put him on death row. They found the actual perpetrator who confessed to the crime. Porter was freed, and the public was shocked at how a near tragedy was averted.

In the late 1990s, the number of exonerations from death row continued to grow, and the issue of innocence received confirmation from another outside source. The advent of DNA testing, which emerged in the 1990s and became more sophisticated and prevalent in the late 1990s, confirmed that people, whom the courts and juries ensured us were guilty and deserving of death, were actually innocent.

DNA testing cast a new light on our criminal justice system. Even though the majority of the cases where inmates were freed from death row did not involve DNA testing, this scientific affirmation exposed deeper problems throughout the system. If DNA testing proved that in some cases the wrong person had been convicted and sentenced to death, then one had to be concerned about the many other cases in which no DNA evidence was available.

The second important contribution to the decline in the use of the death penalty that emerged in the 1990s was the introduction of the sentence of life without the possibility of parole. That has been a gradual process in the United States, and may not seem like progress from the perspective of those concerned about the high rate of incarceration in the U.S. But for the death penalty, it represents a critical alternative.

Jurors in death penalty cases are faced with the difficult task of possibly sentencing someone death, knowing that in 5 or 10 years new evidence might reveal that the wrong person was convicted. In the earlier years of the death penalty, the alternative to a death sentence was a life sentence in which the defendant might someday be released. A life-without-parole sentence has given jurors a middle ground between death and the possibility of release.

The number of death sentences has declined dramatically and the number of people serving life-without-parole sentences has increased. These two developments, innocence and life-without-parole, are changing the face of the death penalty in the United States.

As I mentioned earlier, however, all the change is not in one direction. The federal death penalty is expanding and there are efforts to broaden it even further. The federal death penalty is being aggressively pursued in the 12 states that do not have capital punishment. The number of people on the federal death row has gone up while the number of people on the states' death rows has declined.

Another disturbing development is happening in California. There are 640 people on death row in California. There have been 11 executions over the past 30 years. That is a system that is on the verge of spilling over its damn. In our system, you cannot stop executions indefinitely. Appeals do run out—there are no "endless appeals." Three executions are scheduled in California over the next few weeks. There could be many more, and that could reverse some of the trends I have been describing.

Finally, there are still many lawmakers who believe strongly in the death penalty and are still trying to accelerate executions. There is proposed legislation entitled the Streamlined Procedures Act, which would drastically curtail death penalty appeals. It currently takes an average of 10 years from sentencing to execution in the United States. Some legislators want to shorten this to 5 years. Of course, the danger with such a system is that some of the 122 innocent people who had been freed from death row would have been executed before the evidence emerged to free them. Those cases took an average of 9 years from sentencing until when the inmates were freed to develop the necessary evidence of innocence. If the executions had occurred after 5 years, many of them would be dead.

We will hear from one of these individuals, Kirk Bloodsworth, shortly. His case was the first case where DNA evidence freed a death row inmate in the United States. That case took many years to develop. If we cut the appeals process down from 10 years to 5 years, we run the risk of executing the typical innocent person instead of freeing him.

So there are clearly trends that counterbalance the decline in the use of the death penalty in the U.S. Nevertheless, I believe that the drop in death sentences is the stronger trend because it has occurred not just this year, but consistently over the past 5 years. Moreover, there are other indications that the death penalty may be on the wane: New York recently rejected an effort to restore its death penalty after it was overturned in the courts. New York was the last state to adopt the death penalty in 1995, and now it has abandoned capital punishment. Texas, which leads the country in executions, just this year adopted the sentence of life without parole. I think we will start to see a decline in death sentences in Texas. Illinois has a moratorium on executions. New Jersey has a moratorium on executions. Many states are considering reforms of their death penalty system. I think the prospects for the future are positive, but there are many competing trends. Hopefully, the international movement away from capital punishment will buttress the turnaround on the death penalty that has been slowly emerging in the United States. Thank you.

SOURCE: Dieter, Richard C. Remarks at International Conference on Human Rights and the Death Penalty. Tokyo, Japan. December 6–7, 2005. https://deathpenaltyinfo.org/stories/speech-by-richard-c-dieter-given-at-the-international-conference-on-human-rights-and-the-death-penalty (Mr. Dieter is the former Executive Director of the Death Penalty Information Center in Washington, DC)

ANALYSIS

Richard C. Dieter served as the executive director of the Death Penalty Information Center from 1992 until 2015. A graduate of Georgetown Law School, Dieter has written more than 40 reports on the death penalty. In December 2005, Dieter gave a speech in Tokyo, Japan, where he talked about the decline of the death penalty in the United States.

DID YOU KNOW?

The Case of Kirk Bloodsworth

In this excerpt from his 2005 speech in Japan, Richard Dieter, the former head of the Death Penalty Information Center, specifically mentions the awful case of Kirk Bloodsworth—a former Marine and fisherman wrongfully accused and convicted of murdering a young, 9-year-old girl. The *Bloodsworth* case was an awful case of witness misidentification and prosecutorial misconduct.

It was through DNA evidence that Bloodworth was conclusively excluded as the perpetrator of the crime. Convicted in 1984, Bloodsworth was released from prison in 1993 and, in 1994, was given a full pardon by the then governor of Maryland. The real killer of the young girl was convicted in 2003.

Bloodsworth later became a devoted anti-death penalty advocate and helped lead the repeal of Maryland's death penalty law. He serves as an executive director of the Philadelphia-based group Witness to Innocence, a group that helps exonerated inmates and their families.

FURTHER READING

Junkin, Tim. *Bloodsworth: The True Story of the First Death Row Inmate Exonerated by DNA Evidence.* Chapel Hill, NC: Shannon Ravenel Books, 2005.

He noted that in the previous five years (2000–2005), there was a significant decline in the death penalty from the 1990s, when public support for capital punishment was reliably high. Dieter explained that the revelations in Illinois and other states of actually innocent persons serving time on death row opened the eyes of many.

He also spoke about the incredible impact of DNA technology in death penalty cases. Dieter specifically mentioned Kirk Bloodsworth, a Maryland man who became the first death row inmate exonerated by DNA evidence. Bloodsworth had been convicted of murdering a 9-year-old girl in Rosedale, Maryland. Bloodsworth always maintained his innocence. DNA testing showed that semen on the victim's underpants did not match that of Bloodsworth and that he could not have committed the horrible crime.

Bloodworth was released from prison in 1993, and nearly a decade later, he received a full exoneration. DNA testing actually showed that another man, whom Bloodsworth had served time with in prison, was the real culprit. For many years, Bloodsworth has been an active campaigner against the death penalty, and he was instrumental in getting the death penalty barred in his home state of Maryland.

Dieter also talked about various reforms for death penalty cases in the states—including work toward a national moratorium on capital punishment—and stressed that the international movement against the death penalty served as a model for the United States. Despite these positive developments, however, Dieter also acknowledged that there were still many who support the death penalty, including many state legislators.

FURTHER READING

Dieter, Richard C. "The Future of the Death Penalty in the United States." 49 *University of Richmond Law Review* 921 (2015).

Hanes, Stephanie. "DNA That Freed Man Leads to New Subject." *Baltimore Sun*. September 6, 2003.

- ***Document 39:*** Text of Professor John McAdams' testimony before Senate Judiciary Subcommittee
- ***Date:*** February 1, 2006
- ***Where:*** Washington, D.C.
- ***Significance:*** The testimony of this political scientist and pro-death penalty scholar calls into question the frequent claims that there have been actual innocents executed and that there is rampant racial discrimination in the administration of the death penalty.

DOCUMENT

Legal Scholar John McAdams Testifies in Support of Capital Punishment

There are a huge number of issues that relate to the merits of the death penalty as a punishment, including deterrence, the moral justice of the punishment, the cost of the imposition of the sanction, and even (implausibly) what policies European nations have. But I'm going to concentrate, given the limited time I have, on two issues that I think are key: the issue of "innocents" convicted and sent to death row, and the issue of racial disparity in the application of the punishment.

HOW MANY INNOCENTS ON DEATH ROW?

One of the most compelling arguments against the death penalty, at least of one accepts the claims of the death penalty opponents at face value, is the claim that a great many innocent people have been convicted of murder and put on death row. Liberal Supreme Court Justice John Paul Stevens, just to pick one case out of hundreds, told the American Bar Association's Thurgood Marshall Award dinner that "That evidence is profoundly significant, not only because of its relevance to the debate about the wisdom of continuing to administer capital punishment, but also because it indicates that there must be serious flaws in our administration of criminal justice."

The most widely publicized list of "innocents" is that of the Death Penalty Information Center (DPIC). As of January, 2003, it listed 122 people. That sounds like an appallingly large number, but even a casual examination of the list shows that many of the people on it got off for reasons entirely unrelated to being innocent. Back in 2001, I analyzed the list when it had ninety-five people on it. By the admission of the Death Penalty Information Center, thirty-five inmates on their list got off on procedural grounds. Another fourteen got off because a higher court believed the evidence against them was insufficient. If the higher court was right, this would be an excellent reason to release them, but it's far from proof of innocence.

Interestingly, prosecutors retried thirty-two of the inmates designated as "innocent." Apparently prosecutors believed these thirty-two were guilty. But many whom prosecutors felt to be guilty were not tried again for a variety of reasons, including the fact that key evidence had been suppressed, witnesses had died, a plea bargain was thought to be a better use of scarce resources, or the person in question had been convicted and imprisoned under another charge.

More detailed assessments of the "Innocents List" have shown that it radically overstates the number of innocent people who have been on death row. For example, the state of Florida had put on death row 24 inmates claimed, as of August 5, 2002, to be innocent by the DPIC. The resulting publicity led to a thorough examination of the twenty-four cases by the Florida Commission on Capital Crimes, which concluded that in only four of the twenty-four cases was the factual guilt of these inmates in doubt.

Examinations of the entire list have been no more favorable. For example, a liberal federal district judge in New York ruled, in United States v. Quinones, that the federal death penalty is unconstitutional. In this case, the court admitted that the DPIC list "may be over-inclusive" and, following its own analysis, asserted that for thirty-two of the people on the list there was evidence of "factual innocence." This hardly represents a ringing endorsement of the work of the Death Penalty Information Center. In academia, being right about a third of the time will seldom result in a passing grade.

Other assessments have been equally negative. Ward A. Campbell, Supervising Deputy Attorney General of the State of California reviewed the list in detail, and concluded that: . . . it is arguable that at least 68 of the 102 defendants on the List should not be on the list at all—leaving only 34 released defendants with claims of actual innocence—less than ½ of 1% of the 6,930 defendants sentenced to death between 1973 and 2000.

There is, of course, a degree of subjectivity in all such assessments. The presence of "reasonable doubt" does not make a person factually innocent (although it's an excellent reason to acquit them), and circumstances might conspire to make a factually innocent person appear to even an objective observer to be guilty "beyond a reasonable doubt." The key thing to remember is that the numbers produced by DPIC are "outliers"—grossly inflated. Indeed, staffers of this very committee have pretty much dismantled the DPIC list. Taking at face value the claims of the activists is about as bad as taking at face value the claims of the National Rifle Association about the number of Americans who save themselves from bodily harm because they own and carry guns, or the claims of NARAL about how many "back alley abortions" would result from overturning Roe v. Wade.

HAVE ANY INNOCENTS BEEN EXECUTED?

Worse than putting an innocent person on death row (only to have him later exonerated) would be to actually execute an innocent person. But death penalty opponents can't point to a single innocent person known to have been executed for the last 35 years. They do make claims, however.

In the 1980s, two academics who strongly opposed the death penalty (Hugo Adam Bedau and Michael Radelet) claimed that of 7,000 people executed in the United States in the 20th century, 23 were innocent. This doesn't seem like a large number, especially when we remember that most of the cases they claimed were from an era when defendants had many fewer due process rights than they do today, when police forces and prosecutors were much less well-trained and professional than they are today, and when the media was less inclined to take an "advocacy" role in claimed cases of injustice.

Indeed, Bedau and Redelet produced only one case since the early 1960s where they claimed an innocent man had been executed—that of one James Adams. But even this one case was quite weak. Steven J. Markman and Paul G. Cassell, in a Stanford Law Review article, took Bedau and Radelet to task for "disregard of the evidence," and for putting a spin on the evidence that supported their thesis of

Adams' innocence. Markman and Cassell concluded that there is, "no persuasive evidence that any innocent person has been put to death in more than twenty-five years." In response, Bedau and Radelet admitted to the Chronicle of Higher Education that (in the words of the Chronicle's reporter) "some cases require subjective analysis simply because the evidence is incomplete or tainted." They admitted this was true of all 23 cases that they reported.

The most sober death penalty opponents have apparently given up claiming solid evidence of any innocent person executed in the modern era. Indeed Barry Scheck, cofounder of the Innocence Project, was featured speaker at the Wrongfully Convicted on Death Row Conference in Chicago (November 13–15, 1998), and was interviewed by the "Today Show."

Schenk was asked by Matt Lauer, "Since 1976, 486 people have been executed in this country. Any doubt in your mind that we've put to death innocent people?" Scheck responded "Well, you know, I—I think that we must have put to death innocent people, but if you're saying to me to prove it right now, I can't."

Nothing stops death penalty opponents from making all sorts of claims about innocent people being executed. But in the rare cases when their claims can actually be tested, they turn out to be false. Consider, for example, the case of Roger Keith Coleman, who was tried for a rape/murder, and finally executed by the State of Virginia in 1992. An essay still on the site of the Death Penalty Information Center discusses the case at considerable length, and clearly leaves the impression that Coleman must be innocent. After attacking all the evidence against Coleman, the essay claims that "official misconduct that has left the case against Roger Coleman in shreds" and goes on to claim:

> . . . there is dramatic evidence that another person, Donney Ramey, committed the murder. For one thing, a growing number of women in the neighborhood have reported being sexually assaulted by Ramey in ways strikingly similar to the attack on Wanda McCoy. For another, one of these rape victims, Teresa Horn, has courageously signed an affidavit stating that Ramey told her he had killed Mrs. McCoy. He threatened to do the same to Ms. Horn.

Someone reading the Death Penalty Information Center website, and lacking due skepticism toward the assertions there, would doubtless conclude that Coleman was innocent. Unfortunately, the State of Virginia allowed DNA testing of key evidence in 2005, using technology unavailable in 1992, and proved decisively that Coleman was in fact guilty as charged. The credibility of anti-death penalty activists when making claims of innocence—whether for those on death row or those who have been executed—is tenuous at best.

HOW MANY INNOCENTS ON DEATH ROW ARE ACCEPTABLE?

At this point, death penalty opponents will argue that it doesn't matter if their numbers are inflated. Even if only 20 or 30 innocent people have been put on death row, they will say, that is "too many" and calls for the abolition of the death penalty. If even one innocent person is executed, they claim, that would make the death penalty morally unacceptable.

This kind of rhetoric allows the speaker to feel very self-righteous, but it's not the sort of thinking that underlies sound policy analysis. Most policies have some negative consequences, and indeed often these involve the death of innocent people—something that can't be shown to have happened with the death penalty in the modern era. Just wars kill a certain number of innocent noncombatants. When the FDA approves a new drug, some people will quite likely be killed by arcane and infrequent reactions. Indeed, the FDA kills people with its laggard drug approval process. The magnitude of these consequences matters.

Death penalty opponents usually implicitly assume (but don't say so, since it would be patently absurd) that we have a choice between a flawed death penalty and a perfect system of punishment where other sanctions are concerned.

Death penalty opponents might be asked why it's acceptable to imprison people, when innocent people most certainly have been imprisoned. They will often respond that wrongfully imprisoned people can be released, but wrongfully executed people cannot be brought back to life. Unfortunately, wrongfully imprisoned people cannot be given back the years of their life that were taken from them, even though they may walk out of prison.

Perhaps more importantly, its cold comfort to say that wrongfully imprisoned people can be released, when there isn't much likelihood that that will happen. Wrongful imprisonment receives vastly less attention than wrongful death sentences, but Barry Scheck's book Actual Innocence lists 10 supposedly innocent defendants, of whom only 3 were sent to death row.

Currently, the Innocence Project website lists 174 persons who have been exonerated on the basis of hard DNA evidence. But the vast majority was not sentenced to death. In fact, only 15 death row inmates have been exonerated due to DNA evidence.

There is every reason to believe that the rate of error is much lower for the death penalty than for imprisonment. There is much more extensive review by higher courts, much more intensive media scrutiny, cadres of activists trying to prove innocence, and better quality counsel at the appeals level (and increasingly at the trial level) if a case might result in execution.

Consider the following quote from an article about how prosecutors in Indiana are tending more and more to ask for life imprisonment and not the death penalty because of the cost of getting an execution:

> Criminal rules require a capital defendant to have two death penalty certified attorneys, which, if the defendant is indigent, are paid for on the public dime. Other costs that might be passed onto taxpayers are requirements that the accused have access to all the tools needed to mount a fair defense, including mitigation experts, investigators, and DNA experts. Because the stakes are so high in a death penalty case, the courts believe a defendant is entitled to a super due process. The cost of getting a death penalty is too

> high in some ways (seemingly endless appeals). But in other ways lesser penalties are too cheap (lacking good lawyers, DNA testing, etc.). The system, in fact, it quite unbalanced, with it being relatively cheap and easy to sentence someone to life imprisonment but excessively expensive to have them executed. But until some balance is restored, the death penalty will remain the fairest penalty we have.

Balance will be achieved by ending "dead weight loss" in administering the death penalty (further limiting the number of appeals), while working for more substantive justice where lesser sanctions are at issue.

Playing the Race Card Death penalty opponents tend to inhabit sectors of society where claiming "racial disparity" is an effective tactic for getting what you want. In academia, the media, the ranks of activist organizations, etc. claiming "racial disparity" is an excellent strategy for getting anybody who has qualms about what you are proposing to shut up, cave in, and get out of the way.

Unfortunately, this has created a hot-house culture where arguments thrive that carry little weight elsewhere in society, and carry little weight for good reasons.

Consider the notion that, because there is racial disparity in the administration of the death penalty, it must be abolished. Applying this principle in a consistent way would be unthinkable. Suppose we find that black robbers are treated more harshly than white robbers?

Does it follow that we want to stop punishing robbers? Or does it follow that we want to properly punish white robbers also? Nobody would argue that racial inequity in punishing robbers means we have to stop punishing robbers. Nobody would claim that, if we find that white neighborhoods have better police protection than black neighborhoods that we address the inequity by withdrawing police protection from all neighborhoods. Or that racial disparity in mortgage lending requires that mortgage lending be ended. Yet people make arguments exactly like this where capital punishment is concerned.

A further problem with the "racial disparity" argument—and one underlining the fundamental incoherence of the abolitionist's thinking—is the fact that there are two versions of it, both widely bandied around, and they are flatly contradictory. I have elsewhere described these as the "mass market" and the "specialist" versions of the racial disparity thesis.

The mass market version is the easiest to understand, since it relies on the notion that racist cops, racist prosecutors, racist judges, and racist juries will be particularly tough on black defendants. Jessie Jackson, never one to pass up an opportunity to nurse a racial grievance, has expressed this view as follows:

> Numerous researchers have shown conclusively that African American defendants are far more likely to receive the death penalty than are white defendants charged with the same crime. For instance, African Americans make up 25 percent of Alabama's population, yet of Alabama's 117 death row inmates, 43 percent are black. Indeed, 71 percent of the people executed there since the resumption of capital punishment have been black.

. . .

What the studies do show is a huge bias against black victims. Offenders who murder black people get off much more lightly than those who murder whites. Since the vast majority of murders are intraracial and not interracial, this translates into a system that lets black murders off far more easily than white murderers.

This is clearly unjust, but it leaves open the question of whether the injustice should be remedied by executing nobody at all, or rather executing more offenders who have murdered black people.

Even more relevant is the question: would doing away with the death penalty improve the situation? Here, as elsewhere, death penalty opponents assume that the choices are a flawed death penalty and a pristine system of criminal justice for every other punishment. But the data don't support that.

Scholars who study the death penalty often study several decisions in the process that might theoretically lead to execution. What they almost invariably find is large-scale bias in these earlier decisions, including decisions that would continue to be made if the death penalty were abolished.

. . .

In sum, the system is relatively lenient toward those who kill blacks, and that leniency extends to decisions that would continue to advantage those defendants who have killed blacks even in the absence of the death penalty. All of this makes perfect sense. If the system is biased toward punishing those who murder whites, it is implausible indeed that decisions leading up to sentencing are made with strict racial fairness, and only the imposition of a death sentence is racially biased.

If people want to punish those who murder whites more harshly than those who murder blacks, this is likely to be reflected in prosecutors' decisions to move ahead with a case, in decisions about whether to plea-bargain, in the allocation of staff to a particular case, in the decision to indict on more or less serious charges, and in jury verdicts. . . .

CONCLUSION

It cannot be stressed too strongly that we do not face the choice of a defective system on capital punishment and a pristine system of imprisonment. Rather, nothing about the criminal justice system works perfectly. Death penalty opponents give the impression that the death penalty is uniquely flawed by the simple expedient of dwelling on the defects of capital punishment (real and imagined) and largely ignoring the defects in the way lesser punishments are meted out.

The death penalty meets the expectations we can reasonably place on any public policy. But it can't meet the absurdly inflated standards imposed by those who are culturally hostile to it. But then, no other policy can either.

SOURCE: McAdams, John. Testimony before Senate Judiciary Committee. February 1, 2006. https://www.judiciary.senate.gov/imo/media/doc/McAdams%20Testimony%20020106.pdf

ANALYSIS

Professor John McAdams (1945–2021) was a noted supporter of the death penalty who published an array of works on the subject. In his congressional testimony above from 2005, he advances several arguments on behalf of his position, including assertions that many of the claims made by death penalty opponents are exaggerations.

In his testimony, McAdams takes issue with the idea that the death penalty is a process endemic with errors. In fact, he says just the opposite is true. He says that the enhanced protections given to capital defendants ensure that capital defendants probably are more protected from error than other criminal defendants. In other words, McAdams asserts there are many more people wrongfully imprisoned than wrongfully placed on death row.

McAdams strongly argues against the claim that there have been numerous innocent persons who have actually faced execution. He criticizes the work of death penalty opponents Hugo Bedau and Michael Radelet, who in 1987 produced a study in which they contended that 23 actually innocent persons were executed.

McAdams also criticizes the idea that the death penalty is filled with racial bias and disparities. He even uses the term playing the race card to disparage the idea that race plays such a massive role in the process. He contends that the real bias is against African American victims of crime. He points out that studies show that most murders are intra-racial as opposed to interracial. In other words, the most likely murderer of a white person is another white person, and the most likely murderer of a black person is another black person. McAdams argues that this had led to a system where African American murderers often get more lenient treatment than similarly situated white murderers: "This is clearly unjust, but it leaves open the question of whether the injustice should be remedied by executing nobody at all, or rather executing more offenders who have murdered black people."

For much of his career, McAdams taught at Marquette University. Marquette suspended him in 2014 for criticizing a graduate student. However, McAdams sued the university and won reinstatement from the Wisconsin Supreme Court. McAdams died in April 2021.

FURTHER READING

McAdams, John. "Claims of Racial Disparity in the Death Penalty are Misleading." *New York Times*. April 6, 2014.

McAdams, John C. "Wisconsin Should Adopt the Death Penalty." 79 *Marquette Law Review* 707 (1996).

- ***Document 40:*** Statement of David B. Muhlhausen to Senate Subcommittee on the Constitution
- ***Date:*** June 27, 2007
- ***Where:*** Washington, D.C.
- ***Significance:*** David B. Muhlhausen is best known as the director of the Institute of Justice during the Trump administration. When he gave this 2007 testimony, however, it was in his capacity as a senior policy analyst for the Heritage Foundation, an influential conservative think tank. Muhlhausen asserted in his testimony that the death penalty is an effective crime deterrent.

DOCUMENT

Heritage Foundation Analyst Testifies in Support of Death Penalty

STATEMENT OF DAVID B. MUHLHAUSEN, SENIOR POLICY ANALYST, CENTER FOR DATA ANALYSIS, THE HERITAGE FOUNDATION, WASHINGTON, D.C.

My name is David Muhlhausen. I am a Senior Policy Analyst in the Center for Data Analysis at the Heritage Foundation. I thank Chairman Russell Feingold and the rest of the Subcommittee for the opportunity to testify today. The views I express in this testimony are my own and should not be construed as representing any official position of the Heritage Foundation.

While opponents of capital punishment have been very vocal in their opposition, a recent Gallup opinion poll found that 67 percent of Americans favor the death penalty for those convicted of murder, while only 28 percent are opposed.

Despite strong public support for capital punishment, Federal, State, and local officials must continually ensure that its implementation rigorously upholds constitutional protections, such as due process and equal protection of the law. However, the criminal process should not be abused to prevent the lawful imposition of the death penalty in appropriate capital cases.

As of December 2005, there were 37 prisoners under a sentence of death in the Federal system. Of these prisoners, 43 percent were white, while 54 percent were African-American. The fact that African-Americans are a majority of Federal prisoners on death row and a minority in the overall United States population may lead some to conclude that the Federal system discriminates against African-Americans. However, there is little rigorous evidence that discrimination exists in the Federal system.

To review the Federal death penalty process, the National Institute of Justice awarded the Rand Corporation a grant to determine whether racial disparities exist in the Federal system. The resulting 2006 Rand study set out to determine what factors, including the defendant's race, victim's race, and crime characteristics, affect the decision to seek a death penalty case. To accomplish this mission, three independent research teams were tasked with developing their own methodologies to analyze the data.

When first looking at the raw data without controlling for case characteristics, Rand found that the decision to seek the death penalty is more likely to occur when the defendants are white and when the victims are white. However, these disparities disappeared in each of the three studies when the seriousness of the crimes was taken into account.

The Rand study concludes that the decisions to seek the death penalty are driven by characteristics of crimes rather than by race. Rand's findings are very compelling because three independent research teams, using the same data but different methodologies, reached the same conclusions.

In recent years, a growing number of sophisticated studies having consistently found that capital punishment saves lives. Federal, State, and local officials need to recognize this benefit. Three studies of professors at Emory University support the deterrent effect. The study found that each execution, on average, results in 18 fewer murders. The second study found that implementation of State moratoria is associated with increased incidence of murders. A third study found that each execution prevents three murders and shorter waits on death row reduce murders as well.

Studies by professors at the University of Colorado at Denver found that each additional execution deters five murders. In addition, each additional commutation resulted in five additional murders. And removal from death row by a court resulted in one additional murder.

In summary, Americans support capital punishment for two good reasons: first, there is little evidence to suggest that minorities are treated unfairly; and, second, recent studies have confirmed what we learned decades ago: capital punishment does, in fact, save lives. Each additional execution appears to deter between 3 and 18 murders.

SOURCE: Muhlhausen, David B. Testimony before Senate Subcommittee on the Constitution, Civil Rights, and Property Rights. June 27, 2007. https://www.judiciary.senate.gov/imo/media/doc/muhlhausen_testimony_06_27_07.pdf

ANALYSIS

David B. Muhlhausen was a policy analyst at the Heritage Foundation, a conservative think tank, when he testified to a Senate congressional subcommittee on the

Constitution in favor of enshrining the death penalty in the federal justice system. His testimony defended two major contentions: (1) that there is little evidence of racial bias in the federal system, and (2) various scholarly studies have found that capital punishment deters crime.

Regarding race, Muhlhausen testified there was no evidence of racial bias in the federal system even though more than 50% of the defendants on death row in federal prison are African American. He insisted those death row numbers reflect more the seriousness of the crimes in question rather than race. He also cites studies from the Rand Corporation, several studies at Emory University, and a study at the University of Colorado at Denver that all concluded the death penalty serves to deter other crime.

"The Rand study concludes that the decisions to seek the death penalty are driven by characteristics of crimes rather than by race," he told the Senators. "Rand's findings are very compelling because three independent research teams, using the same data but different methodologies, reached the same conclusions." The analyst also emphasized that there is still popular support for the death penalty with more than two-thirds of those surveyed saying that they approved of the practice.

FURTHER READING

Berk, Richard A., Laura J. Hickman, and Steven P. Klein. "Race and the Decision to Seek the Death Penalty in Federal Cases." RAND Corporation. 2006.

Muhlhausen, David B. "How the Death Penalty Saves Lives." Heritage Foundation. September 30, 2014. https://www.heritage.org/civil-society/commentary/how-the-death-penalty-saves-lives

---

- ***Document 41:*** Statement of Bryan Stevenson to the Senate Subcommittee
- ***Date:*** April 8, 2008
- ***Where:*** Washington, D.C.
- ***Significance:*** Bryan Stevenson, the head of the Equal Justice Initiative, has been a staunch opponent of the death penalty for many years. In this statement to Congress, he contended that the United States had a critical shortage of willing and trained attorneys with the necessary resources to represent defendants in capital cases.

DOCUMENT

Activist Bryan Stevenson Shines Light on Legal Representation Issues in Death Penalty Cases

Thank you for the opportunity to appear before this Committee. There remains considerable doubt about America's system of capital punishment. Although we have now executed 1100 people in this country during the last 30 years, there are fundamental problems with the fairness, reliability and propriety of the death penalty in state and federal courts. In the last few years, we have uncovered a shocking rate of error in death penalty cases.

Nearly 130 death row prisoners have been released from death row after being proved innocent or exonerated. Hundreds of other death row prisoners have had their convictions and death sentences overturned after it was established that they were illegally convicted or sentenced. Most disturbingly, there has been evidence that innocent people may have been executed.

These problems with capital punishment have lead to a decline in the rate of executions and a decrease in the death sentencing rate in recent years. A few months ago, New Jersey became the first state since the 1960's to completely abolish capital punishment. However, capital punishment remains a costly and dominant feature of the state and federal criminal justice system.

Many jurisdictions have implemented no reforms or review of their death penalty schemes and the practice of executing prisoners and imposing death sentences goes on without much reflection or review. Perhaps the single most significant problem with the administration of capital punishment is the inadequacy of indigent defense for capital defendants. Without competent and skilled counsel in death penalty cases, there can be no reliability or fairness in the outcomes of these proceedings.

Last month, I testified as an expert in a death penalty case in Oklahoma where a court was examining whether James Fisher had received adequate legal assistance at his capital trial. It was my second trip to Oklahoma on this case. Ten years ago, a federal appeals court reversed Mr. Fisher's capital murder conviction and death sentence because his appointed counsel maintained a trial schedule "so heavy he sometimes would finish one case in the morning and begin trying a new case in the afternoon while the jury was still deliberating." He was completely unfamiliar with the State's evidence and witnesses, conducted no investigation for Mr. Fisher, and called no witnesses. At the penalty phase, counsel called no witnesses and waived opening and closing arguments. Not surprisingly, Mr. Fisher was sentenced to death.

. . .

LEGAL ASSISTANCE FOR CAPITAL DEFENDANTS AT TRIAL IS INADEQUATE

Unfortunately, examples of inadequate representation are not exceptional. Alabama has no state public defender offices and trial judges appoint counsel, many of whom have little training or experience in capital litigation.

Of the 203 people currently on Alabama's death row, more than half (59%) were represented by appointed lawyers whose compensation for preparing the case was capped at $1000 by state statute. There are very few mitigation experts or investigative services available and even though compensation has improved in recent years, compliance with the ABA Guidelines on Adequate Representation in Capital Cases is almost never accomplished.

There are people on death row in Texas who were defended by attorneys who had investigative and expert expenses capped at $500. In some rural areas in Texas, lawyers have received no more than $800 to handle a capital case. People still on Virginia's death row were provided lawyers who were effectively paid an hourly rate of less than $20 an hour. In Pennsylvania, there are currently death row prisoners who were sentenced to death in Philadelphia in the 1980s and 1990s when 80% of the capital cases were handled by appointed lawyers who received a flat fee of$1700 plus $400 for each day in court. Similar restrictions can be found in many states, especially in states where the death penalty is frequently imposed.

Underfunded indigent defense has predictably caused flawed representation in many cases with corresponding doubts about the reliability and fairness of the verdict and sentence. Indigent accused facing execution have been represented by sleeping attorneys, drunk attorneys, attorneys who are almost completely unfamiliar with trial advocacy, criminal defense generally, or death penalty law and procedure in particular, and attorneys who otherwise cannot provide the assurance of reliability or fairness in the client's conviction and death sentence.

Even in states where there are public defender systems, funding and compensation for attorneys remains low and resources for investigation and experts is scarce.

Lawyers who are appointed to capital cases often do not have the resources, training and experience necessary to defend such a case. Capital cases involve different and complex investigative, preparation, and trial methods than other criminal cases. IS Lawyers who are not aware of these differences cannot be as effective.

This becomes especially important during the penalty phase when defense counsel should present mitigating evidence. Lawyers with insufficient time, resources, or training will not know the best way to proceed in the penalty phase, denying indigent capital defendants an effective and compelling mitigation presentation.

The states with the most active death rows are those that have historically poor records of providing competent counsel to people accused of capital crimes. In such a system, the risk of wrongful convictions and error is unacceptably high.

I currently represent Anthony Ray Hinton who is an innocent man who has been on Alabama's death row for 21 years. Mr. Hinton was charged with two separate shooting murders that occurred during robberies at two fast food restaurants.

There were no eyewitnesses and fingerprints found at each crime scene did not match Mr. Hinton. The only evidence linking Mr. Hinton to the murders was a victim in a third shooting who misidentified Mr. Hinton. He was never charged with this third crime, but State lab technicians said that bullets recovered from all three crimes were fired from the same gun and matched a weapon recovered from Mr. Hinton's mother.

The State conceded at trial that there was no connection between the murders and Mr. Hinton other than the weapon match, and the State has repeatedly acknowledged that without a weapon match, Mr. Hinton should be released.

Beyond that, at the time of the third shooting, Mr. Hinton was working in a locked warehouse 15 miles from the crime scene. His supervisor and other employees confirmed his innocence when they testified to this, as did a polygraph test given by the police. However, Mr. Hinton was still prosecuted for capital murder and the judge would not admit the exculpatory polygraph test at trial.

Mr. Hinton, who is poor, received court-appointed counsel whose compensation for preparing the case was capped at $1000 by Alabama law. This lawyer did not receive adequate funds to hire an expert to challenge the State's faulty gun evidence or to fully develop evidence of Mr. Hinton's innocence. Mr. Hinton was convicted and given two death sentences.

Since Alabama is the only state in the country that does not provide legal assistance to death row prisoners after their convictions are affirmed Mr. Hinton desperately tried to find his own volunteer legal assistance to prove his innocence, and my office ended up volunteering to take on his case.

. . .

The effort to provide adequate legal assistance to capital defendants has proved to be unobtainable in many states and there is a tremendous need for dramatic reform. The failure to provide consistent, reliable legal assistance to capital defendants has deeply compromised and weakened the integrity of the entire criminal justice system and more must be done to confront this problem.

. . .

NO RIGHT TO COUNSEL IN STATE POSTCONVICTION

Deficiencies in state systems result in wrongful convictions and unreliable verdicts and sentences that must be corrected and addressed in postconviction proceedings. However, state postconviction proceedings in many states are non-responsive to these problems and even less reliable than the state trial process.

. . .

The Supreme Court has consistently recognized the need for counsel in criminal proceedings. Starting in 1932 with *Powell v. Alabama*, the Court recognized counsel as "fundamental" to due process. This should extend to postconviction proceedings where the constitutional rights that the claims are based on, such as effective assistance of counsel, are central to the criminal justice system. Lawyers in criminal courts are "necessities, not luxuries."

Without counsel to represent indigent people accused of capital crimes, justice is not served. . . .

Without counsel in postconviction proceedings there are instances where justice simply is not served. This is especially true when many of the people who are innocent are not exonerated until the later stages of the process that become increasingly hard for indigent Alabama inmates to get to. Thus, it is hugely important that there is a system in place to provide counsel to indigent people accused of capital crimes even in postconviction proceedings so that Constitutional claims are not lost due to lack of legal assistance.

CONCLUSION

Effective legal counsel is essential to a fair and reliable criminal justice system. Without it, countless number of people are convicted and sentenced to death without ever having a competent, fair, reliable trial.

Currently, representation in capital cases is inadequate. Too often, prisoners are required to find their own volunteer counsel to right the errors that have been committed by trial counsel.

When some of the most fundamental claims, including ineffective assistance of counsel and Brady violations, are left unheard because of ineffective counselor lack of counsel, our criminal justice system cannot be fair and reliable.

This leads to many innocent people being convicted and having no ability to seek relief.

Federal habeas and State postconviction plays an important role in making sure that tragic errors in capital cases are not insulated from correction that is required by the United States Constitution. Competent counsel is necessary to navigating this appellate process.

Even before that point, though, it is imperative that trial counsel investigates and researches adequately and is given the resources and compensation to be able to do this thoroughly.

It is also hugely important that trial counsel that is appointed is trained and experienced in capital cases and is not someone who is unwilling or unable to take on and do the work required of a capital case.

I appreciate this Committee's time and attention to these very important matters.

SOURCE: Stevenson, Bryan. Testimony before Senate Subcommittee on the Constitution. April 8, 2008. https://www.judiciary.senate.gov/imo/media/doc/08-04-08 StevensonBryanTestimony.pdf

ANALYSIS

Bryan Stevenson, the head of the Equal Justice Initiative, is arguably the nation's foremost attorney fighting to end capital punishment and other inhumane or unconstitutional sentences. He has become well known in part as a result of his book *Just*

Mercy (2014), which was made into a hit movie. The book and film describe Stevenson's representation of Walter McMillan, an African American man from Alabama, unfairly sent to death row for a crime he did not commit.

Stevenson also represented Anthony Ray Hinton, a man who served more than a decade on death row for a crime he did not commit. Stevenson refers to Hinton's case in his testimony before the Senate Subcommittee on the Constitution. Stevenson later achieved a great victory before the U.S. Supreme Court in *Hinton v. Alabama* (2014). Stevenson told the members of the subcommittee that Hinton was an innocent man, and he later was able to obtain vindication for Hinton when the Supreme Court invalidated his conviction.

Stevenson's testimony focuses on the lack of quality legal representation for many Americans facing capital charges. Part of the problem is simply one of funding. As Stevenson explained, there is simply not enough money to be paid to attorneys to handle these cases. Many of those charged with capital crimes are indigent and do not have the funds to hire a private attorney. Thus, appointed attorneys handle quite a few of the capital cases across the country.

Stevenson emphasized that some death penalty attorneys only receive a pittance and are capped out at $1,000 or even less for handling such cases. He also discussed the lack of training for many lawyers who are simply not qualified or prepared enough to handle capital cases.

Another part of Stevenson's testimony focused on the post-conviction phase in capital cases. An inmate found guilty at trial can appeal his or her sentence. This is called the direct appeal. Once the direct appeal is over, the inmate can file what is known as a post-conviction petition in state court, arguing that his constitutional rights were violated at some point during the trial or appeal process. For example, many inmates claim that they did not receive the effective assistance of counsel from their attorneys.

According to Stevenson, adequate provision of counsel for inmates in the post-conviction proceeding does not always exist. "Without counsel in postconviction proceedings there are instances where justice simply is not served," he told the members of the subcommittee. Once an inmate has exhausted state post-conviction proceedings, the inmate may be able to file a federal habeas corpus claim in federal court, contending that his or her constitutional rights were violated. But, once an inmate is convicted and loses on direct appeal, it is often a herculean legal task to try to undo that conviction.

Stevenson concluded that much more needs to be done to ensure that capital defendants receive proper legal representation in their cases.

FURTHER READING

Hinton, Anthony R., with Sara L. Hardin. *The Sun Does Shine: How I Found Life, Freedom and Justice*. New York: St. Martin's Griffin, 2019.

Stevenson, Bryan. *Just Mercy: A Story of Justice and Redemption*. One World, 2014.

- ***Document 42:*** Supreme Court's Decision in *Kennedy v. Louisiana*
- ***Date:*** June 25, 2008
- ***Where:*** Washington, D.C.
- ***Significance:*** This decision narrowed circumstances under which capital punishment could be utilized, eliminating cases of child rape. The decision represented a natural extension of the Court's decisions in *Coker v. Georgia* (1977), *Atkins v. Virginia* (2002), and *Roper v. Simmons* (2005), all of which limited the offenses for which a perpetrator could be executed by the state.

DOCUMENT

Supreme Court Rules Child Rape Not a Capital Offense

The National Government and, beyond it, the separate States are bound by the proscriptive mandates of the Eighth Amendment to the Constitution of the United States, and all persons within those respective jurisdictions may invoke its protection. Patrick Kennedy, the petitioner here, seeks to set aside his death sentence under the Eighth Amendment. He was charged by the respondent, the State of Louisiana, with the aggravated rape of his then-8-year-old stepdaughter. After a jury trial petitioner was convicted and sentenced to death under a state statute authorizing capital punishment for the rape of a child under 12 years of age. This case presents the question whether the Constitution bars respondent from imposing the death penalty for the rape of a child where the crime did not result, and was not intended to result, in death of the victim. We hold the Eighth Amendment prohibits the death penalty for this offense. The Louisiana statute is unconstitutional.

Petitioner's crime was one that cannot be recounted in these pages in a way sufficient to capture in full the hurt and horror inflicted on his victim or to convey the revulsion society, and the jury that represents it, sought to express by sentencing petitioner to death. At 9:18 a.m. on March 2, 1998, petitioner called 911 to report that his stepdaughter, referred to here as L. H., had been raped. He told the 911 operator that L. H. had been in the garage while he readied his son for school. Upon hearing loud screaming, petitioner said, he ran outside and found L. H. in the side yard. Two neighborhood boys, petitioner told the operator, had dragged L. H. from the garage to the yard, pushed her down, and raped her. Petitioner claimed he saw one of the boys riding away on a blue 10-speed bicycle.

When police arrived at petitioner's home between 9:20 and 9:30 a.m., they found L. H. on her bed, wearing a T-shirt and wrapped in a bloody blanket. She was bleeding profusely from the vaginal area. Petitioner told police he had carried her from the yard to the bathtub and then to the bed. Consistent with this explanation, police found a thin line of blood drops in the garage on the way to the house and then up the stairs. Once in the bedroom, petitioner had used a basin of water and a cloth to wipe blood from the victim. This later prevented medical personnel from collecting a reliable DNA sample.

L.H. was transported to the Children's Hospital. An expert in pediatric forensic medicine testified that L.H.'s injuries were the most severe he had seen from a sexual assault in his four years of practice. A laceration to the left wall of the vagina had separated her cervix from the back of her vagina, causing her rectum to protrude into the vaginal structure. Her entire perineum was torn from the posterior fourchette to the anus. The injuries required emergency surgery.

At the scene of the crime, at the hospital, and in the first weeks that followed, both L.H. and petitioner maintained in their accounts to investigators that L.H. had been raped by two neighborhood boys. One of L.H.'s doctors testified at trial that L. H. told all hospital personnel the same version of the rape, although she reportedly told one family member that petitioner raped her. . . .

Eight days after the crime, and despite L.H.'s insistence that petitioner was not the offender, petitioner was arrested for the rape. The State's investigation had drawn the accuracy of petitioner and L.H.'s story into question. Though the defense at trial proffered alternative explanations, the case for the prosecution, credited by the jury, was based upon the following evidence: An inspection of the side yard immediately after the assault was inconsistent with a rape having occurred there, the grass having been found mostly undisturbed but for a small patch of coagulated blood. Petitioner said that one of the perpetrators fled the crime scene on a blue 10-speed bicycle but gave inconsistent descriptions of the bicycle's features, such as its handlebars. Investigators found a bicycle matching petitioner and L.H.'s description in tall grass behind a nearby apartment, and petitioner identified it as the bicycle one of the perpetrators was riding. Yet its tires were flat, it did not have gears, and it was covered in spider webs. In addition police found blood on the underside of L.H.'s mattress. This convinced them the rape took place in her bedroom, not outside the house.

. . .

About a month after petitioner's arrest L.H. was removed from the custody of her mother, who had maintained until that point that petitioner was not involved in the rape. On June 22, 1998, L.H. was returned home and told her mother for the first time that petitioner had raped her. And on December 16, 1999, about 21 months after the rape, L.H. recorded her accusation in a videotaped interview with the Child Advocacy Center.

The State charged petitioner with aggravated rape of a child . . . and sought the death penalty. At all times relevant to petitioner's case, the statute provided:

> "A. Aggravated rape is a rape committed . . . where the anal or vaginal sexual intercourse is deemed to be without lawful consent of the victim because it is committed under any one or more of the following circumstances:
>
> . . .

"(4) When the victim is under the age of twelve years. Lack of knowledge of the victim's age shall not be a defense.

. . .

"D. Whoever commits the crime of aggravated rape shall be punished by life imprisonment at hard labor without benefit of parole, probation, or suspension of sentence.

"(1) However, if the victim was under the age of twelve years, as provided by Paragraph A(4) of this Section:

"(a) And if the district attorney seeks a capital verdict, the offender shall be punished by death or life imprisonment at hard labor without benefit of parole, probation, or suspension of sentence, in accordance with the determination of the jury."

. . .

The jury having found petitioner guilty of aggravated rape, the penalty phase ensued. The State presented the testimony of S.L., who is the cousin and goddaughter of petitioner's ex-wife. S.L. testified that petitioner sexually abused her three times when she was eight years old and that the last time involved sexual intercourse. She did not tell anyone until two years later and did not pursue legal action.

The jury unanimously determined that petitioner should be sentenced to death. The Supreme Court of Louisiana affirmed. . . .

The court acknowledged that petitioner would be the first person executed for committing child rape since La. Stat. Ann. §14:42 was amended in 1995 and that Louisiana is in the minority of jurisdictions that authorize the death penalty for the crime of child rape. . . .

The state court next asked whether "child rapists rank among the worst offenders." It noted the severity of the crime; that the execution of child rapists would serve the goals of deterrence and retribution; and that, unlike in *Atkins* and *Roper*, there were no characteristics of petitioner that tended to mitigate his moral culpability. It concluded: "[S]hort of first-degree murder, we can think of no other non-homicide crime more deserving [of capital punishment]."

On this reasoning the Supreme Court of Louisiana rejected petitioner's argument that the death penalty for the rape of a child under 12 years is disproportionate and upheld the constitutionality of the statute. . . .

We granted certiorari. See 552 U.S. ___ (2008).

The Eighth Amendment, applicable to the States through the Fourteenth Amendment, provides that "[e]xcessive bail shall not be required, nor excessive fines imposed, nor cruel and unusual punishments inflicted." The Amendment proscribes "all excessive punishments, as well as cruel and unusual punishments that may or may not be excessive." . . .

Evolving standards of decency must embrace and express respect for the dignity of the person, and the punishment of criminals must conform to that rule. As we shall discuss, punishment is justified under one or more of three principal rationales: rehabilitation, deterrence, and retribution. It is the last of these, retribution, that most often can contradict the law's own ends. This is of particular concern when the Court interprets the meaning of the Eighth Amendment in capital cases. When the law punishes by death, it risks its own sudden descent into brutality, transgressing the constitutional commitment to decency and restraint.

. . .

Based both on consensus and our own independent judgment, our holding is that a death sentence for one who raped but did not kill a child, and who did not intend to assist another in killing the child, is unconstitutional under the Eighth and Fourteenth Amendments.

The existence of objective indicia of consensus against making a crime punishable by death was a relevant concern in *Roper*, *Atkins*, *Coker*, and *Enmund*, and we follow the approach of those cases here. The history of the death penalty for the crime of rape is an instructive beginning point.

In 1925, 18 States, the District of Columbia, and the Federal Government had statutes that authorized the death penalty for the rape of a child or an adult. Between 1930 and 1964, 455 people were executed for those crimes. To our knowledge the last individual executed for the rape of a child was Ronald Wolfe in 1964.

In 1972, *Furman* invalidated most of the state statutes authorizing the death penalty for the crime of rape; and in *Furman*'s aftermath only six States reenacted their capital rape provisions. Three States—Georgia, North Carolina, and Louisiana—did so with respect to all rape offenses. Three States—Florida, Mississippi, and Tennessee—did so with respect only to child rape.

Louisiana reintroduced the death penalty for rape of a child in 1995. Under the current statute, any anal, vaginal, or oral intercourse with a child under the age of 13 constitutes aggravated rape and is punishable by death. . . .

By contrast, 44 States have not made child rape a capital offense. . . .

The evidence of a national consensus with respect to the death penalty for child rapists, as with respect to juveniles, mentally retarded offenders, and vicarious felony murderers, shows divided opinion but, on balance, an opinion against it. Thirty-seven jurisdictions—36 States plus the Federal Government—have the death penalty. As mentioned above, only six of those jurisdictions authorize the death penalty for rape of a child. Though our review of national consensus is not confined to tallying the number of States with applicable death penalty legislation, it is of significance that, in 45 jurisdictions, petitioner could not be executed for child rape of any kind. That number surpasses the 30 States in *Atkins* and *Roper* and the 42 States in *Enmund* that prohibited the death penalty under the circumstances those cases considered.

. . .

"Rape is without doubt deserving of serious punishment; but in terms of moral depravity and of the injury to the person and to the public, it does not compare with murder, which does involve the unjustified taking of human life. Although it may be accompanied by another crime, rape by definition does not include the death of . . . another person. The murderer kills; the rapist, if no more than that, does not". . . .

We conclude on the basis of this review that there is no clear indication that state legislatures have misinterpreted *Coker* to hold that the death penalty for child rape is unconstitutional. The small number of States that have enacted this penalty, then, is relevant to determining whether there is a consensus against capital punishment for this crime.

Respondent insists that the six States where child rape is a capital offense, along with the States that have proposed but not yet enacted applicable death penalty legislation, reflect a consistent direction of change in support of the death penalty for child rape. Consistent change might counterbalance an otherwise weak demonstration of consensus. . . .

Respondent and its *amici* identify five States where, in their view, legislation authorizing capital punishment for child rape is pending. . . .

Aside from pending legislation, it is true that in the last 13 years there has been change towards making child rape a capital offense. This is evidenced by six new death penalty statutes, three enacted in the last two years. But this showing is not as significant as the data in *Atkins*, where 18 States between 1986 and 2001 had enacted legislation prohibiting the execution of mentally retarded persons . . .

There are measures of consensus other than legislation. Statistics about the number of executions may inform the consideration whether capital punishment for the crime of child rape is regarded as unacceptable in our society. These statistics confirm our determination from our review of state statutes that there is a social consensus against the death penalty for the crime of child rape.

Nine States—Florida, Georgia, Louisiana, Mississippi, Montana, Oklahoma, South Carolina, Tennessee, and Texas—have permitted capital punishment for adult or child rape for some length of time between the Court's 1972 decision in *Furman* and today. Yet no individual has been executed for the rape of an adult or child since 1964, and no execution for any other nonhomicide offense has been conducted since 1963. . . .

Louisiana is the only State since 1964 that has sentenced an individual to death for the crime of child rape; and petitioner and Richard Davis, who was convicted and sentenced to death for the aggravated rape of a 5-year-old child by a Louisiana jury in December 2007, are the only two individuals now on death row in the United States for a nonhomicide offense.

After reviewing the authorities informed by contemporary norms, including the history of the death penalty for this and other nonhomicide crimes, current state statutes and new enactments, and the number of executions since 1964, we conclude there is a national consensus against capital punishment for the crime of child rape.

As we have said in other Eighth Amendment cases, objective evidence of contemporary values as it relates to punishment for child rape is entitled to great weight, but it does not end our inquiry. . . .

We cannot dismiss the years of long anguish that must be endured by the victim of child rape.

It does not follow, though, that capital punishment is a proportionate penalty for the crime. The constitutional prohibition against excessive or cruel and unusual punishments mandates that the State's power to punish "be exercised within the limits of civilized standards."

. . .

Our response to this case law, which is still in search of a unifying principle, has been to insist upon confining the instances in which capital punishment may be imposed. . . .

Our concern here is limited to crimes against individual persons. We do not address, for example, crimes defining and punishing treason, espionage, terrorism, and drug kingpin activity, which are offenses against the State. As it relates to crimes against individuals, though, the death penalty should not be expanded to instances where the victim's life was not taken.

. . .

Consistent with evolving standards of decency and the teachings of our precedents we conclude that, in determining whether the death penalty is excessive, there is a distinction between intentional first-degree murder on the one hand and nonhomicide crimes against individual persons, even including child rape, on the other. . . .

In reaching our conclusion we find significant the number of executions that would be allowed under respondent's approach. The crime of child rape, considering its reported incidents, occurs more often than first-degree murder. Approximately 5,702 incidents of vaginal, anal, or oral rape of a child under the age of 12 were reported nationwide in 2005; this is almost twice the total incidents of intentional murder for victims of all ages (3,405) reported during the same period. . . .

Our decision is consistent with the justifications offered for the death penalty. *Gregg* instructs that capital punishment is excessive when it is grossly out of proportion to the crime or it does not fulfill the two distinct social purposes served by the death penalty: retribution and deterrence of capital crimes.

. . .

It is not at all evident that the child rape victim's hurt is lessened when the law permits the death of the perpetrator. Capital cases require a long-term commitment by those who testify for the prosecution, especially when guilt and sentencing determinations are in multiple proceedings. . . .

Society's desire to inflict the death penalty for child rape by enlisting the child victim to assist it over the course of years in asking for capital punishment forces a moral choice on the child, who is not of mature age to make that choice. The way the death penalty here involves the child victim in its enforcement can compromise a decent legal system; and this is but a subset of fundamental difficulties capital punishment can cause in the administration and enforcement of laws proscribing child rape.

. . .

With respect to deterrence, if the death penalty adds to the risk of non-reporting, that, too, diminishes the penalty's objectives. Underreporting is a common problem with respect to child sexual abuse. . . .

In addition, by in effect making the punishment for child rape and murder equivalent, a State that punishes child rape by death may remove a strong incentive for the rapist not to kill the victim. Assuming the offender behaves in a rational way, as one must to justify the penalty on grounds of deterrence, the penalty in some respects gives less protection, not more, to the victim, who is often the sole witness to the crime. It might be argued that, even if the death penalty results in a marginal increase in the incentive to kill, this is counterbalanced by a marginally increased deterrent to commit the crime at all. Whatever balance the legislature strikes, however, uncertainty on the point makes the argument for the penalty less compelling than for homicide crimes.

Each of these propositions, standing alone, might not establish the unconstitutionality of the death penalty for the crime of child rape. Taken in sum, however, they demonstrate the serious negative consequences of making child rape a capital offense. These considerations lead us to conclude, in our independent judgment, that the death penalty is not a proportional punishment for the rape of a child.

Our determination that there is a consensus against the death penalty for child rape raises the question whether the Court's own institutional position and its holding will have the effect of blocking further or later consensus in favor of the penalty from developing. The Court, it will be argued, by the act of addressing the constitutionality of the death penalty, intrudes upon the consensus-making process. By imposing a negative restraint, the argument runs, the Court makes it more difficult for consensus to change or emerge. The Court, according to the criticism, itself becomes enmeshed in the process, part judge and part the maker of that which it judges.

. . .

The judgment of the Supreme Court of Louisiana upholding the capital sentence is reversed. This case is remanded for further proceedings not inconsistent with this opinion.

SOURCE: Kennedy v. Louisiana, 554 U.S. 407 (2008).

ANALYSIS

The Court's decision represents an extension of its ruling in *Coker v. Georgia* (1977) that a defendant could not receive the death penalty for the crime of rape when the victim did not die. The Court reasoned that the crime of rape—though quite serious and harmful—was simply not as horrible as murder.

More than 30 years later, the Court addressed the subject in a different context and frankly, one that generates even more emotional reactions—child rapists. The argument for extending the death penalty to child rapists focuses on the age of the victims and the lasting and sometimes permanent harm inflicted upon those who are most vulnerable.

Patrick Kennedy, the defendant in the case, was convicted by a Louisiana jury of raping his own 8-year-old stepdaughter in March 1998 and then blaming his heinous crime on two boys in the neighborhood. Louisiana was one of the few states that allowed for the death penalty for the crime of child rape.

As the Supreme Court pointed out, between 1930 and 1964, there were more than 450 persons executed for the crime of child rape across the United States. From 1964 to 2008, however, no one convicted of that awful crime had been executed. Furthermore, in 1925, 18 states had laws on the books that made the crime of child rape a death-eligible crime. In 2008, there were only six states that had such laws on the books and only two defendants in the United States—Patrick Kennedy and another man—on death row for the crime of child rape.

The Court was sharply divided 5–4 in this decision. Writing for the dissenters, Justice Samuel Alito explained: "The harm that is caused to the victims and to society at large by the worst child rapists is grave. It is the judgment of the Louisiana lawmakers and those in an increasing number of other States that these harms justify the death penalty. The Court provides no cogent explanation why this legislative judgment should be overridden. Conclusory references to 'decency,' 'moderation,' 'restraint,' 'full progress,' and 'moral judgment' are not enough."

Alito criticized the Court for concluding that there was an emerging national consensus emerging against imposing death sentences for child rapists. Alito pointed out that several states had passed such laws in recent years and that bills had been introduced to make child rape a death-eligible crime in several other state legislatures.

Politicians all across the political aisle criticized the Court's decision in *Kennedy v. Louisiana*. Barack Obama, then a U.S. senator from Illinois and a presidential candidate, expressed his disagreement with the Court's decision. "I have said repeatedly that I think that the death penalty should be applied in very narrow circumstances for the most egregious of crimes," Obama said at a news conference in Chicago. "I think that the rape of a small child, six or eight years old, is a heinous crime and if a state makes a decision that under narrow, limited, well-defined circumstances the death penalty is at least potentially applicable, that that does not violate our Constitution."

For his part, Patrick Kennedy received a life sentence without the possibility of parole at a sentencing rehearing in 2009.

FURTHER READING

Greenhouse, Linda. "Justices Bar Death Penalty for Rape of a Child." *New York Times*. June 26, 2008.

Stevenson, Caroline. "Louisiana v. Kennedy." *Duke Journal of Constitutional Law & Public Policy* 4, Sidebar 174 (2009).

- ***Document 43:*** Justice Stevens' statement in *Thompson v. McNeil*
- ***Date:*** March 9, 2009
- ***Where:*** Washington, D.C.
- ***Significance:*** Justice Stevens' statement regarding the Court's denial of review in this death penalty appeal highlighted a long-standing critique of the death penalty—that unnecessarily long delays between sentence and execution constituted a form of cruel punishment forbidden by the Eighth Amendment.

DOCUMENT

Justice John Paul Stevens Says Long Delays in Carrying Out Executions Are Cruel

Last Term, in my opinion in *Baze v. Rees* (2008), I suggested that the "time for a dispassionate, impartial comparison of the enormous costs that death penalty litigation imposes on society with the benefits that it produces has surely arrived." . . .

In June 1976, having been advised by counsel that he would not receive the death penalty if he accepted responsibility for his crime, petitioner pleaded guilty to a capital offense. The advice was erroneous, and he was sentenced to death. Since that time, two state-court judgments have set aside his death sentence. At a third penalty hearing—after petitioner presented mitigation evidence about his limited mental capacity and dysfunctional childhood that had previously been barred—five members of the advisory jury voted against a death sentence, but the court again imposed a sentence of death.

Thirty-two years have passed since petitioner was first sentenced to death. In prior cases, both JUSTICE BREYER and I have noted that substantially delayed executions arguably violate the Eighth Amendment's prohibition against cruel and unusual punishment. . . . Petitioner's case involves a longer delay than any of those earlier cases.

As he awaits execution, petitioner has endured especially severe conditions of confinement, spending up to 23 hours per day in isolation in a 6- by 9-foot cell. Two death warrants have been signed against him and stayed only shortly before he was scheduled to be put to death. The dehumanizing effects of such treatment are undeniable. . . . Moreover, as I explained in *Lackey*, delaying an execution does not further public purposes of retribution and deterrence but only diminishes whatever possible benefit society might receive from petitioner's death. It would therefore be appropriate to conclude that a punishment of death after significant delay is "so totally without penological justification that it results in the gratuitous infliction of suffering."

While the length of petitioner's confinement under sentence of death is extraordinary, the concerns his case raises are not unique. Clarence Allen Lackey had spent 17 years on death row when this Court reviewed his petition for certiorari. Today, condemned inmates await execution for an average of nearly 13 years. To my mind, this figure underscores the fundamental inhumanity and unworkability of the death penalty as it is administered in the United States.

Some respond that delays in carrying out executions are the result of this Court's insistence on excessive process. But delays have multiple causes, including "the States' failure to apply constitutionally sufficient procedures at the time of initial [conviction or] sentencing." The reversible error rate in capital trials is staggering. More than 30 percent of death verdicts imposed between 1973 and 2000 have been overturned, and 129 inmates sentenced to death during that time have been exonerated, often more than a decade after they were convicted. Judicial process takes time, but the error rate in capital cases illustrates its necessity. We are duty, bound to "insure that every safeguard is observed" when "a defendant's life is at stake."

In sum, our experience during the past three decades has demonstrated that delays in state-sponsored killings are inescapable and that executing defendants after such delays is unacceptably cruel. This inevitable cruelty, coupled with the diminished justification for carrying out an execution after the lapse of so much time, reinforces my opinion that contemporary decisions "to retain the death penalty as a part of our law are the product of habit and inattention rather than an acceptable deliberative process."

SOURCE: *Thompson v. McNeil*, 556 U.S. 1114 (2009).

ANALYSIS

Justice John Paul Stevens was one of the justices who voted in favor of the Georgia death penalty statute in *Gregg v. Georgia* in 1976. However, over the years he often voted against death sentences. He wrote the Court's opinion in *Atkins v. Virginia* (2002), ruling that it violated the Eighth Amendment to execute defendants who committed murder under the age of 18.

In the case of *Thompson v. McNeil*, William L. Thompson had spent 32 years on death row. He was sentenced to death in June 1976 for the brutal murder, rape, and kidnapping of Sally Ivester. Thompson pleaded guilty on the faulty advice of his lawyer who told him that by pleading guilty, he would not receive the death penalty.

To Justice Stevens—and Justice Stephen Breyer who also wrote separately—the years Thompson had spent on death row were cruel within the meaning of the Eighth Amendment. Stevens also emphasized that Thompson had nearly been executed on two occasions, only to have reprieves. He viewed this as a form of torture of death row inmates who are left guessing for years about their ultimate fate.

However, Stevens and Breyer were the only justices who wanted to raise this issue for consideration. The Court denied review in Thompson's case. Justice Clarence Thomas responded to Stevens' and Breyer's concern about long delays being cruel. Thomas memorably wrote, "'It is the crime—and not the punishment imposed by the jury or the delay in petitioner's execution—that was 'unacceptably cruel.'"

Justice Stevens retired from the Court only a year later, in 2010. Upon his retirement, he wrote a book titled *Six Amendments: How and Why We Should Change the Constitution*. One of his suggested amendments was to change the language and parameters of the Eighth Amendment to prohibit the death penalty.

FURTHER READING

Liptak, Adam. "Justices Rule on Legal Effects of Slow-Moving Cases." *New York Times*. March 9, 2009.

Stevens, John P. *Six Amendments: How and Why We Should Change the Constitution*. New York: Little, Brown & Co., 2014.

6

CONTEMPORARY CAPITAL PUNISHMENT ISSUES

From the beginning of the twenty-first century to the year 2021, 10 states have abolished the death penalty, beginning with New Jersey and New York in 2007. The other states that have followed suit in formally rejecting capital punishment are New Mexico (2009), Connecticut (2012), Maryland (2013), Delaware (2016), Washington (2018), New Hampshire (2019), Colorado (2020), and Virginia (2021).

As of early 2022, there are 27 states that still have death penalty statutes on the books, but in many of them, a death penalty sentence has not been carried out for years. Another significant development is the action of the Virginia legislature. The death penalty always has had more support in the southern part of the country. In 2021, Virginia became the first southern state to abolish the death penalty. Governor Ralph Northam spoke for many in the state when he declared: "The death penalty system is fundamentally flawed—it is inequitable, ineffective, and it has no place in this Commonwealth or this country."

Only 11 persons were executed across the United States in 2021. The Death Penalty Information Center has called this a "historic low." Three of those individuals were executed by the federal government, three by Texas, two by Oklahoma, and one each in Alabama, Mississippi, and Missouri.

Death penalty opponents contend that the death penalty is on life support. However, an April 2021, a Pew Research survey found that a majority of adults in the United States still favor the death penalty. Six in 10 adults, for example, favored the application of the death penalty for convicted murderers. Moreover, in some states, such as Texas and Tennessee, government-sanctioned executions continue to proceed.

FURTHER READING

Cole, David. "Justice Breyer and the Death Penalty." *New Yorker*. June 30, 2015.

Death Penalty Information Center. "The Death Penalty in 2021: Year End Report." December 16, 2021. https://deathpenaltyinfo.org/facts-and-research/dpic-reports/dpic-year-end-reports/the-death-penalty-in-2021-year-end-report. Last accessed January 17, 2021.

Death Penalty Information Center. "State by State: States with and without the Death Penalty—2021." https://deathpenaltyinfo.org/state-and-federal-info/state-by-state. Last accessed October 19, 2021.

Gramlick, John. "10 Facts about the Death Penalty in the U.S." PEW Research Center. July 19, 2021.

- ***Document 44:*** Catholic Leaders' Statement against the Death Penalty
- ***Date:*** September 26, 2011
- ***Where:*** Dayton, Ohio
- ***Significance:*** The action by these leading Catholic theologians at universities across the country was in direct response to the controversial execution of Troy Davis, an African American who always maintained his innocence in the murder of a Georgia police officer.

DOCUMENT

Catholic Theologians Sign Statement Against the Death Penalty

A CATHOLIC CALL TO ABOLISH THE DEATH PENALTY

There were two state-sanctioned executions in the United States on September 21, 2011. In Georgia, Troy Anthony Davis, an African American man, was put to death for the 1989 murder of Savannah police officer Mark MacPhail. In Texas, Lawrence Brewer, a white supremacist, was executed for his participation in the racist hate crime dragging murder of James Byrd in Jasper in 1998. As theologians, scholars, and social justice advocates who participate in the public discussion of Catholic theology, we protest the state-sanctioned killings of both of these men, and we call for the abolition of the death penalty in the US.

Davis' execution is particularly troubling for it shines a stark light upon many longstanding concerns about capital punishment in the US. We mourn the death of Officer MacPhail and express our deepest sympathies to his family for their tragic loss. However, we believe that a grave miscarriage of justice took place with Davis' execution. As many legal experts have pointed out, including former FBI Director and federal judge and prosecutor William S. Sessions, serious doubt remains about Davis' guilt. Until his last breath he maintained his innocence. The failure of the Georgia Board of Pardons and Paroles, a Federal Appeals Judge, the Georgia Supreme Court, and the U.S. Supreme Court to grant Davis a new trial reveals a deeply flawed justice system. We therefore call upon lawmakers and President Obama to immediately repeal the Antiterrorism and Effective Death Penalty Act, which created the legal conditions for executing a man whose guilt was not established beyond reasonable doubt.

Even those who do not share our faith convictions ought to recognize, as Justice William J. Brennan put it, "the death penalty is imposed not only in a freakish and discriminatory manner, but also in some cases upon defendants who are innocent." The horrific legacy of lynching in the US casts its evil shadow over current application of the death penalty. Studies have shown that black defendants are more likely to receive the death penalty. In many states with capital punishment, defendants are from 3 to 5 times more likely to be executed if their victim was white. In states that retain the death penalty, 98 percent of district attorneys are white and only 1 percent are black. Execution is also irrevocable, and innocent people have likely been victims of it. Since 1973, 138 persons have been exonerated from death row, most of whom were people of color and economically poor.

The US Conference of Catholic Bishops stated that "the sanction of death, when it is not necessary to protect society, violates respect for human life and dignity . . . Its application is deeply flawed and can be irreversibly wrong, is prone to errors, and is biased by factors such as race, the quality of legal representation, and where the crime was committed. We have other ways to punish criminals and protect society." In earlier eras, Roman Catholic tradition acknowledged the necessity of capital punishment, in rare cases, to protect citizens from threats to the common good. In recent times, with more secure prison facilities that give us the means to offer such protection without executions, our church leaders have affirmed the need to eradicate the death penalty.

There are, moreover, theological reasons for this stance, and here we speak especially to our sisters and brothers in faith. In calling for the abolition of the "cruel and unnecessary" death penalty, Blessed Pope John Paul II argued that "[t]he new evangelization calls for followers of Christ who are unconditionally pro-life: who will proclaim, celebrate, and serve the Gospel of life in every situation. A sign of hope is the increasing recognition that the dignity of human life must never be taken away, even in the case of someone who has done great evil." Our theological tradition recalls that our Lord Jesus Christ was unjustly and brutally nailed to a cross to die. The great 20th century theologian Karl Barth put the matter this way: "Now that Jesus Christ has been nailed to the cross for the sins of the world, how can we still use the thought of expiation to establish the death penalty?" The Eucharistic celebration calls Catholics to remember all crucified people, including the legacy of lynching, in light of the life, ministry, death, and resurrection of Jesus Christ. His Gospel message of forgiveness and love of enemies presents a difficult challenge, especially to those who have lost loved ones at the hands of a murderer. Yet, the Gospel teaches us how to become fully human: love, not hatred and revenge, liberates us. We need to forgive and love both in fidelity to the Gospel and for our own well-being. The experience of groups like Murder Victims' Families for Human Rights, who advocate against the death penalty, attests to this.

Therefore, in concert with our recent popes and bishops, we oppose the death penalty, whether a person on death row is guilty or innocent, on both theological and practical grounds. While we especially deplore and lament the killing of Troy Davis, we also decry the death sentences of the more than 3,200 inmates on death row and the 1,268 executions since the death penalty was reinstated by the Supreme Court in 1976. We urge our nation to abolish capital punishment, and we also implore our churches to work unwaveringly to end it as well as all other threats to human life and dignity.

SOURCE: Winright, Tobias, Gerald J. Beyer, Emily Reimer-Barry, and Alexander Mikulich. "A Catholic Call to Abolish the Death Penalty." *Catholic Moral Theology* [blog]. October 10, 2011. https://catholicmoraltheology.com/a-catholic-call-to-abolish-the-death-penalty/

ANALYSIS

About 150 Catholic theologians from universities across the country signed on to a statement of faith-based opposition to the death penalty drafted by Tobias Winright, an associate professor in theology at St. Louis University. The religious leaders signed their statement only five days after the controversial execution of Troy Davis, an African American man from Savannah, Georgia, who was convicted and sentenced to death for the alleged killing of a white police officer in 1989.

The religious leaders called the Troy Davis case "particularly troubling" because (1) he steadfastly maintained his innocence of the crime and (2) many observers questioned the evidence in his case. For example, the Catholic leaders note in their statement that former Federal Bureau of Investigation's (FBI) director William Sessions said there were disturbing questions as to whether Davis was guilty of the crime for which he was convicted. Furthermore, seven of the nine witnesses who testified at Davis' 1991 trial later recanted their testimony. Many of these witnesses contended that they were pressured into signing statements.

Equally as disturbing, there was no forensic evidence tying Davis to the crime. No weapon was ever found. Many people across the world supported Davis, and the refrain "I am Troy Davis" became a powerful rallying cry for death penalty opponents.

In their statement, the Catholic leaders also decried the recent execution of Lawrence Brewer, a white supremacist from Texas who participated in the hate crime murder of the African American man James Byrd. There was no doubt about Brewer's guilt, but the leaders mentioned his recent execution to emphasize their opposition to the death penalty in all cases.

The leaders opposed the death penalty on both theological and practical grounds. On theological grounds, they urged the spirit of forgiveness and redemption. On practical grounds, they decried the process that led to the execution of Davis, a man who very well may have been innocent. They urged the political leaders of the United States to abolish the death penalty, which had been reinstituted in the country in *Gregg v. Georgia* (1976).

FURTHER READING

Marlowe, Jen. *I Am Troy Davis*. Haymarket Books, 2013.

McElwee, Joshua J. "Over 150 Theologians Call for Abolition of Death Penalty." *National Catholic Reporter*. September 27, 2011.

Winright, Tobias, Geraldine Beyer, Emily Reimer-Barry, and Alexander Mikulich. "A Catholic Call to Abolish the Death Penalty." Catholic Moral Theology. September 27, 2011.

- ***Document 45:*** Anthony Graves' testimony to Senate Subcommittee on the U.S. Constitution
- ***Date:*** June 19, 2012
- ***Where:*** Washington, D.C.
- ***Significance:*** The story of Anthony Graves, who was exonerated from his death penalty conviction, certainly moved the senators who heard his compelling testimony about the poor conditions on death row. Graves sought to explain in detail to members of Congress just how bad these conditions were.

DOCUMENT

Former Death Row Inmate Testifies before Congress about His Experiences

On November 1, 1994, I heard the gavel fall and the judge announce, "Anthony Graves, I hereby sentence you to death by lethal injection." The jury had already convicted me of murdering six people and burning down their house down to cover up the crime. I was completely innocent: they had the wrong guy. I was scared of dying for a crime I did not commit, but I believed in my innocence and hoped someone, somewhere would make it right.

What I didn't know then was that this wrongful death sentence was only part of the torture I would experience for the next 18-and-a-half years. I didn't know that I would be forced to live in an 8x12 cage. I didn't know I would have to use a steel toilet, connected to my steel sink, in plain view of the male and female corrections officers would walk the runs in front of my cell. I didn't know that for years on end I would have no physical contact with a single human being.

I didn't know that guards would feed me like a dog, through a slot in my door. Instead of providing basic nutrients, the food sometimes contained rat feces, broken glass, or the sweat of the inmate who cooked it. This diet caused me health problems that continue today. The prison gave me no phone to call my loved ones, no television to keep up with the world and local events, and no real medical care. I lived behind a steel door, with filthy mesh-covered windows looking out to the run; my only window to the outside world was a tiny one on the top of the back wall of my cell. With its peeling, old, and dull paint, my cage was the image of an abandoned one-room project apartment. If I had known when I was sentenced all I would have to go through before I would win my freedom, I don't know if even my faith in my own innocence would have been enough to sustain me.

I was proven innocent in 2010, and became death row exonoree number 138. Some people say that my exoneration, and those of 11 other Texas death row inmates, proves that our system works: the system freed me before I was executed. These people don't understand (among other things) that a death sentence for an innocent person in Texas comes with the physical, emotional, and psychological torture of solitary confinement. If the argument is the State can hold death-row inmates until their appeals finish (and they are exonerated like me or their appeals fail and execution can go forward), shouldn't the State at least keep us physically and psychologically healthy for that time period? Shouldn't they keep us whole? Because Texas did not do that for me, I suffer from ongoing problems—body and mind. I'm innocent and I'm free, but I pay for my freedom with mood swings, emotional breakdowns, veins calcified with plaque, sleepless nights, loneliness, and difficulty being in large crowds. And it was even worse for other guys.

I saw guys who dropped their appeals because of the intolerable conditions. Before his execution, one inmate told me he would rather die than continue existing under these inhumane conditions. I saw guys come to prison sane, and leave this world insane, talking nonsense on the execution gurney. One guy suffered some of his last days smearing feces, lying naked in the recreation yard, and urinating on himself.

Some of us on death row were innocent. Some were unlawfully sentenced to death and had their sentences thrown out. We all suffered the same. If you believe in the death penalty, I hope you would at least agree that some of us—the innocent ones and ones unlawfully sentenced to die—did not deserve this torture. Even if you believe in the death penalty, these torturous conditions make no sense. They damaged guys so much they could not repent for their crimes. Guys could not focus on the wrong they had done when they had a legitimate complaint of being tortured on death row by the State of Texas.

And the torture was unnecessary. We all suffered it because since 2000 all Texas death row inmates are incarcerated in solitary confinement, even if they behave. It is the only part of the Texas prison system where an inmate is forced to live in solitary confinement based completely on his sentence, rather than based on whether he can get along in less strict conditions.

Texas's death row is needlessly cruel and inhumane. Before the sentence of execution can be carried out, the row kills men's souls and bodies little by little. Whether an inmate is guilty or innocent like I was, it's just not right.

SOURCE: ACLU. "An Innocent Man's Tortured Days on Texas's Death Row." June 20, 2012. https://www.aclu.org/blog/prisoners-rights-capital-punishment/innocent-mans-tortured-days-texass-death-row

ANALYSIS

The story of Anthony Graves is quite compelling. In 1992, he was convicted of murdering six people in a family in Somerville, Texas. Graves was 26 years old with no history of violence. Three witnesses confirmed that Graves was at his mother's at the time of the awful murder. Furthermore, no physical evidence tied Graves to the crime.

However, the actual culprit—a man named Robert Carter—testified that Graves was the killer. He was convicted largely on the strength of Carter's perjured testimony. Graves spent 18 years in prison—including two provisional execution dates—before his ultimate exoneration in 2010. He later was awarded $1.4 million for his wrongful conviction and imprisonment. The prosecutor, Charles Sebesta, who brought charges against Graves, later was disbarred for knowingly using false testimony and for withholding exculpatory evidence from Graves' defense attorneys.

In our legal system, prosecutors have enhanced ethical duties as so-called ministers of justice. They have an obligation to turn over any evidence that would exonerate or be quite helpful to the defense. This is sometimes known as the prosecutors' Brady obligations after the U.S. Supreme Court's decision in *Brady v. Maryland* (1963).

In June 2012, Graves testified before the Senate Subcommittee on the U.S. Constitution about the conditions of solitary confinement at a prison in Polk County, Texas. Graves compellingly conveyed the awful conditions of confinement that he faced, including being housed in a small cell with a toilet he had to use in full view of both male and female correctional officers. Graves asserted that the horrible conditions on death row caused some inmates to go insane or attempt suicide. He told the senators that the conditions were "needlessly cruel and unusual."

FURTHER READING

American Bar Association. "Former Texas District Attorney Who Sent Anthony Graves to Death Row Is Disbarred." June 1, 2015.

Colloff, Pamela. "Innocence Found." *Texas Monthly*. June 2011.

- ***Document 46:*** Governor Jay Inslee issues moratorium on the death penalty.
- ***Date:*** February 11, 2014
- ***Where:*** Olympia, Washington
- ***Significance:*** The governor's issuance of this moratorium was hailed by opponents of capital punishment as clear evidence that more and more U.S. lawmakers—including some who supported the death penalty in the past—recognize that there are significant problems with the system of capital punishment in the United States.

DOCUMENT

Governor Inslee Issues Moratorium on Death Penalty in Washington State

Good morning.

I'm here today to talk to you about an important criminal justice issue.

Over the course of the past year, my staff and I have been carefully reviewing the status of capital punishment in Washington State.

We've spoken to people in favor and strongly opposed to this complex and emotional issue, including law enforcement officers, prosecutors, former directors of the Department of Corrections, and the family members of the homicide victims.

We thoroughly studied the cases that condemned nine men to death. I recently visited the state penitentiary in Walla Walla and I spoke to the men and women who work there. I saw death row and toured the execution chamber, where lethal injections and hangings take place.

Following this review, and in accordance with state law, I have decided to impose a moratorium on executions while I'm Governor of the state of Washington.

Equal justice under the law is the state's primary responsibility. And in death penalty cases, I'm not convinced equal justice is being served.

The use of the death penalty in this state is unequally applied, sometimes dependent on the budget of the county where the crime occurred.

Let me acknowledge that there are many good protections built into Washington State's death penalty law.

But there have been too many doubts raised about capital punishment. There are too many flaws in the system. And when the ultimate decision is death there is too much at stake to accept an imperfect system.

Let me say clearly that this policy decision is not about the nine men currently on death row in Walla Walla.

This action today does not commute their sentences or issue any pardons to any offender.

But I do not believe their horrific offenses override the problems that exist in our capital punishment system.

And that's why I am imposing a moratorium on executions. If a death penalty case comes to my desk for action, I will issue a reprieve.

What this means is that those on death row will remain in prison for the rest of their lives. Nobody is getting out of prison—period.

I have previously supported capital punishment. And I don't question the hard work and judgment of the county prosecutors who bring these cases or the judges who rule on them.

But my review of the law in Washington State and my responsibilities as Governor

I don't question their guilt or the gravity of their crimes. They get no mercy from me.

This action today does not commute their sentences or issue any pardons to any offender.

I recognize that many people will disagree with this decision. I respect everyone's beliefs on this and have no right to question or judge them.

With my action today I expect Washington State will join a growing national conversation about capital punishment. I welcome that and I'm confident that our citizens will engage in this very important debate.

I'd like to tell Washingtonians about what lead me to this decision.

First, the practical reality is that those convicted of capital offenses are, in fact,

> rarely executed. Since 1981, the year our current capital laws were put in place, 32 defendants have been sentenced to die. Of those, 19, or 60%, had their sentences overturned. One man was set free and 18 had their sentences converted to life in prison.

When the majority of death penalty sentences lead to reversal, the entire system itself must be called into question.

Second, the costs associated with prosecuting a capital case far outweigh the price of locking someone up for life without the possibility of parole.

Counties spend hundreds of thousands of dollars—and often many millions—simply to get a case to trial.

And after trial, hundreds of thousands of dollars are spent on appellate costs for decades.

Studies have shown that a death penalty case from start to finish is more expensive than keeping someone in prison for the rest of their lives—even if they live to be 100 years of age.

Third, death sentences are neither swift nor certain. Seven of the nine men on death row committed their crimes more than 15 years ago, including one from 26 years ago. While they sit on death row and pursue appeal after appeal, the families of their victims must constantly revisit their grief at the additional court proceedings.

Fourth, there is no credible evidence that the death penalty is a deterrent to murder. That's according to work done by the National Academy of Sciences, among other groups.

And finally, our death penalty is not always applied to the most heinous offenders.

That is a system that falls short of equal justice under the law and makes it difficult for the State to justify the use of the death penalty.

In 2006, state Supreme Court Justice Charles Johnson wrote that in our state, "the death penalty is like lightening, randomly striking some defendants and not others."

I believe that's too much uncertainty.

Therefore, for these reasons, pursuant to RCW 10.01.120, I will use the authority given to the Office of the Governor to halt any death warrant issued in my term.

I will take your questions.

SOURCE: Inslee, Jay. "Governor Inslee's Remarks Announcing a Capital Punishment Moratorium." February 11, 2014. https://www.governor.wa.gov/sites/default/files/documents/20140211_death_penalty_moratorium.pdf

ANALYSIS

For most of his political career, Washington governor Jay Inslee was a supporter of the death penalty. Washington State, meanwhile, instituted the death penalty beginning in the early 1980s after the U.S. Supreme Court authorized the reinstitution of the practice in *Gregg v. Georgia* (1976).

In 2014, there were only 9 men on death row in the state of Washington. But Governor Inslee pointed out that since 1982, 19 people sentenced to death for various crimes had their sentences overturned for various reasons. Governor Inslee said that this was concrete evidence that the system was not working.

The governor in his public statement on issuing the moratorium identified five reasons for his action: (1) the high rate of reversals of death sentences; (2) the high costs associated with litigation in death penalty cases; (3) the length of death penalty litigation, which leads to continued grief for the family members of the victims; (4) the lack of evidence that the death penalty is a deterrent to murder; and (5) the unequal application of the death penalty.

In October 2018, the Washington Supreme Court ended the death penalty in *State v. Gregory*, writing that "the death penalty is invalid because it is imposed in an arbitrary and racially biased manner." The high court specifically mentioned the "implicit and overt racial bias against black defendants in this state."

It was the fourth time that the state's high court had ruled the state's death penalty unconstitutional. The first three rulings occurred in 1972, 1979, and 1981.

FURTHER READING

La Corte, Rachel, and Gene Johnson. "Washington State Ends 'Racially Biased' Death Penalty." *Seattle Times*. February 11, 2018.

Mears, Bill. "Washington Governor Issues Moratorium on Executions in the State." CNN.com. February 11, 2014.

- ***Document 47:*** Supreme Court decision in *Hinton v. Alabama*
- ***Date:*** February 24, 2014
- ***Where:*** Washington, D.C.
- ***Significance:*** Anthony Ray Hinton spent years on death row based on faulty expert testimony and other irregularities in his case. The Equal Justice Initiative and its leader Bryan Stevenson advocated tirelessly for Hinton. The Supreme Court's decision in *Hinton v. Alabama* led to the ultimate freedom of an innocent man who spent more than 30 years in prison, the vast majority of those on death row.

DOCUMENT

Supreme Court Orders New Trial for Death Row Inmate Who Received Ineffective Legal Counsel

In *Strickland* v. *Washington* (1984), we held that a criminal defendant's Sixth Amendment right to counsel is violated if his trial attorney's performance falls below an objective standard of reasonableness and if there is a reasonable probability that the result of the trial would have been different absent the deficient act or omission. Anthony Ray Hinton, an inmate on Alabama's death row, asks us to decide whether the Alabama courts correctly applied *Strickland* to his case. We conclude that they did not and hold that Hinton's trial attorney rendered constitutionally deficient performance. We vacate the lower court's judgment and remand the case for reconsideration of whether the attorney's deficient performance was prejudicial.

I

A

In February 1985, a restaurant manager in Birmingham was shot to death in the course of an after-hours robbery of his restaurant. A second manager was murdered during a very similar robbery of another restaurant in July. Then, later in July, a restaurant manager named Smotherman survived another similar robbery-shooting. During each crime, the robber fired two .38 caliber bullets; all six bullets were recovered by police investigators. Smotherman described his assailant to the police, and when the police showed him a photographic array, he picked out Hinton's picture.

The police arrested Hinton and recovered from his house a .38 caliber revolver belonging to his mother, who shared the house with him. After analyzing the six bullets fired during the three crimes and test-firing the revolver, examiners at the State's Department of Forensic Sciences concluded that the six bullets had all been fired from the same gun: the revolver found at Hinton's house. Hinton was charged with two counts of capital murder for the killings during the first two robberies. He was not charged in connection with the third robbery (that is, the Smotherman robbery).

At trial, the State's strategy was to link Hinton to the Smotherman robbery through eyewitness testimony and forensic evidence about the bullets fired at Smotherman and then to persuade the jury that, in light of the similarity of the three crimes and forensic analysis of the bullets and the Hinton revolver, Hinton must also have committed the two murders. Smotherman identified Hinton as the man who robbed his restaurant and tried to kill him, and two other witnesses provided testimony that tended to link Hinton to the Smotherman robbery. Hinton maintained that he was innocent and that Smotherman had misidentified him. In support of that defense, Hinton presented witnesses who testified in support of his alibi that he was at work at a warehouse at the time of the Smotherman robbery.

The six bullets and the revolver were the only physical evidence. Besides those items, the police found no evidence at the crime scenes that could be used to identify the perpetrator (such as fingerprints) and no incriminating evidence at Hinton's home or in his car. The State's case turned on whether its expert witnesses could convince the jury that the six recovered bullets had indeed been fired from the Hinton revolver. According to the Alabama Supreme Court, "the only evidence linking Hinton to the two murders were forensic comparisons of the bullets recovered from those crime scenes to the Hinton revolver."

The category of forensic evidence at issue in this case is "firearms and toolmark" evidence. Toolmark examiners attempt to determine whether a bullet recovered from a crime scene was fired from a particular gun by comparing microscopic markings (toolmarks) on the recovered bullet to the markings on a bullet known to have been fired from that gun. The theory is that minor differences even between guns of the same model will leave discernible traces on bullets that are unique enough for an examiner to conclude that the recovered bullet was or was not fired from a given weapon.

Recognizing that Hinton's defense called for an effective rebuttal of the State's expert witnesses, Hinton's attorney filed a motion for funding to hire an expert witness of his own. In response, the trial judge granted $1,000 with this statement:

> "'I don't know as to what my limitations are as for how much I can grant, but I can grant up to $500.00 in each case [that is, for each of the two murder charges, which were tried together] as far as I know right now and I'm granting up to $500.00 in each of these two cases for this. So if you need additional experts I would go ahead and file on a separate form and I'll have to see if I can grant additional experts, but I am granting up to $500.00, which is the statutory maximum as far as I know on this and if it's necessary that we go beyond that then I may check to see if we can, but this one's granted.'" Hinton's attorney did not take the judge up on his invitation to file a request for more funding.

In fact, $500 per case ($1,000 total) was *not* the statutory maximum at the time of Hinton's trial. An earlier version of the statute had limited state reimbursement of expenses to one half of the $1,000 statutory cap on attorney's fees, which explains why the judge believed that Hinton was entitled to up to $500 for each of the two murder charges. But the relevant statute had been amended to provide: "'Counsel shall also be entitled to be reimbursed for any expenses reasonably incurred in such defense to be approved in advance by the trial court.'" That amendment went into effect on June 13, 1984, which was over a year before Hinton was arrested, so Hinton's trial attorney could have corrected the trial judge's mistaken belief that a $1,000 limit applied and accepted his invitation to file a motion for additional funds.

The attorney failed to do so because he was himself unaware that Alabama law no longer imposed a specific limit and instead allowed reimbursement for "any expenses reasonably incurred." At an evidentiary hearing held on Hinton's postconviction petition, the following conversation occurred between a state attorney and Hinton's trial attorney:

"Q. You did an awful lot of work to try and find what you believed to be a qualified expert in this case, didn't you?

"A. Yes, sir, I did.

"Q. Would you characterize it that you did everything that you knew to do?
"A. Yes, sir, I think so.

"Q. And this case, did it come down to an unwillingness of experts to work for the price that you were able to pay?
"A. Yes, sir, I think it did.

"Q. So your failure to get an expert that you would have been let's say a hundred percent satisfied with was not a failure on your part to go out and do some act, it was a failure of the court to approve what you believed would have been sufficient funds?
"A. Well, putting it a little differently, yes, sir, it was a failure—*it was my failure, my inability under the statute to obtain any more funding for the purpose of hiring qualified experts.*"

Operating under the mistaken belief that he could pay no more than $1,000, Hinton's attorney went looking for an expert witness. According to his postconviction testimony, he made an extensive search for a well-regarded expert, but found only one person who was willing to take the case for the pay he could offer: Andrew Payne. Hinton's attorney "testified that Payne did not have the expertise he thought he needed and that he did not consider Payne's testimony to be effective."

. . .

At trial, Payne testified that the toolmarks in the barrel of the Hinton revolver had been corroded away so that it would be impossible to say with certainty whether a particular bullet had been fired from that gun. He also testified that the bullets from the three crime scenes did not match one another. The State's two experts, by contrast, maintained that all six bullets had indeed been fired from the Hinton revolver.

On cross-examination, the prosecutor badly discredited Payne. Payne admitted that he'd testified as an expert on firearms and toolmark identification just twice in the preceding eight years and that one of the two cases involved a shotgun rather than a handgun. Payne also conceded that he had had difficulty operating the microscope at the state forensic laboratory and had asked for help from one of the state experts. The prosecutor ended the cross-examination with this colloquy:

"Q. Mr. Payne, do you have some problem with your vision?
"A. Why, yes.

"Q. How many eyes do you have?
"A. One."

The prosecutor's closing argument highlighted the fact that Payne's expertise was in military ordnance, not firearms and toolmark identification, and that Payne had graduated in 1933 (more than half a century before the trial) with a degree in civil engineering, whereas the State's experts had years of training and experience in the field of firearms and toolmark examination.

. . .

The jury convicted Hinton and recommended by a 10 to-2 vote that he be sentenced to death. The trial judge accepted that recommendation and imposed a death sentence.

B

In his state postconviction petition, Hinton contended that his trial attorney was "'ineffective to not seek additional funds when it became obvious that the individual willing to examine the evidence in the case for the $1,000 allotted by the court was incompetent and unqualified. Indeed, this failure to seek additional, sufficient funds is rendered all the more inexplicable by the trial court's express invitation to counsel to seek more funds if such funds were necessary.'".

To show that he had been prejudiced by Payne's ineffective testimony, Hinton produced three new experts on toolmark evidence. One of the three, a forensic consultant named John Dillon, had worked on toolmark identification at the Federal Bureau of Investigation's forensics laboratory and, from 1988 until he retired in 1994, had served as chief of the firearms and toolmark unit at the FBI's headquarters. The other two postconviction experts had worked for many years as firearms and toolmark examiners at the Dallas County Crime Laboratory and had each testified as toolmark experts in several hundred cases.

All three experts examined the physical evidence and testified that they could not conclude that any of the six bullets had been fired from the Hinton revolver. The State did not submit rebuttal evidence during the postconviction hearing, and one of Hinton's experts testified that, pursuant to the ethics code of his trade organization, the Association of Firearm and Tool Mark Examiners, he had asked the State's expert, Yates, to show him how he had determined that the recovered bullets had been fired from the Hinton revolver. Yates refused to cooperate.

C

The circuit court denied Hinton's postconviction petition on the ground that Hinton had not been prejudiced by Payne's allegedly poor performance because Payne's testimony did not depart from what Hinton's postconviction experts had said: The bullets could not be affirmatively matched either to one another or to the Hinton revolver.

The Alabama Court of Criminal Appeals affirmed by a 3-to-2 vote. . . .

The Supreme Court of Alabama reversed and remanded. . . .

On remand, the circuit court held that Payne was indeed qualified to testify as a firearms and toolmark expert witness under the Alabama evidentiary standard in place at the time of the trial, which required only that Payne have had "knowledge of firearms and toolmarks examination beyond that of an average layperson." . . . The Alabama Supreme Court denied review by a 4-to-3 vote, with two justices recused. Hinton then filed this petition for a writ of certiorari.

II

This case calls for a straightforward application of our ineffective-assistance-of-counsel precedents, beginning with *Strickland* v. *Washington*. *Strickland* recognized that the Sixth Amendment's guarantee that "[i]n all criminal prosecutions, the accused shall enjoy the right . . . to have the Assistance of Counsel for his defence" entails that defendants are entitled to be represented by an attorney who meets at least a minimal standard of competence. . . .

A

"The first prong—constitutional deficiency—is necessarily linked to the practice and expectations of the legal community: 'The proper measure of attorney performance remains simply reasonableness under prevailing professional norms.'" . . . Under that standard, it was unreasonable for Hinton's lawyer to fail to seek additional funds to hire an expert where that failure was based not on any strategic choice but on a mistaken belief that available funding was capped at $1,000.

"Criminal cases will arise where the only reasonable and available defense strategy requires consultation with experts or introduction of expert evidence." This was such a case. As Hinton's trial attorney recognized, the core of the prosecution's case was the state experts' conclusion that the six bullets had been fired from the Hinton revolver, and effectively rebutting that case required a competent expert on the defense side. Hinton's attorney also recognized that Payne was not a good expert, at least with respect to toolmark evidence. Nonetheless, he felt he was "stuck" with Payne because he could not find a better expert willing to work for $1,000 and he believed that he was unable to obtain more than $1,000 to cover expert fees.

As discussed above, that belief was wrong: Alabama law in effect beginning more than a year before Hinton was arrested provided for state reimbursement of "any expenses reasonably incurred in such defense to be approved in advance by the trial court." Ala. Code §15-12-21(d). And the trial judge expressly invited Hinton's attorney to file a request for further funds if he felt that more funding was necessary. Yet the attorney did not seek further funding.

The trial attorney's failure to request additional funding in order to replace an expert he knew to be inadequate because he mistakenly believed that he had received all he could get under Alabama law constituted deficient performance. . . .

We wish to be clear that the inadequate assistance of counsel we find in this case does not consist of the hiring of an expert who, though qualified, was not qualified enough. The selection of an expert witness is a paradigmatic example of the type of "strategic choic[e]" that, when made "after thorough investigation of [the] law and facts," is "virtually unchallengeable." We do not today launch federal courts into examination of the relative qualifications of experts hired and experts that might have been hired. The only inadequate assistance of counsel here was the inexcusable mistake of law—the unreasonable failure to understand the resources that state law made available to him—that caused counsel to employ an expert that *he himself* deemed inadequate.

B

Having established deficient performance, Hinton must also "show that there is a reasonable probability that, but for counsel's unprofessional errors, the result of the proceeding would have been different. A reasonable probability is a probability sufficient to undermine confidence in the outcome." "When a defendant challenges a conviction, the question is whether there is a reasonable probability that, absent the errors, the factfinder would have had a reasonable doubt respecting guilt."

The Court of Criminal Appeals held, and the State contends in its brief in opposition to certiorari, that Hinton could not have been prejudiced by his attorney's use of Payne rather than a more qualified expert because Payne said all that Hinton could have hoped for from a toolmark expert: that the bullets used in the crimes could not have been fired from the Hinton revolver. . . . It is true that Payne's testimony would have done Hinton a lot of good *if the jury had believed it*. But the jury did not believe Payne. And if there is a reasonable probability that Hinton's attorney would have hired an expert who would have instilled in the jury a reasonable doubt as to Hinton's guilt had the attorney known that the statutory funding limit had been lifted, then Hinton was prejudiced by his lawyer's deficient performance and is entitled to a new trial.

That the State presented testimony from two experienced expert witnesses that tended to inculpate Hinton does not, taken alone, demonstrate that Hinton is guilty. Prosecution experts, of course, can sometimes make mistakes. Indeed, we have recognized the threat to fair criminal trials posed by the potential for incompetent or fraudulent prosecution forensics experts, noting that "[s]erious deficiencies have been found in the forensic evidence used in criminal trials". . . This threat is minimized when the defense retains a competent expert to counter the testimony of the prosecution's expert witnesses; it is maximized when the defense instead fails to understand the resources available to it by law.

Because no court has yet evaluated the prejudice question by applying the proper inquiry to the facts of this case, we remand the case for reconsideration of whether Hinton's attorney's deficient performance was prejudicial under *Strickland*.

* * *

The petition for certiorari and Hinton's motion for leave to proceed *in forma pauperis* are granted, the judgment of the Court of Criminal Appeals of Alabama is vacated, and the case is remanded for further proceedings not inconsistent with this opinion.

It is so ordered.

SOURCE: *Hinton v. Alabama*, 571 U.S. 263 (2014).

ANALYSIS

The case of Anthony Ray Hinton shows a criminal justice system that is badly flawed. Anthony Ray Hinton did not commit the crimes of which he was accused, but he was convicted based on a witness misidentification and the testimony of two state firearms experts who testified that the .38 gun used at the scene of the crimes matched a .38 gun found at the home of Hinton's mother.

Hinton's court-appointed lawyer mistakenly thought that Alabama law only provided him with $1,000 for expert fees. In reality, Hinton's lawyer could have petitioned the trial judge to award additional funds for an expert. Hinton's trial lawyer, not knowing the law, hired an expert who was blind in one eye and was not seen to be as credible as the prosecution's two expert witnesses.

Hinton pursued an ineffective assistance of counsel claim against his original lawyer in appealing his conviction. At a post-conviction hearing at which he was represented by different lawyers, including Bryan Stevenson, Hinton's legal team presented three firearms experts who testified that the gun at Hinton's mother's house was not the gun used to commit the crimes. However, Hinton lost his post-conviction petition.

Ultimately, though, the U.S. Supreme Court agreed that Hinton's trial attorney provided ineffective assistance of counsel. The standard for ineffective assistance of counsel claims comes from the U.S. Supreme Court's decision in *Strickland v. Washington* (1984). Under that standard, an inmate first has to show "deficiency"—that his attorney's performance fell far below the objective standard of reasonableness and competency expected for attorneys.

Even if an inmate shows deficiency of counsel, though, he also has to show that his attorney's deficient performance constituted *prejudice*—a fair likelihood or "reasonable probability" that absent the attorney's deficient performance, the outcome of the trial would have been different.

In this case, the U.S. Supreme Court ruled unanimously in a per curiam ("for the Court") opinion that Hinton's original lawyer provided ineffective assistance of counsel. The Court first reasoned that there was deficiency, because it "was unreasonable for Hinton's lawyer to fail to seek additional funds to hire an expert where that failure was based not on any strategic choice but on a mistaken belief that available funding was capped at $1,000."

Having found deficiency, the Supreme Court also found prejudice. The Court determined that there was a "reasonable probability" that if Hinton's original lawyer had hired a good firearms expert able to refute the state's experts, Hinton never would have been convicted. The Supreme Court ordered a new trial.

Ultimately, a trial judge dismissed the case against Mr. Hinton, because the Alabama Department of Forensics could not determine whether Hinton's gun was the weapon used at the crime scenes. Hinton finally walked out of jail on April 3, 2015. "The sun does shine," Mr. Hinton said as he walked outside as a free man for the first time in more than 30 years.

FURTHER READING

Hinton, Anthony R., with Sara Love Hardin. *The Sun Does Shine: How I Found Life, Freedom and Justice*. New York: St. Martin's Griffin, 2019.

Segura, Liliana. "Anthony Ray Hinton Spent Almost 30 Years on Death Row: Now He Has a Message for White America." *The Intercept*. June 27, 2018.

- ***Document 48:*** Supreme Court decision in *Hall v. Florida*
- ***Date:*** May 27, 2014
- ***Where:*** Washington, D.C.
- ***Significance:*** The Eighth Amendment prohibits the execution of those who are intellectually disabled. Traditionally, an IQ below 70 was necessary to show the required level of intellectual disability. But, this decision enabled capital defendants to show intellectual disability even if their IQ was higher than 70.

DOCUMENT

Supreme Court Strikes Down Florida Death Penalty Law Permitting Execution of Defendants with Intellectual Disabilities

This Court has held that the Eighth and Fourteenth Amendments to the Constitution forbid the execution of persons with intellectual disability. Florida law defines intellectual disability to require an IQ test score of 70 or less. If, from test scores, a prisoner is deemed to have an IQ above 70, all further exploration of intellectual disability is foreclosed. This rigid rule, the Court now holds, creates an unacceptable risk that persons with intellectual disability will be executed, and thus is unconstitutional.

I

On February 21, 1978, Freddie Lee Hall, petitioner here, and his accomplice, Mark Ruffin, kidnaped, beat, raped, and murdered Karol Hurst, a pregnant, 21-year-old newlywed. Afterward, Hall and Ruffin drove to a convenience store they planned to rob. In the parking lot of the store, they killed Lonnie Coburn, a sheriff's deputy who attempted to apprehend them. Hall received the death penalty for both murders, although his sentence for the Coburn murder was later reduced on account of insufficient evidence of premeditation.

Hall argues that he cannot be executed because of his intellectual disability. Previous opinions of this Court have employed the term "mental retardation." This opinion uses the term "intellectual disability" to describe the identical phenomenon. . . . This change in terminology is approved and used in the latest edition of the Diagnostic and Statistical Manual of Mental Disorders, one of the basic texts used by psychiatrists and other experts; the manual is often referred to by its initials "DSM," followed by its edition number, *e.g.*, "DSM-5." . . .

When Hall was first sentenced, this Court had not yet ruled that the Eighth Amendment prohibits States from imposing the death penalty on persons with intellectual disability. And at the time, Florida law did not consider intellectual disability as a statutory mitigating factor.

After this Court held that capital defendants must be permitted to present nonstatutory mitigating evidence in death penalty proceedings, Hall was resentenced. Hall then presented substantial and unchallenged evidence of intellectual disability. School records indicated that his teachers identified him on numerous occasions as "[m]entally retarded." Hall had been prosecuted for a different, earlier crime. His lawyer in that matter later testified that the lawyer "[c]ouldn't really understand anything [Hall] said." And, with respect to the murder trial given him in this case, Hall's counsel recalled that Hall could not assist in his own defense because he had "'a mental . . . level much lower than his age,'" at best comparable to the lawyer's 4-year-old daughter. A number of medical clinicians testified that, in their professional opinion, Hall was "significantly retarded," was "mentally retarded," and had levels of understanding "typically [seen] with toddlers,"

. . .

Hall's upbringing appeared to make his deficits in adaptive functioning all the more severe. Hall was raised—in the words of the sentencing judge—"under the most horrible family circumstances imaginable." Although "[t]eachers and siblings alike immediately recognized [Hall] to be significantly mentally retarded . . . [t]his retardation did not garner any sympathy from his mother, but rather caused much scorn to befall him." Hall was "[c]onstantly beaten because he was 'slow' or because he made simple mistakes." His mother "would strap [Hall] to his bed at night, with a rope thrown over a rafter. In the morning, she would awaken Hall by hoisting him up and whipping him with a belt, rope, or cord." Hall was beaten "ten or fifteen times a week sometimes." His mother tied him "in a 'croaker' sack, swung it over a fire, and beat him," "buried him in the sand up to his neck to 'strengthen his legs,'" and "held a gun on Hall . . . while she poked [him] with sticks."

The jury, notwithstanding this testimony, voted to sentence Hall to death, and the sentencing court adopted the jury's recommendation. The court found that there was "substantial evidence in the record" to support the finding that "Freddie Lee Hall has been mentally retarded his entire life." . . . The sentencing court went on to state that, even assuming the expert testimony to be accurate, "the learning disabilities, mental retardation, and other mental difficulties . . . cannot be used to justify, excuse or extenuate the moral culpability of the defendant in this cause." Hall was again sentenced to death. The Florida Supreme Court affirmed, concluding that "Hall's argument that his mental retardation provided a pretense of moral or legal justification" had "no merit." Chief Justice Barkett dissented, arguing that executing a person with intellectual disability violated the State Constitution's prohibition on cruel and unusual punishment.

In 2002, this Court ruled that the Eighth Amendment prohibited the execution of persons with intellectual disability. On November 30, 2004, Hall filed a motion claiming that he had intellectual disability and could not be executed. More than five years later, Florida held a hearing to consider Hall's motion. Hall again presented evidence of intellectual disability, including an IQ test score of 71. . . . In response, Florida argued that Hall could not be found intellectually disabled because Florida law requires that, as a threshold matter, Hall show an IQ test score of 70 or below before presenting any additional evidence of his intellectual disability. . .

This Court granted certiorari.

II

The Eighth Amendment provides that "[e]xcessive bail shall not be required, nor excessive fines imposed, nor cruel and unusual punishments inflicted." The Fourteenth Amendment applies those restrictions to the States. . . .

The Eighth Amendment "is not fastened to the obsolete but may acquire meaning as public opinion becomes enlightened by a humane justice." To enforce the Constitution's protection of human dignity, this Court looks to the "evolving standards of decency that mark the progress of a maturing society." The Eighth Amendment's protection of dignity reflects the Nation we have been, the Nation we are, and the Nation we aspire to be. This is to affirm that the Nation's constant, unyielding purpose must be to transmit the Constitution so that its precepts and guarantees retain their meaning and force.

The Eighth Amendment prohibits certain punishments as a categorical matter. . . . And, as relevant for this case, persons with intellectual disability may not be executed.

No legitimate penological purpose is served by executing a person with intellectual disability. To do so contravenes the Eighth Amendment, for to impose the harshest of punishments on an intellectually disabled person violates his or her inherent dignity as a human being. . . .

A further reason for not imposing the death penalty on a person who is intellectually disabled is to protect the integrity of the trial process. These persons face "a special risk of wrongful execution" because they are more likely to give false confessions, are often poor witnesses, and are less able to give meaningful assistance to their counsel. This is not to say that under current law persons with intellectual disability who "meet the law's requirements for criminal responsibility" may not be tried and punished. They may not, however, receive the law's most severe sentence.

The question this case presents is how intellectual disability must be defined in order to implement these principles and the holding of *Atkins*. To determine if Florida's cutoff rule is valid, it is proper to consider the psychiatric and professional studies that elaborate on the purpose and meaning of IQ scores to determine how the scores relate to the holding of *Atkins*. This in turn leads to a better understanding of how the legislative policies of various States, and the holdings of state courts, implement the *Atkins* rule. That understanding informs our determination whether there is a consensus that instructs how to decide the specific issue presented here. And, in conclusion, this Court must express its own independent determination reached in light of the instruction found in those sources and authorities.

III

A

That this Court, state courts, and state legislatures consult and are informed by the work of medical experts in determining intellectual disability is unsurprising. Those professionals use their learning and skills to study and consider the consequences of the classification schemes they devise in the diagnosis of persons with mental or psychiatric disorders or disabilities. Society relies upon medical and professional expertise to define and explain how to diagnose the mental condition at issue. And the definition of intellectual disability by skilled professionals has implications far beyond the confines of the death penalty: for it is relevant to education, access to social programs, and medical treatment plans. In determining who qualifies as intellectually disabled, it is proper to consult the medical community's opinions.

. . .

The first and second criteria—deficits in intellectual functioning and deficits in adaptive functioning—are central here. In the context of a formal assessment, "[t]he existence of concurrent deficits in intellectual and adaptive functioning has long been the defining characteristic of intellectual disability."

On its face, the Florida statute could be consistent with the views of the medical community noted and discussed in *Atkins*. Florida's statute defines intellectual disability for purposes of an *Atkins* proceeding as "significantly subaverage general intellectual functioning existing concurrently with deficits in adaptive behavior and manifested during the period from conception to age 18." The statute further defines "significantly subaverage general intellectual functioning" as "performance that is two or more standard deviations from the mean score on a standardized intelligence test." The mean IQ test score is 100. The concept of standard deviation describes how scores are dispersed in a population. Standard deviation is distinct from standard error of measurement, a concept which describes the reliability of a test and is discussed further below. The standard deviation on an IQ test is approximately 15 points, and so two standard deviations is approximately 30 points. Thus a test taker who performs "two or more standard deviations from the mean" will score approximately 30 points below the mean on an IQ test, *i.e.*, a score of approximately 70 points.

On its face this statute could be interpreted consistently with *Atkins* and with the conclusions this Court reaches in the instant case. Nothing in the statute precludes Florida from taking into account the IQ test's standard error of measurement, and as discussed below there is evidence that Florida's Legislature intended to include the measurement error in the calculation. But the Florida Supreme Court has interpreted the provisions more narrowly. It has held that a person whose test score is above 70, including a score within the margin for measurement error, does not have an intellectual disability and is barred from presenting other evidence that would show his faculties are limited. That strict IQ test score cutoff of 70 is the issue in this case.

Pursuant to this mandatory cutoff, sentencing courts cannot consider even substantial and weighty evidence of intellectual disability as measured and made manifest by the defendant's failure or inability to adapt to his social and cultural environment, including medical histories, behavioral records, school tests and reports, and testimony regarding past behavior and family circumstances. This is so even though the medical community accepts that all of this evidence can be probative of intellectual disability, including for individuals who have an IQ test score above 70. . . .

Florida's rule disregards established medical practice in two interrelated ways. It takes an IQ score as final and conclusive evidence of a defendant's intellectual capacity, when experts in the field would consider other evidence. It also relies on a purportedly scientific measurement of the defendant's abilities, his IQ score, while refusing to recognize that the score is, on its own terms, imprecise.

The professionals who design, administer, and interpret IQ tests have agreed, for years now, that IQ test scores should be read not as a single fixed number but as a range. . . .

Despite these professional explanations, Florida law used the test score as a fixed number, thus barring further consideration of other evidence bearing on the question of intellectual disability. For professionals to diagnose—and for the law then to determine—whether an intellectual disability exists once the SEM applies and the individual's IQ score is 75 or below the inquiry would consider factors indicating whether the person had deficits in adaptive functioning. These include evidence of past performance, environment, and upbringing.

B

. . .

Thus, at most nine States mandate a strict IQ score cutoff at 70. Of these, four States (Delaware, Kansas, North Carolina, and Washington) appear not to have considered the issue in their courts. On the other side of the ledger stand the 18 States that have abolished the death penalty, either in full or for new offenses, and Oregon, which has suspended the death penalty and executed only two individuals in the past 40 years. In those States, of course, a person in Hall's position could not be executed even without a finding of intellectual disability. Thus in 41 States an individual in Hall's position—an individual with an IQ score of 71—would not be deemed automatically eligible for the death penalty.

These aggregate numbers are not the only considerations bearing on a determination of consensus. Consistency of the direction of change is also relevant. . . .

In addition to these States, at least five others have passed legislation allowing a defendant to present additional evidence of intellectual disability even when an IQ test score is above 70. . . .

In summary, every state legislature to have considered the issue after *Atkins*—save Virginia's—and whose law has been interpreted by its courts has taken a position contrary to that of Florida. . . .

The rejection of the strict 70 cutoff in the vast majority of States and the "consistency in the trend," toward recognizing the SEM provide strong evidence of consensus that our society does not regard this strict cutoff as proper or humane.

C

Atkins itself acknowledges the inherent error in IQ testing. It is true that *Atkins* "did not provide definitive procedural or substantive guides for determining when a person who claims mental retardation" falls within the protection of the Eighth Amendment. . . .

Respondent's argument also conflicts with the logic of *Atkins* and the Eighth Amendment. If the States were to have complete autonomy to define intellectual disability as they wished, the Court's decision in *Atkins* could become a nullity, and the Eighth Amendment's protection of human dignity would not become a reality. This Court thus reads *Atkins* to provide substantial guidance on the definition of intellectual disability.

D

. . .

In this Court's independent judgment, the Florida statute, as interpreted by its courts, is unconstitutional.

In addition to the views of the States and the Court's precedent, this determination is informed by the views of medical experts. These views do not dictate the Court's decision, yet the Court does not disregard these informed assessments. . . . It is the Court's duty to interpret the Constitution, but it need not do so in isolation. The legal determination of intellectual disability is distinct from a medical diagnosis, but it is informed by the medical community's diagnostic framework. *Atkins* itself points to the diagnostic criteria employed by psychiatric professionals. And the professional community's teachings are of particular help in this case, where no alternative definition of intellectual disability is presented and where this Court and the States have placed substantial reliance on the expertise of the medical profession.

. . .

The flaws in Florida's law are the result of the inherent error in IQ tests themselves. An IQ score is an approximation, not a final and infallible assessment of intellectual functioning. . . .

Intellectual disability is a condition, not a number. Courts must recognize, as does the medical community, that the IQ test is imprecise. This is not to say that an IQ test score is unhelpful. It is of considerable significance, as the medical community recognizes. But in using these scores to assess a defendant's eligibility for the death penalty, a State must afford these test scores the same studied skepticism that those who design and use the tests do, and understand that an IQ test score represents a range rather than a fixed number. A State that ignores the inherent imprecision of these tests risks executing a person who suffers from intellectual disability. . . .

This Court agrees with the medical experts that when a defendant's IQ test score falls within the test's acknowledged and inherent margin of error, the defendant must be able to present additional evidence of intellectual disability, including testimony regarding adaptive deficits.

. . . The Florida statute, as interpreted by its courts, misuses IQ score on its own terms; and this, in turn, bars consideration of evidence that must be considered in determining whether a defendant in a capital case has intellectual disability. Florida's rule is invalid under the Constitution's Cruel and Unusual Punishments Clause.

E

Florida seeks to execute a man because he scored a 71 instead of 70 on an IQ test. Florida is one of just a few States to have this rigid rule. Florida's rule misconstrues the Court's statements in *Atkins* that intellectually dis-ability is characterized by an IQ of "approximately 70." Florida's rule is in direct opposition to the views of those who design, administer, and interpret the IQ test. By failing to take into account the standard error of measurement, Florida's law not only contradicts the test's own design but also bars an essential part of a sentencing court's inquiry into adaptive functioning. Freddie Lee Hall may or may not be intellectually disabled, but the law requires that he have the opportunity to present evidence of his intellectual disability, including deficits in adaptive functioning over his lifetime.

The death penalty is the gravest sentence our society may impose. Persons facing that most severe sanction must have a fair opportunity to show that the Constitution prohibits their execution. Florida's law contravenes our Nation's commitment to dignity and its duty to teach human decency as the mark of a civilized world. The States are laboratories for experimentation, but those experiments may not deny the basic dignity the Constitution protects.

The judgment of the Florida Supreme Court is reversed, and the case is remanded for further proceedings not inconsistent with this opinion.

So ordered.

SOURCE: Hall v. Florida, 572 U.S. 701 (2014).

ANALYSIS

The Eighth Amendment categorically prohibits the execution of those who are intellectually disabled, as the Supreme Court ruled in *Atkins v. Virginia* (2002) in a case involving inmate Daryl Renard Atkins who had an IQ of 59. After *Atkins*, many capital defendants filed petitions, contending that they were intellectually disabled.

DID YOU KNOW?

Attorney Seth P. Waxman

Seth P. Waxman, one of the country's leading lawyers and Supreme Court advocates, argued on behalf of petitioner Freddie Lee Hall in the case *Hall v. Florida* (2014). Waxman is best known for serving as U.S. solicitor general for the U.S. government from 1997 to 2001.

Waxman earned his undergraduate degree from Harvard University and his law degree from Yale Law School. He then clerked for a federal district court judge in New York before entering private practice. In 1997, President Bill Clinton appointed him as the 41st solicitor general of the United States, a position in which he served until January 2001.

Waxman has argued more than 80 cases before the U.S. Supreme Court. *Hall v. Florida* was not even the first death penalty case that Waxman argued before the High Court. For example, he also argued on behalf of Missouri death row inmate Christopher Shawn Simmons in the case *Roper v. Simmons* (2005) and Louisiana death row inmate Robert McCoy in *McCoy v. Louisiana* (2018). Waxman's clients prevailed in all three of these high-profile capital punishment cases.

FURTHER READING

Brand, Madeleine. "Defender Discusses Juvenile Death Penalty Ruling." NPR.org. March 1, 2005.

One such inmate was a Florida man named Freddie Lee Hall, who was sentenced to death for his part in the murder of a sheriff's deputy after he and another man already had killed a young pregnant woman. Hall apparently suffered from intellectual disability his entire life. He had numerous IQ tests that put his IQ between 60 and 80, but the most recent test had pegged his IQ at 71. This was a problem for Hall because Florida law stated that to qualify as intellectually disabled, a person had to have an IQ of 70 or below. Because Hall's IQ was 71 in his most recent test, he was not considered intellectually disabled—even though his attorneys testified that he had the mental capacity of a young child.

The U.S. Supreme Court invalidated Florida's law in *Hall v. Florida.* The Court emphasized that Hall's IQ score was within the standard error of measurement or SEM. The Court also reiterated that medical experts had testified that whether a person is intellectually disabled must be determined by several factors—the IQ test merely being one of the methods.

"The death penalty is the gravest sentence our society may impose," Justice Anthony Kennedy wrote for the majority in a 5–4 decision. "Persons facing that most severe sanction must have a fair opportunity to show that the Constitution prohibits their execution. Florida's law contravenes our nation's commitment to dignity and its duty to teach human decency as the mark of a civilized world."

The Court also clarified that the proper term to use was "intellectual disability" instead of "mental retardation," which was the term the Court used in the *Atkins* decision. The Court's ruling in *Hall v. Florida* meant that other death row inmates could pursue a new sentence if they could establish intellectual disability, even with an IQ slightly above 70. Such inmates need to present evidence that they struggle with adaptive behavior or other evidence that they are intellectually disabled.

FURTHER READING

Liptak, Adam. "Court Extends Curbs on the Death Penalty in a Florida Ruling." *New York Times*. May 27, 2014.

Rahdert, Lise E. "Hall v. Florida and Ending the Death Penalty for Severely Mentally Ill Defendants." 124 *Yale Law Journal Forum* 34 (2014).

Ryan, Meghan. "Intellectual Disability and Uncertainty in Hall v. Florida." *Concurring Opinions*. June 7, 2014.

- ***Document 49:*** Justice Stephen Breyer's Dissent in *Glossip v. Gross*
- ***Date:*** June 29, 2015
- ***Where:*** Washington, D.C.
- ***Significance:*** Justice Breyer's dissenting opinion in this death penalty case energized the abolitionist movement and renewed conversations around the country about the constitutionality and merits (or lack thereof) of capital punishment. The case in question concerned a challenge to Oklahoma's system of lethal injection.

DOCUMENT

Justice Breyer Questions Constitutionality of Death Penalty in Landmark Dissent

For the reasons stated in Justice Sotomayor's opinion, I dissent from the Court's holding. But rather than try to patch up the death penalty's legal wounds one at a time, I would ask for full briefing on a more basic question: whether the death penalty violates the Constitution.

The relevant legal standard is the standard set forth in the Eighth Amendment. The Constitution there forbids the "inflict[ion]" of "cruel and unusual punishments."

. . .

Nearly 40 years ago, this Court upheld the death penalty under statutes that, in the Court's view, contained safeguards sufficient to ensure that the penalty would be applied reliably and not arbitrarily. . . . The circumstances and the evidence of the death penalty's application have changed radically since then. Given those changes, I believe that it is now time to reopen the question.

In 1976, the Court thought that the constitutional infirmities in the death penalty could be healed; the Court in effect delegated significant responsibility to the States to develop procedures that would protect against those constitutional problems. Almost 40 years of studies, surveys, and experience strongly indicate, however, that this effort has failed. Today's administration of the death penalty involves three fundamental constitutional defects: (1) serious unreliability, (2) arbitrariness in application, and (3) unconscionably long delays that undermine the death penalty's penological purpose. Perhaps as a result, (4) most places within the United States have abandoned its use.

. . .

I

"CRUEL"—LACK OF RELIABILITY

This Court has specified that the finality of death creates a "qualitative difference" between the death penalty and other punishments (including life in prison). . . .

For one thing, despite the difficulty of investigating the circumstances surrounding an execution for a crime that took place long ago, researchers have found convincing evidence that, in the past three decades, innocent people have been executed. . . .

Furthermore, exonerations occur far more frequently where capital convictions, rather than ordinary criminal convictions, are at issue. Researchers have calculated that courts (or State Governors) are 130 times more likely to exonerate a defendant where a death sentence is at issue. They are nine times more likely to exonerate where a capital murder, rather than a noncapital murder, is at issue.

. . .

II

"CRUEL"—ARBITRARINESS

The arbitrary imposition of punishment is the antithesis of the rule of law.

. . .

When the death penalty was reinstated in 1976, this Court acknowledged that the death penalty is (and would be) unconstitutional if "inflicted in an arbitrary and capricious manner." . . .

The Court has consequently sought to make the application of the death penalty less arbitrary by restricting its use to those whom Justice Souter called "the worst of the worst." . . .

Despite the Gregg Court's hope for fair administration of the death penalty, 40 years of further experience make it increasingly clear that the death penalty is imposed arbitrarily, i.e., without the "reasonable consistency" legally necessary to reconcile its use with the Constitution's commands.

Thorough studies of death penalty sentences support this conclusion. . . .

Such studies indicate that the factors that most clearly ought to affect application of the death penalty—namely, comparative egregiousness of the crime—often do not. Other studies show that circumstances that ought not to affect application of the death penalty, such as race, gender, or geography, often do.

Numerous studies, for example, have concluded that individuals accused of murdering white victims, as opposed to black or other minority victims, are more likely to receive the death penalty. . . .

Geography also plays an important role in determining who is sentenced to death. And that is not simply because some States permit the death penalty while others do not. Rather within a death penalty State, the imposition of the death penalty heavily depends on the county in which a defendant is tried. . . .

Still others indicate that the racial composition of and distribution within a county plays an important role. . . .

Thus, whether one looks at research indicating that irrelevant or improper factors—such as race, gender, local geography, and resources—do significantly determine who receives the death penalty, or whether one looks at research indicating that proper factors—such as "egregiousness"—do not determine who receives the death penalty, the legal conclusion must be the same: The research strongly suggests that the death penalty is imposed arbitrarily.

. . .

The studies bear out my own view, reached after considering thousands of death penalty cases and last-minute petitions over the course of more than 20 years. I see discrepancies for which I can find no rational explanations. . . . Why does one defendant who committed a single-victim murder receive the death penalty (due to aggravators of a prior felony conviction and an after-the-fact robbery), while another defendant does not, despite having kidnapped, raped, and murdered a young mother while leaving her infant baby to die at the scene of the crime. . . .

The question raised by these examples (and the many more I could give but do not), as well as by the research to which I have referred, is the same question Justice Stewart, Justice Powell, and others raised over the course of several decades: The imposition and implementation of the death penalty seems capricious, random, indeed, arbitrary. From a defendant's perspective, to receive that sentence, and certainly to find it implemented, is the equivalent of being struck by lightning. How then can we reconcile the death penalty with the demands of a Constitution that first and foremost insists upon a rule of law?

III

"CRUEL"—EXCESSIVE DELAYS

The problems of reliability and unfairness almost inevitably lead to a third independent constitutional problem: excessively long periods of time that individuals typically spend on death row, alive but under sentence of death. That is to say, delay is in part a problem that the Constitution's own demands create. Given the special need for reliability and fairness in death penalty cases, the Eighth Amendment does, and must, apply to the death penalty "with special force." . . .

These procedural necessities take time to implement. And, unless we abandon the procedural requirements that assure fairness and reliability, we are forced to confront the problem of increasingly lengthy delays in capital cases. Ultimately, though these legal causes may help to explain, they do not mitigate the harms caused by delay itself.

A

Consider first the statistics. In 2014, 35 individuals were executed. Those executions occurred, on average, nearly 18 years after a court initially pronounced its sentence of death. . . .

The length of the average delay has increased dramatically over the years. In 1960, the average delay between sentencing and execution was two years. . . . By last year the average had risen to about 18 years. . . . And, at present execution rates, it would take more than 75 years to carry out those 3,000 death sentences; thus, the average person on death row would spend an additional 37.5 years there before being executed.

I cannot find any reasons to believe the trend will soon be reversed.

B

These lengthy delays create two special constitutional difficulties. . . . First, a lengthy delay in and of itself is especially cruel because it "subjects death row inmates to decades of especially severe, dehumanizing conditions of confinement." . . . Second, lengthy delay undermines the death penalty's penological rationale. . . .

1

Turning to the first constitutional difficulty, nearly all death penalty States keep death row inmates in isolation for 22 or more hours per day. . . .

The dehumanizing effect of solitary confinement is aggravated by uncertainty as to whether a death sentence will in fact be carried out. . . .

Several inmates have come within hours or days of execution before later being exonerated. Willie Manning was four hours from his scheduled execution before the Mississippi Supreme Court stayed the execution. . . . Two years later, Manning was exonerated after the evidence against him, including flawed testimony from an FBI hair examiner, was severely undermined. . . .

Furthermore, given the negative effects of confinement and uncertainty, it is not surprising that many inmates volunteer to be executed, abandoning further appeals. . . .

2

The second constitutional difficulty resulting from lengthy delays is that those delays undermine the death penalty's penological rationale, perhaps irreparably so. The rationale for capital punishment, as for any punishment, classically rests upon society's need to secure deterrence, incapacitation, retribution, or rehabilitation. Capital punishment by definition does not rehabilitate. It does, of course, incapacitate the offender. But the major alternative to capital punishment—namely, life in prison without possibility of parole—also incapacitates. . . .

Thus an offender who is sentenced to death is two or three times more likely to find his sentence overturned or commuted than to be executed; and he has a good chance of dying from natural causes before any execution (or exoneration) can take place. In a word, executions are rare. And an individual contemplating a crime but evaluating the potential punishment would know that, in any event, he faces a potential sentence of life without parole.

These facts, when recurring, must have some offsetting effect on a potential perpetrator's fear of a death penalty. . . .

But what about retribution? Retribution is a valid penological goal. I recognize that surviving relatives of victims of a horrendous crime, or perhaps the community itself, may find vindication in an execution. And a community that favors the death penalty has an understandable interest in representing their voices. . . .

Finally, the fact of lengthy delays undermines any effort to justify the death penalty in terms of its prevalence when the Founders wrote the Eighth Amendment. When the Founders wrote the Constitution, there were no 20- or 30-year delays. Execution took place soon after sentencing. . . .

3

The upshot is that lengthy delays both aggravate the cruelty of the death penalty and undermine its jurisprudential rationale. . . .

Moreover, review by courts at every level helps to ensure reliability; if this Court had not ordered that Anthony Ray Hinton receive further hearings in state court, he may well have been executed rather than exonerated. In my own view, our legal system's complexity, our federal system with its separate state and federal courts, our constitutional guarantees, our commitment to fair procedure, and, above all, a special need for reliability and fairness in capital cases, combine to make significant procedural "reform" unlikely in practice to reduce delays to an acceptable level.

And that fact creates a dilemma: A death penalty system that seeks procedural fairness and reliability brings with it delays that severely aggravate the cruelty of capital punishment and significantly undermine the rationale for imposing a sentence of death in the first place. . . .

IV

"UNUSUAL"—DECLINE IN USE OF THE DEATH PENALTY

The Eighth Amendment forbids punishments that are cruel and unusual. Last year, in 2014, only seven States carried out an execution. Perhaps more importantly, in the last two decades, the imposition and implementation of the death penalty have increasingly become unusual. I can illustrate the significant decline in the use of the death penalty in several ways.

. . .

That trend, a significant decline in the last 15 years, also holds true with respect to the number of annual executions. . . .

At the same time, use of the death penalty has become increasingly concentrated geographically. County-by-county figures are relevant, for decisions to impose the death penalty typically take place at a county level. . . .

Moreover, the direction of change is consistent. In the past two decades, no State without a death penalty has passed legislation to reinstate the penalty. . . .

I rely primarily upon domestic, not foreign events, in pointing to changes and circumstances that tend to justify the claim that the death penalty, constitutionally speaking, is "unusual." Those circumstances are sufficient to warrant our reconsideration of the death penalty's constitutionality. I note, however, that many nations—indeed, 95 of the 193 members of the United Nations—have formally abolished the death penalty and an additional 42 have abolished it in practice. . . .

V

I recognize a strong counterargument that favors constitutionality. We are a court. Why should we not leave the matter up to the people acting democratically through legislatures? The Constitution foresees a country that will make most important decisions democratically. Most nations that have abandoned the death penalty have done so through legislation, not judicial decision. And legislators, unlike judges, are free to take account of matters such as monetary costs, which I do not claim are relevant here. . . .

The answer is that the matters I have discussed, such as lack of reliability, the arbitrary application of a serious and irreversible punishment, individual suffering caused by long delays, and lack of penological purpose are quintessentially judicial matters. . . .

For the reasons I have set forth in this opinion, I believe it highly likely that the death penalty violates the Eighth Amendment. At the very least, the Court should call for full briefing on the basic question.

With respect, I dissent.

SOURCE: Glossip v. Gross, 576 U.S. 863 (2015).

ANALYSIS

In 1997, Richard Glossip allegedly hired another man, Justin Sneed, to kill their mutual boss, Barry Van Treese. The three men all worked at a local Best Budget Inn in Oklahoma City, Oklahoma. Sneed worked as the maintenance man, Glossip was the motel manager, and Van Treese was the motel's owner.

Sneed avoided the death penalty by agreeing to testify that Glossip planned the murder and hired Sneed to kill Van Treese. Sneed testified that Glossip offered him $10,000 to kill Van Treese. Glossip maintained his innocence and refused to accept a plea deal.

Prosecutors sought the death penalty against Glossip. In July 1998, a jury convicted Glossip of first degree murder and then sentenced him to death. Glossip appealed his conviction to a higher court, as was his right, and the Oklahoma Court of Criminal Appeals reversed the conviction in 2001.

Prosecutors retried Glossip for first degree murder and once again obtained a jury verdict of guilty in 2004. Once again, a jury sentenced Glossip to death. Glossip once again appealed, but this time the Oklahoma Court of Criminal Appeals affirmed the conviction and death sentence.

Glossip remains on death row in Oklahoma. His attorneys and Glossip himself still maintain that he is innocent. Several inmates on Oklahoma death row—including Glossip who became the lead plaintiff—filed a federal lawsuit, alleging that Oklahoma's method of execution, lethal injection, constitutes cruel and unusual punishment.

Oklahoma's lethal injection protocol consists of three drugs: (1) midazolam, (2) vecuronium bromide, and (3) potassium chloride. It is the use of midazolam that is controversial. The drug is used to induce unconsciousness in the inmate. However, according to the plaintiffs, this process and the use of midazolam inflict wanton pain upon those subject to this execution process. For example, one of Glossip's coplaintiffs, Charles Warner—executed in Oklahoma in 2015—stated as he was being executed: "My body is on fire. No one should go through this. I'm not afraid to die."

The case proceeded to the U.S. Supreme Court, which ruled 5–4 that the state's lethal injection protocol did not violate the Eighth Amendment. Writing for the majority, Justice Samuel Alito wrote, "The District Court did not commit clear error when it found that midazolam is highly likely to render a person unable to feel pain during an execution."

Four justices dissented, with two of them—Sonia Sotomayor and Stephen Breyer—writing dissenting opinions. Justice Sotomayor's dissent focused on Oklahoma's lethal injection process and criticized the use of midazolam.

Justice Breyer took a different approach in his dissent. Instead of writing about Oklahoma's lethal injection process, he took the opportunity to question the constitutionality of the death penalty in general.

Breyer's dissent focused on several problems with the death penalty, including "(1) serious unreliability; (2) arbitrariness in application; and (3) unconscionably long delays that undermine the death penalty's penological purpose." Justice Breyer noted that evidence shows that at least a few innocent persons have been executed and that many more innocent persons were barely spared the death penalty, literally being days away from execution before exoneration.

He also warned that the death penalty system does not provide adequate guidance on which convicted murders are the worst of the worse, or the ones that truly deserve the ultimate punishment. This is the rationale that caused the Court to strike down the death penalty years earlier in *Furman v. Georgia* (1972).

Breyer's dissent attracted immediate attention and caused many in the abolitionist movement to hope that perhaps the Supreme Court would examine the constitutionality of capital punishment. Richard Dieter, the head of the anti-capital punishment Death Penalty Information Center, stated, "I think this case [*Glossip v. Gross*] will be remembered more for that dissent than for the decision itself."

FURTHER READING

Bessler, John, ed. *Against the Death Penalty*. Washington, D.C.: Brookings Institution Press, 2016.

Liptak, Adam. "Supreme Court Allows Use of Execution Drug." *New York Times*. June 29, 2015.

Yorke, Jon. "Comity, Finality, and Oklahoma's Lethal Injection Protocol." 69 *Oklahoma Law Review* 545 (2017).

- ***Document 50:*** Justice Steven Breyer's Dissent in *Jordan v. Mississippi*
- ***Date:*** June 28, 2018
- ***Where:*** Washington, D.C.
- ***Significance:*** Justice Steven Breyer was the most consistent critic of the death penalty on the Supreme Court during his last years on the Court (he retired in 2022 and was replaced by Ketanji Brown Jackson). This dissent highlights two issues of particular importance to Breyer: (1) the long periods of time inmates remain on death row and (2) the geographic disparities in the imposition of the death penalty.

DOCUMENT

Justice Breyer Criticizes Geographic Disparities and Long Delays in Death Penalty Cases

In my dissenting opinion in *Glossip v. Gross* (2015), I described how the death penalty, as currently administered, suffers from unconscionably long delays, arbitrary application, and serious unreliability. I write to underline the ways in which the two cases currently before us illustrate the first two of these problems and to highlight additional evidence that has accumulated over the past three years suggesting that the death penalty today lacks "requisite reliability."

I

The petitioner in the first case, Richard Gerald Jordan, was sentenced to death nearly 42 years ago. He argues that his execution after such a lengthy delay violates the Eighth Amendment prohibition on "cruel and unusual punishments." I continue to believe this question merits the Court's attention. . . .

More than a century ago, the Court described a prisoner's 4-*week* wait prior to execution as "one of the most horrible feelings to which [a person] can be subjected." What explains the more than 4-*decade* wait in this case? Between 1976 and 1986, each of Jordan's first three death sentences was vacated on constitutional grounds, including by this Court. . . . In 1998, Jordan was sentenced to death for the fourth time. (He had entered into a plea agreement providing for a sentence of life without parole, but the Mississippi Supreme Court invalidated that agreement and the prosecutor refused to reinstate it). . . .

Jordan has lived more than half of his life on death row. He has been under a death sentence "longer than any other Mississippi inmate." The petition states that since 1977, Jordan has been incarcerated in the Mississippi State Penitentiary and spent "most of that time on death row living in isolated, squalid conditions." . . . In my view, the conditions in which Jordan appears to have been confined over the past four decades reinforce the Eighth Amendment concern raised in his petition.

Jordan, now 72 years old, is one among an aging population of death row inmates who remain on death row for ever longer periods of time. Over the past decade, the percentage of death row prisoners aged 60 or older has increased more than twofold from around 7% in 2008 to more than 16% of the death row population by the most recent estimate. . . . Meanwhile, the average period of imprisonment between death sentence and execution has risen from a little over 6 years in 1988 to more than 11 years in 2008 to more than 19 years over the past year. . . .

II

In addition, both Richard Jordan's case and that of Timothy Nelson Evans, the second petitioner here, illustrate the problem of arbitrariness. To begin with, both were sentenced to death in the Second Circuit Court District of Mississippi. Evans says that district accounts for "the largest number of death sentences" of any of the State's 22 districts since 1976.

This geographic concentration reflects a nationwide trend. Death sentences, while declining in number, have become increasingly concentrated in an ever-smaller number of counties. In the mid-1990's, more than 300 people were sentenced to death in roughly 200 counties each year. B. Garett, End of Its Rope: How Killing the Death Penalty Can Revive Criminal Justice 138–140 (2017). By comparison, these numbers have declined dramatically over the past three years. A recent study finds, for example, that in 2015, *all* of those who were sentenced to death nationwide (51 people in total) were sentenced in 38 of this Nation's more than 3,000 counties; in 2016, *all* death sentences (31 in total) were imposed in just 28 counties nationwide (fewer than 1% of counties). . . .

This geographic arbitrariness is aggravated by the fact that definitions of death eligibility vary depending on the State. This Court has repeated that "[c]apital punishment must be limited to those offenders who commit a narrow category of the most serious crimes," since "the culpability of the average murderer is insufficient to justify the most extreme sanction available to the State." But the statutory criteria States enact to distinguish a non-death-eligible murder from a particularly heinous death-eligible murder and thus attempt to use to identify the "worst of the worst" murderers are far from uniform. . . .

I recognize that only a small fraction of the roughly 8,000 death sentences imposed since 1976 have resulted in executions. Executions continue to decline from the modern peak of 98 executions occurring across 72 counties and 20 States in 1999 to 28 executions in 22 counties across 6 States in 2015. In 2016, 20 people were executed. That number remains the fewest executions in more than a century, just below the 23 executions that took place in 2017. More than 700 people await execution on California's death row but the State, which has executed 13 people since 1976, has not carried out an execution since 2006. The State of Mississippi, which has executed a total of 21 people since 1976, has not carried out an execution in more than six years. This data suggests that the death penalty may eventually disappear. But it also shows that capital punishment is "unusual" (as well as "cruel").

III

Finally, I note that in the past three years, further evidence has accumulated suggesting that the death penalty as it is applied today lacks "requisite reliability." Four hours before Willie Manning was slated to die by lethal injection, the Mississippi Supreme Court stayed his execution and on April 21, 2015, he became the fourth person on Mississippi's death row to be exonerated. . . . Among them are Rodricus Crawford, Rickey Dale Newman, Gabriel Solache, and Vicente Benavides Figueroa, whose exonerations were based upon evidence of actual innocence.

. . .

In my view, many of the capital cases that come before this Court, often in the form of petitions for certiorari, involve, like the cases of Richard Jordan and Timothy Evans, special problems of cruelty or arbitrariness. Hence, I remain of the view that the Court should grant the petitions now before us to consider whether the death penalty as currently administered violates the Constitution's Eighth Amendment.

SOURCE: Jordan v. Mississippi, Nos. 17–7153 and 17–7245. Decided June 28, 2018.

ANALYSIS

After joining the Supreme Court in 1994, Justice Stephen Breyer became known as a staunch, fierce critic of the death penalty. His dissent in *Glossip v. Gross* (2015) remains an epic opinion in the annals of death penalty jurisprudence. Three years later, he dissented from a petition for certiorari by a Mississippi inmate named Richard Gerald Jordan, who was 72 at the time he filed his latest challenge to his death sentence for murdering a woman named Edwina Marter in June 1976.

Even for death penalty cases, Jordan's case is a bit unusual, as he has had four death sentences. The first three between 1977 and 1986 were overturned for different legal reasons. His fourth sentence was imposed in 1998, after which Jordan filed numerous legal challenges to the sentence.

One of the issues Jordan concentrated on in *Jordan v. Mississippi* focused on the sheer amount of time he had served on death row—more than 40 years by 2018. The U.S. Supreme Court refused to hear his case, but Justice Stephen Breyer found that the petition raised some meritorious issues, including the lengthy delays between the sentence of death and the execution and the geographic disparities of the death penalty.

Regarding the length of time, Breyer noted that Jordan is the oldest person on death row in Mississippi and has spent more than half his life on death row. "In my view, the conditions in which Jordan appears to have been confined over the past four decades reinforce the Eighth Amendment concern raised in his petition," Breyer writes.

Justice Breyer identified another issue that he thought merited the full Court's attention—the abject geographic disparities in the death penalty. There are only a few counties in the country that actually execute inmates. "This geographic concentration reflects a nationwide trend," Breyer writes. "Death sentences, while declining in number, have become increasingly concentrated in an ever-smaller number of counties."

FURTHER READING

Dreher, Arielle. "Cruel & Unusual? The Death Penalty's Trials in Mississippi." *Jackson Free Press*. March 22. 2017.

"In Two Mississippi Cases, Justice Breyer Renews Call to Review Constitutionality of Death Penalty." Death Penalty Information Center. July 2, 2018.

- ***Document 51:*** California Governor's Executive Order Ending the Death Penalty
- ***Date:*** March 13, 2019
- ***Where:*** Sacramento, California
- ***Significance:*** This executive action taken by California governor Gavin Newsom to eliminate the death penalty in America's single-most populous state marked a new chapter in the ongoing battle over capital punishment across the United States. It also underscored how blue and red states were increasingly diverging in their assessments of the value and morality of the death penalty.

DOCUMENT

Governor Newsom Issues Executive Order Ending Capital Punishment in California

EXECUTIVE ORDER N-09-19

WHEREAS, California's death penalty system is unfair, unjust, wasteful, protracted and does not make our state safer.

WHEREAS, the state's bedrock responsibility to ensure equal justice under the law applies to all people no matter their race, mental ability, where they live, or how much money they have.

WHEREAS, death sentences are unevenly and unfairly applied to people of color, people with mental disabilities, and people who cannot afford costly legal representation.

WHEREAS, innocent people have been sentenced to death in California. Moreover, the National Academy of Sciences estimates that as many as one in 25 people sentenced to death in the United States is likely innocent.

WHEREAS, since 1978, California has spent $5 billion on a death penalty system that has executed 13 people.

WHEREAS, no person has been executed since 2006 because California's execution protocols have not been lawful. Yet today, 25 California death row inmates have exhausted all of their state and federal appeals and could be eligible for an execution date.

WHEREAS, I will not oversee execution of any person while Governor.

NOW, THEREFORE, I, GAVIN NEWSOM, Governor of the State of California, in accordance with the authority vested in me by the Constitution and statutes of the State of California, do hereby issue the following order to become effective immediately:

IT IS HEREBY ORDERED THAT:

1. An executive moratorium on the death penalty shall be instituted in the form of a reprieve for all people sentenced to death in California. This moratorium does not provide for the release of any person from prison or otherwise alter any current conviction or sentence.
2. California's lethal injection protocol shall be repealed.
3. The Death Chamber at San Quentin shall be immediately closed.

This Order is not intended to, and does not, create any rights or benefits, substantive or procedural, enforceable at law or in equity, against the State of California, its departments, agencies, or other entities, its officers or employees or any other person.

SOURCE: Newsom, Gavin. Executive Order N-09-19. March 13, 2019. https://www.gov.ca.gov/wp-content/uploads/2019/03/3.13.19-EO-N-09-19.pdf

ANALYSIS

At the time of this 2019 executive order, California had 737 inmates on death row—the most of any state. However, there were very few actual executions in California. No one had been executed in the state since 2006. However, there were 25 inmates who had exhausted their state and federal appeals and were subject to execution.

In a press release that accompanied his executive order, Governor Newsom stated, "Our death penalty system has been, by all measures, a failure. It has discriminated against defendants who are mentally ill, black and brown, or can't afford expensive legal representation. It has provided no public safety benefit or value as a deterrent. It has wasted billions of taxpayer dollars. Most of all, the death penalty is absolute. It's irreversible and irreparable in the event of human error."

The governor's statement identifies several oft-stated problems with capital punishment, including its disproportionate impact on defendants who suffer from mental illness or disability, persons of color, and poor people with limited financial resources. He also identified capital punishment's failure as crime deterrent as a key reason for issuing the executive order.

The governor's action was considered bold because voters in California had repeatedly refused to vote to abolish the death penalty. In fact, in 2016, voters approved of a measure to help expedite the legal process in death penalty cases.

However, Governor Newsom is a longtime opponent of the death penalty, and the action was not surprising.

FURTHER READING

Arango, Tim. "California Death Penalty Suspended; 737 Inmates Get Stay of Execution." *New York Times*. March 12, 2019.

Shafer, Scott, and Marisa Lagos. "Gov. Gavin Newsom Suspends Death Penalty in California." NPR. March 12, 2019.

- ***Document 52:*** Supreme Court's decision in *Bucklew v. Precythe*
- ***Date:*** April 1, 2019
- ***Where:*** Washington, D.C.
- ***Significance:*** The decision showed that death row inmates have a difficult challenge in contending that the state's method of execution will cause so much pain that it violates Eighth Amendment bans on "cruel and unusual punishment."

DOCUMENT

Supreme Court Rejects Missouri Inmate's Claim That Lethal Injection Violates the Eighth Amendment

Russell Bucklew concedes that the State of Missouri lawfully convicted him of murder and a variety of other crimes. He acknowledges that the U. S. Constitution permits a sentence of execution for his crimes. He accepts, too, that the State's lethal injection protocol is constitutional in most applications. But because of his unusual medical condition, he contends the protocol is unconstitutional as applied to him. Mr. Bucklew raised this claim for the first time less than two weeks before his scheduled execution. He received a stay of execution and five years to pursue the argument, but in the end neither the district court nor the Eighth Circuit found it supported by the law or evidence. Now, Mr. Bucklew asks us to overturn those judgments. We can discern no lawful basis for doing so.

I

A

In 1996, when Stephanie Ray announced that she wanted to end their relationship, Mr. Bucklew grew violent. He cut her jaw, punched her in the face, and threatened her with a knife. Frightened to remain in the home they had shared, Ms. Ray sought refuge with her children in Michael Sanders' nearby residence. But then one night Mr. Bucklew invaded that home. Bearing a pistol in each hand, he shot Mr. Sanders in the chest; fired at Mr. Sanders' 6-year-old son (thankfully, he missed); and pistol-whipped Ms. Ray, this time breaking her jaw. Then Mr. Bucklew handcuffed Ms. Ray, drove her to a secluded spot, and raped her at gunpoint. After a trooper spotted Mr. Bucklew, a shootout followed and he was finally arrested. While all this played out, Mr. Sanders bled to death. As a coda, Mr. Bucklew escaped from jail while awaiting trial and attacked Ms. Ray's mother with a hammer before he could be recaptured.

After a decade of litigation, Mr. Bucklew was seemingly out of legal options. A jury had convicted him of murder and other crimes and recommended a death sentence, which the court had imposed. . . .

As it turned out, though, Mr. Bucklew's case soon became caught up in a wave of litigation over lethal injection procedures. Like many States, Missouri has periodically sought to improve its administration of the death penalty. Early in the 20th century, the State replaced hanging with the gas chamber. Later in the century, it authorized the use of lethal injection as an alternative to lethal gas. By the time Mr. Bucklew's post-conviction proceedings ended, Missouri's protocol called for lethal injections to be carried out using three drugs: sodium thiopental, pancuronium bromide, and potassium chloride. And by that time, too, various inmates were in the process of challenging the constitutionality of the State's protocol and others like it around the country. . . .

Ultimately, this Court answered these legal challenges in *Baze* v. *Rees* (2008). Addressing Kentucky's similar three-drug protocol, The Chief Justice, joined by Justice Alito and Justice Kennedy, concluded that a State's refusal to alter its lethal injection protocol could violate the Eighth Amendment only if an inmate first identified a "feasible, readily implemented" alternative procedure that would "significantly reduce a substantial risk of severe pain." . . .

While all this played out, pressure from anti-death-penalty advocates induced the company that manufactured sodium thiopental to stop supplying it for use in executions. As a result, the State was unable to proceed with executions until it could change its lethal injection protocol again. This it did in 2012, prescribing the use of a single drug, the sedative propofol. Soon after that, Mr. Bucklew and other inmates sued to invalidate this new protocol as well, alleging that it would produce excruciating pain and violate the Eighth Amendment on its face. After the State revised the protocol in 2013 to use the sedative pentobarbital instead of propofol, the inmates amended their complaint to allege that pentobarbital would likewise violate the Constitution.

C

Things came to a head in 2014. With its new protocol in place and the necessary drugs now available, the State scheduled Mr. Bucklew's execution for May 21. But 12 days before the execution Mr. Bucklew filed yet another lawsuit, the one now before us. In this case, he presented an as-applied Eighth Amendment challenge to the State's new protocol. Whether or not it would cause excruciating pain for *all* prisoners, as his previous lawsuit alleged, Mr. Bucklew now contended that the State's protocol would cause *him* severe pain because of his particular medical condition. Mr. Bucklew suffers from a disease called cavernous hemangioma, which causes vascular tumors—clumps of blood vessels—to grow in his head, neck, and throat. His complaint alleged that this condition could prevent the pentobarbital from circulating properly in his body; that the use of a chemical dye to flush the intravenous line could cause his blood pressure to spike and his tumors to rupture; and that pentobarbital could interact adversely with his other medications.

These latest protocol challenges yielded mixed results. The district court dismissed both the inmates' facial challenge and Mr. Bucklew's as-applied challenge. But, at Mr. Bucklew's request, this Court agreed to stay his execution until the Eighth Circuit could hear his appeal. Ultimately, the Eighth Circuit affirmed the dismissal of the facial challenge. Then, turning to the as-applied challenge and seeking to apply the test set forth by the *Baze* plurality, the court held that Mr. Bucklew's complaint failed as a matter of law to identify an alternative procedure that would significantly reduce the risks he alleged would flow from the State's lethal injection protocol. Yet, despite this dispositive shortcoming, the court of appeals decided to give Mr. Bucklew another chance to plead his case. The court stressed that, on remand before the district court, Mr. Bucklew had to identify "at the earliest possible time" a feasible, readily implemented alternative procedure that would address those risks.

Shortly after the Eighth Circuit issued its judgment, this Court decided *Glossip v. Gross*, 576 U. S. ___ (2015), rejecting a challenge to Oklahoma's lethal injection protocol. . . . In doing so, it reaffirmed that an inmate cannot successfully challenge a method of execution under the Eighth Amendment unless he identifies "an alternative that is 'feasible, readily implemented, and in fact significantly reduces a substantial risk of severe pain.' " . . . .

Despite the Eighth Circuit's express instructions, when Mr. Bucklew returned to the district court in 2015 he still refused to identify an alternative procedure that would significantly reduce his alleged risk of pain. Instead, he insisted that inmates should have to carry this burden only in facial, not as-applied, challenges. . . . Mr. Bucklew later clarified that the lethal gas he had in mind was nitrogen, which neither Missouri nor any other State had ever used to carry out an execution.

. . . Even so, the court held, Mr. Bucklew's claim failed because he had produced no evidence that his proposed alternative, execution by nitrogen hypoxia, would significantly reduce that risk.

This time, a panel of the Eighth Circuit affirmed. . . .

On the same day Mr. Bucklew was scheduled to be executed, this Court granted him a second stay of execution. We then agreed to hear his case to clarify the legal standards that govern an as-applied Eighth Amendment challenge to a State's method of carrying out a death sentence.

II

We begin with Mr. Bucklew's suggestion that the test for lethal injection protocol challenges announced in *Baze* and *Glossip* should govern only facial challenges, not as-applied challenges like his. In evaluating this argument, we first examine the original and historical understanding of the Eighth Amendment and our precedent in *Baze* and *Glossip*. We then address whether, in light of those authorities, it would be appropriate to adopt a different constitutional test for as-applied claims.

A

The Constitution allows capital punishment. . . . Of course, that doesn't mean the American people must continue to use the death penalty. The same Constitution that permits States to authorize capital punishment also allows them to outlaw it. But it does mean that the judiciary bears no license to end a debate reserved for the people and their representatives.

While the Eighth Amendment doesn't forbid capital punishment, it does speak to how States may carry out that punishment, prohibiting methods that are "cruel and unusual." What does this term mean? At the time of the framing, English law still formally tolerated certain punishments even though they had largely fallen into disuse—punishments in which "terror, pain, or disgrace [were] superadded" to the penalty of death. . . .

It's instructive, too, to contrast the modes of execution the Eighth Amendment was understood to forbid with those it was understood to permit. At the time of the Amendment's adoption, the predominant method of execution in this country was hanging. While hanging was considered more humane than some of the punishments of the Old World, it was no guarantee of a quick and painless death. . . .

What does all this tell us about how the Eighth Amendment applies to methods of execution? For one thing, it tells us that the Eighth Amendment does not guarantee a prisoner a painless death—something that, of course, isn't guaranteed to many people, including most victims of capital crimes. . . .

This Court has yet to hold that a State's method of execution qualifies as cruel and unusual, and perhaps understandably so. Far from seeking to superadd terror, pain, or disgrace to their executions, the States have often sought more nearly the opposite, exactly as Justice Story predicted. . . .

In reaching this conclusion, *Baze* and *Glossip* recognized that the Eighth Amendment "does not demand the avoidance of all risk of pain in carrying out executions." To the contrary, the Constitution affords a "measure of deference to a State's choice of execution procedures" and does not authorize courts to serve as "boards of inquiry charged with determining 'best practices' for executions." . . .

III

Having (re)confirmed that anyone bringing a method of execution claim alleging the infliction of unconstitutionally cruel pain must meet the *Baze-Glossip* test, we can now turn to the question whether Mr. Bucklew is able to satisfy that test. Has he identified a feasible and readily implemented alternative method of execution the State refused to adopt without a legitimate reason, even though it would significantly reduce a substantial risk of severe pain? Because the case comes to us after the entry of summary judgment, this appeal turns on whether Mr. Bucklew has shown a genuine issue of material fact warranting a trial.

A

We begin with the question of a proposed alternative method. Through much of this case and despite many opportunities, Mr. Bucklew refused to identify *any* alternative method of execution, choosing instead to stand on his argument that *Baze* and *Glossip*'s legal standard doesn't govern as-applied challenges like his (even after the Eighth Circuit rejected that argument). Only when the district court warned that his continued refusal to abide this Court's precedents would result in immediate dismissal did Mr. Bucklew finally point to nitrogen hypoxia. . . .

First, an inmate must show that his proposed alternative method is not just theoretically "'feasible'" but also "'readily implemented.'" . . .

Second, and relatedly, the State had a "legitimate" reason for declining to switch from its current method of execution as a matter of law. Rather than point to a proven alternative method, Mr. Bucklew sought the adoption of an entirely new method—one that had "never been used to carry out an execution" and had "no track record of successful use." . . .

Even if a prisoner can carry his burden of showing a readily available alternative, he must still show that it would significantly reduce a substantial risk of severe pain. A minor reduction in risk is insufficient; the difference must be clear and considerable. Over the course of this litigation, Mr. Bucklew's explanation why nitrogen hypoxia meets this standard has evolved significantly. But neither of the two theories he has advanced in this Court turns out to be supported by record evidence.

First, Mr. Bucklew points to several risks that he alleges could result from use of the State's lethal injection protocol that would not be present if the State used nitrogen gas. For example, he says the execution team might try to insert an IV into one of his peripheral veins, which could cause the vein to rupture; or the team might instead use an allegedly painful "cut-down" procedure to access his femoral vein. He also says that he might be forced to lie flat on his back during the execution, which could impair his breathing even before the pentobarbital is administered. And he says the stress from all this could cause his tumors to bleed, further impairing his breathing. These risks, we may assume, would not exist if Mr. Bucklew were executed by his preferred method of nitrogen hypoxia.

The problem with all of these contentions is that they rest on speculation unsupported, if not affirmatively contradicted, by the evidence in this case. Nor does the principal dissent contend otherwise. So, for example, uncontroverted record evidence indicates that the execution team will have discretion to adjust the gurney to whatever position is in Mr. Bucklew's best medical interests. . . .

Moreover, to the extent the record is unclear on any of these issues, Mr. Bucklew had ample opportunity to conduct discovery and develop a factual record concerning exactly what procedures the State planned to use. He failed to do so—presumably because the thrust of his constitutional claim was that *any* attempt to execute him via lethal injection would be unconstitutional, regardless of the specific procedures the State might use. . . .

Second, Mr. Bucklew contends that the lethal injection itself will expose him to a substantial risk of severe pain that could be eliminated by adopting his preferred method. He claims that once the sedative pentobarbital is injected he will "lose the ability to manage" the tumors in his airway and, as a result, will experience a "sense of suffocation" for some period of time before the State's sedative renders him fully unconscious. . . .

But here again the record contains insufficient evidence to permit Mr. Bucklew to avoid summary judgment. For starters, in the courts below Mr. Bucklew maintained he would have trouble managing his airway only if he were forced to lie supine, which (as we've explained) the evidence shows he won't be . . .

In fact, there's nothing in the record to suggest that Mr. Bucklew will be capable of experiencing pain for significantly more than 20 to 30 seconds after being injected with pentobarbital. . . .

Of course, the principal dissent maintains that Dr. Zivot's testimony supports an inference that pentobarbital might cause Mr. Bucklew to suffer for a prolonged period. But its argument rests on a number of mistakes about the record. . . .

In sum, even if execution by nitrogen hypoxia were a feasible and readily implemented alternative to the State's chosen method, Mr. Bucklew has still failed to present any evidence suggesting that it would significantly reduce his risk of pain. For that reason as well, the State was entitled to summary judgment on Mr. Bucklew's Eighth Amendment claim.

IV

"Both the State and the victims of crime have an important interest in the timely enforcement of a sentence." Those interests have been frustrated in this case. Mr. Bucklew committed his crimes more than two decades ago. He exhausted his appeal and separate state and federal habeas challenges more than a decade ago. Yet since then he has managed to secure delay through lawsuit after lawsuit. He filed his current challenge just days before his scheduled execution. That suit has now carried on for five years and yielded two appeals to the Eighth Circuit, two 11th-hour stays of execution, and plenary consideration in this Court. And despite all this, his suit in the end amounts to little more than an attack on settled precedent, lacking enough evidence even to survive summary judgment—and on not just one but many essential legal elements set forth in our case law and required by the Constitution's original meaning.

The people of Missouri, the surviving victims of Mr. Bucklew's crimes, and others like them deserve better. Even the principal dissent acknowledges that "the long delays that now typically occur between the time an offender is sentenced to death and his execution" are "excessive." The answer is not, as the dissent incongruously suggests, to reward those who interpose delay with a decree ending capital punishment by judicial fiat. Under our Constitution, the question of capital punishment belongs to the people and their representatives, not the courts, to resolve. The proper role of courts is to ensure that method-of-execution challenges to lawfully issued sentences are resolved fairly and expeditiously. . . .

The judgment of the court of appeals is

Affirmed.

SOURCE: Bucklew v. Precythe, 587 U.S. ___ (2019).

ANALYSIS

Missouri death row inmate Russell Bucklew contended that he should not be executed by the state's chosen method of execution—lethal injection using pentobarbital—because it would cause him unnecessary and excruciating pain. Bucklew suffered from cavernous hemangioma, a rare condition resulting in the growth of blood-filled tumors in his head, neck, and throat.

Bucklew had filed a slew of lawsuits through the years, challenging his execution as violative of the Eighth Amendment. In his latest challenge, he argued that his medical condition meant that he could not be executed constitutionally through the state's chosen method of execution.

A federal district court forced Bucklew and his attorneys to come up with an alternative method that would reduce his pain. They argued a form of nitrogen gas would be a less painful way of death. However, the lower courts and the U.S. Supreme Court rejected that claim.

This decision was another close 5–4 ruling. The majority, per Justice Neil Gorsuch, found that Bucklew failed to show that the state's method would cause him unnecessary and wanton pain. Furthermore, Gorsuch wrote that "[t]he Eighth Amendment does not guarantee a prisoner a painless death—something that, of course, isn't guaranteed to many people, including most victims of capital crimes."

Justice Gorsuch also noted that nitrogen gas was not a feasible alternative for the state of Missouri, which conducts executions through lethal injection. Gorsuch's majority opinion also concluded that Bucklew had failed to show that the use of nitrogen gas would case less pain than the state's method of execution through lethal injection. Finally, Gorsuch's opinion included a warning about last-minute lawsuits and appeals from death row inmates with approaching execution dates. "Courts should police carefully against attempts to use such challenges as tools to interpose unjustified delay," he wrote. Bucklew was executed on October 1, 2019, through the use of pentobarbital.

FURTHER READING

Liptak, Adam. "Rancor and Raw Emotion Surface in Supreme Court Death Penalty Ruling." *New York Times*. April 1, 2019.

York, Hannah. "Bucklew v. Precythe and the Resurgence of the Method of Execution Challenge." *Colorado Law Review*. May 12, 2021.

- ***Document 53:*** Testimony of Rebecca Brown, Policy Director of the Innocence Project, at Ohio State Senate hearing on capital punishment
- ***Date:*** June 21, 2021
- ***Where:*** Columbus, Ohio
- ***Significance:*** As part of legislative hearings in Ohio about abolishing the death penalty in the state, experts on both sides of the issue were called to provide their perspectives. Rebecca Brown is the policy director for the Innocence Project, an organization opposed to capital punishment. In her appearance, she talks about the dangers of wrongful convictions.

DOCUMENT

Innocence Project Policy Director Urges Abolition of the Death Penalty

My name is Rebecca Brown and I am the Director of Policy at the Innocence Project. We work to prove the innocence of people behind bars who have been wrongfully convicted. We also work to forge win-win policy reforms that both prevent miscarriages of justice and help identify the guilty. It is precisely because of the dual nature of our work that I am here today: to provide a somewhat unique and hopefully helpful perspective.

First let me say that I'm so pleased to be in Ohio. We partner with the Ohio Innocence Project whose diligent work—since its inception—has led to the release of 33 wrongfully convicted Ohioans, who collectively served nearly 650 years behind bars.

Ohio stands among the top states for numbers of wrongful convictions. Indeed, an analysis of the first 2400 exonerations in the nation indicated that of the X counties in the U.S., Cuyahoga County is among the top-ten producers of exonerations.

Wrongful convictions have serious consequences, especially when the numbers are as staggering as we now know they are. Every time an innocent person is convicted, the person who really committed the crime escapes justice and may commit other crimes. That's why in addition to working on cases that help free innocent people, the Innocence Project works on reforms that go to the root causes of wrongful convictions—mistaken identification, false confessions, unreliable jailhouse informant testimony, unreliable or the misapplication of forensic science, official misconduct, and poor lawyering among them.

Nationally, since 1973, 185 people have served time on death row only to be later exonerated of all charges related to the wrongful convictions that put them there.

Ohio ranks 6th among the states in this category, with 11 death row exonerations. Meanwhile Ohio has executed 56 individuals. This means that for every five executions, one person has been exonerated in this state.

These and other disturbing numbers indicate that the risk of convicting and executing an innocent person in and beyond Ohio is real. Indeed, every aspect of a case involves a human being. If just one person at any stage makes an error, jumps to a conclusion, or acts on a false assumption, an innocent person can be condemned to a guilty person's fate.

I know this from experience. My colleagues and I have reviewed hundreds of cases. In some, after we have pored over reams of court transcripts, scrutinized piles of police reports, dissected crime lab analyses, sifted through evidence and property logs, and studied scores of witness statements, we have strongly suspected guilt, only later to discover we were wrong. No less often, someone who we strongly suspect is innocent turns out to be guilty. It's that hard.

In 2014, Ricky Jackson set the record for the longest-serving person to be exonerated in U.S. history. He spent 39 years in an Ohio prison for a crime he didn't commit. Jackson and co-defendants Wiley Bridgeman and Kwame Ajamu together served over 100 years in prison for the 1975 killing of a money-order collector at a Cleveland grocery store. The convictions were based on a lie by a then 12-year-old boy who later recanted his story. The Ohio Innocence Project's exhaustive investigation included finding and gaining the trust of witnesses as well as pursuing the release of critical public records. What if they hadn't succeeded? Would we ever have known the truth?

It might be tempting to say exonerations prove the system works. But the 11 men exonerated from death row in Ohio spent an average of over 20 years between conviction and exoneration, and combined, they served almost 216 years incarcerated after their wrongful convictions. And these cases are just the cases we know about. We simply don't know whether Ohio has executed an innocent person.

As I'm sure you know, DNA testing is perhaps our best tool for producing highly reliable—but certainly not infallible—evidence of guilt or innocence. What most people don't know, though, is that criminalists believe that DNA evidence exists in less than 10% of the most serious cases. For instance, DNA evidence is not what helped free Ricky Jackson, Wiley Bridgeman, and Kwame Ajamu.

Most homicide cases turn on eyewitness testimony, confessions, the credibility of witnesses, including incentivized witnesses, like jailhouse informants, or circumstantial evidence—not DNA testing. DNA testing is not a panacea that can prevent wrongful executions. It does not have the capacity to ensure either a fair or accurate application of the death penalty and its finality.

What DNA has done is help us to shed light on the extent of the tragedy of wrongful convictions across the nation. It has provided some very sobering data about the frequency of error in the entire criminal legal system. The nation's 375 DNA exonerations—21 of which included persons who had spent time on death row—have also taught us that any number of factors—sometimes many functioning at once—can yield a wrongful conviction and that the appeals process does not provide the needed protections to detect them. Problems can arise from:

- Juries relying on incorrect, misleading or partial information;
- Public and private defenders providing ineffective assistance of counsel;

- Crime labs mishandling and contaminating evidence; falsifying results; misrepresenting forensic findings; or exaggerating results of testing;
- Witnesses misidentifying innocent people as the actual perpetrators;
- Innocent, often vulnerable, people confessing to crimes that they did not commit;
- Innocent people pleading to crimes they did not commit, particularly when they fear the administration of the death penalty; and
- Unreliable informants acting on the basis of real or perceived incentives.

These are the same reasons that Ohio's 11 death row exonerees and 22 others were wrongfully convicted. And again, those are just the ones that we have found. There are countless others in prison, currently facing execution, or who have already been executed who have been unable to access DNA testing, even when the evidence is there.

As awareness of the prevalence of wrongful convictions has grown, support for the death penalty has declined, nationally and here in Ohio. That is not surprising to me and probably isn't to you. The death penalty's irreversibility is something that can't be fixed by reforms. Yes, all necessary resources must be provided to ensure that every aspect of the system—investigation, defense, prosecution, trial, appeal, and post-conviction—is as fair and accurate as possible. And there are reforms to the criminal justice system that should be considered, such as regulating the use of jailhouse snitches. But even with the best and most extensive reforms, as DNA has proven, an individual's life can hinge on a sloppy report, an inadvertent cue, the work of an overburdened practitioner, or even malice. Just one imperfect element can topple a house of cards. In the end, there is only one reform that you could make that eliminates the unacceptable risk of wrongful execution. Without a means of executing, Ohio's death penalty system appears—at the moment—to be a symbolic exercise. The lessons of the past 40 years have come together in this hearing. They present an opportunity to abandon a policy that has failed to deliver for Ohioans and turn our attention and resources to policies and programs that honor Ohio's commitment to justice. I urge you to take it.

SOURCE: Brown, Rebecca. Testimony on Ohio State Senate Bill 103 Before the Senate Judiciary Committee. June 16, 2021. https://docslib.org/doc/4708643/rebecca-brown-director-of-policy-innocence-project-testimony-on-senate-bill-103-before-the-senate-judiciary-committee-june-16-2021

ANALYSIS

Rebecca Brown of the Innocence Project was one of the witnesses who testified before the Ohio Senate about Senate Bill 103, a bipartisan measure that would abolish the death penalty in the state. She points out that Ohio has a shaky history when it comes to reliable death penalty convictions. She notes there have been at least 11 exonerations from persons serving on death row.

Brown explained numerous problems with the death penalty, focusing on the unreliability of the death penalty process. She pointed out that in Ohio alone, at least 11 people who were once on death row have been exonerated. She highlighted the case of Ricky Jackson, a man who served 39 years in prison for a crime he did not commit. Jackson and two other men were convicted and sentenced to death in 1975 based on the eyewitness testimony of a 12-year-old boy, Eddie Vernon.

However, in 2011, Vernon told lawyers with the Ohio Innocence Project that his testimony was false, that he had been coerced by the police to make the statement. In 2014, prosecutors dismissed charges against Jackson and his two codefendants. Jackson was thus finally exonerated after serving 39 years.

In her testimony, Brown explains that there are numerous causes for faulty convictions. She identifies poor lawyering, jurors receiving incomplete or misleading information, faulty eyewitness testimony, lying jailhouse informants, and faulty crime lab reports as some of the potential causes of problems.

While she notes that DNA testing has exonerated many inmates, she points out that in many cases it is not DNA that sends someone to death row wrongly. For example, Jackson was sent to death row based on the faulty witness testimony of a person coerced by the police to make such an identification.

Brown supports the idea of reforms to capital punishment but urged the Ohio senators to face the fact that only one reform exists that can solve the problem of innocent people being put to death by the state—abolition of the death penalty.

As of May 2022, Ohio Senate Bill 103 remains in committee and has yet to come up for a vote, either in committee or in the full Senate.

FURTHER READING

Brown, Rebecca, "Innocence Project: The Administration Should Reverse Course on Reinstating the Death Penalty." Innocence Project. July 30, 2019.

Russell, Annika. "Ohio Death Penalty Repeal Bill Amasses Bipartisan Support among Legislators and Ohioans." American Bar Association. March 4, 2021.

Shaer, Matthew. "After 39 Years of Wrongful Imprisonment, Ricky Jackson Is Finally Free." *Smithsonian Magazine*. January/February 2017.

BIBLIOGRAPHY

Adams, Randall, with William Hoffer and Marilyn M. Hoffer. *Adams v. Texas*. New York: St. Martin's Press, 1991.

Alford, Roger P. "Roper v. Simmons and Our Constitution in International Equipoise." 53 *UCLA Law Review* 1 (2005).

Amsterdam, Anthony G. "For Sandra Lockett." 10 *ConLawNOW* 117 (2018).

Arango, Tim. "California Death Penalty Suspended; 737 Inmates Get Stay of Execution." *New York Times*. March 12, 2019.

Baldus, David C., George Woodworth, and Charles Pulaski. *Equal Justice and the Death Penalty: A Legal and Empirical Analysis*. Northeastern University Press, 1990.

Baldus, David C., George Woodworth, John C. Boger, and Charles A. Pulaski. "McCleskey v. Kemp (1987): Denial, Avoidance, and the Legitimization of Racial Discrimination in the Administration of the Death Penalty." In *Death Penalty Stories*, eds. John Blume and Jordan Steiker, pp. 229–275. Foundation Press, 2009.

Banner, Stuart. *The Death Penalty: An American History*. Cambridge, MA: Harvard University Press, 2002.

Bassett, Thom. "Risking Cruelty: McCleskey v. Kemp, Retributivism, and Ungrounded Moral Judgment." 52 *Syracuse Law Review* 1 (2002).

Bedau, Hugo A. *The Death Penalty in America: Current Controversies*. Oxford University Press, 1998.

Bedau, Hugo A., and Paul Cassell. *Debating the Death Penalty*. Oxford University Press, 2005.

Benekos, Peter J., and Alida V. Merlo. "A Decade of Change: Roper v. Simmons, Defending Childhood, and Juvenile Justice Policy." 30 *Criminal Justice Policy Review* 102 (2019).

Blume, John H. "Gilmore v. Utah: The Persistent Problem of Volunteers." In *Death Penalty Stories*, eds. John H. Blume and Jordan M. Steiker, pp. 203–228. St. Paul, MN: Foundation Press, 2009.

Blume, John H., Theodore Eisenberg, and Sheri L. Johnson, "Post-McCleskey Racial Discrimination Claims in Capital Cases." 83 *Cornell Law Review* 1771 (1998).

Burke, W. Lewis. "Pink Franklin v. South Carolina: The NAACP's First Case." 54 *American Journal of Legal History* 265 (2014).

Casey, Anthony J. "Maintaining the Integrity of Death: An Argument for Restricting a Defendant's Right to Volunteer for Execution at Certain Stages in Capital Proceedings." 30 *American Journal of Criminal Law* 75 (2002).

Cassell, Paul G. "Overstating America's Wrongful Conviction Rate? Reassessing the Conventional Wisdom about the Incidence of Wrongful Convictions." 60 *Arizona Law Review* 815 (2018).

Cassell, Paul G., and Stephen J. Markman. "Protecting the Innocent: A Response to the Bedau-Radelet Study." 41 *Stanford Law Review* 121 (1988).

Chammah, Maurice. *Let the Lord Sort Them: The Rise and Fall of the Death Penalty*. Crown Publishers, 2021.

Cockburn, David. "Capital Punishment and Realism." *Philosophy* (April 1991), pp. 177–190.

Colbert, Douglas L. "Challenging the Challenge: Thirteenth Amendment as a Prohibition against the Racial Use of Peremptory Challenges." 76 *Cornell Law Review* 1 (1990).

Colloff, Pamela. "Innocence Found." *Texas Monthly*. June 2011.

Cox, Kevin E. "Execution of the Insane Criminal: Ford v. Wainwright." 41 *Southwestern Law Journal* 745 (1987).

Davis, Peggy C. "Reflections on the Sandra Lockett Case." 10 *ConLawNOW* 29 (2018).

Death Penalty Information Center. "Facts about the Death Penalty." Updated July 1, 2021. https://documents.deathpenaltyinfo.org/pdf/FactSheet.pdf

Dieter, Richard C. "The Future of the Death Penalty in the United States." 49 *University of Richmond Law Review* 921 (2015).

Dow, David R. "When Law Bows to Politics: Explaining Payne v. Tennessee." 26 *UC Davis Law Review* 157, 165–176 (1992).

Dreher, Arielle. "Cruel & Unusual? The Death Penalty's Trials in Mississippi." *Jackson Free Press*. March 22, 2017.

Frankel, Joe. "Payne, Victim Impact Statements, and Nearly Two Decades of Devolving Standards of Decency." 12 *City University of New York Law Review* 87 (2008).

Garguilo, Diana L. "The Batson Standard Remains the Applicable Test for Stating a Claim of Jury Discrimination under the Fourteenth Amendment." 44 *Duquesne Law Review* 771 (2006).

Garland, David. *Peculiar Institution: America's Death Penalty in an Age of Abolition*. Cambridge, MA: Harvard University Press, 2012.

Garrett, Brandon L. "Claiming Innocence." 92 *Minnesota Law Review* 1629 (2008).

Garrett, Brandon L. *Convicting the Innocent: Where Criminal Prosecutions Go Wrong*. Cambridge, MA: Harvard University Press, 2011.

Gohara, Miriam S. "In Defense of the Injured: How Trauma-Informed Criminal Defense Can Reform Sentencing." 45 *American Journal of Criminal Law* 1 (2018).

Goldberg, Arthur J., and Alan M. Dershowitz. "Declaring the Death Penalty Unconstitutional." 83 *Harvard Law Review* 1773 (1970).

Greenhouse, Linda. "Death Penalty Is Renounced by Blackmun." *New York Times*. February 23, 1994.

Greenhouse, Linda. "Justices Bar Death Penalty for Rape of a Child." *New York Times*. June 26, 2008.

Greenwald, Helene B. "Supreme Court Review: Eighth Amendment—Minors and the Death Penalty: Decision and Avoidance: Eddings v. Oklahoma (1982)." 73 *Journal of Criminal Law & Criminology* 1525 (1982).

Hanes, Stephanie. "DNA That Freed Man Leads to New Subject." *Baltimore Sun*. September 6, 2003.

Hinton, Anthony R., with Sara L. Hardin. *The Sun Does Shine: How I Found Life, Freedom and Justice*. St. Martin's Griffin, 2019.

Hudson, David L., Jr. "Does Capital Punishment Have a Future? A Resource Guide for Teachers." American Bar Association. 2004.

Ingle, Joseph B. *Last Rights: 13 Fatal Encounters with the State's Justice*. Nashville, TN: Abingdon Press, 1990.

Johnson, Sherri L. "Race and Recalcitrance: The Miller-El Remands." 5 *Ohio State Journal of Criminal Law* 131 (2007).

Karp, David J. "Coker v. Georgia: Disproportionate Punishment and the Death Penalty for Rape." 78 *Columbia Law Review* 1714 (1978).

King, Bernice. "We Must Abolish the Death Penalty." Death Penalty Action. January 15, 2021.
Klarman, Michael J. "The Plessy Era." 1998 *Supreme Court Review* 303 (1998).
Klarman, Michael J. "The Racial Origins of Modern Criminal Procedure." 99 *Michigan Law Review* 48 (2000).
Klarman, Michael J. "Scottsboro." 93 *Marquette Law Review Law Review* 379 (2009).
Klein, Alexandra L. "The Beginning of the End: Abolishing Capital Punishment in Virginia." 77 *Washington and Lee Law Review* 375 (2021).
Klein, Richard. "The Constitutionalizing of Ineffective Assistance of Counsel." 58 *Maryland Law Review* 1433 (1999).
Koocher, Gerald P. "IQ Testing: A Matter of Life or Death." 13 *Ethics and Behavior* 1–2 (2003).
Labi, Nadya. "A Man against the Machine." *NYU Law Magazine*. 2007.
Lesage, C. R. "Death Penalty for Rape: Cruel and Unusual Punishment?" 38 *Louisiana Law Review* 868 (1978).
Liptak, Adam. "Court Extends Curbs on the Death Penalty in a Florida Ruling." *New York Times*. May 27, 2014.
Liptak, Adam. "Justices Rule on Legal Effects of Slow-Moving Cases." *New York Times*. March 9, 2009.
Liptak, Adam. "Rancor and Raw Emotion Surface in Supreme Court Death Penalty Ruling." *New York Times*. April 1, 2019.
Liptak, Adam. "Supreme Court Allows Use of Execution Drug." *New York Times*. June 29, 2015.
Mailer, Norman. *The Executioner's Song*. New York: Little, Brown, 1979.
Mandery, Evan. *Capital Punishment in America: A Balanced Examination*. Jones and Bartlett Learning, 2011.
Mandery, Evan. *A Wild Justice: The Death and Resurrection of Capital Punishment in America*. Norton & Co., 2013.
Masters, Brooke A. "Pat Robertson Urges Moratorium on U.S. Executions." *Washington Post*. April 8, 2000.
McAdams, John C. "Wisconsin Should Adopt the Death Penalty." 79 *Marquette Law Review* 707 (1996).
McClellan, Jane L. "Stopping the Rush to the Death House: Third-Party Standing in Death-Row Volunteer Cases." 26 *Arizona State Law Journal* 201 (1994).
Mello, Michael A. *Dead Wrong: A Death Row Lawyer Speaks Out against Capital Punishment*. University of Wisconsin Press, 1999.
Mitchell, Greg. *Dead Reckoning: Executions in America*. Sinclair Books, 2011.
Mitchell, Greg, and Robert J. Lifton. *Who Owns Death? Capital Punishment, the American Conscience and the End of the Death Penalty*. New York: William Morrow & Co, 2000.
Morris, Errol. *The Thin Blue Line* (documentary). 1988.
Palmer, Louis J. *The Death Penalty in the United States: A Complete Guide to Federal and State Laws*. 2nd ed. Jefferson, NC: McFarland & Company, Inc., Publishers, 2014.
Patton, James R., and Denis W. Keyes. "Death Penalty Issues Following Atkins." 14 *Exceptionality* 237 (2006).
Radelet, Michael L. *Facing the Death Penalty*. Temple University Press, 1990.
Radelet, Michael L., and Glenn L. Pierce. "Race and Death Sentencing in North Carolina, 1980–2007." 89 *North Carolina Law Review* 2119 (2011).
Radelet, Michael, and Kent Miller. "The Aftermath of Ford v. Wainwright." *Behavioral Sciences and the Law*. Summer 1992.
Rahdert, Lisa E. "Hall v. Florida and Ending the Death Penalty for Severely Mentally Ill Defendants." 124 *Yale Law Journal* 34 (2014).
Reinert, Alexander A. "Solitary Troubles." 93 *Notre Dame Law Review* 927 (2018).
Ryan, Meghan. "Intellectual Disability and Uncertainty in Hall v. Florida." *Concurring Opinions*. June 7, 2014.

Sarat, Austin. *The Killing State: Capital Punishment in Law, Politics, and Culture*. Oxford University Press, 1998.

Scheck, Barry, Peter Neufeld, and Jim Dwyer. *Actual Innocence*. New York: Doubleday, 2000.

Scheck, Barry, Peter Neufeld, and Taryn Simon. *The Innocents*. New York: Umbrage Editions, 2003.

Segura, Lilian. "Anthony Ray Hinton Spent Almost 30 Years on Death Row. Now He Has a Message for White America." *The Intercept*. June 27, 2018.

Selby, Danielle. "8 Things You Need to Know about Pervis Payne Who Is Facing Execution." Innocence Project. July 22, 2020.

Shafer, Scott, and Marisa Lagos. "Gov. Gavin Newsom Suspends Death Penalty in California." NPR. March 12, 2019.

Smith, Stephen F. "Has the 'Machinery of Death' Become a Clunker?" 49 *University of Richmond Law Review* 845 (2015).

Snowdon, Marlene A. "The Boykin-Tahl Requirement." 22 *Pepperdine Law Review* 273 (1994).

Songer, Michael J., and Isaac Unah. "The Effect of Race Gender, and Location on Prosecutorial Decisions to Seek the Death Penalty in South Carolina." 58 *South Carolina Law Review* 161 (2006).

Steiker, Carol S. "Furman v. Georgia: Not an End, but a Beginning." In *Death Penalty Stories*, eds. John H. Blume and Jordan M. Steiker, pp. 94–127. Foundation Press, 2009.

Steiker, Carol S., and Jordan M. Steiker. *Courting Death: The Supreme Court and Capital Punishment*. Cambridge, MA: Harvard University Press, 2016.

Stevens, John P. *Six Amendments: How and Why We Should Change the Constitution*. New York: Little, Brown & Co., 2014.

Stevenson, Bryan. *Just Mercy: A Story of Justice and Redemption*. One World, 2014.

Stevenson, Caroline. "Louisiana v. Kennedy." 4 *Duke Journal of Constitutional Law & Public Policy* Sidebar 174 (2009).

Stewart, Malcolm L. "Justice Blackmun's Capital Punishment Jurisprudence." 26 *Hastings Constitutional Law Quarterly* 271 (1998–1999).

Stott, Kim. "Slain Trooper's Family Upset at Overturning of His Killer's Death Penalty." *Oklahoman*. August 1, 1984.

Strieb, Victor. "Rare and Inconsistent: The Death Penalty for Women." 33 *Fordham Urban Law Journal* 609 (2006).

Strom, Linda. *Karla Faye Tucker Set Free: Life and Faith on Death Row*. Shaw Books, 2000.

Sullivan, Shannon S. "Ford v. Wainwright: States Cannot Execute Insane—But How Is Insanity Determined." 20 *John Marshall Law Review* 549 (1987).

Thoma, George A. "A Note on John Stuart Mill's Views on Capital Punishment." *A Journal of the History of Economic Thought* (1981), pp. 49–50.

Totenberg, Nina. "Justice Scalia and the Death Penalty." NPR.org. June 24, 2002.

Turow, Scott. *Ultimate Punishment: A Lawyer's Reflections on Dealing with the Death Penalty*. Picador, 2004.

Weithern, Lois A. "Conceptual Hurdles to the Application of Atkins v. Virginia." 59 *Hastings Law Journal* 1203 (2008).

Wright, R. George. "The Death Penalty and the Way We Think Now." 33 *Loyola of Los Angeles Law Review* 533 (2000).

York, Hannah. "Bucklew v. Precythe and the Resurgence of the Method of Execution Challenge." *Colorado Law Review*. May 12, 2021.

Yorke, Jon. "Comity, Finality, and Oklahoma's Lethal Injection Protocol." 69 *Oklahoma Law Review* 545 (2017).

INDEX

Note: **Boldfaced** page numbers refer the reader documents and to the text of related documents.

ABOUT THE AUTHOR

DAVID L. HUDSON JR. is an award-winning professor at Belmont University College of Law, where he teaches constitutional law and First Amendment law. He is the author, coauthor, or coeditor of more than 45 books.

www.ingramcontent.com/pod-product-compliance
Ingram Content Group UK Ltd.
Pitfield, Milton Keynes, MK11 3LW, UK
UKHW050951290926
15470UKWH00005B/1755

9 781440 875779